John Bernard McGloin, S.J.

CALIFORNIA'S FIRST ARCHBISHOP

MAKERS OF AMERICAN CATHOLICISM
General Editor, John Tracy Ellis
Volume Two

JOSEPH SADOC ALEMANY, O.P.

CALIFORNIA'S FIRST ARCHBISHOP

The Life of Joseph Sadoc Alemany, O.P.
1814–1888

JOHN BERNARD McGLOIN, S.J.

HERDER AND HERDER

1966
HERDER AND HERDER NEW YORK
232 Madison Avenue, New York 10016

Imprimi potest: John F. X. Connolly, S.J.
July 30, 1964

Nihil obstat: James F. Magner, S.S.
Censor Librorum

Imprimatur: ✠Joseph T. McGucken
Archbishop of San Francisco
September 16, 1964

Library of Congress Catalog Card Number: 66-13072
© 1966 by Herder and Herder, Incorporated
Manufactured in the United States

Contents

Introduction

IT is never too late to offer the tribute of our gratitude to the architects and pioneer builders of the sturdy structure of Catholicism in California. It is a pleasure for me, therefore, as the fifth incumbent of the See of San Francisco, to welcome this biographical study of the pioneer Archbishop in California, Joseph Sadoc Alemany, O.P. For with the onrush of problems which beset us who must, in ever-growing California, shepherd this portion of the flock, there comes the danger that the present be too much with us, to the exclusion of useful knowledge of the past. Yet, in a singular manner, we are building on the shoulders of the pioneers, and it would be unfortunate, indeed, if we were to fail our predecessors by not showing due interest in their times and their accomplishments. This life of Archbishop Alemany, the product of more than a decade of research in California and abroad, will help to bring about a proper appreciation of San Francisco's first archbishop.

Happily, Father Junipero Serra, O.F.M., the founder of the mission system in California, has been accorded the recognition and praise of all who are interested in the beginnings of civilizaton and religion in our state. We pray that, in God's good time, the honors of our altars may be accorded to this great missionary and man of God. Up to now, no such tribute has been paid to the "Little Bishop" (as Archbishop Alemany customarily called himself) who, in a real sense, was a second Serra in the story of our faith in California. Alemany was the "great captain" of pioneer days when spiritual giants were required—and he was one; as the reader of these pages will find out, he had been chosen carefully and well (even though it was the earlier refusal of a brother Dominican which caused his selection), and the thirty-four years of episcopal service which this dedicated Dominican gave to California and to Catholicism here entitle him to history's accolade. For three years, 1850–1853, while still in his thirties, Alemany was Bishop of Monterey, and the title meant that he had all of the present state of California under his pastoral care. Where, at this writing, we have two archdioceses and six dioceses in California, there was but one such jurisdiction in the early days of Alemany. From 1853 to 1884, Joseph Alemany served as the first Archbishop of San Francisco and, as indicated, he served in a humble and dedicated manner. Then, full of merits and of days, he voluntarily resigned the see into the capable hands of his esteemed Coadjutor, Archbishop Patrick W. Riordan, and retired to his native Spain, where death claimed him four years later.

We are deeply grateful to the Reverend John Bernard McGloin, S.J., Professor of History in the University of San Francisco, for the painstaking devotion with which he has spent his outstanding talents as an historian to create this memorial to Archbishop Alemany.

✠ Joseph T. McGucken
Archbishop of San Francisco

Editor's Foreword

"Makers of American Catholicism" was inaugurated with a biography of the man who was chosen by the Holy See to head the third ecclesiastical jurisdiction erected in the State of Illinois (1875), the Diocese of Peoria.[1] While Bishop Spalding had his share of perplexing problems, his task in north central Illinois in the 1870's was simple in comparison to that encountered nearly two decades before by the man whose life forms the subject of Volume II in the series. Joseph S. Alemany, the Spanish-born Dominican friar who reached California in December, 1850, at the age of thirty-six, found himself responsible for the spiritual care, not only of the Catholics widely scattered over the immense expanse of California, but as well for those who then inhabited what are today the States of Nevada and Utah, an area with a combined total of over 350,000 square miles! It was little wonder that the young prelate, who had originally come to the United States in 1840 where he had since served in various Dominican missions, should have felt dismayed at the prospect that lay before him. True, in less than three years he was relieved of responsibility for southern California with the appointment of another bishop for that area; yet in his role as Archbishop of San Francisco and the state's first metropolitan, Alemany still had a staggering load to bear.

In this instance the inevitable difficulties that attend the or-

[1] David Francis Sweeney, O.F.M., *The Life of John Lancaster Spalding, First Bishop of Peoria, 1840–1916* (New York: Herder and Herder. 1965).

ganization of a new ecclesiastical jurisdiction were multiplied and aggravated by the general turmoil of the region. Once the cry of "gold" had been heard at Sutter's Mill in January, 1848, life was never again quite the same in many parts of northern California. And when Alemany came on the scene less than three years later there was no place that mirrored that tumultuous period in California's history—aside from the mining towns themselves—more than the new Bishop's See city. At first the sophisticated San Franciscans were said to have shown little interest in the discoveries at Coloma and Mormon Diggings. But then suddenly they too caught the gold fever, with the result that

Overnight carpenters dropped their hammers, masons their trowels, bakers their loaves, clerks their pens, to rush to the American River. Schools were closed as both teachers and pupils deserted; shopkeepers hung signs on their doors—'Gone to the Diggings,' 'Off to the Mines' —and disappeared. By June 15 [1849] San Francisco was a ghost town, with houses and shops empty, and all who could walk, ride, run, or crawl rushing toward the Sierras.[2]

Alemany arrived in time to catch the San Franciscans on the rebound from the mines with their new-found wealth, their numbers by now being multiplied daily by hundreds of newcomers appearing at the Golden Gate from every direction. The impression made by this rowdy aggregation of human beings on many onlookers was probably pretty faithfully reflected in the letter of a seminarian when he exclaimed:

What a port! What a town! What a population! French, English, Germans, Italians, Mexicans, Americans, Indians, Canacs, and even Chinese; white, black, yellow, brown, Christian, pagans, Protestants, atheists, brigands, thieves, convicts, firebrands, assassins; little gold, much bad; behold the population of San Francisco, the new Babylon teeming with crime, confusion and frightful vice.[3]

[2] Ray Allen Billington, *The Far Western Frontier, 1830–1860* (New York: Harper & Brothers. 1956), pp. 219–220.
[3] Joseph Venisse to the Society for the Propagation of the Faith, San Francisco, September 18, 1851, *Annales de l'Association de la Propagation de la Foi,* XXIV (Novembre, 1852), 412. Alemany ordained Venisse for the Picpus Fathers on November 20, 1853.

10

Through the first critical generation in the life of the Archdiocese of San Francisco (1853-1884), Joseph Sadoc Alemany proved in every respect a dedicated and devoted leader. If one were to ask what were the archbishop's most striking characteristics, those most competent to pass a judgment would in all likelihood give first place to his humility and simplicity. They were qualities that were especially becoming in a friar of Saint Dominic, and from the extant evidence it is obvious that the tone they gave to Alemany's life was not lost on his contemporaries. For example, early in 1864 Herbert Vaughan, the future Cardinal Archbishop of Westminster, visited San Francisco where he was particularly struck by Alemany's easy approachability and his complete accessibility to men of every rank and class. Speaking of Saint Mary's Cathedral and boys' school with its adjacent playground, Vaughan stated that in that yard

stands a miserable, dingy, little iron or zinc cottage containing two rooms. One is the Archbishop's bedroom, the other his office where his secretaries work all day. No man in the whole city is more poorly lodged and no man preaches the spirit of evangelical poverty and detachment, in the midst of this money-worshiping city, like this Spanish, Dominican Archbishop of San Francisco.

Under these circumstances it was not surprising that what were described as Alemany's "disinterested zeal, holy simplicity and poverty," should have had a telling effect on the inhabitants, and that they constituted one of the strongest Catholic influences in the community.[4] Nor did the passing years dim this early impression. In fact, it seemed to grow stronger as Father Hugh Lagan, one of his priests, attested when he spoke of his superior as, "a man whose like we shall not see again," a prelate who, he said, was "cruel with himself, indulgent and kind to others, ready to obey, reluctant to command."[5] Nor were those with whom the archbishop had strong differences in matters of policy an excep-

[4] "The Church and California," *Dublin Review*, VI New Series (January, 1866), 30-31.
[5] Lagan to William Fortune, Oakland, October 24, 1876. Archives of All Hallows College, Dublin.

11

tion, as for example, Sadoc Vilarrasa, the Dominican provincial. Thus when in 1885, after thirty years service as archbishop, he learned that his repeated requests to resign his see had finally been granted, Alemany immediately announced the news to Vilarrasa as the latter's subject, said he was writing the Order's master general for another assignment, but meanwhile he would like to have the provincial's permission for several matters. Since he would be receiving some gifts and a pension, might he, he asked, "continue to give some little alms to the poor?"; and since his work for the next few months would still be rather arduous, might he "use some power to dispense myself . . . in matters of fast and abstinence of the Order?"[6] There would not be many archbishops, whether members of religious orders or not, who the day after they learned of the acceptance of their resignation of office, would so readily step once again into the ranks.

Yet Archbishop Alemany's humility was never carried to such an extreme that he abdicated the duty he had to govern. On the contrary, when he felt bound in conscience to differ and to overrule another, he showed the utmost firmness, to the point, as he himself confessed, of stubbornness, for he is said to have remarked more than once, "I am Catalan, i.e., I come from that 'German' part of Spain where people are stubborn."[7] This quality showed up in a number of extended controversies over questions of jurisdiction and property with the Jesuits, his own Dominican friars, and others.

Generally speaking, the first Archbishop of San Francisco displayed a healthy balance between the sensitive virtues of a holy man and the ready decisions of a man of action. Differ he certainly did with some of his clergy and laity—the objective

[6] Alemany to Vilarrasa, San Francisco, January 26, 1885. Archives of the Dominican Fathers, San Francisco.

[7] Testimony of José Alemany Torner, Barcelona, Spain, to the author of this biography. The archbishop's great grandnephew quoted these words and stated that they were a family tradition; moreover, he added, they were true, for "All Catalans are stubborn!"

12

relating of these disputes being no small feature of reader interest in Father McGloin's biography—but he was never unfair, and Alemany was quite free of the pettiness that is so common a vice of little minds. Despite his several prolonged controversies with the Jesuits, after the dust of battle had settled there would probably have been few of the Society who would have disagreed with Father Michael Accolti, S.J., when he told his superior shortly after their arrival in California:

... I must confess for the sake of justice and truth that if we have laid some solid foundation for our future and permanent existence in California, all (this) we owe to the disinterested and charitable liberality of the zealous and wise Prelate, Bishop Alemany.[8]

No bishop can rule an episcopal see for over thirty years without incurring disapproval or dislike from some of his clergy and laity. In this Archbishop Alemany was probably no exception, but the extant evidence makes it clear that by the great majority of the laity, as well as priests and religious, he was held in the highest esteem. One of the outstanding laymen of San Francisco later wrote of him in a way that would have won the assent of most of his fellow laymen when he said:

Though small in stature, and plain to a marked degree in appearance and dress, Bishop Alemany was indefatigable as a worker, though most ascetic in his own life, and of a composure of temper that nothing seemed to disturb. In adherence to principle he was absolutely inflexible, but personal motives seemed to find no place in his springs of action.[9]

And if the laity appreciated Alemany it was due in part to the fact that he, in turn, appreciated them in a far more meaningful way than as mere providers of the free-will offerings that made possible various archdiocesan undertakings. In fact, San Francisco's first archbishop was far in advance of his time in his attitude toward the laity and the role they should play in the

---

[8] Accolti to William Murphy, S.J., Gilbert J. Garraghan, S.J., *The Jesuits of the Middle United States* (New York: America Press, 1938), II, 415.
[9] Bryan J. Clinch, "The Jesuits in American California," *Records of the American Catholic Historical Society of Philadelphia*, XVII (1906), 131.

13

Church. As early as December, 1883, he suggested to the Prefect of Propaganda that there be instituted lay diocesan consultors who, he said, "should have a consultative vote only, but their advice should be sought as well as welcomed by busy Bishops so burdened with many details that they cannot cope well with such problems without such help."[10] It is doubtful if any American bishop of his time or after his time ever so pointedly anticipated the action of Vatican Council II in regard to the laity as did the first Archbishop of San Francisco.

Needless to say, grave public questions constantly arose during the thirty-four years that Alemany served as a bishop in California. During the Civil War feeling ran high in San Francisco where one of President Lincoln's most severe critics was Thomas A. Brady, editor of *The Monitor,* the weekly Catholic newspaper. Although it was not an official organ, so many attributed the views of *The Monitor* to the Catholic Church, that Archbishop Alemany felt compelled to disavow the paper in August, 1863, and in a still stronger pastoral letter of November, 1864, he urged his priests to warn their people against "such deceits and commotions" as, in his opinion, *The Monitor* was then promoting.[11] A decade later the principal disturber of the peace was Denis Kearney (1847–1907) with his noisy agitation against land monopoly, railroad domination, Chinese labor competition, etc. And when Kearney and his followers threatened to go to further extremes, Alemany declared in a pastoral letter (July 25, 1877) that he felt it his duty

in these dangerous times to counsel all to shun suspicious company, to listen to no declaimer conniving at the subversion of quiet and order, to participate in no unauthorized move and to sustain to their utmost the legally constituted authorities.[12]

[10] Alemany to Giovanni Simeoni, San Francisco, October 3, 1883. Archives of the Congregation de Propaganda Fide.
[11] Quoted in John Bernard McGloin, S.J., "Catholic Attitudes in San Francisco during the Civil War," *Records of the American Catholic Historical Society of Philadelphia,* LXXXIII (March-June, 1962), 57.
[12] *Alta California* (San Francisco), July 26, 1877.

If "no man is an island," so no diocese is a vacuum. Archbishop Alemany's more than thirty years on the Pacific Coast witnessed one of the most unruly periods in the history of California, and no small portion of his responsibility was that of trying to bring his flock through those stormy years as much unscathed as possible by the surrounding social and political dangers. That he did not entirely achieve his goal, he would be the first to admit; but that a very real measure of success in this regard attended his efforts was obvious from the over-all picture of the Catholic community at the beginning and at the end of his administration. In his first report to the Society for the Propagation of the Faith (July 19, 1851), he estimated the Catholics under his care to number about 40,000 for whom there were then forty-one priests —not one of whom was California born—twenty-seven churches, and eleven mission chapels or stations. By the year of his resignation, however, the Catholic population of the archdiocese was reckoned at about 200,000 who were served by 175 priests in 128 churches and twenty-five chapels and stations.[13] True, statistics are an inadequate criterion by which to judge a bishop's career; yet they convey some idea of the zeal and competence with which he has executed his high task. In this instance they clearly demonstrated how mistaken Archbishop Alemany was when, nearly twenty years before he finally left California for his native Spain, he had asked his fellow bishops at Baltimore's Plenary Council in October, 1866, to second his resignation of the See of San Francisco, "since I lack the necessary qualities."[14]

Here, then, in Volume II of "Makers of American Catholicism" the reader will find a biography rich in detail, balanced in judgment, and as near to being a definitive life of Joseph Alemany as we are likely ever to have. Father McGloin's careful and prolonged research in ecclesiastical archives both in the United States

[13] *Sadliers' Catholic Directory, Almanac, and Ordo for the Year of Our Lord 1884* (New York: D. & J. Sadlier & Company. 1884), p. 195.

[14] A letter written by Alemany at Baltimore on October 6, 1866, "Acta et Decreta, Plenary Council of 1866." Archives of the Archdiocese of Baltimore.

and in Europe, as well as the intimate knowledge of the history of San Francisco and of California which he brought to the task, show up on almost every page. Thus in providing this scholarly life of the first Archbishop of San Francisco he has not only made a significant contribution to the history of the American Church, but he has contributed as well to the enlightenment and reading enjoyment of the ever-widening audience for the history of the American West, a new chapter in the religious history of that vast and fascinating region.

JOHN TRACY ELLIS

Professor of Church History in the University of San Francisco
General Editor of "Makers of American Catholicism"

Preface

IN a sense, this book was born in San Francisco on Monday evening, March 26, 1951, when, after lecturing on Joseph Sadoc Alemany at a local forum, I had a friendly chat with the Reverend Hubert Ward, O.P., who is, as I write in early 1965, the newly designated Prior Provincial of his Order on the West Coast. I can yet recall the challenger as well as his challenge: "When are you going to write the life of the Dominican Archbishop of San Francisco?" And I can still recall a rather prompt answer: "Never! Dominicans should write the lives of Dominicans and I had better devote myself to some needed lives of earlier Jesuits prominent on the San Francisco scene!"

With the passage of time, though, it became increasingly evident to me that the neglect of the "great captain" of California Catholicism had lasted much too long and that the time was overdue for someone to write his life and thus endeavor properly to assess the man and his place in the history of Roman Catholicism in California. Here now, for better or worse, is such an attempt.

I would wish, first of all, to acknowledge the courteous cooperation of various Friars Preachers in the research which went into its making. This was shown on the local level when the Very Reverend Joseph Aegius, O.P., then prior provincial, offered me every help and stated that what was both needed and wanted was as complete and frank a biographical study as was possible.

17

To Father Aegius and to his helpful secretary and archivist, the Reverend Charles Hess, O.P., my sincere thanks. Extensive delvings in Roman archives found me the recipient of appreciated kind acts from the Very Reverend John A. Driscoll, O.P., American socius to the master general. Foremost was his obtaining of permission from the Most Reverend Aniceto Fernandez Alonzo, master general, for me to consult the archives of the Order at Santa Sabina in Rome. Nor shall I ever forget the many hours of aid given me by the foremost American Dominican historian, Reverend Reginald Coffey, O.P., of Washington, D.C., who in innumerable ways helped this Jesuit who had to be introduced to Dominican usages and terminology. I could not have been in better hands, and I am deeply grateful to Father Coffey, too, for reading the manuscript and making some valuable suggestions. Out of all these contacts came my conviction that here I was seeing the motto of the Order of Preachers—*"Veritas"*—exemplified in a satisfying and complete sense.

I am grateful, also, to two cardinals for significant favors received in connection with this book. I refer to their Eminences James Francis Cardinal McIntyre of Los Angeles and the cardinal prefect of the Roman Congregation de Propaganda Fide, Gregory Peter Agagianian. It was the former's helpful letter to the cardinal prefect which brought about a relaxation in regulations governing the use of the Propaganda archives; this enabled the author successfully to examine all of the extensive Alemany materials preserved there.

Especial gratitude is here expressed, too, to the esteemed members of the Alemany family in Barcelona, Spain. In 1925, the Archbishop's grandnephew, Antonio Alamany (family spelling) Comella, published a life in Spanish and Catalan of his distinguished ancestor. It was a privilege to consult on two visits to Barcelona this distinguished man and his son, José Alamany Torner. Through their kindness, early contact was made with the Reverend Alberto Collell, O.P., of Barcelona, who kindly put

18

at my disposal a most thorough and valuable manuscript life of Archbishop Alemany which had been occupying his spare moments for some years. Father Collell had progressed as far as the consecration of Alemany in Rome in 1850 and was willing to allow me to use any and all of his materials for the first part of this book. I have leaned heavily upon the pages of Padre Collell and am happy to salute him as the closest thing to a collaborator I have had in this work.

Very early in my researches I became acquainted with the truly excellent and unpublished master's thesis of Sister Gertrude Mary Gray of Holy Name of the College of the Holy Names, Oakland, California. Entitled *A Preliminary Survey of the Life of the Most Reverend Joseph Sadoc Alemany, First Archbishop of San Francisco*, this is a superior study, and many a hint and help have I derived from it.

To my Jesuit superiors of the University of San Francisco, who generously provided me with two extensive leaves of absence to search European archives, I return my sincere thanks. Finally, my warmest gratitude goes to Albert Shumate, M.D., of San Francisco, whose modesty prevents him from admitting how much his help has meant to me in the now completed task.

John Bernard McGloin, S.J.
University of San Francisco

Key to Footnote Abbreviations

AAB   Archives of the Archdiocese of Baltimore.

AAPO   Archives of the Archdiocese of Portland in Oregon.

AASF   Archives of the Archdiocese of San Francisco.

AAHC   Archives of All Hallows College, Dublin.

AOB   Archives of the Congregation of the Oratory, Birmingham, England.

AOPSF Archives of the Order of Preachers, Province of the Holy Name, San Francisco, California.

AOPR   Archives of the Order of Preachers, Santa Sabina, Rome.

AOPW   Archives of the Order of Preachers, Province of St. Joseph, Washington, D.C.

APF   Archives of the Sacred Congregation de Propaganda Fide, Rome.

ASJSF   Archives of the Society of Jesus, California Province, San Francisco, California.

ASJSL   Archives of the Society of Jesus, Missouri Province, St. Louis, Missouri.

ASJR   Archives of the Society of Jesus, Rome.

ASPFP   Archives of the Society for the Propagation of the Faith, Paris.

ASV   Vatican Secret Archives, Rome.

AUSF   Archives, University of San Francisco.

MCUND Manuscript Collections, University of Notre Dame.

CALIFORNIA'S FIRST ARCHBISHOP

1

"Wedded to the Church in California"

ON July 3, 1850, the newest and, perhaps, the youngest Dominican bishop in the world sat at this desk in his room in the convent attached to the ancient Roman church of Santa Maria Sopra Minerva. Only three days previously, Joseph Sadoc Alemany had, with reluctance but in obedience to the explicit demand of His Holiness, Pius IX, received episcopal consecration and been designated as Bishop of Monterey in far-off Gold Rush California. Certainly, the events of the last few weeks should be reported to a devoted mother in Catalonia, and they were in the following lines:

> In my good fortune or bad fortune, three days after arriving here I learned that the Bishops of the United States had named me Bishop of Monterey in place of Father Montgomery whose refusal has been accepted because of lack of health, and that the Pope had confirmed me eight days before I arrived here in Rome. I went then to visit the Pope to see if I could free myself from the burden of California; but as they had already told him not to let me resign, I had hardly entered when he began to speak to me in perfect Castilian, and he said, "You are to go to Monterey; you must go to California. Others go there to seek gold; you go there to carry the Cross. God will assist you. The Bishops of the United States have named you, I have confirmed you. Thus there is nothing for you to do but to obey, otherwise you will oppose the will of the Vicar of Christ and the Will of God." I shut my mouth. There was no choice for me there. He just sent me with nice words to California.
>
> Then I had to have an outfit made for a little Lord Bishop, and to

25

make a Retreat. Last Sunday on the Feast of St. Paul, Apostle of the Gentiles, Cardinal Franzoni, Prefect of the Propaganda, assisted by the Patriarch of Jerusalem and by a Dominican Archbishop, wedded me to the Church in California, together with the new Bishop of Pavia.[1]

At first sight, it would appear that a vast distance separates Spain's province of Catalonia from California—yet three of the latter state's earlier bishops came from Catalonia. As we shall see, Bishop Alemany was from the ancient town of Vich, located about thirty miles from Barcelona. Two future bishops of the central and southern part of California, Thaddeus Amat, C. M., and Francis Mora, were likewise natives of Catalonia. When one reflects, too, that the not distant island of Mallorca was the birthplace of Junipero Serra, founder of the Catholic Church in California, the conviction comes that California's Catholicism owes much to this part of Spain. However, since Joseph Alemany, the first Archbishop to serve in California, was born in Vich and, until 1965, was buried in Santo Domingo Church there, we shall now turn our attention to this town with such a long history—even before the advent of the Alemany family there in the seventeenth century. Vich is now distinguished, among other features, in the fact that a prominent thoroughfare is named "Calle Arzobispo Alemany"—proof positive that the old city is proud of this one of its many sons.[2]

The original settlement of Vich dates from Roman times (a Roman temple dating from the second century is there

[1] Antonio Alamany Comella, *Illustrisimo y Reverendisimo Fray Jose Sadoch Alamany Conill, O.P., Obispo de Monterey y Primer Arzobispo de San Francisco de California: Datos Biograficos—Pastorales Cartas Interesantes—Juicios Referentes a Su Actuacion por la Prensa Espanola y Extranjera-Anecdotas,* Vich, 1925, pp. 21–22.

It is interesting to note that the church of Alemany's consecration, San Carlo al Corso in Rome, was the scene, exactly three quarters of a century later (March 19, 1925), of the episcopal consecration of Angelo Giuseppe Roncalli, His Holiness Pope John XXIII.

[2] Although most modern San Franciscans are quite unacquainted with the origin or the meaning of the name "Alemany," it is worthy of note that a prominent freeway, Alemany Boulevard, daily traversed by thousands, is named after San Francisco's first Archbishop.

26

still), and it bears the distinction of being one of the earliest episcopal sees of Spain. One reason for early prominence is its geographical location, for it is divided by the Meder River across which early trade caravans passed. Its population has never been very large (about 20,000 today), but its devotees, which would seem to include all of its present inhabitants, proudly point out that its illustrious sons and daughters have given Vich an importance far out of proportion to its real size. Its Casa Consistorialis exhibits, in a special room, a "Gallery of Illustrious Men" which includes Alemany prominently among its number. Notables besides San Francisco's first Archbishop include the famous philosopher, Jaime Balmes (1810–1848), and St. Anthony Claret (1807–1870), founder of the religious congregation known after him as the Claretians. Presumably, archbishops as well as others are allowed expressions of legitimate pride regarding their city of origin and Joseph Sadoc Alemany is no exception, for he remarked more than once during his California years: "I am Catalan," and he always showed affection and filial reverence for his native Vich; this he manifested finally with the request that his remains be interred there.

The Alemany family first entered the history of Vich around 1610 when a certain Sebastian Alemany, a knife-maker by trade, removed across the Pyrenees from the city of Salies in southern France into Catalonia. Establishing himself at Vich, he married Catalina Ros, daughter of a fellow artisan; these were the first in the Catalan lines of ancestors of Archbishop Alemany. It would appear that some of the Catalan sturdiness which marked Alemany's years in California came from the hard-working artisans who had preceded him as his ancestors. Indeed, Alemany's strength of will and genuine spirit of sacrifice were inbred. He once remarked that he knew that he was a stubborn man because, he said, "I come from the German or hard-headed part of Spain!"

Towards the end of March, 1777, Antonio Alemany y Font

27

was born in Vich where, in due time, he followed his father's trade of blacksmith. His reputation for solidly honest characteristics was a deserved one and, on November 1, 1809, at the age of 32, he married the 18-year-old Micaela de los Santos Cunill y Saborit, daughter of a local chocolate maker. The twelve children who blessed their marriage were to add a significant page to the religious history of Vich. Of the twelve, in addition to Joseph Sadoc, who was the third child, two became priests of the Diocese of Vich (Ignacio, 1812–1893, and Miguel, 1819–1889), while two other sons became Dominican friars even as the Archbishop (Manuel, 1817–1903, and Juan, 1826–1882). Lest the male offspring be alone in their religious dedication, a daughter, Josefa (1823–1872), entered the Carmel of Vich, and Micaela (1829–1899) followed her as a Dominican sister in her native Vich. Two children died in infancy, Rafaela in 1815 and Ramon in 1828, but the family line was continued by the marriages of three sons, Antonio (1811–1880), Luciano (1821–1870), and Francisco (1825–1864). Seven of the family of twelve died during the lifetime of Archbishop Alemany, while four survived his death in 1888. He was always devoted to his family and the several visits he paid to Vich as first Archbishop of the Church in California were always times of great joy for his townsfolk and, needless to say, especially for members of the Alemany family.

Joseph Sadoc Alemany was born on Wednesday, July 13, 1814, and like Serra who was born a century earlier (1713) on the island of Mallorca, he was brought to the baptismal font on the very day of his birth. Padre Salvador Armengol of the Cathedral staff christened him Jose Buenaventura y Ramon Alemany (the "Sadoc" came with his Dominican profession later) and when only nine months old, on April 12, 1815, he was confirmed in the chapel of the episcopal palace by the Bishop of Vich, Francisco de Veyan y Mola. The firm faith of both of

28

his parents was exhibited in countless ways all during his forma-
tive years and, on one occasion, in referring to the Church of
Santa Clara close to his home, Alemany mentioned that this
church, which was attached to the Dominican Convent next
door, had been the scene where "our saintly mother offered us
to the Virgin Mary as soon as we were born." Another time,
when recalling the memory of his father, he remarked that he
was regular in the reception of the sacraments and rarely omitted
the daily recitation of the rosary. Similar testimony is to be found
in the birthday congratulations which Fray Manuel addressed to
his Archbishop-brother in 1875: "What is the reason that five
brothers chose an ecclesiastical calling while two daughters became nuns? The first reason is a religious education, added to the
exemplary lives of our parents and the constant care they took
of all the family; the more I reflect on the life of my parents,
the more I admire their Holy Christian life and the more I
realize that I owe my good training, under God, to them." These
are sentiments with which the Archbishop found himself in complete agreement. In 1865, at the time of his mother's death,
Alemany expressed his pride and admiration for her thus: "We
are greatly consoled by the well-founded confidence that our
mother does not need our prayers while we certainly need hers.
I am sure, in fact, that none of us ever noticed any voluntary
faults in her. She was absolutely innocent and just, serene and
imperturbable, in the face of all vicissitudes." With such a background, it is hardly a surprise, then, to come on evidence all
during Alemany's life of a genuine spirit of prayer and a constant and solid practice of the Christian virtues.

Piety is not enough if not accompanied by other facets of
training as well, and it is not surprising to learn that Alemany's
father was a strict man with regard to such family upbringing.
Later on, some found an unbending rigor in Archbishop
Alemany's character which pleased them little or not at all

29

—and this, perhaps, can be attributed in part to just such early training. At any rate, whether excessive upon occasion or no (there were those who maintained that the rigor was always directed towards himself and rarely, if ever, towards others), the firmness and strength of character which constantly marked him would seem to have been natural results of his earlier training. Nor did Jose have to wait until later years for a chance to show such fortitude for, almost from his earliest years, his native city of Vich was rocked with scenes of disorder and anarchy, especially from 1820-1823 when the supporters of the so-called constitutional movement succeeded in profoundly agitating the town and countryside. Anticlericalism manifested itself in sacrilegious profanations which culminated with the murder of the local bishop who was torn from his Cathedral and barbarously killed after having been brought to the fortress of Barcelona. However, despite these sad outbursts, it would appear that Jose Alemany, together with others of his family, was able to acquire a good education in the primary schools of Vich. At the age of 10, he was enrolled in the diocesan seminary where he began the study of Latin and the humanities and where the registers of this institution list him from 1824-1828. A tribute to the intrepid spirit of the youth of Vich—or, perhaps, to the same spirit of their parents—is to be found in the fact that, even at the height of the excesses already mentioned, approximately 400 youths from Vich and vicinity were enrolled in the seminary. The three years spent by Alemany in these surroundings found him diligent in his application to study and exemplary in his piety. The next step in his education came when he was sent to nearby Moya to attend classes in the Institute there taught under the title of the "Escuelas Pias de Moya." Unfortunately, this school was destroyed by fire so that all of its records were destroyed leaving no information concerning Alemany's work during these two years. An account which would seem to date from

1850 but remains unsigned thus sums up this part of Jose Alemany's earlier years:

His upbringing was such as you might expect from a father who never lost his children from sight and who, on holidays, accompanied them in their jaunts into the country . . . at the proper age, he attended courses at the diocesan seminary in Vich for three years and with the Padres Escolapios of Moya for two years of humanities. That he repayed the paternal solicitude shown him is amply testified to by his teachers—all of whom remember him with tender affection and are pleased yet to speak of his lively intelligence, diligent application and exemplary behavior.[3]

[3] Quoted in Alberto Collell, O.P., *Biografía del Exco. y. Rdmo. Fray Jose Sadoc Alemany, O.P., Primer Arzobispo de San Francisco de California,* p. 12. This is an unpublished manuscript with excellent and accurate details on the early years of Alemany which the author, Padre Collell, a Dominican friar resident in Barcelona, graciously made available to the present author.

2

First Years in the Dominican Order, 1830–1840

ALTHOUGH the disturbed state of things in Spain regarding religion and the treatment of religious orders was well known to young Jose Alemany, he determined to enter the Dominican Order as soon as such entrance might be allowed him. This decision to enter religious life can be easily understood in the light of what has been mentioned concerning his earliest upbringing. It would appear that the young lad was fortunate in his spiritual director, Padre Fortian Feu of the Oratorian fathers of Vich. That this affection for his director was extended to the work of the Oratorians themselves became evident many years later when Alemany, as the newly consecrated Bishop of Monterey, entered into negotiations with Father John Henry Newman of the London Oratory concerning the possibility of sending some Oratorian fathers to help him in California.

Having obtained his parents consent and blessing, Jose Buenaventura y Ramon Alemany, aged sixteen, entered the Dominican Order in the Priory of Santo Domingo in his native Vich. This entrance was made with the taking of the holy habit in middle September, 1830. Although, at present, there is no male Dominican foundation in Vich, there was one from 1571 up to the dispersal of the Order from Spain in the 1830's. Alemany was fortunate in having as his novice master Father Pedro Vaquer, a celebrated preacher and distinguished Catalan Dominican of the day. Father Manuel Alemany, the Archbishop's brother, who also had Vaquer as novice master, later recalled him as an "exemplary man with a deep understanding of youth." A key to the further understanding of the missionary stirrings which seemed ever to animate Alemany's soul (made evident later on by his oft-expressed desire to resign the See of San Francisco and to resume his life as a Dominican missionary) is found in the fact that, after listening to an account of his Order's missionary apostolate in the Philippine Islands, he decided to offer himself for membership in the Missionary Province of the Most Holy Rosary there. His director advised him to wait until he had completed his spiritual and intellectual formation in Europe before proceeding, and the young novice was docile to this direction. On September 23, 1831, having completed his canonical year of novitiate, he pronounced solemn vows (then customary immediately after the novitiate year) while choosing to add to his baptismal name of Joseph that of the Prior and head of the Dominican martyrs of Sandomierz in Poland, Blessed Sadoc, who had been martyred in the thirteenth century. (Henceforth, his other baptismal names "Buenaventura y Ramon" do not occur in his signature while the religious name of "Sadoc" is frequently there encountered.) With the pronouncing of his religious vows of poverty, chastity, and obedience, Brother Joseph Sadoc became both a member of the Aragon Province of the Dominican Order as well as, more specifically and as required by Dominican usage, a son of the Dominican Priory of Vich.

Some days later Brother Joseph Sadoc was sent to take the three-years course of philosophy in the more inland city of Tremp at the priory of his Order called San Jaime de Pallars. He seems early to have demonstrated his intellectual acumen, for near the conclusion of his philosophical studies he was entrusted, on April 17, 1834, with a public defense of the materials proposed in his philosophical course. That he was, also, well liked is testified to by a letter written to his family by a brother Dominican who taught him during these years. In 1850, when writing to congratulate the family on the appointment of Bishop Alemany to Monterey, Father Jose Sentanera expressed himself as follows: "It is neither exaggeration or hiding the truth but a sincere expression of affection to state that the student Alemany always made himself loved by his teachers."[1] Although Alemany was naturally gratified at the success of this public demonstration of his mastery of the philosophical course, his happiness was marred a month later, on May 29, 1834, with the death of his beloved father in his fifty-seventh year.

Four days after this public defense, Alemany was sent to begin his theological studies at his Order's celebrated Priory "de la Anunciacion" at Gerona, not far from Vich. This house traced its foundations back to the middle of the thirteenth century and was, therefore, one of the earliest of the Dominican Order. After his arrival, Brother Joseph Sadoc wrote to his family that there were fifty friars there, among whom there was one destined to become celebrated (along with the future Archbishop himself) —Father Francisco Coll, called the "Apostle of Catalonia." Because of his subsequent career and because of the close friendship which united them, Bishop Alemany tried unsuccessfully on several occasions to have Father Francisco transferred to California to help him with the work of his far-flung diocese. For one year, both of the young Dominicans applied themselves diligently to the traditional course in fundamental theology called the "*De Locis Theologicis*" of Melchior Cano, O.P. This peaceful phase of his earlier Dominican life came to a rude close in 1835 when the same forces of anti-religion already mentioned caused a Secularization Law to be passed which closed all the religious houses in Spain. On August 10, 1835, the friars were expelled from their Gerona convent and sad acts of vandalism occurred which rendered their going all the more poignant. Alemany, along with

[1] Collell, *Biografia*, etc., p. 17.

34

the others, was forced to don a civilian suit in lieu of his beloved habit, and, thus attired, made his way back to his family home in Vich. However, this was not considered a safe refuge and he decided to take advantage of an offer to repair to his grandmother's country home in the parish of Gurb, not far from Vich. There, for about a year, 1835–1836, he lived with a devoted uncle and aunt while applying himself privately to the study of the *Summa* of St. Thomas. In these studies, he was aided by the tutoring of a lector of his Order, the competent Father Lucia Costa, and in order to offer some service to those among whom he lived, the young friar also occupied himself with the teaching of some grammar classes. It was not until the middle of 1836 when what was, certainly, an unsatisfactory position for a professed religious was resolved in favor of a more regular form of life. By then, it had become evident that there was to be no immediate improvement in religious conditions in Catalonia, and, when a cordial invitation reached the dispersed Dominican students from their brethren in Italy, the decision was made voluntarily to exile themselves in the hope that they would be able to continue their theological studies there. Accordingly, having decided to go to Turin, Brother Joseph Sadoc, together with another Dominican and four other clergymen, embarked from the port of Barcelona on August 23, 1836. Before embarkation, reports had reached them of an outbreak of cholera in Turin and vicinity and this caused them to change their plans in favor of Rome where they planned to present themselves to the master general of their order, and to await his decision as to their future. After a journey which included storms and other dangers, they arrived at Cività-Vecchia on September 8, 1836. A few days later they arrived in Rome where they were cordially received by their master general, Father Tommasso Jacinto Cipolleti, who ordered that the religious habit of their order be immediately granted the wanderers while he told them to spend two weeks seeing the glories of Rome before proceeding to further study. This was the first of what were to be several visits to Rome for Alemany, and it is interesting to reflect that could the young Catalan exile have foreseen the future, he would have been amazed to think that, only fourteen years later, after a decade of missionary labors in the United States, he would be consecrated a bishop in Rome, while, in 1869–1870, as an archbishop, he would take a prominent part in the First Vatican Council there. Such things, of course, were far from his vision and he simply reported, in letters home, how great and complete was his joy in the opportunities afforded him to visit the religious shrines of Rome.

Pilgrimages to St. Mary Major and to St. John Lateran, together with several visits to St. Peter's Basilica, reached their climax when an audience was arranged for him and for his companions with Pope Gregory XVI. His Holiness received the exiles most graciously and blessed them *"ex intimo corde"* while praising them for their fidelity to their religious calling in the midst of trials. There were ten Catalan friars who, like Alemany, were in Rome awaiting assignment and soon the news came that six of these, including Alemany, were to go to Viterbo, where they were to continue their theological studies in either of two Dominican houses there.[2] Brother Joseph Sadoc was assigned to that called

[2] Viterbo, situated about fifty miles north of Rome, is the site of an ancient episcopal see and possesses the splendid Romanesque Cathedral of San Lorenzo, dating from the twelfth century. One Dominican convent, to which Alemany was assigned, was located near the ancient gate and, therefore, was called "Santa Maria ad Gradus" or "dei Gradi." Several miles from the city was the Convent of Santa Maria della Quercia. In 1873, the Italian government converted the Dominican Convent of S. Maria dei Gradi to a prison, and it still serves as such now. The lovely old church in which Alemany sang his first Mass on Easter Sunday, March 26, 1837, is now included in the jail area. In 1927, the studium generale of the Dominican Order was removed from La Quercia to Rome, and His Holiness Pope Pius XI decided that the ancient convent which had served the Dominican Order, 1515–1927, should be converted for use as a regional major seminary. Thus one of the oldest continuous Dominican foundations in Italy came to an end. The adjoining church, still complete with Dominican choir stalls, is in the care of the secular clergy.

S. Maria dei Gradi and he was in residence there by September 29, 1836. His appreciation for his master general's kindness found expression in the following letter:

Reverend Father Master of the Order of Preachers,
The undersigned novice with his companions, not only because of politeness, but even more because of the very intense affection in our hearts aroused and strengthened by the many and great benefits given to us, wish to inform Your Most Reverend Paternity, that God granted us a happy journey and that we arrived at our religious home where we have been received by the Superiors with the greatest benignity and charity. We also wish to be remembered to the Reverend Fathers of your convent whom we greet with full hearts.

The least of the subjects of Your Most Reverend Paternity,
Fray Joseph Sadoc Alamany

In the Convent of S. Maria ad Gradus in Viterbo,
30th of September, 1836.[3]

It is not surprising that soon the promising qualities of the young Catalan friar pleased his Italian Dominican superiors to the extent that they decided, despite his youth, to obtain necessary dispensations for him to make quicker progress towards priestly ordination. On November 9, 1836, he was approved for the reception of minor orders in preparation for priesthood and these he received two days later. On Saturday, December 27, 1836, he received the subdiaconate, while on February 18, 1837, another milestone was reached with the reception of the diaconate. These orders were conferred upon him at Toscanella near Viterbo and the ordaining prelate was the same Bishop who raised him to priesthood on Saturday, March 11, 1837, in the San Lorenzo Cathedral of Viterbo. This was Gaspar Bernardo Pianetti (1780–1862), who, in 1840, was made a cardinal by Gregory XVI. In February, Brother Joseph had written to his

[3] Joseph Alemany to Thomas Cipolletti, Viterbo, September 30, 1836. AOPR.

brother Antonio to ask him to notify his parents and other relatives of his forthcoming reception of priestly powers:

> Although at the beginning of my stay here in Viterbo I wrote you a long letter in which I promised to write again . . . I want to let you know that last November I received the Tonsure and Four Minor Orders, at Christmas the Subdiaconate, and on the 18th of this month the Diaconate, and also that I passed the examination and am approved to be ordained the 11th of next month of March. Therefore with divine help, if within three weeks the dispensation arrives, on the 12th of March or on St. Joseph's Day, our Lord will grant me the grace of celebrating my first Mass. But if these three weeks are not time for the dispensation to arrive, then I will sing my first Mass on Easter Sunday at eleven o'clock. Tell Mother and ask her to commend me to God so that everything will come out all right. If I could fly and bring her with me, I would do it. Please let my nurse know all this, and give them both loving remembrances.[4]

Father Joseph Sadoc Alemany's joy was complete when, having received holy orders while more than a year below the canonical age, he sang his first Mass on Easter Sunday, March 26, 1837, "with the greatest happiness to be imagined"—as he reported in a letter home, adding that "there was also the joy of having Father Provincial present and of being assisted by two Catalan friars as deacon and subdeacon."[5] This Mass was offered in the Dominican church of Santa Maria dei Gradi, Viterbo, the father prior yielding the dignity of celebrant of the conventual Mass on the Church's greatest feast to the newly ordained priest. His letters home are filled with the sentiments customary with young priests on such occasions and are concluded with the fervent petition that God be asked to grant him the grace to be and to remain a "good priest."

An indication of the worth with which the newly ordained Father Alemany was regarded within his own order is to be

---

[4] Joseph Alemany to Antonio Alemany, Viterbo, February 21, 1837, in Alamany Comella, *Fray Jose Sadoc Alamany*, etc., p. 15.

[5] Joseph Alemany to Antonio Alemany, Viterbo, April 4, 1837. *Op. cit.*, p. 15.

found in the fact that, shortly after ordination, he was appointed as assistant master of novices in his convent of La Quercia. The novice master under whom he served, Padre Conti, was genuinely fond of him and made good use of his services in the office of training the novices of the order. Meanwhile, Father Alemany continued to distinguish himself in his class work, and it is said that a classical aphorism not unknown to Dominicans was used concerning him: "In the choir and in matters spiritual, he behaved as if he had no thought of study; in his studies, he behaved as if he had never heard of choir!" His constant companion during these months was the *Summa* of St. Thomas, and he repeatedly demonstrated his competency with regards to its contents. On Saturday, May 5, 1838, the feast of the great Dominican preacher St. Vincent Ferrer, Father Alemany preached publicly for the first time in the pulpit of Santa Maria dei Gradi. A pious chronicler, bent perhaps more on edification than on historical accuracy, finds a lesson in the fact that Alemany started his career of preaching (which he was to continue for so long in the nineteenth century) on the feast of the Dominican who had similarly distinguished himself in the fifteenth century.

He was again chosen for a public defense—this time in theology, and on April 23, 1839, this exhibition was successfully acquitted as part of the customary exercises connected with the provincial chapter which met in Viterbo then. That he was conscious of the importance of the appointment was indicated by a letter to his Dominican friar-uncle in which he wrote: ". . . Tell my mother that, in April, if God wills, I will have to defend some theological theses in the provincial chapter which will be held in my convent."[6] Added importance was had in the fact that

[6] Alemany to Jacinto Cunill, Viterbo, January 3, 1839. Quoted in Collell, *Biografía,* etc., p. 70. An official record notes that, on December 14 (1838), letters patent were issued to "Fathers Brother Augustine Borelli and Brother Joseph Allemanny" by which they were allowed to count the years of theology in the convent of S. Maria ad Gradus just as if they had pursued these studies in the studium generale of St. Dominic in Perugia. Regestum

among those present was Monsignor Giacomo Antonelli, the future cardinal secretary of state of Pope Pius IX. Another who admired Father Alemany's performance was Père Jean Baptiste Henri Lacordaire (1802–1861), who had arrived in Viterbo only two weeks before to enter upon his novitiate as a Dominican. A firm friendship developed between the two friars and, later on, Alemany referred several times in various letters to the esteem in which he held Lacordaire while expressing his hope that the latter would succeed in his project of restoring the Dominican Order in France. Both, indeed, proved to be among the lights of the Dominican Order, the one in the fullness of priesthood in distant California and the other in the fullness of the spoken word in France.

On June 17, 1839, together with his Dominican brother Manuel, Father Joseph Sadoc had the happiness of assisting in Rome at the first Mass of their brother Ignacio, ordained for the Diocese of Vich. While still there, it seems, the new Dominican master general, Angelus Ancarani, who served from 1838–1844, developed plans to further the career of the promising friar from Vich. This plan took the form of an assignment to the venerable Church of The Minerva, Rome, where Alemany was to have an early taste of priestly ministry while continuing his studies. There followed some busy months which gave him great satisfaction and, concerning which in a letter to his uncle, he wrote that "I have an assignment which, although oftentimes allowing me to rest peacefully at night, sometimes does not give me that opportunity."[7]

It will be recalled that, while yet a novice in Vich, Alemany

---

Romanae Provinciae O.P. ab an. 1837 ad an. 1858, p. 26. Dominican Archives, S. Maria Sopra Minerva, Rome.

[7] Alemany to Jacinto Cunill, no date given, but probably late November or early December, 1839. Collell, *Biografia*, etc., p. 81. That he was successful in these studies is also attested to in Dominican records where under date of February 1, 1840, he is recorded as having been awarded the "Laurea Lectoratus" in theology with twenty-one affirmative votes while only four were opposed: Regestrum Collegi Divae Thomae de Urbe, Vol. III, p. 296. Archives S. Maria Sopra Minerva, Rome.

had wished to volunteer his services in the cause of the Philippine missions of his order. Now, with his newly enjoyed priestly ministry, the same desire to become a missionary of his order began once more to overwhelm his thoughts and prayers and, repeatedly, he besought the requisite permission from the master general, Father Ancarani. He was, indeed, to receive the mandatum of a missionary from Ancarani, but his mission was not to be in Asia, but in America. This unexpected development, which was to change his career completely and was to institute a chain of events which would find him ultimately serving as the first Archbishop of San Francisco, came about as a result of the choosing in 1837 of Richard Pius Miles, O.P. (1791–1860), as the first Bishop of Nashville in Tennessee in the United States. This Dominican Prelate, destined to be known as the "Father of the Church in Tennessee," was almost entirely destitute of all resources including clergy and he thus represented his needs to the master general in Rome. What more fitting, thought Ancarani, than that the eager and zealous friar from Spain be prepared for a missionary career in the challenging and largely unchurched frontier of the United States? A letter of Father Alemany written to his uncle in early December, 1839, explains his change of destination.

I do not now pursue my theological studies but occupy myself according to the orders of Father Master General to the study of Moral Theology and to the study of the English language because this is the language of the United States. I have always noticed that my Superior has, in a certain way, opposed my going to the Philippines. On the other hand, in the United States, the weather is similar to our own, we have houses there and there is as much, if not more, need than in the Philippines. I leave it all to the Lord.[8]

[8] Alemany to Jacinto Cunill, Collell, *Biografía,* etc., p. 82. An undated letter of Alemany written in 1839 at Santa Sabina, Rome, to Ancarani, adds an interesting and important detail here; he mentions that he was moved to the missionary apostolate in America by Bishop Flaget's description of the great need the Dominican Bishop Miles had for priests in his vast diocese. In the same letter, Alemany praises the holiness of Bishop Flaget and mentions that to Flaget was even attributed the power of working miracles.

41

The last months of Father Alemany's stay in Rome in 1839 found him enrolled as a student in the Urban College of Propaganda Fide where he endeavored to penetrate the mysteries of the English language and in various other ways to prepare himself for the apostolate of the foreign missions. His completion of the Dominican course of studies came with the awarding of the degree of lector in sacred theology at The Minerva in Rome[9] and, on January 24, 1840, he addressed a letter to Ancarani informing him that, as he had about completed his preparations for departure to America, he was writing to get a paternal blessing for himself and for his companion, another Spanish Dominican, Francisco Cubero, similarly assigned to North America. Several weeks previously, he had written to his brother Antonio: "I have already my orders to go to the missions, since the Father General has sent me to help our Dominican Bishop in Tennessee, U.S.A."[10]

[9] The lectorate in sacred theology is one of the three traditional degrees granted in the Dominican Order to those friars who have successfully satisfied the requirements. The others are the bachelor degree and that of master of sacred theology.

[10] Alemany to his brother Antonio, SOPRA Minerva, Rome, January 6, 1840. Conill, p. 86. *Biografía.*

3

Missionary Years in America, 1840–1849

AT the beginning of February, 1840, Father Alemany and his companion, Father Cubero, prepared for their departure from the Eternal City to the United States. They were able to arrange this out of the port of Leghorn in northern Italy, and this caused them to cancel previous plans to depart from England. An older friar, Father Eugene Hyacinth Pozzo, en route to serve as novice master for his Order in America, joined them in their departure for the United States.[1] On February 12, the three Dominicans set sail and, in an early letter which Alemany wrote to his parents from the United States, he thus reveals the touch of nostalgia which he felt as his ship passed along the Catalonian coast:

I stretched my vision to discover Montseny and at least, in this manner, to take leave of my country. On the ship's map, this peak was

[1] Francis Cubero, O.P., was born in the Province of Aragon, Spain, in 1807 and died in 1883 at St. Catherine's Convent near Springfield, Kentucky. Ordained at Viterbo in Italy in 1837, he labored in Ohio and Kentucky for many years. Father O'Daniel, Dominican historian (see n. 5), characterizes him as a "somewhat bluff, but staunch, Friar Preacher."

Hyacinth Pozzo, O.P., was born in Piedmont, Italy, in 1808. Ordained in Italy in 1831, he taught at St. Joseph's near Somerset, Ohio. He returned to Italy in 1851 or 1852 and died there in 1862. "A capable scientist and theologian," O'Daniel calls him. Alemany's worth is thus assessed by a contemporary: "Of the venerable Dr. Alemany, the only survivor of the three [this was written in 1884] who has filled for so many years the archiepiscopal See of San Francisco, it is not necessary that anything should be here said. His admirable work in the field committed to his charge speaks more loudly in his praise than can tongue or pen. God grant that he may long survive to edify those he has so earnestly endeavored to serve." Benjamin J. Webb, *The Centenary of Catholicism in Kentucky*, Louisville, Ky., 1884, p. 209.

43

pictured as rising high but we hit rough and high waters as well and I had to bid adieu to the plains of Vich while saying the Holy Rosary and, on God's sea, to beg for His protection.[2]

It would be long before Father Alemany and the others would forget the stormy crossing which was theirs to New York. An indication of the slowness of their passage is had in the fact that it was not until February 25 (two weeks after departure from Leghorn) that they finally put out into the Atlantic. Veering south after passing Gibraltar, they had hardly passed the isle of Madeira when, unexpectedly, they found themselves deprived of the winds while a disturbing calm seemed to have kept their vessel glued to a glassy sea; true Dominicans that they were, the friars began a novena to St. Catherine of Siena, asking their patroness to send them a favorable wind. From the sequel, they considered themselves fortunate that their prayers were not answered exactly as they wished for, after the captain had decided to change course somewhat, it was discovered that the area of the ocean into which they would otherwise have entered had become the scene of a tempestuous storm which might well have sent them to the bottom of the sea. Even so, their own course was marked by anything but peaceful weather and, on March 19, the feast of St. Joseph, they were almost swamped by a huge wave which well-nigh engulfed their ship. Pious strategy was here employed as the friars threw into the sea a piece of the "veil of Our Lady of Livorno, patroness of storms at sea," and they rejoiced to note that the stormy weather gradually subsided as they proceeded westward. However, the crossing of the gulf of Florida was not without its tense moments as currents out of Mexican waters again agitated their ship. In the same letter quoted above, Alemany wrote: "During almost all the trip, we had occasion to admire the workings of the Divine Providence."[3]

[2] Alamany Comella, *Fray Jose Sadoc Alamany Conill,* p. 17. Montseny is a peak which stands between the plain of Vich and the sea. The name of the ship on which Alemany sailed to America remains unknown.

[3] Alemany to his family, Somerset, Ohio, April 26, 1840—in Alamany Comella, *Fray Jose,* etc., p. 16.

We may well imagine that all aboard the ship were happy on Thursday, April 2, 1840, when, fifty days out of Leghorn, their craft dropped anchor in New York harbor. After remaining there about a week to make arrangements to continue their journey (in the letter already quoted above, Father Alemany expressed his interest in and admiration for the metropolis of New York), the friars left New York City on April 7, en route to Philadelphia and Pittsburgh. This was the barge and canal age in what was then a part of frontier America, and it was an interesting experience so to travel to Pittsburgh after going part of the way by train. On Palm Sunday, April 12, 1840, they arrived there about noon and the piety so characteristic of Alemany was thus reported several weeks later from Ohio:

On Palm Sunday, in the morning, I was told that it would be impossible for me to offer Mass since we would arrive late; but I (who have always been a bit different) did not wish to be without the celebration of Mass . . . arriving at the Redemptorist church where we were to stay, I discovered that a solemn Mass was in progress at the only altar. Recalling that, in Rome, we were permitted to offer Mass until one o'clock, I waited and then was able to offer my Mass.[4]

The Redemptorist fathers proved themselves to be excellent hosts and invited their Dominican confreres to remain with them for the solemn celebration of Holy Week. However, since they had already determined to go on, they left Pittsburgh on the next day, April 13, for Cincinnati by way of the Ohio River. By daybreak on Holy Thursday, April 16, having anchored at Cincinnati, they made their way to the cathedral to make their paschal communion. It was an especial joy for Father Alemany there to encounter the Bishop of Nashville, Richard Pius Miles, O.P., who was spending some days in Cincinnati as the guest of Bishop John B. Purcell of that city. Since it had been Miles's request for helpers in his frontier diocese that had caused Alemany to be assigned to America, the meeting of the two Dominicans was a source of gratification to both. It was not difficult for them to

[4] Ibid.

keep engaged during the solemn triduum of Holy Week, and the following days, including Easter Sunday, saw Father Alemany and his companions assisting the two prelates in various pontifical functions.

Evidently, however, it was not long before Bishop Miles told them, while expressing his gratification at the arrival of his Dominican brethren, that (not having heard from the master general of their Order in Rome concerning his request for new helpers) he had been able to procure several priests to help him. At the moment, therefore, he considered it best that they not go to Tennessee with him, but rather continue on to St. Joseph's Convent, Somerset, Ohio, where they could rest a bit after their extensive travels and continue their study of English in preparation for future labors on the Dominican missionary frontier in Ohio, Tennessee, and Kentucky.[5] Accordingly, the friars accompanied Bishop Miles to Somerset, which he planned to visit while en route to the Fourth Provincial Council of Baltimore which was to begin on the following May 17.

So it was that, with a cordial greeting from the brethren at St. Joseph's, Father Alemany found himself in the second of the principal convents of the Dominican province which dated from 1805 when Fathers Edward Fenwick and Thomas Wilson had made their pioneer foundation at St. Rose, near Springfield, Kentucky. It had been from St. Rose that the early Dominicans had made their way as missionaries through Kentucky and into Ohio. In Perry County, Fenwick built the first Catholic church and convent in the state of Ohio, while from this nucleus the town of Somerset developed as a Catholic community and served as the logical center for missionary activity in central Ohio. By the time of Father Alemany's arrival on Friday afternoon, April 24, 1840, the Dominican foundation, while hardly out of the pioneer stage, was rather solidly established. One of their hosts, Father Nicolas

[5] The history of St. Joseph's Province of the Dominican Order has been told in several volumes by Victor O'Daniel, O.P. (1868–1960). Although highly opinionated and, at times, exhibiting excessive loyalty to his Order, Father O'Daniel's various volumes are standard in the field.

Young, thus wrote to another friar, Father Raymond Van Zeeland, about their arrival:

> Two Spanish priests have arrived at St. Joseph's a few days since. They appear very zealous and are busily engaged in learning English. One, in particular, is making much progress.[6]

Less than a week after their arrival at Somerset, the two Spanish friars addressed a letter to Father Ancarani in Rome. They mentioned that, after a long but happy journey, they had arrived at St. Joseph's, where they now beheld their brethren "working tirelessly for souls." They had become acquainted with the fact that much pressure was being exerted to have them remain in Ohio rather than, ultimately, to proceed to Tennessee to help the Bishop of Nashville, but they added that they were committed to Bishop Miles through obedience even though, in deference to his expressed wishes, they were not going to Tennessee until they had perfected themselves in English.[7] In this connection, we may quote a later interesting reflection of a student of the Alemany story as to the change which now awaited the young friar:

> The transition of a twenty-six year old Dominican from the center of Christendom to a pioneer country where priests were regarded with suspicion, and from one of Rome's most beautiful churches and monasteries to the frame convent of St. Joseph's in Somerset, must have been a difficult adjustment.[8]

[6] Nicolas Young, O.P. (1793–1878), "co-apostle of Ohio and a priest of the highest merit," says O'Daniel.

Father Young's correspondent was a Dutch Dominican named Raymond Van Zeeland. A copy of this letter, written from St. Joseph's, Ohio, and dated April 14, 1840, is preserved in AOPW.

[7] Alemany and Cubero to Ancarani, Somerset, Ohio, April 29, 1840. Copy in AOPW. On August 10, 1840, Father Charles Montgomery, O.P., wrote to Ancarani from the Somerset convent. "The two Spanish Fathers are with us and are doing well. They wish to be affiliated with this Province. This is also our wish. . . ." AOPR.

[8] Sister Gertrude Mary Gray, *A Preliminary Survey of the Life of the Reverend Joseph Sadoc Alemany, O.P., First Archbishop of San Francisco.* Unpublished master's thesis, Catholic University of America, Pacific Coast Branch, San Rafael, California, 1942, p. 15.

47

A year later, Father Alemany thus referred to the matter in a letter to Bishop Purcell of Cincinnati: "I thought good to write to you these lines and to beg your assistance . . . you know how strange it is for a priest to come from Rome to celebrate Mass in a wooden unplastered church."[9] Similar testimony was given by Father Francis Vilarrasa, the Dominican friar who was to loom large in the future Alemany story in Ohio and in California, who thus described Ohio missionary life and hardships in a letter written to his family in Barcelona in 1847:

> The convent is two miles from Somerset, a little city surrounded by forests with a few scattered homes. The people are for the most part Irish and German, almost all Catholics. . . . On feast days the faithful come great distances to hear Mass and Vespers in spite of the snows, bad weather, and poor roads. Mass is said at eight o'clock and after the Mass the catechism is taught in the German language. At ten o'clock the Rosary is recited and the catechism explained in English, and Mass is sung, always concluded with a sermon in English. . . . The hardships of the priests on the missions are very great. They can never count on sleeping in the convent. Many times it happens that one arrives tired out and thinking he can rest, when he must leave at once on horseback and go where he is called without stopping through the rain and snow . . . There is exact regularity in the convent in all that pertains to the Constitutions of the Order, and though poor, we are happy. Our dinner consists of bread, soup, apples, potatoes, cooked greens and vegetables, and sometimes eggs . . .[10]

[9] Alemany to Purcell, Zanesville, Ohio. August 18, 1841. MCUND.

[10] Vilarrasa to his family, July 5, 1847. Somerset, Ohio. Published in Revista Catholica, Barcelona, 1851.

O'Daniel, *The Dominican Province of St. Joseph,* etc., has the following information concerning Vilarrasa. Francis Sadoc Vilarrasa was born in La Pobla de Lillet, Province of Catalonia, Spain, August 9, 1814. (This was only about three weeks after Alemany's birth, July 14, 1814.) He took his vows as a Dominican at St. Catherine's Convent, Barcelona, on September 25, 1830. O'Daniel adds: "He went to Italy and his name is first found on the records there [the priory of La Quercia, near Viterbo, Italy] in 1836 and continues to appear on them until 1839. His first signature for saying Mass is on May 13, 1837, which most likely means that he was ordained the day previous, and by Archbishop [later Cardinal] Gaspar Bernardo Pianetti of Viterbo. The little dark man is said to have just attained the height required by canon law for admission to the priesthood. However, the

It would seem that the language problem was rather quickly solved by Alemany for, in a letter to his brother, Father Manuel, he mentioned that, by August 7, 1840 (little more than three months after his arrival at St. Joseph's, Somerset), he was assigned to the near-by Dominican church at Zanesville, Ohio, as an assistant. The 6,000 inhabitants of Zanesville included a very substantial proportion of Catholics—largely because of zealous activities there on the part of the earlier Dominicans—and Father Alemany was soon hard at work in this ministry which he had long ambitioned. A letter to his brother Antonio, dated January 5, 1841, confirmed the fact that he was a busily engaged assistant pastor during the fall months of 1840. He mentioned the usual routine activities and his constant sharing in the ministries of the parish. Reference has been made to the fact that a notable element in Alemany's character was his conviction that God had called him very specially to the vocation of a missionary. Undoubtedly, this conviction was strengthened by the phase of his apostolic career which now began in Ohio as he commenced a series of peregrinations in search of opportunities to be of service to the many unchurched of that frontier region. Father Alemany offered Mass in private homes and there administered the sacraments and thus succeeded in bringing his official and personal character to bear where it counted most—and it would seem no exaggeration to suppose that these were among the happiest days of the friar who, wiry and still less than 30 years of age, combined bodily strength with an apostolic vigor.

---

records of La Quercia show that, while small of body, he was great of mind, an industrious student, an observant religious and of a character that won the hearts of all. . . . September 26, 1844, he started on this journey to the United States. . . . He was not of the missionary, but contemplative type. . . . Later on, he accompanied Bishop Alemany to California, where, in Monterey, he started the Dominican Province of the Holy Name in an adobe shanty. . . . He spent most of the rest of his life in Benicia, California, beloved and venerated by all, especially his confreres. He died on March 17, 1888 and was buried in his community's cemetery. It is rare that a superior makes his way down so deep into the hearts of his subjects. . . ."

An interruption, however, came when his prior provincial, Father Charles Pius Montgomery (whose refusal of the mitre of Monterey later was to be the reason for Alemany's consecration as bishop of that see) decided to send him to Cuba on a begging tour. A new and spacious church was planned for Somerset and other alterations and additions were planned for the existing building there; hence, to obtain some of the requisite financial help, it was decided that the Spanish-speaking Alemany would go on a begging tour of the island of Cuba. He arrived in New Orleans on January 3, 1842, and left for Cuba on January 12. Almost immediately, he encountered difficulties with the Cuban government in the matter of collecting funds for his worthy objective and, were it not for the direct aid of ecclesiastical authorities there, his mission would not have been successful. He could not be said to have failed in governmental circles through a lack of contacts for, shortly after his arrival, he met with the Spanish governor and captain general of Cuba, Jeronimo Valdes Noriega y Sierra, who, however, refused his request to be allowed to solicit funds. Although the See of Havana was vacant, its apostolic administrator was a fellow Dominican from Aragon. This prelate received Alemany kindly and offered to provide some help so that he might not have to return empty-handed to Ohio. Ultimately, with this support, Father Alemany returned to Ohio with about $700 as well as several gifts of church furnishing for the new edifice at Somerset; most distinguished in this regard was a large crucifix, still above the main altar at St. Joseph's Church there, and still considered to be one of the finest of its kind in the United States. Alemany's Cuban mission was marred in part by an attack of yellow fever which put him to bed for a period, but his wiry frame served him well in his recovery from an ailment which not infrequently proved almost fatal. On April 28, 1842 he bade farewell to Cuba with his departure on the *S.S. Alabama* for New Orleans. Many years later, in a letter written on December 11, 1878, from San Francisco to the Prior of St. Joseph's Convent, Somerset, Ohio, Archbishop Alemany recalled his mission to Cuba as a time of many difficulties and hindrances. Refused permission to offer Mass because he had been ordained in Italy without the permission of Queen Christina of Spain, he managed to do so by finding a friend in a pastor of a church who "didn't believe that Christina had ecclesiastical jurisdiction!"

The Captain General took Alemany for a spy of Don Carlos, pretender to the throne of Spain, rather than a begging friar, and "wishing to ascertain my true character he catechized me about the number and order of sacraments. He corrected me when I placed the Holy Eucharist before Penance—but having heard from me that St. Thomas argues that Penance is better placed after the Holy Eucharist because Penance is medicine and the Eucharist is food—and a child needs food before medicine—he seemed satisfied, but I was not. I asked him for some donation and he ordered his secretary to give me an ounce of gold." After arrival in New Orleans Alemany continued his return journey up the Mississippi and into the Ohio River where he disembarked at Marietta, from whence he proceeded to Somerset, arriving there about the middle of May. A quick return to his familiar missionary apostolate followed. Although he still felt some of the weakness left him by his recent bout with yellow fever, he was able to make his missionary circuit with success and without any recurrence of the dread disease.

Chief among the memories of his native Spain which Alemany had at this time was that of the meddlesome interference of its government in the affairs of the Church and of his religious order in particular; as has been mentioned, it had been just such policies which had forced the young Catalan friar into exile in Italy. Small wonder, then, having now arrived in the United States, he became so strong in his admiration of the provisions of its Constitution that he promptly (on April 15, 1841) filed his Declaration of Intention to become an American citizen in the court of the County of Muskingum, Ohio. Subsequently, he was naturalized when, on October 27, 1845, he took his oath to support the American Constitution and renounced all allegiance to the King of Spain before Judge Ephraim W. M. King in Memphis, Tennessee. His later actions while occupying the See of San Francisco, notably his policies during the Civil War years, amply testified to his sincere loyalty to his adopted country.

Evidence that Alemany's presence among them was acceptable to his Dominican brethren is shown by a letter written in his behalf by the Prior Provincial, Father Charles Montgomery, to Father Ancarani at the end of 1841 requesting active and passive voice for Alemany—this meant that it was desired that he be affiliated to the American Province rather than remain with the rather uncertain status of a "missionary apostolic."[11] This petition was, a few months later, supported by a like letter written by Father Nicolas Young from Somerset which was also addressed to the master general. Young referred to the desire of Alemany, joined with that of Cubero, also at Somerset, to be "affiliated to our province where they desire to consecrate their services in the future to the province and to the community that received them when they were rejected by Bishop Miles: —the community that has shared with them for the past two years our temporal wants and instructed them in that language by the acquiring of which they now begin to be of service to the Province."[12] A reply from Ancarani in Rome in mid-August informed Young that he could do nothing about the desired affiliation of Alemany and Cubero to St. Joseph's Province, stating as his reason that, since they were from Spain and the monarch there reserved the asserted right to exercise effective control over the friars in just such matters, his hands were tied.

---

[11] Montgomery (1806–1860) to Ancarani. Somerset, Ohio, December 18, 1841. Later Father Montgomery will be further identified in connection with his refusal of the See of Monterey in 1850. Copy in AOPW.

[12] Young to Ancarani, Somerset, Ohio, July 1, 1842. Copy in AOPW. Father Young wrote to Ancarani on December 21, 1842: "Bishop Miles has taken from us Fr. Allemany [sic] . . . his loss will be felt most severely. . . ."

Bishop Miles of Nashville had not forgotten the zealous friar from Spain who had come originally to help him in his work there, and he thereupon saw to it that Father Alemany was next assigned to help him in his scattered missionary activities. This began a three-year residence for Alemany at the Cathedral of the Holy Rosary in Nashville, 1842–1845. It had not been easy for Miles to get Alemany released to him for work in his diocese, and he soon had the friar occupied in such manner that none could claim that his services were unneeded.

Father Alemany was the first Dominican missionary assigned to help Bishop Miles in the state of Tennessee. Soon after his arrival in Nashville, he was asked by Miles to draw up a report for the Congregation de Propaganda Fide in Rome as to the present status of the diocese. He listed a total population of 850,000 with only eleven hundred Catholics ministered to by the bishop and seven priests.[13] It was not long before Alemany was made the director of an incipient diocesan seminary located in the Bishop's own house. This was an impermanent foundation, for after 1848 it is not mentioned in the official "Catholic Almanac." However, an extant letter written by Alemany to Bishop Anthony Blanc of New Orleans, in which he makes inquiries concerning the "morals and conduct of Mr. ———, that young man who lived with you at the end of 1841 . . . be so good as to give me . . . this . . . information, which will oblige me still more and keep stronger in my memory the kindness and attention used by you and your whole house in my passing through New Orleans, going to and coming from Habana,"[14] —serves to confirm O'Daniel's opinion that, in Alemany's selection as seminary rector, "no stricter or more conscientious man could have been selected for the place."[15]

---

[13] A summary of this report is in O'Daniel, *The Father of the Church in Tennessee, or the Life, Times and Character of the Right Reverend Richard Pius Miles, O.P., The First Bishop of Nashville*, Washington, D.C., 1926, pp. 399–400.

[14] Alemany to Blanc, Nashville, Tennessee, January 21, 1844. MCUND.

[15] O'Daniel, *The Father of the Church in Tennessee*, etc., p. 399.

In the summer of 1845, a French priest, John M. Jacquet, came from Europe to take charge of this seminary, and Father Alemany was now able to resume his missionary work. Accordingly, he was sent as assistant to Father Michael McAleer at St. Peter's Church in Memphis, Tennessee. This city counted about 8000 inhabitants at the time, of whom about 500 were Catholics. An interesting reference to Father Alemany's work there was made by a correspondent of the New York *Freeman's Journal* in November, 1845:

> Several years since, the Catholics of this city . . . erected a fine brick church. . . . The congregation now numbers about five hundred Catholics and is rapidly on the increase.
>
> Latterly our pastor, Mr. McAleer, has been assisted in his arduous and laborious ministerial duties by the Rev. Joseph Alemany, a Spanish priest of the Order of St. Dominic, who was educated in Rome and emigrated to America in 1840. His aid promises to be truly efficient and useful, and we confidently look for the most brilliant success to attend their combined efforts. . . .[16]

An indication that at least two of his Dominican brethren were convinced that Alemany had the qualities of a future superior in his order is found in a letter which Father Pozzo, who had come with Alemany from Europe, wrote to Ancarani in early 1845. He suggested a further expansion of Dominican efforts with the establishment of a foundation in St. Louis and suggested that Father Alemany be made its first superior. He mentioned that Father d'Arco, another Italian Dominican on the scene in Somerset, joined with him in this recommendation.[17] It would appear, then, that these two older friars were quite favorably impressed with their Catalan Dominican brother.

[16] O'Daniel, *op. cit.*, p. 410.

[17] Pozzo to Ancarani, Somerset, Ohio, January 21, 1945. Copy in AOPW. Januarius d'Arco, O.P., was born in Naples in 1818 and died in Indianapolis as a secular priest in 1899. He saw service as a Dominican in Ohio, according to O'Daniel, and he is said "to have combined zeal and kindliness with not a little self will."

The two years spent by Father Alemany at St. Peter's Church in Memphis found him again engaging in his favorite form of priestly ministry as he journeyed about the western part of the state as a missionary. When Father McAleer, who was a diocesan priest, obtained leave to go to help Bishop John Hughes in New York, a Dominican priest, Father Thomas Grace of St. Rose's, Kentucky, replaced him, and Alemany continued as assistant pastor with the additional consolation of now living with one of his own religious brethren. The sources serve to confirm the fact that Father Alemany left a record for zealous service in Memphis; there are mentions of his campaign for church funds, his organization of an altar society, and his efforts to obtain subscribers for the *Catholic Advocate*.[18]

Further indication that Alemany was being observed favorably by those of his order came in the fall of 1847 when the Dominican chapter held at St. Rose, Kentucky, elected him to the important office of master of novices there. At the end of November, therefore, he left Memphis to take up his new task in Kentucky. But he was not destined to remain long in the position of novice master because of a series of events which soon saw him elevated to the post of prior provincial of all of the American Dominicans. In that same chapter which had elected him novice master, a deadlock had been reached with regard to the election of a prior provincial. Father George Wilson, writing to the newly elected master general in Rome, Vincent Ajello, who served from 1844–1850, reported from the St. Rose's meeting that the friars, after voting from the morning through the afternoon without electing (Father Charles Bowling lacking one vote for election), had agreed to send to the master general a list of those they considered eligible for the office of prior provincial. First on this list was Father Bowling, with second and third places going to Fathers Alemany and Cubero. Father Wilson is emphatic in his own desires in the matter as he adds:

18 Sister Gertrude Mary Gray, *A Preliminary Survey*, etc., p. 19.

I earnestly beg of you . . . not to name Father Bowling . . . but to name either Father Alemany or Father Cubero, who are both men animated with great zeal for the good of the Order and will be tempted by nothing that is not for its best interest. . . .[19]

Father Pozzo, who by this time had returned to Italy after serving as novice master in America, also expressed himself at this time in a letter written to the master general from Turin— he wrote that, if Father Alemany were appointed provincial, he would like to return to America, where he had served for six years, with seven other friars who would like even as himself to serve under Alemany.[20]

With these recommendations, coupled with the fact that Father Ajello had known Alemany in Italy, it was not entirely unexpected when the master general exercised his privilege of appointing a prior provincial for the province of St. Joseph in the United States. A notation of the appointment of Alemany is found in the Dominican archives in Rome where, under date of May 2, 1848, it was recorded:

The Very Reverend Father, Brother Sadoc Alemany, is appointed Provincial of the Province of St. Joseph in the United States of Northern America and there were sent to him letters patent and official confirmation of the acts of the Chapter held in the convent of St. Rose, Kentucky, on the Saturday before the third Sunday in October . . .[21]

A confirmation of this appointment is found in the register of the prior provincial of the American Province with a notation, in the handwriting of a secretary, as follows:

On September 16, 1848, the Letters Patent by which Father Master General has appointed me Provincial of this Province were read before the entire community of St. Rose's Convent.

Fr. Joseph Allemany [sic][22]

[19] Wilson (1807–1884) to Ajello, St. Rose, Kentucky, October 22, 1847. Copy in AOPW.
[20] Pozzo to Ajello, Turin, Italy, November 19, 1847. Copy in AOPW.
[21] Copy in AOPW.
[22] *Registrum Prioris Provincialis Prov. S. Josephi Stat. Foederatorum Amer. Septentrionalis ab anno 1845*, p. 9. AOPW.

Before proceeding with the activities which marked Father Alemany's term as provincial, which he was not to finish because of his appointment to the See of Monterey in California, it will be well to briefly sketch here the split in the American Dominican ranks which had caused an appeal to Rome for the appointment of a prior provincial. A key to the background of the disagreement is furnished by a letter which Alemany's compatriot, Father Vilarrasa, sent to the master general between the date of Alemany's appointment and his confirmation in the office of prior provincial at St. Rose's in September, 1848. Writing from Somerset, Ohio, under date of July 5, 1848, Vilarrasa mentioned that the letters patent of the new Provincial had not yet arrived, but that all knew that Father Alemeny was to be named in his stead. Vilarrasa was emphatic in expressing his view that the fathers of the province were "unanimous" in the opinion that, were either Grace or Alemany named, "it will be the ruin of the Province." For six years, Vilarrasa continued, Alemany had lived outside his convent on the missions until his recent assignment to St. Rose's as confessor of nuns and master of novices. "In these last eight months," continued Vilarrasa's indictment, "he has shown that he has lost all the spirit of and desire for regularity and has clearly indicated that, if he becomes Provincial, he will change everything." Vilarrasa also added that he did not think that Alemany was an effective confessor of nuns either! He reminded the Master General that two convents of the province had already written to Rome against the appointment of either Alemany or Grace as provincial. With a dramatic flair, Vilarrasa asked a rhetorical question for which he had a ready answer: "Why, then, was Alemany recommended in the first place? Because of what was known of him before he went on the missions! No one could then realize that his attitude towards regular life had so changed. Today, he would not receive one vote . . ."[23]

[23] Vilarrasa to Ajello, Somerset, Ohio, July 5, 1847. Copy in AOPW.

It is known that the most serious disagreements sometimes occur between completely sincere persons—and the above letter of the indignant Vilarrasa would seem to serve as confirmation. One is puzzled, at first, at these earlier accusations concerning Alemany, especially when one reflects that the later Archbishop Alemany was always regarded as a very conscientious and even rigorous man. His early acceptance of correct religious values in his life and his constant endeavor, in his personal life, to exemplify the ascetical practices of his order are quite evident. But Alemany was also a realist—and this would seem to furnish the key to his unacceptability to some of the friars such as Vilarrasa. The latter was for strict conventual observance first, last, and always—and, whenever he detected, or thought he did, a lack of respect for these observances, he was not slow to write such letters as that quoted above. Alemany was just as much a dedicated son of St. Dominic as was Vilarrasa, but he was more convinced concerning what he considered to be the realistic approach to the situation in America. Obviously, in the years of missionary wanderings which he spent in the states of Ohio, Tennessee, and Kentucky, it was largely impossible for Alemany to practice such community observances to which he was accustomed and from the spirit of which, presumably (despite the somewhat harsh strictures of Vilarrasa) there is no evidence that he had departed. In essence, then, the disagreement was between those who suspected adaptability as a form of decadence and those who accepted situations as they arose in certain given and necessary circumstances. However, Alemany surely stands unconvicted of any disloyalty to his Dominican vocation or to any of the venerable observances of his order.[24] Indeed, an indication of the careful thought given by Alemany to difficulties pro-

[24] These observations are based on a series of conversations with the Reverend Reginald Coffey, O.P., Archivist of the St. Joseph Province, Dominican House of Studies, Washington, D.C. Father Coffey's extensive knowledge of American Dominican history, together with his shrewd insights, made the present author's task in this chapter considerably lighter.

posed by his subjects when he was prior provincial is evidenced by the following letter written to one of his friars in late December, 1848:

. . . In regard to the vow of poverty, do as Fr. General Ancarani told me to do himself when in Nashville—i.e. to act according to the direction of the confessor. In everything else, allow me to advise you to go on with prudence, edifying all with good example, kind and charitable to all, principally to the poor to the sick and to the children—instructing these with all patience and perseverance for, if the children be neglected, religion must go down. . . .[25]

In passing, it may be observed that these hardly sound like the words of a lax or unobservant religious.

From the spring of 1848, Father Prior Provincial Alemany was in residence at Somerset, Ohio, which had become, some years previously, the seat of government for the Dominican Province of St. Joseph. (Actually, there was but this one province in the entire United States at this time, so Father Alemany was the only Dominican provincial in the entire federal union.) Although Somerset was the official headquarters, it was necessary for Alemany to be absent quite frequently on visitations to the various convents of his order which were now his principal concern; occasionally, however, he was still able to act the part that pleased him most—that of Dominican missionary. In 1849, he decided to send Father Augustine Anderson to California, and this decision is thus recorded in the Register of his provincialate:

1849—Feb. 22—Peter Augustine Anderson is sent to the Californias [*sic*] or to Santa Fe where efforts are being made to restore our missions.[26]

[25] Alemany to Orango (1820–1909), Somerset, Ohio, December 28, 1848. Copy in AOPW.

[26] *Registrum*, etc., p. 10, AOPW. Peter Augustine Anderson, O.P., was born in or near Elizabeth, New Jersey, in 1812. Ordained at St. Rose's near Springfield, Ky., in 1840, he was sent to California in 1849. On November 27, 1850, his death occurred there. Nine days after his death, Alemany sailed into San Francisco Bay as the newly appointed Bishop of Monterey in California. Undoubtedly, he was quickly made acquainted with Anderson's recent death.

To this same Father Anderson was reserved the distinction of becoming the first priest to die as a martyr of charity in California, for, in Sacramento, where he had established the first Catholic church in the fall of 1850, Father Anderson contacted typhoid fever while ministering to others in an epidemic, and died on November 27, 1850.

That all was not well among the friars who were not happy in the imposition of Alemany as their prior provincial by the Master General is made evident from a formal warning sent to him by Fathers Young, Montgomery, and Wilson to remind him that the intermediate chapter required by the Dominican constitutions must be held![27] Ten days later, these same friars informed Alemany that, by virtue of authority granted them in the general chapters of 1629 and 1647, they had taken it upon themselves to convoke this same chapter "to meet on the Saturday before the third Sunday of October."[28] More than a mere touch of Catalan firmness is evident in the reply which Father Montgomery received from the displeased Prior Provincial who wrote to him on October 6, 1849, that, because of the disturbed state of affairs in Europe, it was extremely doubtful whether it would be possible to have the required general chapter in Italy; "Therefore, I now use the authority, granted me by the Master General, to cancel the Intermediate Chapter proposed by you and transfer it to the first Sunday after Epiphany, 1850." That Father Alemany meant what he said is confirmed by a final remark: "Beware to oppose your private judgement to the authority of your Superior!"[29]

[27] Young, et al. to Alemany, September 18, 1849, St. Joseph's, Somerset, Ohio. AOPW. According to Dominican rule in force at this time, the intermediate chapter had as its purpose to express approval or disapproval of the administration of the incumbent provincial. If judged competent in his administration, a petition was sent to the master general recommending his continuance in office; if otherwise, then a petition was sent urging his removal from office. Intermediate chapters are no longer held.
[28] Ibid.
[29] Alemany to Montgomery, October 5, 1849, AOPW.

However, it would appear that the embattled friars had just begun to fight. A month later, a report went to Rome from the definitorium, or consultors of the province, in which six conditions were proposed that, in their judgment, Alemany should be made to meet under penalty of being suspended from office— the most pointed was that which said: "He should admit that, as Provincial, he does not enjoy such inspiration from the Holy Ghost as to make him infallible." The four friars who signed this letter included Fathers Montgomery, Wilson, Vilarrasa, and even the same Father Pozzo who, previously, had been prepared to die with and for Alemany! Lest the master general should miss the point they had in mind, the signers ended their letter to Rome by recommending that Alemany be removed from the office which he held.[30] Less than a week later, Fathers Young, Pozzo, Wilson, and Vilarrasa returned to the attack with another letter from Ohio to Father Master General Ajello who, by this time, must have realized that all was not well with the American Dominicans. In this long letter many charges are made against Alemany, none of them involving his personal character so much as reflecting the dissatisfaction the signers felt with his administration of affairs. Thus, they again accused him of failing to observe the constitutions of the order as regards the observances of the common life. He should, indeed, be suspended from office because of his failure to convoke the intermediate chapter already mentioned, etc. The letter is in the distinctive handwriting of Father Vilarrasa and, later on, in Rome, when Alemany was acquainted with its contents and author, it could hardly have helped the relationship between the two friars from the same part of Spain.[31] Whatever may have been the ultimate motives of the complainers, they and their complaints were not to prevail for, almost two years later, a laconic notation in the master general's *Register* records that, on July 21, 1851, "all of these

[30] Montgomery, *et al.*, to Ajello, October 23, 1849, Somerset, Ohio. AOPR.
[31] Young, *et al.*, Somerset, Ohio. October 29, 1849. Copy in AOPW.

things are declared null and void by the Master General."[32] Further evidence that Alemany had not lost the confidence of his order is had in another entry in the same *Registrum* and under the same date: ". . . A new Province may be erected in either of the Californias . . . immediately subject to the Master General over which, until a chapter be called on the third Sunday of October, 1850, Bishop Joseph Alemany, O.P. may preside. . . ." By this date, Alemany was already more than a year a bishop in California where he had new and different problems to face than those indicated by the definitorium of the province which he had formerly headed.

Although it may be presumed that Father Alemany had no way of knowing it, he had now reached the two years which were to mark such a decisive change in his future career. These were 1849, when a series of circumstances brought his name to the attention of the American hierarchy, and 1850, which was to see his unexpected consecration in Rome. In 1849 the American bishops met in Baltimore for the Seventh Provincial Council and, in his official capacity of prior provincial of the American Dominicans, Alemany was in attendance. Among the acute problems studied there was the spiritual destitution of the Church in California, concerning which passing mention only shall be here made since the next chapter will endeavor to present the sombre picture more accurately. Suffice it to note here that, in these meetings at Baltimore, the American bishops came to know Alemany; he was present, for example, when they selected his brother Domin-

---

[32] *Registrum Generalium O.P.*, entry of July 21, 1851. AOPR. From some observations of O'Daniel, *The Dominican Province of St. Joseph, Historico-Biographical Studies* (Washington, D.C., 1942), p. 170, it would appear that Alemany had, with reluctance, agreed to hold the intermediate chapter after all. However, adds O'Daniel: ". . . From the same source [papers in the general's archives, Rome] we learn that good Father Alemany was not above all retaliation. He had unwillingly convoked the chapter. So, on his arrival in Rome, he had its acts annulled by Father Jerome Gigli, who was temporarily vicar general of the Order. This was after Alemany's consecration as Bishop of Monterey, and it was all the more uncalled for because they contained nothing but what was most reasonable. . . ."

ican (and critic) Father Charles Montgomery, for the See of Monterey. Indeed, one of the final notations found in the provincial register before Alemany's departure for Europe in 1850 to attend the general chapter of his order summoned, but never held, for Naples, is as follows:

1850. Feb. 25. Rev. Fr. Charles Montgomery has received a Bull from the Holy See by which he is chosen as Bishop of Monterey in California—which [appointment] he has refused.[33]

On March 24, 1850, with the necessity of leaving for Europe facing him, Alemany appointed Father Dominic Bowling (not one of the signatories of the letter of complaint about his stewardship) as vicar general "during my absence at the General Chapter."[34] A week later, just before leaving the country for Europe, he wrote from Buffalo to Bishop Purcell of Cincinnati:

I believe that my religious duty requires me to attend the General Chapter of our Order to be held in Naples about the middle of next May for the election of a new General and the transaction of other business of the Order. I would feel very thankful to you if you would recommend me, in the same or separate paper, to the charities of the faithful in general and, in particular, to the Associations for the Propagation of the Faith established in France and Germany. We have at present 12 novices at St. Joseph's and 11 at St. Rose's. Our sisters, both in Ohio and in Kentucky, have several orphans under their care. I hope, Bishop Purcell, you will be so kind (though, perhaps, we do not deserve it) as to recommend me to the charity of the faithful in Europe. Please to direct to me in New York, where I shall be detained for awhile.[35]

Significant news awaited Alemany when he arrived at the Paris convent of his order. Word had been received there that by command of his Holiness, Pius IX, the anticipated general chapter

[33] *Registrum Prioris Provincialis,* etc., p. 14, entry of February 25, 1850. AOPW.

[34] *Registrum Prioris Provincialis,* etc., p. 14, entry of March 24, 1850. AOPW.

[35] Alemany to Purcell, Buffalo, New York, March 31, 1850. MCUND.

was not to be held after all. Another hand than that of Alemany thus noted the news later on in the official register of the province:

1850 April 20. While journeying to the General Chapter, on our arrival at our convent in Paris, we learned that the Council will not be held.

J. Allemany [sic][36]

While in Paris, Father Alemany thus decided to address himself directly to the Paris branch of the French Society for the Propagation of the Faith to obtain needed financial aid:

Respected Sir,

As our American Missions are rather poor, I now find myself without the means to return to America: and as I have charge of all the Dominican Missions in the United States, being the Provincial of all, even the Dominican Sisters, I have to ask for all in their need. Hence I humbly beg the charitable Association to be so good as allow me at present for my actual need $150, which will be nearly all necessary to return to Kentucky, some 900 miles west of Boston. If the Association can afford it, I would also humbly ask now the same sum of $150 for my brother Dominican Priest in Italy, who wrote to me that he desired to go to our Missions in America.

In the second place I also respectfully beg the Association to be so good as to assign us some alms or contributions, to be divided among our Dominican establishments in the United States; so as to enable us to pay the debts which we necessarily contracted, to carry out better our Noviceships, our Academies, and all our Missions.[37]

Even though the general chapter which was the main reason for his coming to Europe was now officially cancelled, there seems to have been no doubt in Alemany's mind that his office demanded that he continue to Rome to present himself and his problems to the general definitorium, which was a commission of several friars which Pius IX had instituted to rule the order

---

[36] *Registrum Prioris Provincialis,* etc., p. 14. Entry of April 20, 1850. AOPW.

[37] Alemany to director of Society for the Propagation of the Faith, Paris. Letter undated. ASPFP.

in the interval between successive masters general. He first visited Vich en route and there must have followed a very affectionate reunion with his mother and with the other members of his family. It will be recalled that he had left his native city in 1836, fourteen years previously, when he had been forced to choose exile in Italy in order to continue his priestly studies in the Dominican Order. After a stay, the exact duration of which it is impossible to determine, Father Alemany went to Barcelona and thence to Marseilles and on to Genoa, from whence he made his way to Rome, arriving there on June 8, 1850. Here we may leave him for awhile as we turn our attention now to what was to be his biggest problem in just a few months—the state of religion in California.

4

Catholicism in California, 1697–1849

ON Monday, May 3, 1535, the conqueror of Mexico, Hernando Cortes, sailed into that bay of Lower California which is now called La Paz. In accordance with traditional Spanish custom, he named what he saw spread before him after the feast day of the Church; consequently, since May 3 was the feast of the Finding of the Holy Cross, Cortes called this land "La Tierra de Santa Cruz"—"The Land of the Holy Cross." This would appear, then, to be the first name given by the white man to California.

In relating the religious phase of the California story, it is almost a commonplace to mention that its justly celebrated Franciscan mission system was first started in San Diego in 1769, reaching completion in Sonoma, north of San Francisco, in 1823. However, the fact is that California, viewed historically, comprised both Lower and Upper California; hence, one should say rather that its mission system was first started in Baja California on a permanent basis on October 25, 1697, with the founding of the mission of Our Lady of Loreto by Padre Juan Maria Salvatierra, acting under the direction of his Jesuit superior, Padre Eusebio Kino.[1] Between 1697–1767, a total of twenty-one out-

[1] More properly, then, it is Father Salvatierra rather than the later Father Serra who should be called the Father of Catholicism in California—in the sense mentioned in the text. Perhaps, though, equal honors should go to Father Kino who had urged on Salvatierra the foundation of a mission at Loreto. Today, the restored mission at Loreto bears a proud and historically

posts of spiritual empire were founded by a devoted group of Jesuit missionaries working in what their modern historian has called a "hard land" and who succeeded, despite incredible odds, in the laying of a solid foundation for future apostolic works.[2] These twenty-one missions, together with one founded by the Franciscan, Junipero Serra, in 1769 at a northern point of Baja California when joined with the nine missions founded by Dominican friars in Lower California, 1774–1834, form an important prelude to the later Franciscan missions of Upper California, 1769–1823.

The next epoch in this brief overview of California's religious past concerns the short episcopal rule of the first bishop of both Upper and Lower California. This was the Franciscan friar Francisco Garcia Diego y Moreno (1785–1846), who served California as its pioneer prelate from 1840–1846. The earlier and heroic labors of Serra and his confreres, as well as their Dominican and Jesuit predecessors, were crowned with the consecration of Bishop Garcia Diego in Mexico City in 1840. However, the years of this prelate were to be both short and sad, for his was the burden of sustaining the cares of the secularized missions of Alta California which were made to bear the full brunt of an unwise and unjust governmental policy.[3]

Even though it is quite commonly admitted now that this process of secularization was, indeed, a "spoilation of the missions"—a phrase first used by Hubert Howe Bancroft, a California historian not notably enamored of Catholicism, —there

accurate inscription on its facade; "Cabeza y Madre de las misiones de Baja y Alta California"—"The Head and the Mother of all of the missions of Lower and Upper California."

[2] For the best discussion of the Jesuit missionary work in Baja California, see Peter M. Dunne, S.J., *Black Robes in Lower California*, Berkeley, 1952. Father Dunne's first chapter is appropriately entitled "A Hard Land."

[3] On the career and distress of California's pioneer prelate, see Francis J. Weber, *A Biographical Sketch of Right Reverend Francisco Garcia Diego y Moreno, First Bishop of the Californias, 1785–1846*, Los Angeles, 1961.

are phases of the California Catholic past even during this period which have suffered, perhaps, from occasionally being treated with bucolic overtones. To William Gleeson, author of an ambitious but now outdated account of the Catholic Church in California, the first quarter of the nineteenth century was a brilliant time, as fifty thousand Indians dwelt in peaceful abodes erected for them through missionary zeal. His conclusion is expressed thus:

> So happy and contented, therefore, was their condition before the baneful influence of a ruinous Mexican policy was felt in the land, that one is in every sense justified in regarding their state as among the most favored of any neophyte Christian community of the world.[4]

This may well have been so, but we need not deny that critics of certain phases of the California mission system are entirely without justification for their views. Thus, for example, a Catholic layman, Joseph Warren Revere, who had seen for himself the sad effects of secularization in a naval tour of duty in the California of the 1840's, noted with sadness that those who were once the very best of Christian Indians seemed to have become the "very worst of horse thieves on the same principle that a relapse is worse than the original disease."[5] While freely admitting that the Franciscan fathers were earnestly devoted to the welfare of their docile pupils, Revere gives it as his opinion that, "being fond of making proselytes, they sometimes used means

---

[4] William A. Gleeson, *A History of the Catholic Church in California*, two vols., San Francisco, 1872, I, pp. 21–22.

[5] Joseph Warren Revere, *A Tour of Duty in California, Including Descriptions of the Gold Region and an Account of the Voyage Around the Horn*, etc., New York, 1849, pp. 124–125. Revere (1812–1884) was a nephew of the celebrated Paul Revere, and, commissioned as a naval lieutenant in 1841, he was assigned to duty in California. His was the distinction, on July 9, 1846, of first raising the American flag at Sonoma, after hauling down the pennant of the short-lived Bear Flag Republic. Out of this and many other interesting experiences came the above mentioned book. He later resigned his naval commission, and, during the Civil War, was advanced to the rank of brigadier general in the United States Army. He died at Hoboken, New Jersey, on May 8, 1884.

not entirely justifiable to that end," although he is quick to add that, in the main, their conduct compared favorably with that of missionaries elsewhere, especially those "from our own country boasting a faith which assumes to be more enlightened." Finally, it is his conclusion that, even though the American government must never identify itself with the interests of any single church, since "all sects are now at liberty to settle in California, it would be good policy on the part of the white population to encourage the return of the worthy Padres to their shepherdless flocks." Wherever the exact truth may lie, it is beyond dispute that many and grievous were the worries and woes which marked the six years of Bishop Garcia Diego's rule in California. To these worries must be attributed his premature death, in 1846, at Santa Barbara. Behind him he left a dispirited and orphaned flock while, with his demise, a series of events started which would ultimately culminate in the selection of Joseph Sadoc Alemany as his successor. However, the years which intervened before Alemany's arrival in California in 1850 were even sadder than those which had marked Garcia Diego's episcopal rule. Abundant testimony to this fact is to be found in the letters which were written by various individuals during the period, and one who reads them a century and more later is struck by the unanimity which characterized them all: their theme was that Catholicism in California was well nigh on the way to extinction unless vigorous means were applied by responsible authority to see that a despoiled fabric did not ultimately become the tomb of what had been Serra's ambitious design to bring all in California to Christian knowledge and faith. For example, Edward H. Harrison, a Catholic employee of the Quartermasters Department in California, wrote in early 1848 to a prominent bookseller of Baltimore, Francis Lucas, to bewail what he had seen in his tour of duty in California. He had found only about 200 Catholics in San Francisco, and, since very few were conversant with the Spanish language, there was an immediate need of a priest who spoke English and who could care for the spiritual needs of this flock. Mission Dolores he found completely inadequate to the fulfillment of these needs for, he reported, the cleric there (the Mission was at a distance of three miles from the town itself) commanded little or no respect from either foreigners or, indeed, from native Californians. He noted how the once beautiful mission structures had now declined and had become a mass of ruins; "beautiful plains, once under cultivation, have now become a barren waste and the Indian, who looked up to his padre with reverence, has again returned to his native wilds and has become the terror of the Californians." Harrison concluded his informative letter by asking Lucas to present these details to Archbishop Samuel Eccleston of Baltimore so that the latter might be moved to act in behalf of the Catholics of California before it would prove to be too late.[6]

Six months after Harrison had written this letter, Frederick Chatard, serving in the United States Navy, also unburdened himself concerning the same sad situation. Writing directly to Eccleston, Chatard reported that he had found San Francisco a veritable religious wilderness composed of "a wild motley set of all nations and creeds and no one to guide them." As for the morals of San Francisco, "you can imagine what they must be," wrote Chatard, "when the Golden Calf alone is worshipped." He added that a priest who came out from the United States, however, would not lack support, for a good number of Catholics had already made it evident that they would be both ready and willing to help such a minister of their faith. He had checked

---

[6] Harrison's letter, from which these details were taken, was dated "San Francisco, Upper California, March 16, 1848." AAB. His reference to the priest at Mission Dolores concerns Prudencio Santillan, of mixed Mexican and Indian blood, who had been ordained by Bishop Garcia Diego at Santa Barbara on January 1, 1846. He served as pastor of Mission Dolores under the trying conditions of its secularization as well as those connected with the Gold Rush Days of '49; correctly judging that he was in no way prepared to cope with such problems, he retired to Mexico in 1850.

and found that there were, when he wrote, only thirteen priests in all of Upper California, some of whom were "very old, others very ignorant and others again, I am sorry to say, but it is true, very bad; none of them, I expect, suitable for the present population emigrating to Upper California." Chatard had also come upon the fact that church property was commonly squatted upon by illegal possessors, that is, emigrants who cared not a whit for church rights or the inviolable rights of private property. He had been told by a priest at Monterey that, against his remonstrance, the alcalde, the Reverend Walter Colton, formerly chaplain of an American frigate, had sold church lots quite near to the edifice itself.[7]

The situation continued to worsen, as predicted and expected, through the early months of the eventful year of 1849. Again, we are indebted to Revere for further information in this regard. Addressing himself, as had Chatard, to Archbishop Eccleston, Revere mentioned that he had arrived in San Francisco in February to find California in a singularly unstable condition because of the influx of gold seekers. He observed that the wildest tales were told everywhere and believed by many concerning the abundant riches in gold waiting for the Argonauts, and then, turning his attention to details which he knew would be of prime interest to Eccleston, he mentioned that, due to the huge influx of immigrants, "it will become more necessary than ever to send to the country many enlightened and liberal priests and to appoint a bishop, or even two, at the earliest practicable moment. Those Fathers and Sisters whose vocation it is to teach youth should be sent immediately." Revere added that even though the greater

[7] Frederick Chatard to Samuel Eccleston, San Francisco, November 29, 1848. AAB. Chatard, a native of Baltimore, had entered the United States Navy in 1824, and, as indicated, did a tour of duty in California as had Revere. Subsequently, in 1855, he was advanced to the rank of commander. Samuel Eccleston (1801–1851), served as fifth Archbishop of Baltimore, 1834–1851.

portion of the native Californians were Catholic, in all of California, as of the preceding summer, there was not "one single Catholic clergyman of education, intelligence or superior virtue." He noted with sadness the lamentable fact that the entire clerical functions of the province were in the hands of a few scattered Mexican priests, "none professing the respect of the population, apart from their clerical character, for reasons, which notorious as they were in the country, I should hesitate to name." Revere had known the dead to remain unburied, and dying Catholics to have been frequently deprived of all spiritual aid; he reported to Eccleston that in Sonoma, with a population of 2,000, Mass had been offered only twice in six months. This informative report concluded with Revere's words that "anyone of education and personal dignity of character, appearing as a priest of the Roman Catholic Church, no matter what his country or his language, would be warmly received."[8]

It is interesting to note that Catholic concern, such as indicated by the foregoing testimonies, was matched by that of Colonel Jonathan D. Stevenson who, while identifying himself as a non-Catholic, wrote in a similar vein to Archbishop Eccleston. His letter, written in the middle of 1848 from Los Angeles, mentioned that, since the abandonment of the Franciscan missions in California, while many of the priests had died, "of the few that remain, some are aged, sick and infirm and others, by a careless and dissolute life, have forfeited the respect of their parishioners."[9]

Obviously, the concern of the laity was matched by that of the estimable Franciscan administrator of the diocese, Jose Maria Gonzales Rubio, who had for long been at his wits end trying

[8] Revere to Eccleston. AAB. Undated, no place of composition indicated.
[9] Jonathan D. Stevenson, USA, to Eccleston, Los Angeles, California, May 1, 1848, APFR. Seemingly because of Stevenson's prominent position in the Army, Eccleston forwarded the former's letter to Propaganda in Rome. Colonel Stevenson figures prominently in the military history of California during these years.

to provide for the needs of his flock. Early in 1849 Padre Gonzalez wrote to the superior general of the French Congregation of Picpus with headquarters in Paris to ask for aid. This congregation had already furnished several priests to California by way of the Sandwich Islands, and the Franciscan Administrator implored Archbishop J. D. Bonamie, the superior general, to send several more fathers to California. He concluded with the justifiably gloomy prophecy that, unless a shepherd be sent soon, there would be little or no flock remaining among the Catholics of California.[10] Further and more direct evidence of the pastoral solicitude which seems ever to have animated Gonzalez Rubio is furnished in a pastoral letter which he addressed to the Catholics of California in June, 1849. Mentioning that from the very day when he had been forced to assume the burden of the government of the Church in California his efforts had been directed

[10] Jose Maria Gonzalez Rubio to the Most Reverend J. D. Bonamie, superior general of the Congregation of the Sacred Hearts of Jesus and Mary (Picpus fathers) Santa Barbara, February 1, 1849. Copy in Franciscan Archives, Santa Barbara, California. Father Gonzalez Rubio (1804–1875) deserves the title of saviour of the California Catholic Church during the years between the death of the Franciscan Garcia Diego and the coming of Alemany, 1846–1850. Writing in 1872, when Gonzalez Rubio was still alive, Gleeson paid him this deserved tribute:

> He is the oldest missionary now in the country, having come to California in the palmy days of the missions . . . now, after a missionary career of nearly two generations . . . it may truly be said of him that, while he represents the true characteristics of the apostle, he recalls most forcibly the spirit, zeal and devotion of that ancient body of religious who first introduced religion into the country.

History of the Catholic Church in California, II, pp. 174–175

Another indication of how far things could drift in California came with the arrival there, in May, 1849, of an impostor, who called himself Juan Bautista Brignole and who claimed that he was a bishop and apostolic delegate "Urbis et Orbis, Reformer of the Catholic Church and of the clergy both secular and regular in the Republic of Mexico and adjacent areas." His unwelcome and unauthorized presence caused the true administrator, Gonzalez Rubio, to write to the governor of Monterey, May 28, 1849, that "the man must be either a fool or an impostor—and in either case, he should be stopped, for he is doing harm, etc." He does not seem to have lasted long on the local scene.

73

toward the recruitment of more priests for the country, Padre Gonzalez Rubio noted the great difficulties which he had encountered in the fulfillment of his design. The missionary colleges of Mexico could no longer fulfill the need as they had done so generously in the past; one could not hope that the secular clergy of Mexico could be persuaded to come to California, for they would find no benefices to provide for their legitimate support. However, a heartening note was that a few European priests were willing to come, although there were no funds to bring them to California. "The Church here has no property, as the revenues it formerly had from the mission system, the Pious Fund, as well as other sources, have disappeared. It is necessary, then," concluded the harrassed Administrator, "to depend principally upon the charitable offerings of those of the flock who could afford to give of their means to provide for the necessities of their dying Church." A warning followed that, if this help were not forthcoming, whatever of divine worship was yet had in California would continue to disappear; the administrator's final plea was both poignant and eloquently expressive of his feelings:

> The administration of the sacraments, the training of the young and, lastly, the conversion of the Indians, cannot be obtained without gospel laborers who will give to these objects their talent, their toil, and even their lives at need. All of you, dear Christians of the diocese, who truly love Jesus Christ and His holy religion, who desire it to take root and to thrive among us, who wish to sanctify your own souls and help them on the road to Heaven must, with free hand, give the help we need.[11]

It was abundantly clear, then, to all concerned at the time with the weakened state of Catholicism in California that prompt succour was all that would save the very existence of the Church. That these representations concerning the need for the renewal

[11] Gonzalez Rubio to the "Catholics of California," etc. Pastoral letter dated June, 1849. Copy in Franciscan Archives, Santa Barbara, California.

of episcopal authority were to bear fruit will next be indicated as we note how the hierarchy of the United States, in the person of some of its more prominent members, expressed themselves as to what precisely was to be done for the Catholic Church in California.

5

The Mitre of Monterey, 1849–1850

THERE is abundant evidence that the various reports concerning the sad state of Catholicism in California, which have been previously mentioned, actually did cause concern in Baltimore, where the American bishops were accustomed to gather in council, and, ultimately, in Rome itself. Obviously, the most significant single effect was the selection of Joseph Sadoc Alemany to be the bishop so much needed in California. Before various details are presented as to how his selection came about, it will be of interest to have an admiring Dominican's judgment on Alemany:

> It is universally admitted that vain would have been the search to find another clergyman in the United States better adapted or more competent for the new See in the Far West than Alemany. During his ten years of labor in Ohio, Kentucky, and Tennessee, he had imbibed our American ways and spirit. This fitted him for meeting the great influx of gold hunters from the east. His knowledge of the Spanish language and character adjusted him for directing the strong Mexican element still existing in California. Though somewhat low of stature and slight of build, the swarthy bishop had a strong constitution and an energy that seemed never to tire. The two archdioceses and three dioceses now in California—are the fruits of the seed sowed by his faithful hands.[1]

Many, indeed, were the problems resulting from the formal acquisition of California for the United States by the Treaty of

[1] O'Daniel, *The Dominican Province of St. Joseph, Historico-Biographical Studies*, pp. 172–173.

Guadalupe Hidalgo which, on February 2, 1848, concluded the War with Mexico. An example of the wish of the victor to proceed with due caution is found in the following letter, which was written by a Department of State official to Archbishop Eccleston of Baltimore just six weeks after the signing of the treaty:

Most Rev. and Dear Sir:

Mr. Buchanan, the Secretary of State, has requested me to write to you to ask you to be so good as to give me a letter, addressed either to myself or to the Archbishop of Mexico, stating that the Catholics in this country are in the enjoyment of the fullest privileges of citizens —that they are perfectly satisfied, and that the property of the church is completely protected. He is very desirous that I should take such a letter from you to Mexico, believing that it would have the most salutary effect.

I am glad of this opportunity of calling myself to your recollection, etc.

Robert M. Walsh[2]

Eccleston was also informed by a long letter from the American Commandant of the Southern Military District of California —Colonel J. D. Stevenson—of some of the problems that were naturally presenting themselves with the changeover from Mexican to American rule. (Part of this letter was cited in the previous chapter.) Colonel Stevenson was properly sympathetic with the particular problems concerning religion in his area of command, praised the Franciscan Administrator in the manner of other testimony previously quoted, and noted that some action would have to be taken by responsible Catholic authorities if their religion was to survive in California. He added:

I am not, Sir, of the Catholic faith, but desire that every man be permitted to worship God according to the dictates of his own conscience, and should not, perhaps, as a military officer, permit myself to interfere in any manner with the religion of the country . . . but I highly esteem the people of this country . . . and have, therefore,

[2] Robert M. Walsh to Samuel Eccleston, Washington, D.C., March 15, 1848. AAB.

deemed it an act of humanity as well as an imperative duty in me to use my best efforts to rescue these people from their present ignorance and degradation which must follow if no relief be afforded them, and I know of no channel through which relief can flow except it be through the ministers of that faith they have been taught to venerate and live by and in which they hope to die. . . . My determination to write to you has been fully communicated to Father Gonzalez and has given much pleasure, and all have expressed an anxious desire and hope that they might be taken under the clerical protection and care of the Church in the U.S. to which they look for succor and relief. . . .[3]

It would appear that Archbishop Eccleston was sufficiently impressed with this letter of the ranking military officer in Southern California to cause him to forward it to the Prefect of Propaganda, Cardinal Franzoni. (At this time and until 1908, all of the United States was under the jurisdiction of this arm of the Catholic Church.) Eccleston's covering letter explained to the Cardinal that he was conscious of his obligation to report such things to competent authority and to ask for advice and suggestions as to what was being planned with regard to taking action concerning the sad situation in California.[4]

Nor was it enough for Eccleston to consult Rome; prudence dictated that he inform some of his brothers in the American hierarchy of all these matters and, consequently, his letter books began now to exhibit copies of various communications of this sort. For example, a letter to Bishop Francis Patrick Kenrick of Philadelphia sent from Baltimore on December 19, 1848, told of his forwarding of the Stevenson report to Rome, adding these comments:

The great influx of sectarian adventurers with their gold hunting parsons makes the sending of some representative indispensable. But it seems to me that anyone appointed for the purpose of securing the property of the Church should, if practicable, speak the English lan-

[3] Colonel Jonathan Stevenson, USA, to Eccleston. Headquarters, Military District of California, Los Angeles, May 1, 1848. Original sent by Eccleston to Sacred Congregation de Propaganda Fide, Rome. APF.

[4] Eccleston to Franzoni, Baltimore, September 4, 1848. APF.

guage and have a previous understanding with our government at home. From a little incidental correspondence which I lately had with Mr. Secretary Buchanan, I have no doubt that he would, if in his time, afford every facility. How would Bishop Timon do?[5] He is a man of business and understands these wild regions. One other doubt on the subject has occurred. How can the functions of the Prefect Apostolic or other envoy be made to harmonize with the feelings and authority of the Bishop of Monterey or other resident ecclesiastical superiors?[6]

Of equal or even greater prominence with Kenrick in the American hierarchy of the day was the redoubtable Bishop John Hughes of New York.[7] He, too, had been the recipient of a letter from California concerning the state of things there, and he informed Eccleston of his own concern, too. He warned the Archbishop of Baltimore that the "country is now [December, 1848] inundated with Protestant missionaries to whom it would be a double triumph if they could plant themselves in the deserted habitations of the old Catholic missions. They are impudent enough to attempt it and, if there be no one to represent the church properly there or to advise the government reasonably here in regard to the matter, they may succeed." Hughes had a ready solution, though; he proposed that Eccleston enter into proper negotiations with Washington to insure proper titles to all the property held by the Catholic Church in California under Mexican days. He thought that "such a reasonable request will be instantly granted if the matter be taken in time," but he went on to warn that he feared "there might be danger in delay—these fellows might get up a mock title to the most valuable portion of it, either by quasi-purchase from parties having no right to sell or by taking undisputed possession." More

[5] John Timon (1797–1867) was first Bishop of Buffalo, New York, 1847–1867.

[6] Eccleston to Francis Patrick Kenrick (1797–1863), Baltimore, December 19, 1848. Copy in Eccleston Letter Book, AAB. Kenrick was third Bishop of Philadelphia, 1842–1851.

[7] John Hughes (1797–1864) was fourth Bishop of New York, 1842–1850.

important was his concluding suggestion concerning the appointment of a bishop for California:

> It strikes me also that, at the next Council, the Bishops should recommend to the Holy See the importance of appointing one or more Bishops for that and other recently acquired portions of United States territory.[8]

Additional evidence of Hughes' interest in the recovery of Catholicism in California is to be found in a letter of inquiry which he wrote about two weeks before that just quoted. It was written to a distinguished and worthy Catholic leader then residing in Santa Barbara, Don Jose de la Guerra y Noriega (1779–1858).

> New York, December 12, 1848
> John Hughes, Bishop of New York to
> Don Jose de la Guerra y Noriega.
> My Very Esteemed Friend:
> . . . Since it has come to my knowledge you are one of the oldest residents of Santa Barbara, that you are deeply interested in the advancement of our faith, and that you are one of the foremost protectors and advisors of the missionaries, I do not doubt, Senor Don Jose, that you are one of the persons most capable in that province to give me confidential information regarding the present state of the Church and missions there.
> Because of the territory ceded to the United States . . . the Bishops of this country will probably take into consideration the state of religion in that province in order to set before the Holy See the most necessary means requisite for the protection, both spiritual and temporal, of the faithful residing in that region . . .[9]

Bishop Hughes then went on to ask several pertinent questions concerning these matters and informed Don Jose that "the bishops of the United States will hold a meeting this coming May . . . and will then urge the Pope to choose one or two

[8] Hughes to Eccleston, New York, December 23, 1848. AAB.

[9] Hughes to Jose de la Guerra, New York, December 12, 1848. Quoted in Joseph A. Thompson, O.F.M., *El Gran Capitan. Jose de la Guerra, a Historical Biographical Study,* Los Angeles, 1961, pp. 220–221.

Bishops for the province of California. Fortunately, there are in this country several Spanish priests from whose number one will be gladly selected for such a bishopric."

An illustration of the length of time necessary to communicate with California is shown by the fact that Don Jose did not address his reply to Hughes until April 18, 1849, which he mentioned was only a few days after his reception of the letter. De la Guerra went into satisfying details in answer to the questions asked of him:

> As to what you add, that it [the See of California] ought to be occupied by a Spanish priest, I judge that to be fitting, because the Catholics of this country are almost all Spanish American, with whom the Spaniards are in sympathy; however, if this might not be accomplished, I think at least that as an indispensable requisite, the bishop or bishops who are appointed should be proficient in Spanish.

De la Guerra thus discussed the question of the number of Catholics in California:

> Before the discovery of gold, they could be calculated at about twenty-five or thirty thousand, but since then, the influx of people from the Spanish Americas, and such as are expected from every part of the continent, Oceania, Asia, etc. . . . has made it impossible to form a judicious estimate of how many will be in this country within the next six years. . . .[10]

An indication of the scarcity of clergy in California at the time of writing was thus phrased by de la Guerra:

> The whole clergy that at present exists in this Alta California consists of four secular priests, four outside priests, one Dominican religious and seven Franciscans. Of these latter, one is the Governor of the miter [Father Gonzalez Rubio], another is about to depart for Mexico City . . . and, of the remaining five, only two are capable of giving their all to the ministry, the others being too old and too infirm. The Dominican belongs to the missions of Baja California which

[10] De la Guerra to Hughes, Santa Barbara, California, April 18, 1849. Quoted in Thompson, *op. cit.*, pp. 221–225, *passim*.

province he left, so I am informed, because of some revolts there, for which reason I presume his stay here will be of short duration. Of the four alien priests, two were sent here at the request of the Rev. P. Gobernador of this miter by the Illustrious Lord Bishop of the Sandwich Islands; another was sent by the Illustrious Lord Archbishop of Oregon, also at the insistence of the aforesaid Gobernador; while the other came here on his own account and who, because he acknowledges no prelate, will, it is feared, become discontented for any reason whatever and leave the country. Of the four secular priests, the one is always so sick that he is often unable to celebrate Mass, but the other three fulfill their ministry.

This, then, Most Illustrious Lord Bishop, is the number and circumstances of the priests, both religious and secular, living in this extensive land, from which it can be easily understood how great is our need for an increase in the number of priests to administer to us.[11]

Several days later, Archbishop Eccleston referred to the Hughes letter when, again writing to Kenrick, he mentioned that he was leaving for Washington immediately to confer with responsible authorities concerning Catholic Church property in the territories newly acquired from Mexico by conquest.[12] Indeed, he was able to report on the next day that his interview with Secretary of State James Buchanan had found the latter suggesting the sending of a commission to California to survey the situation and then to make due report.[13] Two weeks later, Eccleston confided to Kenrick that "every daily paper that I open impresses me more and more with the necessity of not letting ourselves be headed by the gold hunting parsons."[14]

Other plans relative to California were afoot at this time. This was made evident by another letter from Eccleston to Kenrick in which mention was made that the Jesuit provincial, at Eccleston's suggestion, had written to the general of the Society

[11] *Ibid.*
[12] Eccleston to Kenrick, Baltimore, December 26, 1848. Copy in Eccleston Letter Book, AAB.
[13] Eccleston to Kenrick, Georgetown, D.C., December 27, 1848. Copy as above, AAB.
[14] Eccleston to Kenrick, Baltimore, January 10, 1849. AAB.

"requesting his authorization and aid to take initiatory measures to form a branch of the Order in California," adding that, so far, he had received no answer and, hence, he could not, in consequence, "pledge myself to furnish a chaplain for a party of Catholics who proposed to go from Philadelphia to California."[15] But, if the Jesuits were not so prepared to assist, consolation was afforded by the fact that the "Superior of the Dominicans in Ohio [Alemany] had offered the services of Rev. Father A. P. Anderson to go to California in quest of souls with a view to the establishment of a permanent branch of their Society there."[16]

The next significant step is to be found in a letter to Kenrick from Eccleston in which, after remarking that he was quite in the dark concerning the "newspaper intelligence of the appointment of a French Bishop to California (may it be apocryphal, unless he may have given evidences of an extraordinary vocation!)," he goes on to the important detail that he had finally received an answer from Rome to his former communication sent there some months previously. The desired answer authorized Eccleston to propose the matter of an episcopal appointment to California at the forthcoming council to be held in Baltimore —with the consequent forwarding of any action to the same Roman congregation.[17] At last, the American prelates could move forward with Roman sanction.

It is hardly to be wondered at that the continued delay in the appointment of a bishop for the California Church should have caused another prelate closer to the scene to interpose his ideas on the subject. On June 10, 1849, Archbishop Francis Norbert Blanchet of Oregon City[18] wrote to Cardinal Franzoni reminding him that, while Monterey was the present capital of California, it appeared likely that San Francisco would continue to grow

---

[15] Eccleston to Kenrick, Baltimore, March 12, 1849. AAB.
[16] *Ibid.*
[17] Eccleston to Kenrick, Baltimore, January 3, 1849, AAB.
[18] Francis Norbert Blanchet (1795–1883) to Franzoni, Oregon City, June 1, 1849. APF.

in importance and, hence, the bishop who was to be designated for California should be left the freedom of designating his episcopal seat there. With that forthrightness which had caused him to be appointed archbishop of Oregon City in what now seems a quite premature arrangement, Blanchet sent another letter, which he directed to Pope Pius, suggesting either of two Canadian priests for the proposed See of California and requesting that the new diocese be made suffragan to his archiepiscopal See of Oregon![19]

An organization to which the Catholic Church in the United States must always owe a large debt of gratitude for aid rendered is that known as the "Oeuvre de la Propagation de la Foi en Faveuré de Missions Etrangeres des Deux Mondes," with joint headquarters in Paris and in Lyons. One of the most fruitful sources of information, indeed, for the history of the Catholicism in the United States is to be found in the well preserved records of this Society and, among such records, there are pertinent mentions of its concern with matters in California. On December 8, 1849—actually, some six months before the appointment of Alemany to California—the president of the council of the Lyons branch of the Society informed Monsignor Alessandro Barnabò, secretary of the Congregation de Propaganda Fide in Rome, that it had become acquainted with the California situation because of information given it by an American prelate en route to Rome with the reports of the recently concluded Council of Baltimore. He had told them, said the president, of the sad situation and had added that it was surely not to be long before the Holy See would designate a bishop for California. Accordingly, moved by the genuine needs presented to them, it had been decided to authorize financial help to this bishop, and word to this effect had been sent to Archbishop Eccleston of Baltimore. His reply, thanking them for the generosity implicit in such an action, had

[19] Blanchet to Pius IX, Oregon City, June 10, 1849. Blanchet was first Archbishop of Oregon City, 1846–1880. APF.

informed them that no such bishop had yet been appointed. Hence it was desired that, when and as soon as such an appointment was made, the Paris president be so informed so as to be able to present the subsidy in favor of California and its newly designated prelate. Final inquiry is made concerning two points:

1. Has the Holy See, in fact, appointed such a Bishop for California?
2. If so, who is he?[20]

Presumably, the prelate who later tried, unsuccessfully, several times to resign the archiepiscopal See of San Francisco, the future Archbishop Alemany, had little sensitivity in his knowledge of the fact that he had not been Rome's original choice for the mitre of Monterey. In fact, he seems never to have deviated from his conviction that it would have been far better for the Church had someone else been appointed and made to serve in his place. That such a one was so appointed, but succeeded in avoiding episcopal consecration and consequent service in the See of California, is the next matter for consideration here. He was a brother Dominican whom we have already mentioned—Father Charles Pius Montgomery.

Father Montgomery, the successful eluder of Monterey's mitre, was born in Kentucky in 1806 and professed as a Dominican at St. Rose's, Kentucky, in 1822. Ordained in 1830, his first years of priestly service (1830–1833) were spent at St. Rose's, with a transfer to Zanesville, Ohio, following in May, 1833. There ensued some zealous and successful years as pastor and, undoubtedly, the reputation which he made during these years helped to place him on the list of those suitable for episcopal dignity in the United States. Additionally, from 1838 to 1843, Father Montgomery served his order as prior provincial of the St. Joseph Province. On November 20, 1849, Pius IX appointed him to

[20] "President of the Council, Society for the Propagation of the Faith" (name illegible) to Alessandro Barnabò, secretary of the Sacred Congregation de Propaganda Fide, Lyons, France, December 8, 1849. APF.

85

the newly constituted See of Monterey in California. Barnabò informed Eccleston concerning this appointment as follows:

> Since matters in California have reached such a state as to induce His Holiness to appoint a Bishop for Monterey immediately, he has authorized Apostolic Letters given at Naples, by which B. P. [*sic*] Montgomery is appointed to this task. Kindly see to it that these Apostolic Letters . . . are transmitted to the Bishop-Elect and urge him to accept consecration as soon as possible.[21]

The ever-systematic Eccleston noted, on the bottom of this letter, that on February 18, 1850, he had received and forwarded these bulls.[22] However, it quickly became evident that Montgomery's refusal of the See of Monterey was not long delayed—for we have his letter so stating which he wrote to Eccleston from Zanesville, Ohio, only four days later, on February 22, 1850.

Most Reverend Sir:

I received the documents from Rome sent on by you and beg leave to return the same through you, with my reasons for non-acceptance:

1. I feel not the least vocation to that state; neither have I the knowledge nor other qualities with which to fulfill it with benefit to religion.

2. My constitution is broken down and my health is gone. I am scarcely able to say the last Mass and dare not venture to sing anything, being afflicted with bronchitis. . . . I am almost certain that anxiety, with arduous duties, would very soon end my earthly existence. Under these circumstances, I think that it would be worse than useless for me to accept such an office. Knowing your kindness, I am sure that you will communicate the above to the Holy Father and I beg you to use your influence to have me relieved from further anxiety on the subject. It will be a favor for which I will ever be thankful. In the meantime, believe me,

Your humble and obedient servant,
Charles P. Montgomery[23]

[21] Barnabò to Eccleston, Rome, December 21, 1849. AAB.
[22] *Ibid.*
[23] Montgomery to Eccleston, Zanesville, Ohio, February 22, 1850. AAB.

One of the earlier press announcements of Montgomery's appointment appeared in the Pittsburgh *Catholic*, March 9, 1850, where it was credited as a reprint from the Cincinnati *Catholic Telegraph*:

> We take great pleasure in transferring to our columns the following auspicious announcement of the election of Rt. Rev. Charles P. Montgomery, O.P., of Zanesville, as Bishop of Monterey. Mr. Montgomery is a native of Kentucky, of the Order of Saint Dominic, and has been for many years an active and efficient missionary as well as an exemplary priest of this diocise. He will find many of his former parishioners in the Valley of Sacramento by whom his presence will be hailed with more joy than the discovery of a placer.[24]

Perhaps it was soon brought home to Father Montgomery that there is a certain amount of correspondence in connection with the refusal of the episcopal burden, for we find him, in a letter written to Bishop Purcell of Cincinnati, again mentioning his reasons for refusing the appointment as bishop of Monterey.[25] Montgomery's refusal was a clear cut one, but there were, nevertheless, conflicting reports concerning it. This is made evident by the following letter from Eccleston to Purcell:

Baltimore, Holy Saturday,
(March 30) 1850

> I was lately informed by a young French clergyman that he heard from your *eveche* [*sic*] that the Rev. Mr. Montgomery was to be consecrated in the Cathedral at Cincinnati. . . . I naturally inferred that he [Mr. Montgomery] had reconsidered his declination and submitted to the yoke. But I am truly sorry to see in a late number of the *Telegraph* that I had been misinformed. . . . Poor California is thus again

[24] Pittsburgh *Catholic,* March 9, 1850. Unless otherwise indicated, the copies of the early American Catholic papers used were consulted in the extensive collection of the American Catholic Historical Society of Philadelphia. These are housed in the library of St. Charles Seminary, Overbrook, Pennsylvania.

[25] Montgomery to Purcell (1800–1883), Zanesville, Ohio, March 16, 1850. Purcell was serving at this time as second Bishop of Cincinnati, 1833–1850. MCUND.

thrown back. The second on the list is Rev. Mr. Lamy. But, he being first on the list for the Vicariate of Santa Fe, it appears that the mitre should fall on the head of the Rev. Thomas Grace, O.S.D., in the diocese of Nashville. Before urging his nomination, would it not be prudent to ascertain his future? He is a stranger in these parts. . . .[26]

What was evidently an attempt on the part of Eccleston to have Montgomery reconsider his decision gave rise to a further remonstrance on the latter's part in which he firmly reiterated his decision to continue to refuse the episcopal dignity.[27] Montgomery's "episcopal" mail was not yet at an end, for he soon received a letter from the Society for the Propagation of the Faith informing him that his future needs would be considered by this Society when, as occasion offered, he would acquaint the missionary organization of his more pressing needs.[28]

Although not true in the case of several others of those who were later to be appointed to sees in California, Father Montgomery's determined refusals bore fruit—consequently, with his being freed from the burden of the episcopal dignity, the way was now open for a second choice, that of Joseph Sadoc Alemany, for the See of Monterey. Before the actual details are furnished of how a startled and somewhat dismayed friar was informed of his selection as bishop for California, we shall trace the American phase of his selection for this important post.

The first known mention of Alemany's possible appointment to the vacant see was contained in a letter written by Bishop Purcell of Cincinnati to Eccleston when, after mentioning other possible candidates, he wrote that Alemany had finally been selected for the position.[29] A month later, the Dominican Bishop Pius Miles of Nashville wrote to Eccleston to express regret over Montgomery's refusal and to praise Alemany's recog-

---

[26] Eccleston to Purcell, Baltimore, March 30, 1850. MCUND.

[27] Montgomery to Eccleston, Zanesville, Ohio, March 31, 1850. AAB.

[28] "Director of Society for the Propagation of the Faith" to Montgomery, Lyons, France, January 1, 1850. AAB.

[29] Purcell to Eccleston, Cincinnati, Ohio, April 3, 1850. AAB.

nized piety and learning.[30] Two days earlier, Eccleston had informed Bishop Martin Spalding of Louisville as to what had been done in the matter of a selection of a bishop for California; he mentioned that Alemany had been placed first in a list of three names which had been sent to Rome.[31] We may here quote this letter which the Baltimore Prelate had sent to Cardinal Franzoni:

> Since Father Montgomery, whose health grows poorer, has legitimately (in my opinion) refused the See of Monterey, I beg leave to forward the names of the following priests who have merited approval by our Counciliar Fathers in their last meeting.
>
> 1. Joseph Alemany, a Spaniard, Dominican Provincial, of sufficient age and adorned with both piety and learning—(he has just gone to Naples to assist in electing a General of his Order). Therefore, if it please the Holy See, he could receive episcopal consecration before his return to the United States.[32]

In addition to his own personal letter to Cardinal Franzoni, Eccleston, in a circular letter which was dated April 17, 1850, requested all the American bishops to write to Rome and express their views to the same Cardinal Prefect of Propaganda regarding a selection for Monterery. On April 27, 1850, Michael O'Connor, Bishop of Pittsburgh, while praising Father Alemany as a "good religious," expressed doubts as to whether he had manifested sufficient force of character for the task to be done in California. Also, he added, Alemany's Spanish blood, though ostensibly a recommending feature, might prove just the opposite in practice since the Californians of Mexican extraction had no love for Spain! Finally, Bishop O'Connor remained unconvinced that Alemany's admittedly imperfect knowledge of English would enable him to speak it in public utterances so as to dignify

[30] Richard Pius Miles, O.P. (1791–1860) to Eccleston, Nashville, Tennessee, April 18, 1850, *AAB*, Bishop Miles served as first Bishop of Nashville (1837–1861).

[31] Eccleston to Martin John Spalding (1810–1872), Baltimore, April 16, 1850. Copy in AAB.

[32] Eccleston to Franzoni, Baltimore, April 16, 1850. APF.

the episcopate. He concluded his frank analysis with mention of the fact that he did not consider Alemany the possessor of such outstanding qualities as to merit his selection.[33] Bishop Martin Henni of Milwaukee was not satisfied with acquainting a Roman cardinal with his views: his letter he addressed directly to His Holiness Pope Pius IX. In it, he informed the Holy Father that he proposed, in the first place for Monterey, "Very Rev. Joseph Alemani [sic], O.S.D., who, in addition to the necessary virtues which he has, also enjoys a knowledge of the Spanish and of English tongues."[34] From St. Louis, Archbishop Peter Richard Kenrick wrote to Cardinal Franzoni that he agreed with Archbishop Eccleston in placing Father Alemany first on the list for Monterey, adding that he thought Alemany possessed the necessary learning in matters theological and that his competency in the Spanish and English languages should stand him in good stead were he selected for California.[35] In the opinion of the Jesuit Bishop James Van de Velde of Chicago, Alemany would do quite well in California, and that his proficiency in Spanish would merit him well both of the older inhabitants as well as with the "aborigines" who would be under his pastoral care. The objection that a Spanish-born bishop might be resented by the Californians was neatly disposed of by Bishop Van de Velde in his remark that such a candidate was being proposed not by the Spanish government with consequent complications, but by a council made up of American bishops—hence, there should be no trouble since California was now American.[36] Bishop Anthony

[33] Michael O'Connor (1810–1872) to Franzoni, Pittsburgh, April 27, 1850. *APF*. O'Connor was first Bishop of Pittsburgh, 1843–1860.

[34] Martin Henni (1805–1881) to Pius IX, Milwaukee, April 30, 1850. APF. Henni was first Bishop of Milwaukee, 1843–1875.

[35] Peter Richard Kenrick (1806–1896) to Franzoni, St. Louis, May 2, 1850. Kenrick served as second Bishop of St. Louis, 1843–1847, and as first archbishop there, 1847–1895. APF.

[36] James Van de Velde, S.J. (1795–1855), to Franzoni, Peoria, Illinois, May 8, 1850 APF. Van de Velde served as second Bishop of Chicago, 1849–1853. APF.

Blanc of New Orleans, while professing confidence in Alemany's character and worth, changed him from first to second place in his letter to Franzoni.[37] The reason for his selection of Father Purcell of Cincinnati for Monterey for first place was brought out in another letter which Blanc wrote to Bishop Purcell, the brother of the one favored by him:

> On my arrival here, I found a letter of the Archbishop of Baltimore relating to the new proposed candidates for Monterey. I will tell you frankly that I am not in favor of the appointment of professed religious (particularly when they occupy high places in their own Order) beyond cases of real necessity, which I doubt is not [sic] the present one and, as it is generally admitted that the Professed religious do not accept the ecclesiastical dignities unless they be especially enjoined to do so by the Sovereign Pontiff, we yet run the risk of another refusal. . . .[38]

Bishop Kenrick's comments from Philadelphia concerning the selection for Monterey found him admitting frankly that the "one who is in first place is unknown to me, but he has been praised by numerous Bishops."[39] He went on to propose that Bishop Andrew Byrne of Little Rock be translated to the new see in California, for, as Kenrick noted, this Prelate had already expressed his desire to be transferred from his present charge, and had declared himself willing to assume the burden of episcopal rule in California even though he was aware of the lack of immediate financial resources which, seemingly, would be part of the episcopal burden in California.[40] As it developed, nothing came out of the offer of the Arkansas Prelate with regard to the See of Monterey.

That Rome itself was not inactive in the matter is proven by

---

[37] Anthony Blanc (1792–1860) to Franzoni, New Orleans, May 9, 1850. APF. Blanc was second Bishop of New Orleans, 1835–1851.
[38] Blanc to Purcell, New Orleans, May 10, 1850. MCUND.
[39] Kenrick to Franzoni, Philadelphia, June 12, 1850. APF.
[40] *Ibid.*

several documents which record the interesting sequence of events which were to make Alemany a bishop. On May 19, 1850, Cardinal Franzoni, in an audience with Pope Pius IX, explained Montgomery's refusal and suggested that Alemany be appointed to Monterey. He obtained the approval of His Holiness, who ordered the customary apostolic letters to be prepared. On the following day, May 20, Franzoni caused the following letter to be sent to the secretary of briefs of the Vatican secretariat of state:

> Since Rev. Fr. Montgomery has asked to be freed from the acceptance of the See of Monterey in Upper California because of his weakened health, the Sacred Congregation of Propaganda, in the person of the undersigned, its Secretary, has asked that the dignity of this position be given to the Very Rev. Joseph Alemany, whose virtue, learning and prudence are well established by the testimony of many. . . .[41]

It now belonged to the secretary of briefs to draw up the customary document or apostolic letter, dated May 31, 1850, which would authorize the consecration of Father Alemany. This brief followed the usual form in stating that Pius IX, "mindful of his obligations as Supreme Shepherd, had decided to provide for the pressing needs of the Church in Monterey in Upper California, United States of America." It went on to announce to "our beloved son and priest Alemany [sic]" that, after consultation, reflection, and prayer, His Holiness had decided to name him to the See of Monterey and admonished him to accept the "burden of the Lord which is thus imposed on your shoulders with willingness of spirit so that you may thus enter upon the ruling of your diocese with prudence and devotion." Finally, authorization was given Alemany to arrange for his episcopal consecration by any bishop in communion with the apostolic see.[42] This

---

[41] Franzoni to the "Secretary of Briefs, Vatican Secretariat of State, Rome." ASV.

[42] *Ibid.* Brief is dated May 31, 1850.

document, filled with implications not only for Alemany but for the future of Catholicism in California, was noted as having been "given at Rome at St. Peter's, under the Fisherman's Seal, on May 31, 1850, the fourth year of Our Pontificate."[43] As Father Alemany was soon to find out, Rome had spoken in his regard and the will of the Pope was to be final and not subject to change.

Thus far, in the story of Alemany's promotion to episcopal dignity, we have presented the official aspects of the promotion; obviously, though, it should prove interesting to learn of the first reactions of Alemany himself. We are fortunate in having a diary kept by Alemany for the years 1850–1853, which starts with the event which was to so change his life—his notification that he was to be a successor of the Apostles in California.[44] From this diary, we are able to reconstruct the main details quite satisfactorily. Thus, for example, Friar Joseph Sadoc noted, after his arrival in Rome on June 6, 1850, that Cardinal Franzoni had informed him on June 11 that he was to be the Bishop of Monterey and that he must soon prepare himself for consecration. The next day the dismayed friar consulted his confessor, who suggested that he present his objections to Father Jerome Gigli, then acting as vicar general of the Dominican order. Father Gigli was quite sympathetic and gave his leave to Alemany to refuse the dignity by making a "humble and modest resignation" if this proved agreeable to the Holy Father who had appointed him. The next Sunday, June 16, found Father Alemany in private audience with Pius IX himself, and this pivotal event is recorded as follows:

> Before allowing me to refuse, he said that it is necessary that I go to Monterey. "You *must* go to California; there is no alternative.

[43] *Ibid.*
[44] Francis J. Weber, *Long Lost Ecclesiastical Diary*, Los Angeles, 1964. (A translation of 24 pages of notes in the hand of Joseph Sadoc Alemany, O.P. Chancery Archives, Archdiocese of Los Angeles.) The present writer is indebted to Father Weber for permitting the use of this *Diary*.

where others are drawn by gold, you must go to carry the Cross. God will assist you."

"Holy Father, while it is not my wish to oppose the will of God, I must point out my lack of qualifications for the Bishopric and ask Your Holiness for permission to refuse the nomination." The Pontiff answered, "I appreciate the prudence which prompts your reply, but it is for me to judge in this matter. According to St. Thomas, prudence and obedience are equally necessary virtues and the wish of Christ's Vicar is the Will of God for you. Do not ponder over what to say or do for the Lord will direct you at the proper time."[45]

The next day Father Alemany again met with Cardinal Franzoni, as well as with Father Gigli. Presumably both concurred in their decision that the die was cast and, on the next day, the Dominican Vicar General gave him the formal and necessary permission to accept the nomination. A spiritual retreat of eight days followed at the ancient Dominican convent of Santa Sabina in Rome, June 21–29, and the bishop-elect concluded it most appropriately by offering Mass on the last day, the feast of Sts. Peter and Paul, at the altar of the tomb of St. Peter.[46]

Since the Dominican Church of Santa Maria sopra Minerva was undergoing extensive renovation and repair at this time, it was decided that Bishop Alemany would receive episcopal consecration in the basilica of San Carlos al Corso which, since completion in 1672, had been one of the outstanding churches of Rome. On Sunday, June 30, 1850, the feast of St. Paul the

[45] Weber, *Diary*, etc.

[46] Even though Father Vicar Gigli had allowed Alemany to proceed to his consecration, the matter was not concluded here. According to the Dominican constitutions, a friar who has been selected for episcopal dignity must obtain permission to assume the office from the master general. If one should proceed to consecration without obtaining the required permission, it is explicitly provided that, on his death, none of the prescribed prayers of the order, including Masses, etc., be applied to his soul. On July 21, 1850, three weeks after his consecration, the commission of friars which, with the vicar general, was governing the order at the time, formally confirmed Gigli's permission in the following words which were entered into the *Acta* of their meeting of that day: "Permission is granted to the Brother Provincial, Joseph S. Alemany, to accept the bishopric of California and this permission is hereby confirmed." (Translated from Latin by the author.) AOPR.

Apostle, California's newest apostle, who was to walk in the steps of Paul and of Serra, received episcopal consecration at the hands of the cardinal prefect of Propaganda, Cardinal Franzoni. The co-consecrators were the patriarch of Jerusalem, Archbishop Joseph Valerga, and a brother Dominican prelate, Giovanni Stefanelli, titular Archbishop of Trajanopolis. With him was consecrated Angelo Ranazotti, destined for the Italian See of Pavia. After the long and impressive ceremony, Bishop Alemany was a guest of Cardinal Franzoni at a festive dinner at the Propaganda, following which he made an *ad limina* visit to that tomb of St. Peter where he had offered Mass the day before.

In a letter of only a few days later which he wrote to his mother in Vich, Bishop Alemany thus recorded the event:

Everything went off well, except the heavy book of the Gospels which the Cardinal placed on my shoulders weighed a little heavy, but I hope our Lord will aid me in carrying it, as our Holy Father told me. The function lasted three hours attended by all the Dominicans who were able to come. Afterwards the Cardinal gave us a wedding dinner. And now they want me to start as soon as possible for California, for the diocese has been three years without a Bishop. . . . As soon as I finish my visits, I shall start for Paris, London, New York, Panama, and California, now my beloved bride, to live there the life of altar boy, vicar, missionary, pastor and bishop.[47]

[47] Rome, July 3, 1850. Quoted in Comella, *Biografia,* etc., pp. 21–22.

6

From Rome to Monterey in 1850

MONDAY morning, July 1, 1850, saw the newly consecrated Bishop Alemany in conference with the board of cardinals who ruled the Congregation de Propaganda Fide.[1] Although nothing more than the cryptic entry that such a meeting took place is to be found in the Alemany *Diary*, it is obvious that the discussion must have centered around the information which had reached their eminences concerning the sad state of Catholicism in California. Alemany must have been heartened by the interest shown in his work and the attention paid to his preliminary assessment of his problems. On July 4, he went to the Basilica of St. Paul Outside the Walls to offer Mass there, following which he visited the traditional site of the martyrdom of St. Paul close by. On Saturday, July 6, accompanied by Father Vilarrasa (who had, on July 3, been assigned to accompany him to California), Bishop Alemany had another audience with Pius IX, his two priest brothers also forming part of the group. Alemany offered the Pope the sum of $100, which Pius refused to accept. Instead, the Pope gave him a silver chalice for his personal use in California.[2] The young Prelate was busy with many things during the next few days—even over-busy, for on July 22 he

[1] Testimony as to a visit to the tomb of St. Peter by Bishop Alemany on June 30, 1850—the day of his episcopal consecration—is to be found in a printed form, duly filled out and, undoubtedly, brought by him to California, which is preserved in AASF.

[2] Weber, *Diary*, entries for July 1, 4, 6, 1850.

noted in his *Diary* that he had "suffered the fever for seven days." However, he was sufficiently recovered to offer his first pontifical Mass on July 28. Finally, on July 30, he left Rome and proceeded to Cività Vecchia on the first stage of his long journey to California. Earlier in the month, shortly after his consecration, he had thus written to his mother in Vich:

> If I were able, I would come to Vich to see you again, and invite you to become the housekeeper of the Bishop from the Pyrenees; but I do not believe that you would have the courage to make a trip equivalent to four thousand walking hours. If Michael were willing to go with me and to be pastor in California, I would pass there to take him. Do not bother sending me congratulations. I beg you all to recommend me to God, so that Our Lord, Who makes me walk upright in this world, will not let me walk upside down in the next. God bless us all.
>
> I would like to come to visit you, but to go just to have you see my biretta, all three points adorned and crowned with green trimmings, does not seem to me worthwhile. . . .[3]

Even though it was to be months before Alemany would arrive in the United States, word of his new appointment preceded him. On August 9, 1950, Cardinal Franzoni wrote to Archbishop Eccleston to give official confirmation to the decrees of the Seventh Provincial Council of Baltimore; in this letter, Franzoni added the welcome news of Alemany's consecration and his departure for Monterey.[4] Nor did the 36-year-old Bishop leave Rome without having been liberally granted numerous "faculties" or permissions which he would need in California. Even before Alemany had been notified as to his selection for Monterey, Monsignor Alessandro Barnabò, secretary of the Congregation of Propaganda Fide, had obtained for Alemany from Pius IX a liberal grant of such permissions. Given to him for a

---

[3] Alemany to his mother. Rome, July 3, 1850. Quoted in Comella, *Biografía,* etc., pp. 21–22. The reference to "Michael" is to his brother, Miguel Alemany (1819–1889), who was already a priest of the Diocese of Vich in Spain.

[4] Franzoni to Eccleston, Rome, August 9, 1850. APF.

period of five years, they covered certain matters which would be part of his daily concern in his new diocese.[5]

Bishop Alemany arrived in Città Vecchia in early August, for there is a letter written by him to Barnabò from there on August 5. In it he requests authorization to have a certain Father Semeria, "canonist and theologian," released to him for service in California with the object of having him inaugurate a seminary there.[6] Nothing is known as to what transpired, but Father Semeria seems never to have arrived in California. Another letter, this one of gratitude, was sent from the same place to a fellow Dominican, Father Prior Aquaroni, to thank him for hospitality while in Rome. This note concluded: "I shall never forget the good heart of Father Aquaroni, Prior and Master of Sacred Theology," and concludes with evidence that the Bishop of Monterey still considered himself a son of the Dominican order although removed from its immediate jurisdiction by elevation to the episcopate—for the letter is signed: "Bro. Gui. Sadoc Alemany, O.P., Bishop of Monterey."[7]

Alemany seems to have wisely determined to make his progress to his see with some carefully planned European stops in the hope of obtaining co-workers and financial support. Arriving in Marseilles on August 8, he was able to assemble three large packages of "books, medals, rosaries and pictures" which he sent on to California by way of New York. Two days later, he arrived in Lyons, where one of the branches of the Society for the Propagation of the Faith had its headquarters. This visit established a valuable contact which later on was to result in substantial financial help being accorded to him. Pressing on to Paris, and there visiting the other office maintained by the Association, Alemany noted that he was immediately rewarded with a gift

[5] Listing of these "faculties" is in APF.
[6] Alemany to Franzoni, Città Vecchia, Italy. August 5, 1850. APF.
[7] Alemany to Aquaroni. Città Vecchia, Italy, August 5, 1850. AOPW.

of 10,000 francs which had been designated for Monterey in 1849 and which had not been forwarded in the absence of a bishop there. Now that Alemany had appeared with proper credentials, the welcome gift was his—with a promise that, in March, 1851, he would receive a similar allocation.[8]

A visit in Paris to the Dominican Convent of the Holy Cross proved providential indeed, for, under date of August 21, 1850, Alemany noted that "a good Third Order Dominican sister of Paris offers to come to my diocese as does her Superior provided that she can live in a convent of the Second Order. Both are good teachers." The former was Sister Mary Goemere, a Belgian novice who was to accompany Alemany to California and there found the first religious community of women in the state—the Dominican Congregation of the Holy Name. As things worked out, Sister Goemere was accompanied to America by two postulants from a Dominican convent in Toulouse.[9]

Paris was also the occasion of a visit which he made to the superior general of the Daughters of Charity, Very Reverend Jean Baptiste Etienne, C.M., to whom he made a request for a foundation of sisters for Monterey. This request was to be answered with the arrival of the Daughters of Charity in San Francisco in 1852. Another facet of the Paris visit is provided by an informative letter which he wrote while there to his Dominican confrere, Father Peter Anderson, already in California, in which he told him of the circumstances which had resulted in his consecration as bishop of Monterey. Alemany concluded this letter

---

[8] From 1853–1884, the Archdiocese of San Francisco received the not inconsiderable amount of $45,600 in annual stipends from this Society; in addition the Diocese of Monterey-Los Angeles, 1849–1877, received almost an even $100,000—some part of which must certainly have been of help to Alemany during his three years, 1850–1853, as Bishop of the Diocese of Monterey. These figures are to be found in Edward J. Hickey, *The Society for the Propagation of the Faith: Its Foundation, Organization and Success, 1822–1922,* Washington, D.C., 1922, p. 188.

[9] Memoir of Mother Mary of the Cross Goemere. Copy in AOPC.

with the hope that God would give His blessing to the Church in California "and to its pastor that needs it so much."[10]

On August 30, having satisfactorily transacted his business in Paris and made contacts which were to prove invaluable to him later on, Bishop Alemany left for London. On the next day, he offered Mass at the Oratory there and talked with Father Frederick Faber about the possibility of sending some Oratorian fathers to help him in California. Since Faber suggested that he go to see Father John Henry Newman at the Oratory in Birmingham, where the latter was in charge, Alemany did so and the visit resulted in some encouraging words from Newman, who asked Alemany to survey the situation upon his arrival in California and then to send a report to Birmingham where it would be studied with a view to sending several priests to help him.

The next important stop made by Bishop Alemany was in Ireland, at the missionary college of All Hallows, located at Drumcondra on the outskirts of Dublin, and only eight years old at the time of Alemany's visit in September, 1850. Several seminarians offered their services for California, but the most noteworthy volunteer was Father Eugene O'Connell (1815–1891), a seminary professor who had been ordained in 1842 and who was willing to go to California "on loan" for a few years. Father O'Connell's willingness to go to California must have gladdened the heart of the young Bishop who was seeking volunteers, for O'Connell was already known as a scholarly theologian as well as a man of zeal. Both qualities would be of use to Bishop Alemany in the diocese of Monterey.[11]

After having arranged with Father Robert White, a Dublin

[10] Alemany to Anderson, Paris, August 24, 1850. The original of this letter has been lost but it is reproduced in Joseph Riordan, S.J., *The First Half Century of St. Ignatius Church and College*, San Francisco, 1905, p. 34.

[11] Much additional material concerning O'Connell is to be found in Henry L. Walsh, S.J., *Hallowed Were the Gold Dust Trails*, University of Santa Clara, 1942, *passim*. Alemany's words in his *Diary* concerning O'Connell are significant: "Receive Fr. Eugene O'Connell, a very good priest, who

Dominican friar, concerning several possible clerical students who might wish to join him, Alemany paid two satisfactory visits to St. Patrick's College, Maynooth, and to the college of the same name in Carlow. Then it was time for him to return to England and to proceed to Liverpool, which was to be his embarking port. Since he had now had time further to think through the matter of obtaining some Oratorians, he sent a letter on the subject to Father Newman:

> I am very glad to see that Almighty God has granted me your cooperation towards establishing the Children of St. Philip in my Diocese. I hope the Spanish Fathers will also feel themselves moved and decided. Your proposals to me by Father Flanagan are very reasonable, and in what I am concerned I accept of them, at least as far as I can see in the matter of the present. I think you will permit me to ask, not as a required condition or obligation but as a favor, that your Fathers may, for some few years at least, baptize and marry, etc. in their Church, and do all parish duties about their place which would not interfere materially with their Institute. . . . As to the climate I cannot say much, but the American Minister in Rome told me that he had been in Monterey, and that the climate of this city is most delightful. I should suppose the climate of Calif. considerably warmer than that of England, and a little damper in the winter, but by no means infected with any contagious or prevailing fevers. I expect to be in California about the end of November or beginning of December next; and as soon as I will have examined places, I will write to you and give you all possible information as to the best place to make the establishment, the best way to reach there, and also how money may be obtained there. I expect to sail for America in one or two days. Excuse my hasty letter; please to recommend me and my Mission to St. Philip and the Blessed Virgin.[12]

Before leaving for the United States, Alemany recorded several other items of interest in his *Diary*. On September 7, he

wants to come to California if his College of All Hallows can allow it. The President [Father Moriarity] agrees if an annual sum of five pounds can be set aside to provide for his elderly mother . . ." (September 5, 1850).

[12] Alemany to Newman, Liverpool, England, September 9, 1850. AOB. Cardinal Franzoni, Alemany's consecrator, had ordained Newman to the priesthood in Rome on June 1, 1847.

noted that "the news from All Hallows concerning O'Connell is favorable. He may return with a few Indians [!] to be trained in Ireland." On departure day, Wednesday, September 11, he mentioned that he had sent an encouraging letter to Father O'Connell.[13]

The eventful day of his departure for America was thus recorded by Bishop Alemany: "September 11, 1850—Pay Captain McCarran of the ship *Columbus*, ninety pounds sterling for the passage of seven people, and leave for New York. Good wind until the night of the 17th."

Fortunately for all concerned, the *Columbus* made a relatively uneventful journey to New York, with the weather predominately favorable. This is attested to by the fact that both Bishop Alemany and Father Vilarrasa were able to offer Mass almost every morning, while on Sundays the Bishop exercised his pastoral office by offering Mass and preaching to more than five hundred passengers and crew members.

Alemany's imminent arrival in the United States was a source of constant expectation among his Dominican brethren and others. Two days before his embarkation at Liverpool, Alemany's arrival was thus mentioned in a letter written by Father Nicolas Young, O.P., to his fellow Dominican, Father George Young:

> St. Rose, Kentucky, 9 Sept. 1850
>
> . . . I received a long letter a few days ago from Fr. Anderson, who you know, is now in San Francisco—in which he urges me and some of the rest of our brethren to join him there. He gives a fine account of the country and says that San Francisco is one of the most flourishing towns he knows, having about 40,000 settled inhabitants and that he has no doubt in 20 years will rival New York.
>
> You have already seen that our Provincial, Fr. Alemany, has been consecrated Bishop of Monterey. We expect his arrival from Europe any day. That some of our Fathers will accompany him I have no doubt. . . .[14]

[13] Alemany *Diary, passim.*

[14] Nicolas Young, O.P., to George Young, O.P., St. Rose, Kentucky, September 9, 1850. AOPW.

Another Dominican, one who looms large in the history of his order in the Middle West, Father Samuel Mazzuchelli, seems to have had some interest in California and in the prospective arrival of Bishop Alemany. Mazzuchelli thus wrote to Bishop Matthias Loras of Dubuque:

New Diggings, September 26, 1850

. . . Bishop Alemany will be in St. Rose, Kentucky, Washington Co., near Springfield, on the 3rd Sunday of next month, for he has to be there with some of our Fathers who have to meet for the election of a new Provincial . . . with regard to my going to California, it is doubtful whether as a simple missionary I am as well employed here at present as I would be there. My present situation is more pleasing to me than any I have had before in America, and it would be a great sacrifice to leave it. . . . Bp. Alemany will find many willing to go for the gold either of this or of the next world.[15]

For several years the Catholic press of the United States had been carrying reports concerning the discovery of gold in California, as well as the consequent upheavals taking place there. Small wonder, then, that the news of an appointment of a bishop in California should merit space in their columns. One is from the Pittsburgh *Catholic* for September 14, 1850. It would appear that a previous mention of such appointments had been greeted with a certain skepticism:

THE NEW APPOINTMENTS

The items we copied last week from the TRUTH TELLER respecting our new Bishops appear to want confirmation. A report prevails that Rev. Mr. [*sic*] Alemany has been consecrated at Rome for California. We shall know how much of these rumours are true in due time. —*Catholic Herald*

Our authority, friend Herb, was as reliable as any on the continent and time will show it to have been such. —*Truth Teller*

Among ye be it, gentlemen! Perhaps both may be disappointed. Nous Verons![16]

[15] Samuel Mazzuchelli, O.P. (1806–1864), to Matthias Loras (1792–1858). Loras was first Bishop of the Diocese of Dubuque, 1837–1858. "New Diggings" (?), September 26, 1850. Copy in AOPW.
[16] Pittsburgh *Catholic*. September 14, 1850.

In its next issue, the Pittsburgh *Catholic* returned to the subject with the following item, not without inaccuracies:

Monsignor Alemani [*sic*], Bishop of Santa Fe [*sic*] and of all California, who has been in Paris for some years [!] at the Dominican convent, left yesterday for Dublin to recruit some Irish priests for the missions among the British settlers in California. Monsignor Alemani is a Spaniard and was Provincial of the Dominican friars. . . . The French mission in California is served by friars from Valparaiso [!] and some priests from France.[17]

The Philadelphia *Catholic Herald* adopted a more lofty tone in reporting Alemany's appointment:

THE CHURCH OF CALIFORNIA

We believe it is now a settled fact that the Rev. Mr. Alemany has been appointed Bishop of California. As this gentleman is admirably qualified for that particular field of labor, his selection inspires us with high expectations on behalf of the old faith among the motly people of that extensive country. We hope that Bishop Alemany will succeed in securing for those distant and arduous missions a large band of zealous priests and other coadjutors—men like himself, endowed with strong faith, indomitable energy, earnest and ardent piety and a large share of prudence and wisdom.[18]

On October 12, 1850, the day on which Alemany arrived in New York, the St. Louis *Shepherd of the Valley* reprinted an item concerning him from the *Tablet* of London, which appeared to have been more than merely vague about Alemany and his new episcopal see in California.

On Monday morning last, Rt. Rev. Dr. Alemany, Bp. of Monterey, California, arrived in this town [London] and celebrated Mass after which he communicated the purport of his mission, which is to prevail upon some priests to accompany him to the almost totally destitute missions of the gold region.

His Lordship is Spanish and a Dominican and was ten years Bishop

17 Pittsburgh *Catholic*. September 21, 1850.
18 Philadelphia *Catholic Herald*. October 3, 1850.

of the State of Missouri [!] from which he was translated to his present See. He has lately visited his native country and succeeded in obtaining the services of three of the Oratorian Fathers of Vich. What success he has met with in this country, I do not know; but he hopes to obtain a large accession to his number in Ireland where, by this time, he has arrived.[19]

On November 2, 1850 the New York *Freeman's Journal* reported Alemany's departure for California:

Bishop Alemany took his departure for his See on Monday. Previous to going, he expressed his grateful thanks to Messrs. Howland and Aspinwall and to Messrs. Howard and Son for special and valuable courtesies extended to him in the matter of his passage to Chagres.[20]

Despite these journalistic inaccuracies, it is possible to trace Alemany's itinerary from New York to San Francisco. His actual arrival date in New York Harbor appears to have been October 11, with the landing taking place on the following day. Here the party split temporarily, with Vilarrasa accompanying the two nuns from Toulouse to Somerset, Ohio; there he spent some time at St. Joseph's Priory gathering the personal belongings of the bishop as well as his own. Meanwhile, Alemany occupied himself advantageously by travelling to Baltimore for a visit with Archbishop Eccleston, who briefed him on some details of the situations he would have to face there.

On October 27, 1850, the party met again in New York, and on Monday, October 28, Bishop Alemany, Father Vilarrasa, and Sister Mary Goemere sailed on the steamer *Crescent City* for the Isthmus of Panama. During the night of November 6, they arrived at Chagres and, according to Vilarrasa's account, they set out on the following morning on the river in a small boat operated by three Indians. It was to mean three and a half days of uncomfortable journeying—each of which saw them travelling,

[19] St. Louis *Shepherd of the Valley.* October 12, 1850.
[20] New York *Freeman's Journal.* November 2, 1850.

with the night spent either in Indian huts or in small and primitive inns. On November 10, they arrived at Las Cruces and, on the following day, departed on muleback for Panama City, reaching there on November 12. They obtained welcome hospitality at the local seminary, and during their short stay Father Vilarrasa sang a solemn Mass at which Alemany preached. On Saturday, November 16, the group sailed on the steamer *Columbus*, which arrived at Acapulco on November 24; their stop there was only of a few hours duration, and they sailed in through the Golden Gate on the night of Friday, December 6, 1850. On the next day, December 7, 1850, they went ashore.

On October 29, 1850, the day before Bishop Alemany took passage for Chagres, he reported the interesting news of his arrival in America to Father Newman in England; inasmuch as it is Alemany's first recorded letter written from America, it may be quoted here:

Very Rev. Dear Father,

God granted us to arrive safely here the 11th inst. Every day I hear better news in regard to the prospects of my distant diocese and to the climate of Calif. The Archbishop of Baltimore told me a few days ago, that Calif. is going to be one of the most beautiful and promising missions in the world. I hope the Spanish Fathers will not feel so much attached to the souls in their country, as to deprive me from having their and your services in my very needy missions. I leave tomorrow for the Isthmus, and hope to be in Monterey within five or six weeks, and soon after I will write you a longer letter.[21]

Shortly after Alemany's departure for Panama, journalistic mention was made of some difficulties which would probably be

[21] Alemany to Newman, New York, October 27, 1850. AOB. The evident discrepancy as to the dates of Alemany's arrival in New York—he mentions "October 11" and other sources state it as "October 12"—is easily explained when one recalls that passengers on board arriving vessels in American ports were customarily detained for some time for inspections, etc. Undoubtedly, then, Alemany is referring to the fact that he arrived in the harbor of New York on Friday, October 11, and that he disembarked on the following day, Saturday, October 12.

his upon his arrival in California—the New York *Freeman's Journal* thus mentioning these matters:

THE BISHOP OF MONTEREY, AND HIS MISSION IN CALIFORNIA

A statement, not ill-intended but calculated to do no good, appeared lately in the *Philadelphia Times,* and has thence been copied elsewhere, to the effect that the Rt. Rev. Dr. Alemany "in addition to the exercise of his religious duties as a spiritual head of the Church of California, has been made a representative of the Pope, for the purpose of examining and displaying the titles of the old Jesuit property in California."

Now we take the liberty of stating, not officially indeed, but on the very best authority, that upon his arrival in New York, Bishop Alemany was totally ignorant of the fact that there was Church property in dispute in California, and that, according to the very best knowledge of Bishop Alemany, the Pope was equally unaware of the fact; at any rate His Holiness in his frequent interviews with the Bishop talked much about his interesting Mission, but never alluded to the matter of the Mission property.

We may further state that when we related the position of the Mission property in California at the present time to the good Bishop he was unaffectedly distressed; he had anticipated that the weighty charge of the spiritual management of his Diocese was all that he would have to regulate. He had supposed that there was very little property in California belonging to the Church besides the Church edifices, and expressed his concern on finding that his conscientious duties to the pious bequests of the dead, and the claims of justice on the part of the Church, would compel him to engage in possible complications and litigations so foreign to the heart and life of his past missionary career.[22]

On Sunday, December 8, 1850, Bishop Alemany offered Mass in St. Francis Church, San Francisco. He noted in his *Diary* that he preached at this Mass both in English and in Spanish, and, in an afternoon service, in French. He added: "The Catholics

[22] New York *Freeman's Journal.* November 2, 1850. It would seem that the forthright explanation here given was by James A. McMaster (1820–1886), who served as editor of the New York *Freeman's Journal,* 1848–1886. McMaster ranks as one of the foremost defenders of the interests of the American Catholic Church: he here exhibits this concern in the matter of Bishop Alemany's problems in California.

joyfully received me in the schoolroom after High Mass." On Monday, Father Anthony Langlois, who had previously been appointed vicar general by the administrator of the see, arrived in San Francisco, and having examined Alemany's credentials, as prescribed by Church law, knelt to receive his blessing, thus acknowledging the fact that the Church in California had again received a shepherd.

Bishop Alemany was accorded an official reception several days after his arrival in San Francisco. Although his flock had been given no official news of his coming, they were not tardy in their joyful greeting to their new Bishop. The reception was held on Tuesday evening, December 10, at St. Francis Church. Previously, a committee composed of eight prominent Catholic laymen had met and appointed one of their number, John A. McGlynn, to voice the official welcome to Alemany, and this he did in the presence of a large number of well-wishers. After expressing gratitude to God for the arrival of a sorely needed spiritual leader, McGlynn praised the choice made by Rome for California, referring to Alemany in the traditional manner in which a bishop is greeted: "Behold a great priest who in his time pleased God and was found just." A brief account of the history of Catholicism in California was then given by McGlynn, who assured Bishop Alemany of the gratitude of all present for Rome's solicitude in providing so auspiciously for their spiritual needs. Adding that the Protestants of the city would also rejoice in his coming, especially when they learned of his decade of previous service in the United States as well as the fact of his being an American citizen, the speaker concluded by invoking God's choicest blessings on their Bishop who, it was hoped by all, had arrived among them to long "carry on the work of the ministry for His glory and the salvation of souls." As expected, Bishop Alemany's reply was warm and apropos; thanking all for their sincere sentiments, he recalled the length of the journey from Rome to San Francisco, and mentioned how consoling it was to find, at its end, such devoted Christians and such a sincere outpouring of affection for the Church which he served and which they evidently loved so well. "Two or three years ago," Alemany remarked, "the insignificant town of San Francisco would scarcely meet the eye of the student of geography; today, the name of this large and important city resounds throughout the world." He briefly recalled the growth of Catholicism in America, predicting that, with equal devotion from the faithful in California, "equal prosperity may be prophesied." He then imparted his episcopal blessing on all those present. Finally, a sum in excess of $1,400 was presented to Alemany to defray the expenses which were shortly to be his as he journeyed through his diocese to become acquainted with his people.[23] Thus, in a manner befitting the man and his mission, was Joseph Sadoc

[23] A special "broadside" was printed in English, Spanish, and French to commemorate this official reception to Alemany. The English version is to be found as an appendix to this volume. A rare copy was made available to the author by Miss Frances Molera, member of an old California family; the original has long been in her possession as one of the cherished heirlooms of her family. According to Bishop Alemany's *Diary,* $1000 of the purse presented to him on this occasion was in gold dust worth $10 an ounce (*Diary* entry for December 10, 1850).

Writing a week after Alemany's arrival, Father Flavian Fontaine, a Picpus father stationed at Mission Dolores, informed his religious brethren in Belgium of the Bishop's arrival:

Monseigneur Joseph Alemany, of Catalan origin, formerly a missionary in the United States, happily arrived here on last Saturday. His Grace has not yet decided on the location of his episcopal headquarters. The clergy and faithful of California have received the news of his coming with incredible joy. For too long a time they have been without a guide. Monseigneur speaks many languages, is a very industrious person, a man of action, and quite young (36 years old). Although of small stature, he is strong in health, although not robust. His gentle and affable manner have made him loved from the very start. His piety is, in itself, a living sermon.

Flavian Fontaine, C.ss.C. to "his brethren"
"Mission of San Francisco, of Sorrows,
California" December 15, 1850, Archives
Picpus Fathers, Rome.

Alemany made welcome to San Francisco and to his pastoral care of the entire state of California.

Nine days after his arrival in San Francisco, Bishop Alemany wrote to Father Newman concerning his journey thither while recording some first impressions:

> God in his goodness granted us to arrive here safe, having made the journey from Liverpool to N. York in 28 days and from N.Y. to San Francisco in 40. Though I have not been here but a few days, I have have seen enough to convince me that I was not mistaken in thinking that your services would be very useful in this diocese. The people shows a good desire to secure good Priests, and if the Spanish Catholics of California could secure the good services of those Spanish Fathers together with those of some of your English Fathers, as we were arranging, I can see they would consider that a very great acquisition. I cannot as yet (so lately arrived) come to particulars. I merely write to beg you to do all in your power to accomplish the proposed project. The Providence of God will, no doubt, be good to us. I find the Catholics here very generous. The Sunday before last the donation at the offertory of the last Mass was 23 pounds st. I find the climate better than I anticipated. Considerable rain falls in the three months of the winter, but this season is always very mild, the rains are not continual, and through the year the climate is not bad, it is rather good, and some say the best in the world. It is by no ways sickly, though in a few places there is just now some cholera, which no doubt, God will be so good as to remove from us after a while. I will write again. I will be looking for some good letters from you or some of your good Fathers, whom please to salute and to pray to commend California to God, as well as its unworthy Pastor.[24]

[24] Alemany to Newman, San Francisco, December 15, 1850. AOB. On the same day Bishop Alemany wrote to the Dominican master general, Vincent Ajello. Among other things he passed on some details of the arrival of the other Dominicans who came with him. He also requested more explicit directions for the erection of a Dominican province in California. He also asked permission to have several hundred books, kept for him in Memphis by the Dominicans, sent to him in California. On February 15, 1851, Father Ajello answered Alemany from Viterbo. While promising cooperation in the matter of a prospective Dominican foundation in California, the Master General reminded Bishop Alemany that "a religious elevated to the episcopate cannot take anything belonging to the Order away with him—however, because of your needs in California, I give permission

That the joy felt by the Catholics of San Francisco on the arrival of Alemany was likewise a matter of civic satisfaction is established by the following item in the most prominent daily paper of the city:

The Catholics of this city meet this afternoon [Tuesday, December 10] at the church of St. Francis to greet, by an address and public welcome, Rev. Joseph Alemani [*sic*], Bishop of California who arrived here on the *Columbus*. This Divine comes among us with a very enviable fame for ability and scholarship, which we can readily believe, knowing that the Roman Catholic Church would place in so responsible and important a station none other than one in whom it had great reliance—and for good cause. The Reverend gentleman is, we believe, of Spanish origin, but has resided a long while in the United States, and will thus be able to do and assist in doing a vast amount of good to both races. May this be the result of his residence and ministrations among us, giving and receiving happy evidences of the peaceable and glorious reign of Prince Emmanuel.[25]

---

to have those books sent to you for your use—with the stipulation that they now and always will belong to our Order and must never be diverted permanently to your diocese." A further and more important point was made when he added, "It is entirely forbidden to any Dominican religious elevated to the episcopacy to retain any jurisdiction in the Order, itself; this is clear in our Constitution and confirmed, if I mistake not, by a bull of Benedict XIII. Since I am unable to give you the authority to establish our Order in California, I send with this answer letters patent to Father Vilarrasa to do so." AOPR. Possibly the earlier permission granted by Vicar General Gigli to Alemany to preside over the beginnings of any such foundation was granted before it was known that Vilarrasa would accompany Alemany to California; it was certainly supplanted by the above decision making Vilarrasa the responsible head of any such Dominican foundation.

[25] San Francisco *Daily Alta California*. December 10, 1850. San Francisco Public Library. Perhaps the editor wished to repair for such earlier inaccuracies as had appeared several days previously in reporting Alemany's arrival; e.g. *Daily Alta California*, Saturday, December 7, 1850:

Passengers, per steamer *Columbus* from Panama
   Rt. Rev. Francis Villarasa [*sic*]
   Rev. Joseph Alemany
   Sister Mary Goemere.

The same issue carried the following news item: "St. *Columbus* arrived last night c. 11 o'clock—it brought up 95 passengers, among whom we noticed the names of Rt. Rev. Francis Vilarrasa, Rev. Joseph Alemany and Sister Mary Goesnerd" (!).

After this reception by the Catholics of San Francisco there remained the important matter of Alemany's presenting himself to Father Gonzalez Rubio, who now had served as administrator of the diocese from 1846–1850. To this friar who had the official title of "Governor of the Mitre" Alemany had to show his credentials and thus establish himself as the legitimate bishop sent by Rome. Accordingly, as Gonzalez resided in Santa Barbara, Alemany decided to go there for this purpose. On December 14, accompanied by Father Anthony Delmas, he left San Francisco by ship, arriving in San Pedro (Santa Barbara was not one of the ports of call on this voyage) on December 18. From San Pedro he proceeded immediately to what he called, in his *Diary* entry of that day, the "Pueblo de Nuestra Senora de los Angeles, which has about 5,000 inhabitants. Father Jose Jimeno and Francisco Sanchez, both Franciscans, are the good priests here." On December 20, he travelled to San Fernando, remaining there two days before going on to San Buenaventura. His first Mass on Christmas Day was offered in the early morning, and he then left for Santa Barbara, arriving at eleven o'clock, to be greeted by a large number of people. After offering the two other Masses of Christmas, Alemany showed his credentials to Gonzalez Rubio. Later on, realizing as he did the importance of this act, he supported his *Diary* item concerning it with the following statement in a book of official records:

I show my bulls to the Vicar Capitular who, with Father Jose Jimeno and Father Francisco Sanchez, recognize them as genuine and acknowledge me the long expected Bishop of Monterey, and as such, I take possession of the diocese, formerly called the Diocese of Both Californias—and preach to the assembled people at the Old Mission.[26]

[26] Alemany, entry of December 25, 1950, in the *Libro Borrador*—his volume of official records in which he continued such notations as were made 1840–1846, by his predecessor as bishop of California, Garcia Diego, O.F.M. The *Borrador* is preserved in the AASF. Delmas, who accompanied Alemany to southern California, was the Reverend John Mary A. Delmas of the Diocese of Cahors, France, who, after arriving in San Francisco in mid-1850, served as assistant at Mission Dolores.

The several weeks of Bishop Alemany's stay in Southern California were marked by conferences with Father Gonzalez and with other priests and laity who could properly inform him of the many details of diocesan administration now unfolding before him. A pastoral letter written by his Franciscan predecessor in California, Bishop Garcia Diego, was given to him by the Administrator, and this spurred him on to the writing of his own first such letter, which he was to issue within a month. Alemany got his first glimpse of the California Indians in their native habitat when, on December 27, he journeyed to the rancho called San Francisco Xavier, located several miles from Santa Barbara. Upon his arrival, two hundred Indians who lived there in huts fell to their knees to receive Alemany's blessing. He was relieved to learn that General Stephen W. Kearney, military commander in California, had ordered that, until and unless Washington decided otherwise, the priests were to remain at their posts in the various missions of California. Two final notations in Alemany's *Diary*, those for December 29 and 30, mention that the pontifical instruments belonging to the former bishop, including his crozier, had been handed over to him together with an important account book by Father Gonzalez Rubio.

New Year's Day, 1851, was a memorable one for Bishop Alemany as well as for his flock at Santa Barbara, for it was marked by his celebration of a pontifical Mass before a crowded congregation in the mission church. On the occasion, Alemany preached after the Gospel and concluded the ceremony by imparting his pontifical blessing. Much of the time remaining to him in Santa Barbara was devoted to a detailed study of the claims to Church property which he intended to press with the United States government; in this connection, he was pleased to discover that some official documents of the Mexican government itself had made it quite clear that such properties belonged to the Church and not to the state.

As a conclusion to his first visit to the southern part of Cali-

113

fornia, Bishop Alemany performed the first of the dedication ceremonies which were to mark his long episcopal rule in the state. This was the blessing of a small chapel for the Indians at a place designated as "Sieneguita" near Santa Barbara where Alemany blessed the chapel under the invocation of St. Francis Xavier. Soon afterwards, he left for his return voyage to Monterey, which he called his "titular city" and where he arrived on January 28, 1851.

7

The See of Monterey, 1850–1853

OUR present concern is the three years Bishop Alemany spent as the ordinary of the Diocese of Monterey in California.[1] And at the very outset we are confronted with a rather interesting problem. Alemany's predecessor, the Franciscan Bishop Garcia Diego, had been correctly called the "Obispo de las Ambas Californias," "Bishop of Both Californias," —whereas Alemany was consecrated with the title "Bishop of Monterey, Upper California." Apparently, the change of title must be attributed to the American annexation of California as a result of the Treaty of Guadalupe Hidalgo, signed on February 2, 1848; and moreover, it was only natural to name the new diocese after a prominent city than after the entire region of both Lower and Upper California. Although the Latin form of Bishop Alemany's title varies con-

[1] Some of what must necessarily be recorded here can be found in printed sources already known to students of the American phase of California Catholicism. Two such sources are William Gleeson, *History of the Catholic Church in California*, and Zephyrin Engelhardt, O.F.M., *Missions and Missionaries of California*, 2 vols., San Francisco, 1908–1915. However, it is felt that these materials can be supplemented here by other gleanings from archival sources both at home and abroad. In the former case, one immediately thinks of the Archives of the Archdiocese of San Francisco, which most certainly were never completely used in former accounts; and in the latter case one thinks of the Archives of the French Society for the Propagation of the Faith, in Paris, never before used in this connection, as well as the collection of the Propaganda Fide Archives in Rome and the valuable Archives of the Dominican Master General in Rome.

CALIFORNIA'S FIRST ARCHBISHOP

siderably in different sources,[2] in California itself the new Bishop came soon enough to be known as the "Bishop of Monterey." (Nevertheless, the printed report of the speeches of welcome to Bishop Alemany is entitled, "Arrival of the Rt. Revd. Joseph Alemany, Bishop of California,"[3] while Father Langlois, in San Francisco, blended in curious fashion the old title with the new: "December 6, 1850, at 11 o'clock, the steamship *Columbus* brought us the Rt. Rev. Joseph Alemany, Bishop of Monterey and California."[4]) However, despite these verbal discrepancies, the impressive fact remains that one of the largest ecclesiastical jurisdictions in the United States was committed to the care of the Bishop of Monterey. At the time of his arrival in 1850, his diocese included all of both Upper and Lower California, although in 1853 Lower California was made subject to Mexican ecclesiastical jurisdiction. In addition to this vast territory, the Diocese of Monterey included all of the present state of Nevada, most of Utah, and the southernmost part of Arizona.

Since mention has been made of Lower California as part of Alemany's pastoral care, we might here indicate the lengthy negotiations which preceded its final separation from the Diocese of Monterey. Alemany was not slow to see the anomaly of an American bishop claiming jurisdiction over Mexican territory. Indeed, when the Mexican government first heard of the appointment of an American citizen to Monterey, it had immediately petitioned Rome for the appointment of a Mexican vicar apostolic for Lower California. The Congregation de Propaganda

---

[2] Various forms of Alemany's episcopal title are as follows: "Ecclesia de Monterey in California," "Diocesis Montereyensis," "Sedes Montisregis," "Episcopus Montisregis, Californiae Superioris," "Episcopus Montisregii," "Ecclesia Montisregensis." All of these forms appear in various documents; Monterey was far distant from Rome and only vague notions were had concerning it.

[3] Engelhardt, *Missions and Missionaries of California*, IV, p. 682, n. 36.

[4] Anthony Langlois: *Journal*, quoted in Riordan, *The First Half Century of St. Ignatius Church and College*, p. 35.

116

Fide countered with the reply that such an appointment would be promptly made only if and when the Mexican government would promise to see to the support of such a prelate in his missionary territory—something which it had not done, despite pledges, in the case of a Mexican citizen, Bishop Garcia Diego. This, until 1853, was as far as the matter went.

There was yet another complication resulting from this awkward situation. A diocese is customarily part of an ecclesiastical province headed by a metropolitan archbishop, and to what metropolitan was Alemany to be subject? His predecessor, Garcia Diego, was a suffragan of Mexico City, but Alemany could hardly want this affiliation in American California. The nearest metropolitan see to the north was that of Oregon City, established on July 24, 1846, but how could Alemany desire affiliation there while still encumbered with the rule of Lower California, a part of Mexico? While the obvious solution would have been simply to separate all the Mexican territory from Alemany's diocese, it would seem that the Holy See was not anxious to divide the old diocese of Bishop Garcia Diego. Instead, another expedient was adopted; remaining a simple diocese, Monterey was declared to be immediately subject to the Holy See,[5] thus, solving the problem of affiliation with a metropolitan see. Meanwhile, as Mexico still seemed recalcitrant in the matter of providing for the proper support of a vicar apostolic for Lower California, Alemany was continued, more nominally than otherwise (for he did not visit Lower California in his pastoral role), as bishop of Lower California. Padre Gonzalez Rubio seems to have served Alemany as vicar forane for this part of his immense diocese. Finally, and after a definite refusal on the

[5] Alemany's anomalous position was cleared up by a Roman decree dated December 21, 1851—more than a year after his arrival in California. Although the fact was known in Baltimore by May, 1852, it would appear that the Roman document did not reach Alemany until much later (November 28, 1852).

117

former's part to accept the mitre as vicar apostolic of Lower California, Alemany received official word on April 17, 1853, that Rome had separated Lower California from the Diocese of Monterey.[6]

That the Holy See had favored the Church of California with a solicitous shepherd soon became clear by the dispatch with which Bishop Alemany entered upon his pastoral duties. One of the main means of communication from a bishop to his flock, clerical as well as lay, is the pastoral letter, and Alemany had his first ready by January 13, 1851. At the time of its publication he was still in Santa Barbara. This first pastoral letter had a benevolent and fatherly tone which was not lost, presumably, upon those to whom it was addressed; after telling the people that he would try to visit them all in due time, Alemany recalled the sudden appointment which had been his in distant Rome; and then, having thus established his official position, he turned to some spiritual considerations which he thought worthy of note. The pastoral charge concluded with the acknowledgment that the young shepherd of the Church of Monterey was well aware of his serious responsibilities in the care of a widely scattered flock.[7]

In several months, an approving editorial voice was heard from as far away as New York in praise of this first pastoral of Bishop Alemany; on April 12, 1851, the New York *Freeman's Journal* and the *Catholic Register* thus commented:

PASTORAL OF BISHOP ALEMANY
We have received a copy of the Pastoral of the Bishop of Monterey, Upper California. We make from it a very long extract because of its great beauty and universal applicability. It is cheering and glorious to hear this true successor of the Apostles thus lifting his voice against

[6] It is clear, then, that Alemany, as Bishop of Monterey, had jurisdiction over Baja California from December 25, 1850, to April 17, 1853.
[7] Pastoral letter of the Right Reverend Joseph Alemany, O.P., Bishop of Monterey, Upper California, Santa Barbara, California, Octave Day of the Epiphany, 1851 (San Francisco, 1851). AUSF.

the three evils that intelligent travellers have told us are threatening California society with utter ruin—forgetfulness of old principles and practices, an insatiable thirst for gold, and a most profligate unchastity.[8]

That Alemany was to be a man of pastoral action as well as of pastoral words is evident from his early occupations in the first year of his episcopal rule in California. The main activities are sufficient indicated in the official records which were meticulously kept by him.[9]

By the end of January, 1851, Bishop Alemany had established himself at Monterey, where he was greeted with traditional hospitality, lodging with the Gonzalez family. He noted the kindness of Don Manuel Jimeno and others.[10] He was cheered also by the gracious lines of welcome which he soon received from Archbishop Francis Norbert Blanchet of Oregon City:

Allow me to offer my felicitations to Yr. Grace in the occasion of your nomination as Bishop of New [sic] California and at your happy arrival in the midst of your flock. The Holy See, in giving to that country a "priest according to the heart of God" and according to the heart of its new ruler and numerous immigrants, has again given proof of profound wisdom. I rejoice very sincerely. Under the wise administration of the first pastor formed of an illustrious Order . . . a new church, erected after a long time marked by so many and so serious calamities—has now come to life again.[11]

Alemany's first administration of the sacrament of confirmation took place in late January upon his arrival in Monterey. He thus records the event:

Jan. 28, 1851
I arrive in Monterey where the Catholics show great joy at my coming. I start a visitation here and in Carmel Mission and administer Confirmation in both places.[12]

[8] New York *Freeman's Journal,* April 12, 1851.
[9] A listing of these various official records will be found in the "Essay on Sources" at the end of this present volume.
[10] *Libro Borrador,* entry dated February 4, 1851. AASF.
[11] Blanchet to Alemany, Portland, Oregon, February 14, 1851. AAPO.
[12] *Liber Visitationis Episcopalis,* etc., entry of January 28, 1851. AASF.

Since San Francisco was the largest of all the areas committed to his care, on February 8, 1851, Alemany returned to where he had first been welcomed to California. On February 16, at Mission Dolores, he confirmed thirty persons. A week later, on February 18, he officiated in a similar capacity at San Jose, and several days later he visited Santa Clara Mission. By February 23, he had gone as far as Sacramento where, he noted, "I bless a small church there as 'St. Rose of Lima.' "[13] The next few months saw no lessening of the pace, for after a return to Monterey, Bishop Alemany visited Benicia, Stockton, and Santa Cruz. The dedication of the church in Sacramento caused the following to be printed in the New York *Freeman's Journal*—additional proof of the interest of the New York paper in ecclesiastical events in the new state of California:[14]

Sacramento, Feb. 24th, 1851

Yesterday, in accordance with public notice, the new Catholic Church, corner of K and 7th Streets, was solemnly dedicated by the Rt. Rev. Dr. Alemany, Bishop of California, assisted by the Rev. Mr. Langlois, Vicar-General, from San Francisco, Rev. Mr. Llebaria, of Marysville, and Rev. Mr. Ingoldsby, Pastor of the congregation in this city.

The Church was densely crowded at an early hour, and many left who were unable to get within sight or hearing of the impressing [*sic*] ceremony.

[13] *Ibid.,* entry of February 23, 1851. AASF. On February 14, 1851, Alemany wrote two letters to Rome, one to Franzoni of Propaganda, the other to Ajello of his order. In this first report to the cardinal who had consecrated him a bishop, Alemany told of his *"buon viaggio"* to California, where he had arrived in *"buona salute la vigilia della Concepzione Immaculate della SS Vergine."* He rejoiced to find that the interregnum period had been accomplished in proper form but informed the Cardinal of his sadness at seeing the fabric of the former California missions so disintegrated. He also reminded Franzoni that his authority would not be recognized in Lower California by the Mexican government and asked for a solution. The letter to the master general was also signed by Vilarrasa and consisted mostly of a plea that one, or, better, two friars be sent immediately to California to aid in the establishment of the contemplated foundation. APFR: AOPR.

[14] The correspondent who signed himself "Philos." was Dr. Gregory J. Phelan (1822–1902), a physician from Philadelphia who came to Sacramento in Gold Rush days and who remained there for many years.

120

We were forcibly reminded of the astounding progress of this country, for on entering this neat little chapel that stands where a few months ago there was scarce a vestige of civilization, we beheld a neat altar and tabernacle, a mitred Bishop in gorgeous vestments and crosier with priestly attendants, assisting in the solemn High Mass.

During the service a sermon was preached by the Bishop appropriate to the occasion. There was also an address in Spanish and French.

During the afternoon Vespers, the Bishop again preached a short, but instructive sermon. Immediately after he was waited upon by a number of gentlemen of different denominations, and tendered, through Murray Morrison, Esq., in a brief but very appropriate address, the hospitalities of the city. To which the Bishop replied with that characteristic humility that marks the sincere laborer for the welfare of mankind.[15]

Attention was again called to Alemany's activities by the *Freeman's Journal* which soon printed another report from California:

Mission of Santa Clara
April 14, 1851

To the Editor of the New York Freeman's Journal:

Mr. Editor, —Yesterday being Palm Sunday, the church of Santa Clara was filled by a large and attentive congregation. Bishop Alemany, with a priest and two Sisters of Charity, arrived in the morning. His presence added much to the interest of the ceremonies of the day. Before Mass the palm was blessed and a procession formed, which passed down the church, out the front door and around the cross planted in front. The Bishop and priests then chanted the parts as usual on such occasions, after which the procession entered the church and passed to the Sanctuary. High Mass was sung by the Bishop assisted by Rev. John Nobili, S.J., and two other clergymen. After the reading of the Gospel, the Bishop ascended the pulpit and preached in Spanish and English.

The Bishop has been making a visitation of a portion of his diocese, and yesterday afternoon started for Monterey, where his presence is much needed, having only remained part of the day at Santa Clara.[16]

Appropriately, Bishop Alemany officiated at the pontifical ceremonies of Holy Week in the Royal Presidio Chapel of Mon-

[15] New York *Freeman's Journal,* April 12, 1851.
[16] *Ibid.,* May 24, 1851.

terey, which he had previously designated as his cathedral. His solemn blessing of the holy oils on that occasion was memorable in that it represented the first time since Bishop Garcia Diego's death in 1846 that such a pontifical blessing was possible. Gone, happily, were the days when it was necessary for the Franciscan administrator of the mitre to petition Archbishop Blanchet of Oregon to send some consecrated oil to California.

The beginning of a new phase of San Francisco's Catholic story is found in the notation that, on May 20, 1851, Bishop Alemany authorized Father John Maginnis to start a new St. Patrick's parish in a section of the city designated as "Happy Valley."[17] On July 6, still another notable event was recorded:

I bless St. Francis Church, in the city of San Francisco, erected last winter in Vallejo Street.[18]

Another aspect of his many activities was indicated on July 30, 1851, when Alemany visited the New Almaden Mines (near San Jose) and there blessed a cemetery for the use of the "many Catholics who work there in the mines."[19] The month of August was extremely busy as Alemany travelled down the coast, visiting such old Franciscan missions (then mostly in decay) as Soledad, San Miguel, San Luis Obispo, La Purissima, and Santa Ines. Actually, this trip took him as far south as San Diego while he administered confirmation all along the way. His plan to pontificate in his cathedral at Monterey on Christmas day was thwarted by some rough weather which he encountered while sailing there, for he arrived several days after the feast. Thus concluded the first year of Bishop Alemany's episcopal rule in California. This brief overview will serve to indicate the pattern of the many busy years which were to follow in the career of California's solicitous shepherd.

[17] *Liber Visitationis Episcopalis,* etc., entry of May 20, 1851. AASF.
[18] *Ibid.,* entry of July 6, 1851. AASF.
[19] *Ibid.,* entry of July 30, 1851. AASF.

Mention has been previously made of the friendly relationship which Alemany had formed with John Henry Newman, England's future cardinal. Alemany wrote twice to Newman, just a few months after his arrival in California. The first letter read in part as follows:

Monterey, California, May 1, 1851

Very Revd. Dear Father,

Soon after my arrival here I wrote you, giving you what information I could then give of this diocese. Now I have visited many places of this state, and I feel obliged to state that, with the exception of San Francisco, there is perhaps no place in the diocese where you might have an establishment, without having to perform all the duties of parish-priests. The Catholic population is rather too small in each of the existing missions or congregations, except in San Francisco, where we are making preparations to build a small Church (besides the tolerably large one built a year ago) for the French Catholics. San Francisco will soon need, and commences to need another Church for the Spanish and English Catholics; and that Church I will keep for your Fathers, if you send them, as I hope you will. Even in such Church, I believe it would be necessary that the Fathers would perform some parroquial [sic] duties which, however, I think would not interfere with the duties of the Fathers. I should consider myself very happy to have in the Babylon of San Francisco the children of that admirable sanctifier of souls, St. Philip Neri.[20]

A few days later, Alemany again wrote to Newman:

San Francisco, Calif. May 11th, 1851

Very Revd. Dear Father,

By the last steamer I informed you that unless your Fathers could discharge all Pastoral duties, I did not think they could, for the present, establish themselves out of San Francisco, owing to the small number of Catholics in the other places. I stated that I would be very glad they could come to San Francisco and attend to the Spanish and English in a new Church that I expect will soon be constructed. Yet as I fear I did not explain sufficiently clear, I feel I must explain that even after two years it might be necessary to have

[20] Alemany to Newman, Monterey, May 1, 1851. AOB.

123

one who could preach in English. Most probably some of the Spanish Fathers by that time could speak English; if not, I believe it would be required that at least one of the English Fathers would still continue with them.

It is my sincere regard for the true zeal of the children of Saint Philip Neri that makes me desire to have them in this diocese; yet I must be candid in explaining the actual condition in California. In any case I shall always treat them as my brothers, and do all in my power for them.

A large portion of the best buildings in this city was destroyed by fire a week ago; but in a very few months it will be built up again. Pray for my dear California and its unworthy pastor.[21]

Bishop Alemany also found it necessary to engage in extensive correspondence with the Paris headquarters of the Society for the Propagation of the Faith, which, it will be recalled, had awarded him 10,000 francs for use in the Monterey diocese. This organization had set up rules, of course, which had to be observed before financial help was accorded. Each bishop who asked for aid was required to fill out an extensive questionnaire as to his needs as well as to his resources; these reports were carefully assessed at both the Lyons and the Paris headquarters of the Society, and all of them were carefully preserved. They provide us, therefore, with a solid source enabling us to bridge some wide chasms in former estimates as to the Catholic picture in California in early American days. For example, in July, 1851, Bishop Alemany, for the first of what was to be many times, addressed himself to the President of the Council of the French Society:

San Francisco, California, July 19, 1851

Highly Respected Sir:

Enclosed please to find a sketch of the condition of this diocess [*sic*], and a communication on the Missions of California.

The principal object of this is to sollicit humbly from you and the

[21] Alemany to Newman, San Francisco, May 11, 1851. AOB.

124

respected Council in Paris the appropriation of some funds to assist us in carrying on the good work of the Missions. Our diocese was in the most miserable condition in regard to education. The poor boys and girls must be left a prey to Protestantism and immorality, if we do not exert ourselves to open some good institutions. We have commenced this work: and we are already in debt. Some of the old Churches have to be repaired and some new ones have to be built, and although there is money, yet all is exceedingly dear. Your aid will greatly relieve us.[22]

Bishop Alemany accompanied this plea for help with a rather detailed portrait of his diocese as it appeared in 1851. He estimated the number of Catholics at about 40,000 and the number of Protestants at 30,000; he also stated that he would number the unbaptized, among both Indians and white, at approximately 130,000. He had forty-one priests, not one of whom was native to California. There were twenty-seven churches and eleven chapels under his jurisdiction. Alemany listed a "college and seminary" at Santa Ines, "founded some seven years ago, directed by two clergymen; but owing to the confused state of society and its being in a remote or desert place, it has only a small number of inmates. It has no funds." Next were listed Santa Clara College, "conducted by the Jesuit Fathers, just commencing, with little or no funds," and the College of Los Angeles, "just commenced by the Fathers of Picpus with little funds." Two female schools were accounted for as "St. Catherine's Female Academy at Monterey by Dominican Sisters—no funds" and "Female Academy at Pueblo [San Jose] by Sisters of Notre Dame—no funds." Under general observations, Alemany noted that California's Indian missions had been mostly ruined by secularization, while "plans are being studied to organize some new ones away from the white population." He minced no words concerning some of the grimmer effects of the Gold

[22] Alemany to the "President of the Central Council of the Work for the Propagation of the Faith," San Francisco, July 19, 1851. ASPFP.

Rush in California, remarking that "the great emigration brings Protestantism and immorality. Most of the old mission churches will serve for the coming Catholics. But more churches are needed. Good schools and colleges are of the utmost importance. Debts have been necessarily contracted. We hope you will assist. There is money in California and some are liberal in giving, but the expenses are very great and labour very dear. To build churches and schools is exceedingly expensive; to help in this, I have not been able to build to myself [sic] a small house. So I humbly and respectfully beg you to be so kind as to send us some funds to meet the necessary expenses of the year."[23]

Evidently, Bishop Alemany showed early signs of that persistence which was so characteristic of him. Never one to do things by halves, he supported the communication with another longer one in which he gave some of the historical background of the Church in California; apparently, he surmised correctly that the French directors were quite ignorant of the situations which had brought his present problems.

Commencing his account with the founding of Catholicism in California by Padre Junipero Serra and his Franciscan confreres, Alemany explained the sad process of secularization which had effectively ruined the fabric erected so laboriously. He next informed the Parisian directors of the immense changes brought to California by the Gold Rush and, while expressing the somewhat forlorn hope that he might be able to turn his attention to the reestablishment of mission churches for the Indians, he pointed out that his primary concern must be with providing for the spiritual and educational needs of the thousands who had come to California in search of gold and who were now destined to remain there. Alemany requested earnest prayers from the members of the Paris Propagation group that God help him to meet at least some of his many necessities. A literary flourish was added to this letter when he thus expressed his views as to

[23] Alemany's report of same date which accompanied above letter. ASPFP.

the earlier and sad fate which had come upon the Church in California:

And thou, Spain! Oh Catholic Spain! How glorious for thee was the day, in which thou didst send from the most eastern shores to this finis terrae of America such Apostolic men as FF. Serra . . . and many others! How deservedly didst thou wear the name of *Catholic* when thou didst foster the spirit of those holy, religious, and apostolic men, whose missionary field of labour was the world, and who did not dread to cross two oceans to go and live both among the bears and savages of California, hoping that God would deliver them from the terrors of the former, and that the divine spirit of the Catholic Church would convert the ferocity of the latter into the mildness of the lambs of the children of Christ! Catholic Spain! Missionaries from thy shores effected a perfect change on the face of California!—thy arts, thy trades, thy music, thy language, hospitality, honesty, piety, thy Catholic Faith were engrafted and nurtured with success in this vast region of the farthest west:—thou didst stud these misterious [*sic*] shores with a variety of monuments, whose picture along makes the anglosaxon pause and admire the greatness of the enterprise. Catholic Kingdom! How truly Catholic thou wert, when thou didst foster those rich monuments of faith, those apostolic institutions, those Missionary colleges—those Religious Orders, from whose bosom walked out so many Apostles to evangelize the most distant regions of the east, and the barbarous unexplored confines of the west! But, oh! how uncatholic thou wert, when in a raving fit of impiety thou didst exclaustrate those holy cloisters! How uncatholic that hour, in which thou didst refuse admission into thy dominions to the noble Catholic Work of the Propagation of Faith for the Foreign Missions, for fear that thy own poor (Judas was thy inspirer) should suffer from it! Blot out, my country, blot out those two black stains from thy history, efface them from its bright pages, for they give the lie to thy name of *Catholic*. Let the world know, that thou art no longer ashamed to admit into thy catholic precincts men who practice the Catholic apostolic counsels of the gospel, poverty, chastity, obedience and apostolic zeal. Let the head of the Catholic World know, that thou art one of those cristian [*sic*] nations, who charitably send their alms to the Catholic and most glorious Work of the Propagation of Faith.[24]

[24] This second communication, which has the same date of July 19, 1851, was evidently intended to serve as background material on the Catholic

127

As we shall see, Alemany's pleas for financial help were generously answered by his Parisian friends.

We now turn to another activity of the Monterey years of Bishop Alemany's rule. In this instance he acted in another capacity which was his by delegation of the vicar general of the Dominican order in Rome. This was the establishment of what may rightly be called the cradle of the religious life in California—the Dominican convent of St. Catherine in Monterey, which was canonically erected by Alemany on March 7, 1851. Before leaving Rome to journey together to California, Alemany and Vilarrasa had jointly petitioned the Dominican vicar general, Father Jerome Gigli, for permission to establish a new province of their order in California. They asked that it be designated as the Province of the Holy Name of God, and that it embrace the territory of both Upper and Lower California. Further, they asked that it be made immediately subject to the master general of their order when he should be elected, and that Bishop Alemany be named the first prior provincial to serve for the next six years, that is, until the calling of a provincial chapter in October, 1856, when he might stand for reëlection. Father Gigli approved of all these points in a document which he signed at "Santa Maria sopra Minervam," Rome, on July 18, 1850. Alemany sent the original of this petition to the Dominican vicar of the Province of St. Joseph, Father Charles Dominic Bowling. He also mailed this document to Father Bowling of St. Rose's Priory, Springfield, Kentucky, with the postmark indicated as "Liverpool, England, September 11, 1850."[25] Al-

---

Church in California. ASPFP. Evident is the uncompromising tone of Alemany's Catholicism—part, no doubt, of his Catalan background.

The secularization of the California chain of Franciscan missions was accomplished from 1810–1846. Originally announced as a simple replacement of the friars with secular priests (hence the name), the process became, historically, the ruination of the whole mission system as white settlers and/or predatory government officials enriched themselves at the expense of the mission properties. Cf. Gerald J. Geary, *The Secularization of the California Missions, 1810–1846* (Washington, D.C., 1934).

[25] The original petition and Gigli's approval are in AOPC. According to

though, on February 25, 1851, Father Alexander Jandel, newly serving as vicar general, appointed Vilarrasa as his commissary with authority to erect convents of his order in California, the word of his appointment did not reach California for some time. This is attested to by the fact that Bishop Alemany was the one who erected the first convent of the Dominican order in California, and several days after the event he thus attested to the legality of his act:

We, Brother Joseph Sadoc Alemany of the Holy Order of Preachers of God, and Bishop of the Apostolic See of Monterey, also Prior Provincial of the Province of the Most Holy Name of Jesus of Upper and Lower California—in virtue of these presents and by the authority granted to us by the Most Reverend Father, Brother Jerome Gigli, Vicar General of our Order, under letters given at Rome, July 18, 1850, do erect and found the convent of Sisters of our Third Order in the city of Monterey of Upper California under the invocation of St. Catherine of Siena, and thus instituted, founded and erected, we incorporate in the province of the Most Holy Name of Jesus of Upper or Lower California and declare it under the jurisdiction of the Prior Provincial of said province pro tem.[26]

---

the Reverend Reginald Coffey, O.P., Dominican archivist, Province of St. Joseph, Washington, D.C., there was an illegality in Bishop Alemany's assuming the title of prior provincial—since no Dominican bishop may act as such, although he *may* act as vicar or commissary general by delegation of the order's master general. In the absence of further evidence, it may be presumed that Almany, being ignorant of this provision, acted in good faith in the matter. A decree of July 21, 1850, issued by authority of the Dominican definitorium generale in Rome, was phrased as follows: "Permission is granted to erect a new Province for either part of California [that is, Upper or Lower] with the title of the Most Holy Name of God which will be immediately subject to the Master General and which will be governed up to the Chapter to be convened on the Third Sunday of October, 1856, by Bishop Brother [*sic*] Joseph Sadoc Alemany, O.P." Actually, though, there was no such province until much later; therefore, in fact, Bishop Alemany did not serve as prior provincial.

Father Bowling's title as "Vicar of the Province of St. Joseph" is accounted for by the fact that his was a temporary or interim appointment made necessary by Alemany's promotion to the See of Monterey.

[26] Archives, Dominican sisters, Congregation of the Holy Name, San Rafael, California. An interesting distinction of this first Convent in California was that the celebrated Concepcion Arguello (1791–1857), known in religion as Sister Mary Dominica, the first native daughter to enter reli-

This first Dominican convent was previously known as La Casa Arnel and had served as the residence of the well-known William Hartnell of Monterey. Built of adobe in 1825, it was opened as a convent on April 1, 1851.

Evidently, another of Alemany's pressing problems concerned itself with the clearing of title to the properties of the Catholic Church in California. This was to cause much anxiety as he entered upon wearisome negotiations with civil authorities to see what he could do in regard to the restoration of title to those properties which had been lost to the Church as a consequence of the secularization of the mission system of California in the 1830's and afterwards. Another problem came because certain Americans had effectively "squatted" upon Church prop-

---

gious life in California, entered the Dominican Order there. Her betrothal to Rezanov, Russian envoy, has been told many times, in considerably garbled form, by lovers of the romantic in California history. Thomas C. Russell (in Langsdorff's *Narrative of the Rezanov Voyage*, San Francisco, 1927, p. 144), thus sums up this phase of her story: "When the first convent and seminary for females in California was founded at Monterey in 1851 by the Dominican sisters, the Dona Concepcion, though sixty years of age, was the first novice to enter. On April 11, 1851, she received the white habit of Saint Dominic at the hands of Bishop Jose Sadoc Alemany, and with it the name of Maria Dominga [*sic*]. This convent, opened under the protection of Saint Catherine of Siena, was in 1854 moved to Benicia and there Sister Maria Dominga lived until her death on December 23, 1857. Two days later, the body was laid to rest in the convent cemetery."

An unpublished master's thesis (University of San Francisco, 1963) by Sister Jane Mast, S.H.F., entitled *The Concepcion Arguello Story—Fact Versus Fiction,* represents a scholarly endeavor to put this distorted story in focus and perspective.

It would seem that Bishop Alemany was determined to get any such Dominican (or prospective Franciscan) foundation off to a canonically correct start; this would seem to be the point of a petition which he addressed directly to Pius IX from Monterey in November 4, 1851. Citing the need of zealous sons of St. Dominic and St. Francis in his vast territory and stating that he could look for no further recruits from Mexico for the two orders, he asks permission to found novitiates for both so that he may have "religious endowed with a true spirit of poverty and zeal for souls who may assist me in my tasks here" (APF). Under dates of February 21–22, 1852, both the Franciscan and Dominican authorities expressed their approval of Alemany's plans in letters they sent to Barnabò, secretary of Propaganda, who evidently had asked them to pass on the proposals.

erty—notably around the old Franciscan missions themselves.

When less than a month in California, Bishop Alemany discovered, after conversing with the old Franciscan missionaries (as he records in his *libro borrador*[27]), that it was their conviction that the mission lands were really the property of the Indians who cultivated them under the direction of the missionaries and, more especially, under the direction of their own *alcaldes* or officers elected by the Indians themselves under the supervision of the Fathers. However, these same missionaries insisted that the "church, edifices, stores, cemeteries, orchards and vineyards with their aqueducts should be considered as the property of the Catholic Church."[28] As is evident, this was to be not only a helpful distinction for Alemany, but it was to form the basis of his claims in the whole matter of these ecclesiastical properties. He was to win final success, but only after his efforts extended over a period of five years.

It might be mentioned parenthetically that Alemany was not entirely without knowledge of this problem, for, while in New York in October, 1850, he had consulted the bishop of New York, Rt. Rev. John Hughes, "on the claims of the Missions of California or the rights of church property. I also consulted the Archbishop of Baltimore, the Most Rev. Dr. Eccleston."[29] Further consultation took place in May, 1851, with the first American governor of California, this fact being duly attested to by another notation: "I consult with Gov. Peter Burnett on the prosecution of my claims of Mission church property."[30] The next month saw similar consultations being held between the Bishop and "Lawyers Botts and Emmett—and I consult Judge Pacificus Ord of Monterey."[31] That these consultations had al-

[27] *Libro Borrador,* entry of December 26, 1850, Santa Barbara, California. AASF.

[28] *Ibid.*

[29] *Libro Borrador,* notation dated "October, 1850." AASF.

[30] *Libro Borrador,* "May, 1851." AASF.

[31] *Libro Borrador,* "June, 1851." AASF.

ready induced Alemany to action is shown by the request he made in writing to Rome that, "for the preservation of ecclesiastical property, we here in California should be under the decrees of Baltimore—hence we should be detached from any ecclesiastical connection with Mexico, etc."[32] Earlier, we mentioned that this separation was finally arranged, and Alemany was relieved when he received word that, under date of June 14, 1851, it had been decided that the Baltimore decrees should apply to the California Catholic Church.[33] More important from the standpoint of American law, of course, was the decision which was finally handed down by the "United States Commissioners for Ascertaining Private Land Claims, etc.," when, on December 18, 1855, a year and a half after Alemany had become archbishop of San Francisco, Commissioner Alpheus Felch delivered the opinion of the board in the matter. After reviewing the case for the return of the Church lands as presented by Alemany, Felch thus rendered the decision of the commission which he headed:

These concurrent proofs bring us irresistibly to the conclusion that, before the Treaty of Guadalupe Hidalgo, these possessions were solemnly dedicated to the use of the Church, and the property withdrawn from commerce. Such an interest is protected by the provisions of the Treaty, and must be held inviolable under our laws.

A decree of confirmation will therefore be entered in the case.[34]

While justice was honored by this decision, an attempt to overthrow it was made by parties who would be dispossessed of their

[32] Alemany to Pius IX, March 31, 1851, San Francisco. APF.

[33] Letter to Alemany of "Secretary for Extraordinary Ecclesiastical Affairs, Sacred Congregation de Propaganda Fide," Rome, July 8, 1851. AAS.

[34] Case no. 709, *Lands of the Catholic Church: Opinion of the Board of Commissioners Confirming the Claim Delivered by Commissioner Alpheus Felch,* San Francisco, December 18, 1855. Photostatic copy in AUSF. On September 20, 1857, Alemany sent a report to Propaganda Fide containing a map of California missions and other properties restored to Church. He also included a printed copy of the Felch decision. APF.

habitations, many acquired through squatters rights. All such attempts were rejected by competent authority, and the final patents confirmatory of the Land Commission decision were signed by President Lincoln on March 18, 1865, only a month before his tragic death.

Closely allied with the matter of establishing title to former Church property was that concerning the so-called "Pious Fund" —one of the more celebrated examples of injustice shown to the Catholic Church by the Mexican government. The Pious Fund of the Californias was a name given to a substantial sum originally collected by Jesuit missionaries associated with the establishment of missions in Lower California. Dating from 1698, when Fathers Salvatierra and Ugarte successfully begged the nucleus of this fund from some wealthy Mexican benefactors, the fund had gradually increased until, after undergoing several vicissitudes at the hands of hostile and avaricious Mexican administrators, it was seized in 1842 by President Santa Anna with the pretext that, after selling the property administered by the Fund, all the money would be given to the Church together with a 6 per cent interest rate. In other words, Mexico was merely borrowing the Fund on a temporary basis, but, as feared, it eventually reneged on its obligations and, even though Alemany received some partial payments, Mexico to this day has refused to make good on its obligations regarding this Fund. Rather than enter into a more detailed history of this Fund, it is proposed only to indicate Alemany's valiant efforts to have restored the income legitimately accruing to the Church from it. Frustration dogged practically every step of his path here. In defense of the Church's indubitable rights, Alemany journeyed to Washington as well as to Mexico City and elsewhere; however, finally he had to acknowledge that no completely satisfactory results had come from these earnest efforts.

In May, 1852, Bishop Alemany attended the First Plenary Council of Baltimore and, at its conclusion, he consulted Chief

Justice Taney of the United States Supreme Court concerning the various claims of the Church. This he did because the Committee on Temporal Affairs at the Council had advised Alemany to take immediate action with the American government in all matters affecting property rights of the Church in California. (It was Taney who advised that the Bishop, upon his return to California, file his claims with the U.S. Land Commission there, and it was this good advice which eventually resulted, as we have just seen, in the favorable decision of 1855.) But Taney could be of little help with regard to the Bishop's perplexities regarding the Pious Fund because, in this case, the Mexican government was directly at odds with the Church, and he seems only to have confirmed Bishop Alemany in his intention to return to California by way of Mexico City in an endeavor to see what might be done about the matter. Previously, Alemany had again consulted with various American prelates to obtain their advice as to how to proceed. On his return to California, after wearisome months of almost fruitless negotiations, Alemany noted its various stages in his *libro borrador*; he recorded that, in July, 1852, he pressed his claim in Mexico City concerning the Pious Fund as the successor of Bishop Garcia Diego. This work occupied him into August when, as he noted, "after many delays, they notified me that they could not acceed [*sic*] to my demands and I left the capitol."[35] In a detailed report concerning various matters affecting his diocese which he dispatched to Rome in November, 1852, Alemany summed up his unsuccessful efforts to move the Mexican government towards justice in

[35] *Libro Borrador,* notation of "July-August, 1852." A large ledger, preserved in AASF, contains many original letters of Alemany and of others, including some from Mexican governmental officials, concerning these wearisome negotiations. Another large ledger, which is inscribed "From the year 1872 to 1879—Letters numbered from 292–600 inclusive," contains much more of the same. While several accounts of the Pious Fund exist (see Gerald Geary's *The Secularization of the California Missions,* Washington, 1934), there is need of a more detailed and adequate account.

134

the matter of the Pious Fund.[36] Although, as an extremely conscientious bishop, Alemany was to write frequently concerning
the cares of his diocese to the successive cardinals prefect of
Propaganda, he was helped in this practice by a letter which
was written to him by his consecrator, Cardinal Franzoni, in early
1852, exhorting him to write frequently concerning the state of
affairs in California; for this, wrote the Cardinal, is "not a bother
but it is a pleasure to hear from you."[37]

Another important matter which occupied Bishop Alemany
in 1852 concerned his summoning of the first synod ever called
in the history of the Catholic Church in California. A synod is
comparable, in certain respects, to a general meeting or council
of the universal Church although, obviously, it is restricted to
the territory administered by a bishop or archbishop. Its purpose
in this present case was to formulate and promulgate various
regulations which were to govern the life of the Church in the
Diocese of Monterey. On January 21, 1852, in a document
issued from Monterey, and addressed to clergy and laity, Bishop
Alemany summoned such a synod to assemble at St. Francis
Church, San Francisco, on March 18, 1852.[38] The prelate indicated his will that the clergy should assemble on March 10 to
begin a series of spiritual exercises before entering upon the work
of the synod. This was done, with Alemany in attendance and
presiding at these Exercises, while the synod itself was begun on
Friday, March 19th, and continued through March 23rd. This
important meeting was reported by the California correspondent
of the New York *Freeman's Journal*:

[36] Alemany to Franzoni, November 14, 1852, San Francisco. APF. Later,
under date of February 19, 1856, Alemany again reported to Franzoni on
the Pious Fund—"the matter is still in a state of flux, etc."

[37] Franzoni to Alemany, Rome, February 10, 1852. AASF.

[38] The summons for the convocation of this synod is dated Monterey,
January 21, 1852, and has the following signature: "Fr. Josephus Sadoc,
Epis. Montisregis, Cal. Sup" (Brother Joseph Sadoc [*sic*], Bishop of Mon-
terey, Upper California). AASF.

Sacramento, California, April 3, 1852

During a part of last month, a retreat and conference of the clergy was held at San Francisco under the direction of our distinguished and beloved Bishop Alemany. There were from 23–25 priests present, among whom were several of the old missionaries who have resided in California for many years.[39]

The decrees which emerged from this synod concerned themselves principally with such subjects as ecclesiastical tithes and the question of clandestine marriages between Catholics and non-Catholics. These decrees were forwarded to Rome where they received final approval on August 5, 1854.[40]

On December 2, 1852, Alemany wrote from Monterey to the Parisian Director of the Society for the Propagation of the Faith that he had just returned from the Council of Baltimore where he had heard great praise for the help extended to various American Bishops by the Paris organization. He expressed gratitude for aid already received which had enabled him to begin work on various projects dear to him, and noted that "several precious establishments have been founded and are now in successful

[39] New York *Freeman's Journal*, May 8, 1852. Among the "old California missionaries" in attendance were the Franciscan padres Gonzalez Rubio, Jose Jimeno, and Francisco Sanchez.

[40] Father Engelhardt brings out the interesting point that the usually meticulous Alemany made sparse official mention of this synod in either the *Libro Borrador* or *Libro de Gubierno*; in fact, such mention is restricted to the following notation: "March 10 [*sic*]. All the priests of the Diocese assembled in Diocesan Synod concur with me in urging the U.S. Land Commission to confirm to the mission property." Engelhardt notes further, with regard to the date discrepancy—that is, March 10—before the synod had met: "Should doubtless be March 20, as the session began March 19th and continued to March 23rd. The Bishop frequently made entries later, and then supplied the dates ʿrom memory, it would seem." Engelhardt, *Missions and Missionaries of California*, IV, p. 693. See *Catholic Historical Review*, April, 1905, pp. 30–37, for a short resume of this first synod. Weber notes (*Right Reverend Joseph Sadoc Alemany, Bishop of Monterey*, p. 58, n. 112) that this synod seems to have been largely forgotten as far as later mention is concerned; for example, he notes that there is no mention of it in the *Acta et Decreta Concilii Sancti Francisci Primi (1874)*. However, he adds, mention is made of this first synod in the Appendix of the account of the *Synodum Secundum Diocesanum* held in Los Angeles, April, 1869.

136

operation; several priests and seminarians and sisters have been enabled to pay the long journey to this remote country; several churches have been built and some are about being erected." Since Alemany realized that such a missionary group as that in Paris was directly concerned with the evangelizing of the primitive inhabitants of an area, he hastened to add that he had now in hand the "grand work of doing something direct [*sic*] towards christianizing the savage Indians, whose number is immense." Moving on to a consideration of his other pressing needs, he reported that a fire has burnt his fine church in Sacramento, while there was need in San Francisco itself of another new church "where, in one of the three churches, we must have the French, the English, the Spanish and the German congregations." Adding that the city, too, needed the services of some Christian Brothers, Alemany remarked that there "are many new towns which ask for churches and priests. If I had means enough, I could do much for them." He then concluded his appeal for aid:

. . . and to enable me to do more for our holy Religion, I hope and earnestly beg that your Charitable Society will send me this year a large appropriation. This is a large diocess [*sic*] and the great number of emigrants find it in many places without Churches or Priests. Some people in the mines, and some in the great cities make money; but most of it goes to other parts of the world and although some give us, yet it is not half sufficient. Building materials and labour and every thing else is very dear here. I will therefore repeat my ardent petition to you, Mr. President, and to all the Members of your Society, that you would vouchsafe to send me a large alms to meet my necessities.[41]

As he had in 1851, Bishop Alemany accompanied this letter with a detailed account of the state of the diocese as of late December, 1852. In the year since his first report, he noted an increase of Catholics from about 40,000 to 52,000 while he listed the number of Protestants as 40,000—up 10,000 from the

[41] Alemany to the "President of the Council, Society for the Propagation of the Faith" (Paris), Monterey, December 2, 1852. ASPFP.

previous figure. Alemany estimated the number of unbaptized at 148,000—up 18,000 from the figure furnished in 1851. That there was still a dearth of priests in his large diocese is testified to by the small increase: forty-seven in contrast to the previously listed forty-one. However, there had been a small but satisfying increase in the number of churches—1851 saw a listing of twenty-seven churches; a year later the figure had risen to thirty-four with the number of chapels remaining at eleven. Three of these churches were in San Francisco with the others scattered in the towns of the Mother Lode gold country as well as among the older missions of the Franciscan period. Alemany noted that there were simply no resources from the properties of the diocese, although he was able to list "receits [*sic*] from Churches, Colleges, Associations—$6,000"; "contributions for support— $3,500"; and "free offerings of the faithful—$12,000." However, he also listed the "expenses for bishop and clergy— $18,000, for clergymen and sisters coming from Europe and from the eastern states." This part of the revealing report concluded with the listing of "expenses to be incurred in building churches and paying debts on colleges already built—$20,000."[42] Under "colleges, academies, seminaries," Alemany reported that his diocesan seminary at Santa Ines "is in danger of being lost to the diocese from the change of government in California and the violent usurpation of some emigrants." In addition to the Dominican school at Benicia and that opened by the Sisters of Notre Dame at "the Pueblo of San Jose," the diocese had been strengthened with the arrival, in 1852, of several Daughters of Charity from Emmitsburg, Maryland, who had established a much needed Orphan Asylum in San Francisco. Finally, there were some general observations with which he concluded this report to Paris:

A small Seminary is kept in San Francisco.
A Dominican Convent has been commenced in Monterey.

[42] *Ibid.*

138

The Dominican Sisters have bought a house in Monterey for their Academy, they owe yet $3,000.00.

A College was prematurely commenced in the Mission of San Jose; its debt, $5000.00.

A lot has been bought in San Francisco for $2,000.00 where a brick Church much needed will cost $25,000.00.

The late large conflagration of the city of Sacramento burnt also our Church; a new one must be rebuilt, which will cost $10,000.00.

The property of the Old Missions is in danger of being lost to the Church, unless with lawyers I try to save it, which is also expensive.

I have made arrangements to commence Missions in the interior for the conversion of the savage Indians. This grand work cannot be done without pecuniary means: which I hope and beg that God may send me through your great charity.[43]

Before turning to the details which, in 1853, preceded the erection of the Archdiocese of San Francisco, it should prove of interest to mention a description of the Bishop of Monterey which appeared in 1852 in an eastern Catholic paper:

We have been favored with a full and interesting extract from the correspondence of a lady recently become resident in San Francisco:

The principal church of San Francisco is built of wood and is attended by a Bishop (a Spaniard) and 7 priests, one of whom, Fr. Scanlon, is an Irishman. . . . The good Bishop is a most amiable and venerable [40 years old!] ecclesiastic, his simplicity of manners so childlike and his benevolence so truly Christian—an instance, apparently, of Divine Grace in turning or transforming the man even of this earth into the saint. The Divine Sacrifice of mass is celebrated and continued every morning at this church from 5 A.M. to 10 A.M. The Bishop and clergy are truly apostolically poor and live in a small wooden house, over the door of which is placed . . . a rude wooden cross.[44]

Although San Francisco in the early 1850's is more frequently portrayed as a lawless town requiring Committees of Vigilance, etc., this same correspondent may be cited in an opposite, if somewhat idyllic, vein:

43 *Ibid.*
44 Pittsburgh *Catholic,* April 17, 1852.

139

Nothing strikes a European here on arrival with more astonishment than to find in this city generally prevailing, with few exceptions, the utmost regularity and order as far as I am able to judge—as much so as in any city in Europe and that, too, without a shadow of a soldier or a policemen . . . petty larceny is seldom heard of and crimes of a more serious nature are promptly punished. We could leave all of our possessions out of doors; no-one would think of molesting them.[45]

Despite such allegedly ideal conditions it would seem that Bishop Alemany had been unable to find complete satisfaction with all his priests; this is testified to by a letter from Father Eugene O'Connell to the President of All Hallows College in Ireland:

San Francisco, February 13, 1853

Dear Father Moriarity:

The Bishop has transferred me from Santa Ines to this rising city in order to assist him in training up some seminarians . . . he has just commissioned me to ask you to select for him two choice students who shall have finished or are about finishing their studies at All Hallows. Doctor Alemanni [sic] hopes that you will send to him two talented young men if possible, but what he lays the principal stress upon is piety and zeal. . . . The Irish missioners that have hitherto figured here didn't reflect much credit upon our country. If the Californian missioner be not disinterested in a country where avarice is the ruling passion, he can do no good but an immensity of evil. . . .[46]

By 1853, Bishop Alemany had already determined that the wooden structure known as St. Francis Church on Vallejo Street in San Francisco was unsuitable for further use as his pro-cathedral. (Although the royal presidio chapel of Monterey was his official cathedral, Alemany had, between 1851–1853, made St. Francis Church the scene of many of the episcopal ceremonies— he designated it, then, as his "pro-cathedral.") A pastoral letter issued in June, 1853, explained Bishop Alemany's plans for a

45 *Ibid.*

46 Eugene O'Connell to "Father Moriarity, President of All Hallows College, Dublin, Ireland," San Francisco, February 13, 1853. AAAC.

new and permanent cathedral in San Francisco. He recalled that the Catholics there had, in the early part of 1850, built a temporary church on Vallejo Street which had served as a pro-cathedral for several years. Now the time had arrived, wrote Alemany, to lay plans for a cathedral worthy of the city and of the Catholic Church. Saying that a large lot had been purchased "at the northeastern corner of California and Dupont Sts.," and that "a chaste and elegant design in the gothic style of architecture had been prepared by Messrs. Craine and England, architects, for the contemplated St. Mary's Church," Alemany asked for liberal support of this important project.[47]

Further evidence that the progress of Catholicity in California at the time was being observed by a number of Catholic editors in the eastern states is had in the following comments found in the *Catholic Register* of Philadelphia:

THE CATHOLIC CHURCH IN CALIFORNIA

California is a fast place, and San Francisco is a fast city in religious movements as well as in other things. We noticed a few weeks ago the purpose of the Catholics to built another Church in San Francisco, on the corner of California and Dupont streets, to be called St. Mary's. Bishop Alemany, on June 1st, issued a pastoral in which he recounts the steps of Church building for the last three years.

The Bishop then mentions the intention of building a new church, and commends the cause to the zeal of Catholics. The San Francisco *Catholic Standard* of the next week informs us that, although but a few comparatively had yet been called on, the amount subscribed already was nearly $20,000! And that some of the most liberal contributors were non-Catholics. They do things in a big way on the Pacific coast. One Thousand, and Five Hundred dollars are the standard of personal contributions.[48]

By the time this item was printed, Bishop Alemany had already laid the cornerstone of his new St. Mary's Cathedral. The

[47] This pastoral dated San Francisco, June 1, 1853, was reprinted in several Catholic papers in the eastern states; the present version is from the Cincinnati *Catholic Telegraph and Advocate*, July 23, 1853.

[48] Philadelphia *Catholic Register*, July 14, 1854.

significant event took place on Sunday, July 17, 1853. The ceremonies were imposing in the extreme, and those present correctly guessed that they marked the beginning of a newer and finer period for Catholicism in California. At noon, the northeast corner of California and Dupont streets was alive with spectators as Bishop Alemany commenced the ceremonies. The foundation of the new edifice was sufficiently complete to allow him to walk in procession around it and to bless the substructure with holy water and ritual prayer. Father Hugh Gallagher, the orator of the day, addressed the multitude, explaining the ceremonies and furnishing a translation of the Latin document which was deposited in the cornerstone. There is a reminder, though, of the relative paucity of the clergy in San Francisco at the time when one reads that Bishop Alemany was attended by "the Reverend Clergymen, John Francis Llebaria, Vicar General, Eugene O'Connell, Superior of the Seminary, Hugh P. Gallagher, Pastor of St. Mary's, Anthony Jimeno, missionary of the College of San Fernando, Flavian Fontaine, Pastor of the Mission of San Francisco and three seminarians."[49]

We may now turn to the details which were to culminate in the selection of Bishop Alemany as first metropolitan Archbishop of San Francisco. As will be seen, his choice was an indication of the confidence which the Holy See had in his administrative ability. It was likewise extraordinary that a prelate only consecrated three years and only thirty-nine years old should be selected for such an honor. An earlier account of the establishment of the Archdiocese of San Francisco thus phrased it:

The rapid increase in the Catholic population during the two years immediately following the discovery of gold and especially the extent over which the people were scattered, demanded towards the beginning of 1852 the services of an additional prelate. A representation

---

[49] San Francisco *Daily Herald,* July 18, 1853. Alemany's *Diary* records that the collection on this occasion was $419.88 (July 14, 1853).

to this effect having been made to the proper authority, the country was divided and San Francisco created into an archdiocese, with Monterey and Los Angeles as suffragan.

To the newly-founded archdiocese of San Francisco, Dr. Alemany was transferred in the month of July, 1853. In the following year, Right Rev. Dr. Amat succeeded to the bishopric of Monterey and Los Angeles.[50]

When the First Plenary Council of the American hierarchy met at Baltimore on May 9, 1852, no time was lost in entering into discussions concerning the status of religion in Bishop Alemany's vast territory. At the first of the private meetings, which was attended by five archbishops and twenty-five suffragan bishops, the status of the Monterey diocese was discussed. A report of this discussion eventually made its way to the Congregation of Propaganda Fide in Rome. Under date of May 10, 1852, the document reports that the bishops had decided that the diocese of Monterey should not be made subject to any metropolitan see then existing because of its remoteness from any of these. Due recognition was made of the importance of San Francisco, which had emerged as the metropolis of the Gold Rush in California, and the decision was agreed upon that here was the logical site for the new archdiocese which should be created. Agreement was also reached that Bishop Alemany should be elevated from the Diocese of Monterey to his newest dignity, while three names were proposed for consideration by the Holy See, as possible successors of Alemany in Monterey. They were Fathers Thaddeus Amat, a Vincentian priest who was in charge of the Philadelphia diocesan seminary; Eugene O'Connell, formerly stationed at Santa Ines seminary in California—although it was pointed out that he was barely thirty years old and therefore quite young for episcopal office; while the third choice was

[50] *William Gleeson, History of the Catholic Church in California,* II, pp. 216–217.

Father John Nobili, the Jesuit founder of Santa Clara College in California.[51]

Ecclesiastical secrets sometimes have a way of being known rather quickly and it is interesting to find a reference in a letter written by a Dominican priest in Baltimore that current report at the Council had it that Bishop Alemany was to be named the first Archbishop of California.[52] Events followed rather rapidly as the following sequence will make clear: under date of July 19, 1853, a decree of the Sacred Congregation of Propaganda Fide, duly signed by its prefect, Cardinal Franzoni, indicated that, on June 26, at an audience with Pius IX, approval had been obtained for the erection of the metropolitan See of San Francisco with Bishop Alemany's separation from Monterey and promotion to San Francisco also winning approval.[53] It is quite possible that the Holy Father might well have recalled the dismay of Father Alemany three years before when he had informed him of his decision to send him to California; presumably, Pius IX was happy in the thought that the three years of Alemany's stewardship had proven him correct in thus selecting him. Ten days later this decree was followed by the customary brief, confirming the selection of Bishop Alemany as San Francisco's first archbishop.[54] Territorial limits of the new archdiocese were established as follows: in the north, the 42nd parallel (that is, the boundary line between California and Oregon); to the west, the Pacific Ocean; to the east, the Colorado River; and to the south, the "pueblo of San Jose." The Diocese of Monterey had its limits set as all the remainder of California south from San

[51] *Acta Secretioris Concilii in Concilio Baltimorensi Plenario,* Baltimore, October 1, 1852. California *Acta* under date of May 10, 1852. APF.

[52] Robert A. White, O.P., visitator general of the Province of St. Joseph, to James P. Leahy, O.P. AOPW.

[53] ASV.

[54] Pius IX to his "venerable brother, Joseph Alemany of the Order of St. Dominic of Preachers, presently called Bishop of Monterey," Rome, July 29, 1853. ASV.

144

Jose to the Mexican border, as well as from the Pacific Ocean to the Colorado River on the east.[55] Among the distinctions which attended the creation of the new Archdiocese of San Francisco may be mentioned that it was only one of six such archdioceses created by Pius IX in the longest pontifical reign on record—thirty-two years.[56]

A letter which the newly appointed Archbishop sent to Father Gonzalez Rubio at Santa Barbara indicated how this news of his appointment had reached him:

. . . Yesterday, I received the documents, one a Bull from the Pope in which San Francisco is erected into a metropolitan See; another is a Bull by which I am separated from the See or Diocese of Monterey; finally, a brief by which I am authorized to exercise, before receiving the Pallium what without said Brief I could not have exercised before receiving the Pallium. I should have preferred the smaller labor of Monterey, but there has been no option. I am glad that the burden has been divided and thus the Diocese of Monterey can receive better care. You will see that the boundaries of the diocese of San Francisco are the southern parallel of the pueblo of San Jose. Over the country

[55] APF.

[56] Alemany's *Libro Borrador* has his own notation concerning his promotion to the newly created Archdiocese of San Francisco: "1853. July 29. I am appointed by the Holy Father Archbishop of San Francisco with powers to continue to administer the diocese of Monterey." AASF. That this date was later "backdated" by Alemany is shown by a letter which he addressed to Franzoni on August 15, 1853. In it he makes no reference to his new appointment which, clearly, was unknown to him; instead, he discusses such matters as the reception of the Roman decree definitively separating Lower California from his jurisdiction and separating him from any subjection to a Mexican metropolitan archbishop. Also, he asks that all the "privileges, faculties and dispensations" which have been accorded to the various dioceses of the United States be given to his Diocese of Monterey. He also asks that the feast of the Immaculate Conception be explicitly granted as the patronal feast of his California diocese (as it was of all the United States) in lieu of the feast of Our Lady of Guadalupe, which was patronal for all of Mexico. Undoubtedly, Alemany knew that, very shortly, California would be admitted to the federal union; actually, it was only three weeks later, on September 9, 1850, that this was done and California became the thirty-first star on the American flag. (The Alemany letter referred to is in APF.)

south of this, I have no longer any jurisdiction. The new Bishop of Monterey is the Rt. Rev. Thaddeus Amat of Barcelona, a Father of the Congregation of St. Vincent de Paul, a man, I am assured, very distinguished for his humility and learning. . . .[57]

[57] Alemany to Gonzalez Rubio, San Francisco, October 17, 1853. Santa Barbara Mission Archives.

146

8

The First Decade in the
See of San Francisco, 1853–1863

THE long administration of Patrick William Riordan who, in 1884, succeeded Archbishop Alemany in the See of San Francisco, is properly commemorated as the "Age of the Builder"— for it was Riordan who built many of the parochial schools of San Francisco and environs. Always, though, the second archbishop freely admitted his debt to his pioneer predecessor, Archbishop Alemany, for it was the latter who succeeded in bringing several groups of sisters to San Francisco who, later, furnished teachers for the Catholic schools. Although a number of these sisterhoods arrived in California during Alemany's years as bishop of Monterey, 1850–1853, they did not begin to make their influence felt on the local scene until the first decade of his archiepiscopal rule; hence, it has seemed better to summarize the stories of their pioneer beginning here.

It was perhaps most appropriate that a Dominican bishop should be responsible for bringing some sisters of his own order to California with him in 1850, for it is the distinction of the Dominican sisters that they were the first women religious to work in California.

As we have already mentioned, on his way to California shortly after his consecration in Rome, Bishop Alemany stopped at the Dominican monastery of the Holy Cross in Paris. He

147

there made an appeal for helpers to "go over to Macedonia" to which he had been missioned by the Holy Father. As a result of his August visit, Sister Mary Goemere, a Belgian religious, received leave to accompany Bishop Alemany together with two other Dominican novices. The three sisters went on from New York to the Dominican convent of St. Mary's in Somerset, Ohio, where the novices were exchanged for two other professed sisters who were destined for later service in California. On December 6, 1850, Sister Mary Goemere entered the Golden Gate with Bishop Alemany on board the *S.S. Columbus.* "The echoes of the last gunshot that celebrated the admission of the free and sovereign state of California [September 9, 1850] to her place in the Union had hardly died away when Bishop Alemany and his companions arrived in San Francisco."[1] A warm welcome was given to this pioneer religious, and after a few days and according to the plan proposed by Bishop Alemany, Sister Mary Goemere made her way to Monterey, California, situated about 140 miles south of San Francisco. No time was lost in establishing a school in the little adobe generously offered her by the visitador general of the missions, William Hartnell, for, on July 18, 1851, the school of Santa Catalina was opened with the formal approbation of Bishop Alemany. The date of incorporation of this first convent in California was March 13, 1851, when, as previously mentioned, Santa Catalina Convent was formally declared to be a Dominican foundation, while Sister Mary Goemere was appointed by Alemany as first prioress. Among the most significant happenings of the early months was the reception into Dominican life on April 11, 1851, of the one who was to become so famed in California history—Concepcion Arguello, who received the religious name of Sister Mary Dominica.[2] In 1854, again with

[1] *The Dominicans of San Rafael: A Tribute from Many Hands,* San Rafael, 1940, p. 6.
[2] Concerning Alemany's first educational foundations, we here quote a laudatory mention of this phase of his episcopal rule. James A. Burns,

Alemany's explicit sanction, this pioneer Dominican foundation was moved to Benicia, north of San Francisco.[3] By 1862, the sisters were ready and able, with gentle prodding from Archbishop Alemany, to open St. Rose Academy, at first located on Brannan Street in San Francisco, which for more than a century has served the city as a Catholic school for girls.

A second sisterhood to arrive was that of the Sisters of Notre Dame who, having made their way to Oregon from their Belgian motherhouse at Namur in 1844, arrived in California in March, 1851. The discovery of gold in California in 1848 had contributed largely to the depopulation of the Oregon country; with the arrival of two sisters from Oregon to help in the many tasks facing Alemany, a new phase began, for, by advice of Father Michael Accolti, S.J., in California since 1849 but formerly a warm friend of the sisters in Oregon, it was decided that they should transfer their activities from the Oregon country to California.[4] On July 4, 1851, the pioneer convent of Notre Dame opened its doors to its pupils in San Jose; until 1923, when a change was made to Belmont, closer to San Francisco, this pioneer foundation of the Notre Dame sisters was an important part of the educational scene in San Jose.

The Daughters of Charity of St. Vincent de Paul are truly world-wide in the scope of their multiple activities. Here we may

---

C.S.C., thus writes of it in the *Catholic Encyclopedia,* XIII (1912), p. 580 (article entitled "Schools in the United States"):

". . . Great Bishops like a Blanchet in Oregon and an Alemany in California . . . were called upon to do heroic pioneer labors in the founding of schools. . . ."

[3] "At the expense of $500, Mother Mary chartered a schooner that belonged to Captain Edward Josselyn and transported the Convent of Santa Catalina from Monterey to Benicia"—*The Dominicans of San Rafael,* etc., p. 34.

[4] For an accurate account of the removal of the Notre Dame Sisters to California, looked upon with considerable disfavor by Archbishop Blanchet of Oregon City, see Sister Mary Dominic McNamee's *Willamette Interlude,* Palo Alto, 1959, *passim.*

149

recall that they, too, formed part of the pioneer picture in the early years of Bishop Alemany's rule. We have mentioned another visit which Bishop Alemany had made in Paris in August, 1850, to the Reverend Jean Baptiste Etienne, Superior General of the Vincentian Fathers and of the Daughters of Charity. Alemany had then asked that some of the Daughters be allowed to go to California. Wisely, the Father General told the young Bishop to make his request anew at their Emmittsburg, Maryland, Motherhouse and, after the usual negotiations, it was decided that, not immediately, but as soon as feasible, such a foundation should be made. In June, 1851, at the request of Father Maginnis, newly appointed pastor of St. Patrick's Church in San Francisco, acting with the approval of Bishop Alemany, seven sisters left Emmittsburg for California. Head of this group was Sister Francis Assisium McEnnis, and she was to have the sad experience of burying two of her companions on the Isthmus of Panama when they succumbed to yellow fever. On August 17, 1851, the five other Daughters arrived in San Francisco aboard the steamer *Golden Gate*. Justifiably, one of the sisters wrote: "It is impossible to describe the joys of our hearts as we caught sight of the first view of San Francisco."[5]

That the first phase of the work of the Daughters in San Francisco was not without trials and tribulations came out in a letter written two years later by Sister Francis:

Knowing you would always hear from our dear Mother how your children were getting along in California, I did not write before. In fact, my beloved Father, I had not the heart to write to anyone, our prospects were so bad. I was truly disappointed and not only myself, but everyone is so, when they come here. It is so different from what we expected but God had dealt with us for the best. It was His Holy Will that we should suffer, and we ought to obey Him under all circumstances. Nothing was heard from the mouths of my dear com-

[5] Manuscript journal—"San Francisco." Archives, Daughters of Charity, Marillac Seminary, Normandy, Missouri.

panions but the ready *Amen* to His appointments and indeed, my Father, I think it was my sainted Sisters' prayers that upheld our fortitude under such circumstances. Our mission I hope bears the proper stamp.

Our prospects are brighter now; it seems to me as if the sun was under a cloud since we have been here. The last time the Bishop was in the city I went to see him. I was much pleased and I find he will do anything he can for us. He even told me, if he could get Sisters of Charity he preferred them to any other Order. I must tell you that I was not much pleased with the Bishop when I first saw him, but indeed, I am now. . . .

This is a strange place, a real bad place. Immorality seems to be the favorite virtue here. God pity us! We need prayers and good fervent ones, for we see nothing good in this miserable place.[6]

Despite the frank opinions expressed in this letter, it had been found possible to open St. Vincent's School in October, 1852. Part of the small structure used by Father Maginnis as St. Patrick's Church furnished space for this first educational foundation of the Daughters of Charity in Bishop Alemany's diocese. Soon an orphanage was added and the nuns were solidly entrenched in their work in San Francisco.

In 1854 two more teaching congregations of sisters made pioneer foundations in San Francisco within a few weeks of each other. Early in that year, Archbishop Alemany had sent Father Hugh Gallagher to Ireland to ask for more recruits from among the sisterhoods there. Father Gallagher arranged to have five Presentation Sisters leave their convent at Middleton, County Cork, in answer to Alemany's plea. On November 13, 1854, this group entered the Golden Gate, and, lacking a convent of their own, they were received hospitably by the Daughters of Charity. In the amazing time of little more than two weeks, on

[6] This letter, dated "March, 1853" and written in San Francisco, was addressed to the Reverend Francis Burlando, C.M. (1814–1873), who, from 1853–1873, was the director of the Daughters of Charity in the Province of the United States.

151

December 1, 1854, the Presentation Sisters opened a free school on Green Street; after the usual pioneer trials, the sisters were able to lay the cornerstone for a permanent foundation on Powell Street. This was on August 10, 1855, and historical significance is had in the fact that this became the first Presentation motherhouse in the United States.

Only a few days after the arrival of the Presentation Sisters, more fruits of Father Gallagher's successful foray in Ireland were manifested with the arrival, on December 8, 1854, of eight Sisters of Mercy from Kinsale, Ireland. Their work first consisted in furnishing aid and comfort to the sick with house visiting while, shortly afterwards, they were granted leave to visit the sick in the City Hospital, which was then located not far from their first home on Vallejo Street. It was in the autumn of the following year, 1855, when the dreaded cholera made its appearance in San Francisco, that the Sisters of Mercy made a lasting impression upon its citizenry as, with signal devotion, they nursed many of the sufferers at the risk of their own lives. From what has been here briefly summarized, it will be seen that Alemany counted it as one of his greatest blessings that God had furnished such devout auxiliaries to aid him in his pioneer apostolate in northern California.

As we continue to examine the first years of Archbishop Alemany's tenure, it becomes increasingly evident that we are dealing with an extremely conscientious prelate. This is apparent as one delves into the considerable correspondence between Alemany and the successive prefects of the Roman Congregation de Propaganda Fide. Frontier California is well and frequently represented in the letters of various bishops of the day but, in signal manner which reveals the man, Alemany reported his problems to Rome for final decision. Frequently he inquired as to the application of certain Church laws to conditions in post-Gold Rush California—notably in the case of laws affecting

152

matrimony. In all of the simply phrased requests of this nature, there is revealed that submission of obedience to the pope (represented here by the prefect of Propaganda) which he had earlier vowed at his episcopal consecration.

In 1853, when Alemany assumed his new dignity as first archbishop of San Francisco, the religious picture in his see city had just been assessed as follows by an eastern periodical:

> There are, at present, thirty churches in San Francisco, California. This is about one to each thousand inhabitants. The Methodists have four; the Episcopalians, Presbyterians and Baptists have two each; the Congregationalists, Roman Catholics, Swedenborgians and Welsh one each.[7]

Actually, of course, the figure concerning the number of Catholic churches in San Francisco is inaccurate: there were three, St. Francis (1849), St. Patrick (1851), while the Old Mission Dolores (1776) still had the services of a resident priest. However, even with these three, it was evident to Alemany that there was much more to be done in San Francisco and, indeed, all throughout his vast archdiocese. Subsequent pages will make it evident with how much devotion and perseverance the youngest archbishop in the United States of his day performed his many tasks. Rome had prepared him for his work by granting him additional and necessary "faculties" or permissions which were dated July 3, 1853—almost a month before the official decree establishing the archdiocese.[8]

Another interchange of letters between Alemany and Father Newman of the Oratory took place only several weeks after the former's elevation to the See of San Francisco. The future Cardinal Newman had undergone a severe trial in a civil suit filed against him by Achilli, an apostate from the faith. This matter caused Alemany to thus express himself:

[7] *The National Magazine* (New York), May, 1853, p. 478.
[8] "Facultates Concessae a SS. D.N. Pio Divino Provid. PP. Pius IX, R.P.F. Josepho Alemanny [*sic*] Archiep. S. Francisci in California." APF.

San Francisco, California
Aug. 25th, 1853

Very Rev. Dear Father,

The Catholics of California, and in particular, myself and the Clergy, take great pleasure in giving echo, from the shores of the Pacific, to the general sympathy justly expressed, towards you, from countless places in the old and new world. You have nobly defended the Faith, from the shameful cant of the shameless apostate! Hence we deemed it our duty, to address you, as the *"true" Defender of the Faith*; expressing this our sympathy, for you, in your late trial and triumph, in letters of California gold, formed into a ring, surmounted by one of our specimens, in the shape of a heart. The expression is in Latin, the language of the Church, and suitable to our Rev. Clergy, who are from Mexico, Ireland, France, Spain, Italy, Belgium, Germany, etc., and who beg me to ask of you to accept their sincere and warmest regards.[9]

That these lines and the accompanying gift, delivered to him by Father Michael Accolti en route to Rome, were deeply appreciated by Newman is evident from the following reply:

My dear Lord Archbishop,

You may fancy with what extreme satisfaction and gratitude I have received the very munificent mark of their charity which the clergy and laity of California have sent me, conveyed to me by your good priest, Father Accolti, which is still more welcome as coming to me with the sanction and cooperation of your Grace, whom I have never ceased to remember with sentiments of deep veneration from the day that you so kindly allowed me and mine to make your acquaintance and ask your blessing. The only alloy in my feelings or qualification is my deep consciousness how unworthy I am both of the consideration you have shown me and the words you use of me. But to dwell on such thoughts, however well founded, would be a very ungracious way of meeting the warm hearted sympathy of such friends, and therefore I put them aside and do but thank God that He has deigned to make me, such as I am, an object of it.

The present from California has a singular interest in itself. All people here feel the utmost curiosity to see so beautiful a specimen of the far

[9] Alemany to Newman, San Francisco, August 25, 1853. AOB. Alemany's signature as "Bishop of Monterey" is explained by the fact that he had not yet received word from Rome of his promotion to the See of San Francisco as its first archbishop.

famed gold fields of California. I should not be surprised if soon it was not the wonder of all Birmingham and, if St. Philip blesses us, it will go down in this house to posterity and will be gazed upon when we are gone, as the precious relic of an era which then will have become historical.[10]

Previous mention has been made of the extensive financial help given to Alemany by the Paris Society for the Propagation of the Faith. From 1853 to 1884, that is, the span of Alemany's rule as archbishop, this generous group sent a total of $45,600 to aid him. It may be recalled that this not inconsiderable sum had an increased value much above that of present-day money. To obtain it, he had to continue to furnish detailed statements of his needs, but the chronicler of his life is fortunate that he had to do so—for these same reports provide him with an accurate picture of ecclesiastical affairs during the Alemany tenure.[11] While we shall summarize some later reports, Archbishop Alemany's first official communications to Paris since his promotion merit partial quotation; as will be seen, the two reports were written within two weeks of each other:

San Francisco, California, U.S.
N. America. 15th Nov. 1853

I enclose a Report of passed [sic] and present condition of this diocese of San Francisco, which, you will be aware, has lately been erected by the Holy See out of a portion of that of Monterey, and to which

[10] Newman to Alemany, Birmingham, January 22, 1854. Copy in AOB. The unique gift attracted the attention of the *Catholic Herald* of Philadelphia which, on September 15, 1853, reported concerning it:

Rev. Dr. Newman

The Catholics of California have prepared a gold ring for Dr. Newman. It is described as a large plain ring of great thickness, having the nugget in its original grotesque shape. . . . It weighs more than seventeen ounces and . . . bears the following inscription: "Reverend. Admodum Doctor J. H. Newman, Vero Fidei Defensori, Catholici Californiae."

[11] The donations of this Society were indeed impressive and helpful, as Alemany testified many times. In addition to the $45,600 received by the Archdiocese of San Francisco, 1853–1884, the Marysville Vicariate which was succeeded by the Diocese of Grass Valley and then by the Diocese of Sacramento received, 1860–1876, the sum of $36,200.

though most unworthy I have been transferred. It is the most difficult part of California, for it is here that new towns are formed, and many new comers settle: they need Churches, Priests, Orphan Asylums, Colleges for young men, Academies for young ladies, Hospitals, etc. and I may say all has to be created at once, without having much time to do it. I do not say it to praise myself, but to show the great need in which we are, when I state, that I have to preach every Sunday, and go to the sick and do the work of a missionary, notwithstanding my other important business in the administration of the diocese. Our Churches are not able to contain the people. In one of them we have sermons every Sunday in various languages: we should build a Church for the Chinese, very numerous here, and some of them are Catholics. Oh! my good, and respected President, my wants are many and rather pressing; I know that you have applications from every part of the world; but you will pardon me for such a detail of wants; I do so, because necessity presses me. It is true, that there is gold in California, and that our people assist me considerably; but the wants are so many and so sudden, that I cannot but humbly and ardently beg of you and of the whole Council to make me a large appropriation in the coming exercise of distribution.[12]

In the final portion of this report, Alemany listed the number of Catholics under his care, as of November 15, 1853, as numbering 55,000; "heretics" were numbered at 40,000 and "infidels" as 100,000. His clergy numbered only twenty-four, of whom none was native-born. There were the same number of churches as previously reported—viz., twenty-four, and three smaller chapels in the archdiocese. However, there was a not unimpressive total of 13,000 persons listed as having made their paschal communion. Finally, Alemany thus summed up his more immediate needs:

1. College for young men.
1. Seminary to educate students for the Priesthood.
2. Female Academies of Sisters educating young ladies.
2. Orphan Asylums.

[12] Alemany to the "President of the Pontifical Work for the Propagation of the Faith, Paris." San Francisco, California, November 15, 1853. ASPFP.

3. Religious Houses; i.e. one of Jesuit Fathers: one of Sisters of Charity: and one of Sisters of Notre Dame.

Five years ago in this portion, now the Metropolitan See of San Francisco, there were only 6 Churches, 3 Priests, with no institution. Now, with the blessing of God and your great aid, it has 24 Churches, 24 Priests, 11 Seminarians and some good Institutions. But now we greatly need a good College in this great city, more Academies, 12 Priests more, some more Churches, principally a good one of brick, for of wood [sic] is exposed to our frequent conflagrations: we have commenced this, which has to be the Cathedral, and have spent for it $20,000.00 but as materials and labor are so high here, we beg a large appropriation to finish it soon, as the increase of population requires it. We need and purpose [sic] building next year an Hospital. We need many more things, and trust in Providence and your holy Work.[13]

In an article written in November, 1853, a Sacramento correspondent thus reported concerning Catholic activities in the archdiocese:

The Rev. H. P. Gallagher, Pastor of St. Mary's Cathedral, which he has been laboring to erect, goes to New York in the steamer that leaves San Francisco to-morrow. Before returning he will probably visit Ireland and Rome, where, I suppose, he will receive the Pallium of Archbishop Alemany. I hope that on his return he may be accompanied by many zealous Priests, and some religious communities; they are much needed here. Father Gallagher is much beloved by his people, and all wish him a safe passage and speedy return.

Yours truly. Philos.[14]

Obviously, Archbishop Alemany could not content himself with the problems of San Francisco alone. A bishop must visit his flock, administer confirmation, and tend to its needs in dispersed places; since the record proves abundantly that Alemany was always a missionary at heart, we are not surprised to find him unwearying in his frequent visitations all over his diocese.

[13] *Ibid.*
[14] New York *Freeman's Journal*, December 28, 1853.

For example, confirmations in early 1854 in Sacramento and in the Mother Lode region are thus reported:

> On Sunday, 29th inst., Archbishop Alemany administered Confirmation to 14 persons, 5 of whom were adults. He left this morning for Jackson and Drytown, where he will also administer this Sacrament. His health is very good: indeed, it requires good health to make a visitation of so extensive an Archdiocese.[15]

That San Francisco Catholicism, yet in its pioneer American phase, had its prouder moments is shown by the following report of Easter there:

1854: EASTER IN SAN FRANCISCO

We have in this city people from every quarter of the globe . . it is, indeed, a strange blending of the races of the Old and the New world, but, so far as regards the Catholic Church, it is, we believe firmly, destined to produce an amount of permanent good to our religion which those outside our new State cannot realize. In true piety and exact conformity with the discipline of the Church, Catholics of this city, it has been made manifest to those best qualified to judge, stand unsurpassed even in the most faithful portions of the Old World.

During the Lent, and more especially from Holy Thursday to Easter Sunday, there were more communicants in proportion to the population than any of our clergy have seen round the altar in any place before.

On Easter Sunday, the first Mass was celebrated at six o'clock and each clergyman who celebrated from that hour until High Mass commenced was engaged nearly an hour in administering Holy Communion. From five o'clock until half past twelve, the Church in Vallejo St. was crowded to a most inconvenient degree. . . .

Such sure indications of a living faith must bring consolation, not only to the pastors of the Church but to all true Catholics, and we have no doubt but a knowledge of the flourishing condition of the Faith amongst us, would induce multitudes who have hitherto been deterred by the reports of the immorality which prevailed here formerly, to come here with their families and settle amongst us. . . .[16]

[15] *Ibid.*, January 31, 1854.
[16] *Ibid.*, June 3, 1854. Reprinted from San Francisco *Catholic Standard*, date not indicated.

It was probably some such wanderings to even more remote parts of his archdiocese that inspired Archbishop Alemany's consent to a petition of the Franciscan fathers for the establishment of an apostolic college in Santa Barbara to prepare friars to resume the Franciscan apostolate in California among the long-neglected Indians. Alemany warmly endorsed their petition in a letter to Cardinal Franzoni in Rome. It is interesting to read in this document his warm commendation, too, of the "regular observance of the Dominican Fathers here" with the accompanying request that he be allowed to transfer title to them of church property in Benicia.[17] This is significant, indeed, in the light of the subsequent and serious disagreements between the Dominicans and Jesuits and himself in this same matter of the transference of such titles.

One of the more important helpers of Archbishop Alemany during these earlier years was that Father Hugh Gallagher (1815–1882), who at Alemany's request had set out to Europe in 1854 to obtain priests and sisters for California. Father Gallagher was an extremely talented and competent priest and he produced good results. Among other evidence, this is demonstrated by the earnestness of his appeals for help, one of which, in Latin, was addressed directly to the Congregation of Propaganda while he was in Rome.[18] His success in obtaining recruits was thus reported in the New York *Freeman's Journal*:

DEPARTURE OF MISSIONARIES AND RELIGIOUS FOR CALIFORNIA
On Monday last the Very Rev. H. P. Gallagher, the Rev. Father Congiato, S.J., eight Sisters of Mercy, five Sisters of Notre Dame, two Jesuit lay

[17] Alemany to Franzoni, San Francisco, March 31, 1854. APF.
[18] Petition of "Hugo Patritius Gallagher e diocesi S. Francisci" to the "Eminentissime Princeps Cong. de Prop. Fide"—undated. APF. Father Gallagher pointed out in this petition that Catholicism in California has had to make a new start after the virtual destruction of the earlier Franciscan mission system. He asked for such donations as books for the seminary in San Francisco and for a diocesan library, as well as for "vestments, chalices and missals for our churches and chapels."

brothers, and a number of friends of these parties, sailed in the steamer Star of the West, via San Juan and the Nicaragua route, for San Francisco. We congratulate the Catholics of San Francisco on so important an accession as this. A number of Ecclesiastics and Religious left a few weeks ago for the same destination.

As every day places on record the occurrence of fearful and grave disasters, by land and sea, Rev. Mr. Gallagher humbly solicits for himself and those placed in his charge, in obedience to the call of duty, now on their way to San Francisco, the prayers of the clergy and religious, and through them the suffrages of the orphans and the humble faithful during the voyage; of whom, in return for their Christian charity, he will make commemoration in the Holy Sacrifice.[19]

The subsequent arrival of Father Gallagher and his welcome helpers also received notice in the *Freeman's Journal*:

Sacramento, Dec. 15th, 1854

To the Editor of the New York *Freeman's Journal*:

Mr. Editor:—The steamer *Golden Age* arrived at San Francisco yesterday, bringing the New York mail of November 20th, and about two hundred and fifty passengers.

Last week Rev. H. P. Gallagher, who has been on a visit to the Atlantic States and Europe, returned. He brought with him a number of Jesuits and secular Priests, also five nuns of the Presentation Order, five Sisters of Notre Dame, and eight Sisters of Mercy. The Presentation Nuns have commenced an establishment in San Francisco. The Sisters of Notre Dame have gone to San Jose, where there is a very flourishing academy conducted by their Community. Probably four of the Sisters of Mercy will remain in San Francisco, and the other four will come to this city to conduct a school for girls. The building recently used as a church will be converted into a residence and school.

Our people throughout the State are much rejoiced at this desirable accession to the number of the clergy and Religious.

Philos.[20]

A week previous to the account, an event of major importance in the history of Catholicism took place in Rome. This was the solemn proclamation of the dogma of the Immaculate Conception of the Blessed Virgin Mary. Writing on November 15,

[19] *Freeman's Journal,* November 18, 1854.
[20] *Freeman's Journal,* January 20, 1855.

1854, Alemany had expressed his regrets to Cardinal Franzoni for his inability to be present for this significant ceremony to which he had been invited by the Holy Father; Alemany mentioned how willingly he would have attempted the journey were it not so far, saying that the distance would make it impossible for him to be on time for the proclamation. He also professed his full faith in the dogma of the Immaculate Conception and said, not without legitimate pride, that the faithful of his archdiocese would gather in late December to dedicate their new cathedral, the cornerstone of which had been laid a year ago, *"sub titulo Immaculatae Conceptionis B. V. Mariae."*[21]

The dedication of St. Mary's Cathedral took place at the Christmas Midnight Mass, 1854, six weeks after Alemany had written to Franzoni. Surely, one would pardon any feelings of legitimate pride felt by Archbishop Alemany as he pontificated at this dedication Mass. Barely more than four years had passed since his arrival in San Francisco, aged thirty-six, as the Bishop of Monterey; now, he stood at the altar in a beautiful new brick cathedral which had the distinction of being the first in the entire world dedicated to the Immaculate Conception after the proclamation of this dogma. The dedication of St. Mary's Cathedral was of such interest to the citizenry of San Francisco that, long before the pontifical ceremonies commenced, the structure was filled beyond capacity—while a huge overflow congregation stood outside on the sidewalks of California and Dupont Streets. Two days later the young Prelate, heart filled with gratitude and joy, thus wrote to his mother in Spain:

The Cathedral of which I sent you the plan is large, [but] not so large as that of Vich, and all were surprised to see it as full as an egg. One

21 Alemany to Franzoni, San Francisco, November 15, 1854. It is noteworthy that Alemany, even at this late date when he had been acting as Archbishop of San Francisco for over a year, still signed himself as "Epis. Electus S. Francisci"—the reason, undoubtedly, was that he had not yet been invested with the pallium, which would formally have conferred upon him the title of archbishop.

hour before the ceremony the people were hurrying to the bell tower and to the galleries which, at present, have nothing but the beams. I do not remember having seen a church more crowded, and they told me that more than a thousand people had to turn back, not being able to enter. . . . I offered a low Mass in the morning and sang a second Pontifical Mass in the late morning, The music was splendid. I delivered two sermons and, in the evening, we concluded the dedication with solemn Vespers, benediction with the Blessed Sacrament and the recitation of the Rosary.[22]

As 1854 ended—his first full year as Archbishop of San Francisco—Alemany thus reported the state of things to his financial supporters in Paris: his approximations placed the number of Catholics at a growing 60,500, and the number of Protestants as 60,000, and the "unbaptized" at 60,600. Paschal communions for the year were listed as about ten thousand, while the number of his priests had grown, if slowly, to thirty, none of whom was yet a native of the diocese. There were twenty-eight churches and three chapels under his jurisdiction. With real gratitude for favors already rendered to him by the Paris Society Alemany wrote:

With the blessing of God and your great assistance our diocesan Seminary goes on well, new Churches have been built, a large Orphan Asylum has been constructed, and I hope, (thanks to our good God) the progress of Religion is marked in the increase of every thing, principally in . . . . attendance to the Church and to the frequenting of the Holy Sacraments.

We had no room enough in this city for its numerous Catholics, a large brick Cathedral was commenced last year, and is now nearly completed: and its expenses are very great, for all materials and labor are exorbitant here. The people have contributed very generously, but I have been forced to contract a debt of some $20,000,00 and this debt will press very heavily on my mind unless for one or two years you with the other members of the Council will be so kind as to send me a large appropriation. Except some small sum which I borrowed at a low interest, I have to borrow here at a very high rate of interest. I could not do

[22] Antonio Alamany Comella, *Biografía,* etc., pp. 27–28.

otherwise, for I could not leave the Church undone and unoccupied another year.[23]

The Alemany diaries and records are filled with cryptic and interesting comments about the pioneer conditions which he endured so frequently in his apostolic wanderings about his diocese; ordinarily his conveyance was the stagecoach of the day where his favorite position, so he mentioned, was up on the seat alongside the driver.[24] Usually he travelled alone and his few and scattered priests soon came to know that their Archbishop wanted the least possible recognition of his high office. In his words, he wanted only "to borrow a bed" and be of help to the priests whom he visited. Such simplicity made the most favorable impression on Catholics and non-Catholics alike, although not all of the latter shared a complete respect for Catholicism. For example in the fall of 1855, Drytown, Amador County, was the scene of an anti-Catholic outbreak, in the course of which a Catholic church there was burned down, as Alemany records, by "irresponsible Americans," adding, in his journal, that someone in the crowd had shouted: "Hang the priest!"[25] But such incidents happened rarely and Alemany was almost always treated with due respect.

One of the attractions in visiting the Mother Lode country

[23] Alemany to Paris Society, etc., San Francisco, November 30, 1854. ASPFP.

[24] Once, after a ride alongside the driver when on a confirmation tour of the Mother Lode country, Alemany recalled being put in his place when, forgetting his green and battered carpet bag in which he kept his belongings, he was called back by the driver who, shouted: "Come back here, old man, you forgot your violin!"

[25] Alemany journal, entries from January 1, 1855—January 30, 1863, p. 26. AASF. Here are some examples of the somewhat laconic entries found in this journal:

Nov. 7 [1856]. Confirmation administered at Robinson's Ferry. Hard place. . . . Nov. 11. Church at Jesus Maria—a hard place. . . . Nov. 18. We gave man last rites at West Point—a hard place.

Evidently, the Archbishop had come on some real pioneer conditions in his apostolic wanderings.

in California today is to be found in the re-creation of the scenes of over a century ago when Archbishop Alemany dedicated a good number of the churches there; some are still in use, others tell their story in reflective silence, and even abandonment— but they all speak to those who know something of their stories of the days when a zealous Prelate seconded the efforts of his scattered clergy in the preserving and spreading of the Catholic faith in the mining districts. While it must be supposed that some of the seed was scattered upon infertile soil, this was not always so: under date of September 28, 1855, Alemany records that he visited the mining town of Downieville and exhorted the people to build a church there, while, two days later, he blessed the Immaculate Conception Church at nearby Goodyear's Bar. But he was back in Downieville on June 22, 1856, to dedicate a small church there "under the title of the Assumption of the Blessed Virgin."[26]

In the middle of 1855, Archbishop Alemany wrote yet another of his informative letters to Paris. As usual, he protested his sincere gratitude for all the help which had been given to him while portraying the many needs which remained to be filled. In this instance, he told the directors in Paris that he had just returned from a journey of nearly a thousand miles throughout his diocese, in the course of which he had dedicated several new churches. On his return, he writes, his heart had been made glad by the generous allocation of funds in his behalf which the Propagation of the Faith Society in Paris had sent to him. New churches are being built, he reports, while the Church has assumed the burden of educating upwards of 1500 children in San Francisco alone; added joy was afforded the Archbishop recently when he had ordained two priests and three subdeacons, among whom he singled out for particular mention "a fine well promising Parisian, Louis A. Auger."

[26] *Ibid*. This little church at Downieville, rebuilt along original lines and still containing some of the original furnishings, still serves the Catholics there.

Among the most important milestones in the life of California's first archbishop was Alemany's reception of the pallium in San Francisco on Sunday, November 18, 1855. It will be noted that a long time had elapsed between his appointment as archbishop (July 29, 1853) and this reception of the symbol of his jurisdiction as a metropolitan archbishop. There was the problem of distance not easily appreciated today, as well as the difficulties of communication between Rome and California. That Alemany had not been remiss in making the required request for the pallium is made evident by a letter which he addressed to Cardinal Franzoni, shortly after he had received word of his appointment. In it he referred to his unworthiness to hold the new office, and made the request that someone, perhaps Father Gallagher while in Rome, should bring the pallium with him to San Francisco. In the end, it was to be Bishop Amat, his successor in the See of Monterey, who, after some delays, brought the pallium for Archbishop Alemany.[27] The bestowal was, of course, a new experience for the Catholic Church in California, and thus attracted due attention in the press of the day. In fact, the San Francisco *Daily Evening Bulletin* seems to have done some fruitful research on the subject as its reporter duly informed his readers of the meaning and symbolism of the pallium:

> The ceremony of presenting the Pallium sent by the Pope of Rome to the Rev. Bishop Alemany will take place in St. Mary's Cathedral tomorrow, immediately after High Mass. The Rt. Rev. Dr. Amat, who brought it from Rome, will officiate. The Pallium is an ornament, made of lamb's wool spotted with purple crosses, and is worn as a token of spiritual jurisdiction over the Churches of the Province. It is regarded as an emblem of humility, charity and of innocence.[28]

[27] February 10, 1854. APF. Alemany had received the bulls of his appointment in late October, 1853.

[28] San Francisco *Daily Evening Bulletin,* November 17, 1855. The "Pope of Rome" reference, with its unfriendly connotation, may possibly be explained in the fact that James King of William, frequently hostile to Catholicism, was editor of the *Bulletin* at this time.

On the day after the ceremony, the same paper mentions that the cathedral had been filled to capacity for this significant ceremony.[29] Another San Francisco newspaper called the pallium a "consecrated garment from Rome" which is a sign of "pontifical partiality."[30]

That such an event, of real significance in the history of Catholocism in California, should have attracted notice in other parts of the country was not too surprising: all of the United States was long since conscious of California because of the Gold Rush and the subsequent admission of the state in 1850. The Cincinnati *Catholic Telegraph and Advocate*, in commenting on the event, added some details not mentioned in the local press, such as the fact that the ceremony took place in the presence of the "largest, within-doors assemblage ever held in the state." The *Telegraph* account went on to quote a San Francisco paper to the effect that "a magnificent gold chalice, manufactured from native gold, is about to be presented to Archbishop Alemany by his congregation to evince the regard in which he is held by them and as a memorial of his elevation to his present dignity."[31]

Finally, in a letter about many things which Alemany wrote to Franzoni several weeks after this ceremony, he formally thanked him and the Holy Father for this bestowal of the sign of his archiepiscopal authority. In writing to Rome, for the first time he signed himself as "Josephus Sadoc Alemany, Archiep. S. Francisci."[32]

By the end of 1855, the number of Catholics under Alemany's

---

[29] *Ibid.*, November 19, 1855.

[30] San Francisco *Daily Alta California*, November 19, 1855.

[31] Cincinnati *Catholic Telegraph and Advocate*, December 29, 1855.

[32] Alemany to Franzoni, San Francisco, December 4, 1855. APF. Alemany noted his reception of the pallium: "A.D. 1855, Die 18 Novembris, Sacrum Pallium jam antea debite petitum, ac concessum, ob Illo Revdo Dmo Thaddae Amat pro me Romae traditum, post Missam Pontificalem a Dmo. Amat celebratam in ecclesia cathedrali S. Francisci servatisque a Pontificale praescriptis, ab eodem Dmo Thad. Amat mihi imponitur." AASF. Journal, 1855, p. 15.

pastoral care had grown to 68,000. Forty-six priests served the diocese (again, all foreign-born), but encouragement was to be found in the fact that a diocesan seminary, located at Mission Dolores but called St. Thomas Seminary, contained ten students for the diocese. Moreover, fifteen other aspirants were studying for San Francisco in the Irish seminaries of All Hallows and Carlow and in the Roman College de Propaganda Fide. The City Hospital, conducted by the Sisters of Mercy, was caring for 200 sick persons. There were two orphan asylums, one housing thirty boys at San Rafael and one for girls under the Sisters of Charity in San Francisco with one hundred in residence. There was a convent of Dominican Fathers in Benicia, as well as "Female Academies, number of ladies, two hundred."[33]

While the over-all picture here given of the Archdiocese of San Francisco at the end of 1855 certainly represented steady and solid progress, Alemany was able to record some other observations in what now was amounting to his annual letter to the Paris Society for the Propagation of the Faith. While he was liquidating the considerable debt on his new Cathedral very quickly, the exorbitant rate of interest (18 per cent!) which he had to pay made it imperative that he ask for still more financial help. He expressed the conviction that, if such help could be sent him, he could extinguish the entire debt on the cathedral within a year. By this time, experience could father the reflection which he thus put in writing:

This infant diocese had the wants of an old one all at once—and to do little was to leave the field to the enemy. It was necessary to undertake and make provision for great wants. God has been so good as to help us much, though we are so unworthy, in a land of such forgetfulness of God: we hope that, after some little time more, the wants of the diocese will be much provided, and hence greatly reduced.[34]

[33] Alemany to Paris Society, etc., December 19, 1855. ASPFP.
[34] Ibid. In these letters to Paris, it is apparent that Alemany was not without shrewdness for he made frequent references to his pastoral activities on behalf of the French in San Francisco.

167

That the first shepherd of the metropolitan See of San Francisco was industriously and successfully cultivating the apostolic fields committed to his care is made even more evident by contrasting two accounts compiled by him in 1857. One was written at the beginning and one at the end of this year, and both afford a study in progress which amply proves the zeal of Alemany and of his helpers among the clergy and laity. In early 1857, for example, Alemany estimated a Catholic population in his archdiocese of about 73,000, while at year's end the number had increased to 80,000. During the year, five churches were opened in his territory. Among the more pressing needs at the beginning of this year were the completion of the "yet unplastered Cathedral" and the building of a "humble house for the clergy of the Cathedral," as well as the reduction of the debt contracted by the purchase of a Protestant edifice in San Francisco which had been opened anew as Notre Dame des Victoires Church for the French Catholics of the city.[35] In the report written at the end of 1857, Alemany mentions that the last September had seen the opening of a new convent for the Sisters of Mercy in Sacramento, while the cathedral, "until now unfinished," was being completed and plastered. The number of converts had increased, which fact is attributed by Alemany to the "good example and instruction of the Sisters." He had spent $3000 in enlarging the seminary at Mission Dolores and had been able to send various sums to European colleges (notably to All Hallows and other Irish seminaries) to pay for the education of future priests for the archdiocese; lest his Parisian benefactors conclude that the pioneer conditions and needs were finished, Alemany adds: "But, please, continue your large allocations in behalf of this infant diocese, which has yet so many pressing necessities."[36]

In light of the great expansion of the Church in California in

[35] Alemany to Paris Society, etc., January 4, 1857. ASPFP.
[36] Alemany to Paris Society, etc., December 4, 1857. ASPFP.

the last century, and of the greatly increased standard of living that all America is now accustomed to, the financial details which Alemany furnished to the Paris Society may not seem so pressing, but in 1857 they were indeed: expenses "for the Archbishop," he estimated, would amount to $1000, while his estimate for those of the clergy was put at $36,500. Money which would be expended in building projects—that is, "churches, academies, presbiteries [*sic*] and paying debts on old ones"—was listed at $60,000, and expenses to be incurred for new ones would amount, Alemany thought, to about $25,000. The debts on his churches and institutions came to $45,000, while the sum of $28,000 must be found during the next year to care for "pressing debts." Under income, Alemany put a laconic "zero" as his expected revenue from "properties, rents or the Government"—while from the customary "collections, subscriptions, offerings and the like" he expected about $100,000.[37] From all these details, it may be seen why Archbishop Alemany found it necessary to call on outside help to meet his everpressing obligations in his growing archdiocese. No wonder, too, that he entertained such sincere sentiments of gratitude for the charity so constantly shown him by the board of managers of the Paris Society for the Propagation of the Faith. This society proved itself the truest of friends in his years of serious want.

In the spring of 1858, three Irish Catholics of San Francisco established a weekly paper which they called the *Monitor*. When William G. Hamill, James P. Marks, and Patrick G. Thomas did so, it was with the intention of providing an organ for the publication of "Irish and Catholic news," and it was not until 1877, almost twenty years later, that it became the official organ of the Archdiocese of San Francisco. In its pioneer phase, the *Monitor*, editorially speaking, was as rough and tumble as were most of the papers of the day; one who reads the available files (there is no complete file because of destruction by fire) is

[37] *Ibid.*

struck by the vigor of the language used. This was proven at the beginning by one of the first editorials published in the paper when an attack was launched on the evidences of corrupting books which the editors found on all sides and which they considered to be one of the outstanding problems of their day—evidently, if the facts nearly approximate their presentation in the *Monitor*, Archbishop Alemany would agree that the moral atmosphere of his see city left more than a little to be desired:

YELLOW COVERED ABOMINATIONS

Again we return to attack the greatest moral and social evil among us. . . . Parents have made the sad statement to the Police Magistrate of our city that they had found under the very pillows of their children obscene and corrupting books. . . . Here we have the young and innocent defiled, corrupted and debased by the thousand—and all to make a few dollars for the beastly dealers in infamy. . . . Fathers of families, let us have a little plain speaking on this subject. What have you come to California for? Let us ask what are the objects for which you seek wealth? Is not the paramount one the happiness, honor and security of your children? Yet, while you toil for them under your very eyes, the poison is entering their souls! The fair young girl you love to call daughter is seduced to gloat over the description of the vilest scenes of depravity, while the ill-judging boy, your hope and pride, is erecting Dick Turpin for his hero worship and studying with anatomical nicety the tinselled intricacies of sin![38]

In this same year, 1858, Alemany furnished some more revealing information in his customary reports to Paris. Writing on May 27, the Archbishop mentioned his return that very day from an episcopal visitation which had served to convince him both of steady progress and of the debt he owed to the Paris Society for making possible much of this progress. He related how, only the day before, he had visited a "church in the woods" which, commenced several years before, had been enlarged three times and was even yet too small to contain all those who wished to worship within it. He was heartened at the prospect of de-

---

[38] San Francisco *Monitor*, March 20, 1858.

parting shortly once again for another area of his diocese where he would soon dedicate "six or seven new churches."[39]

Several months later, after returning from this visitation, Alemany wrote to Paris to tell the directors of the Society that he had, indeed, dedicated five churches and laid the cornerstone for a large brick church to take the place of another wooden one which had been thrice enlarged. Adding that he hoped "this fall, to bless three or four churches more," he assured his friends in Paris that "in all of them, the prayers of the faithful will, I am sure, go up to Heaven for the benefactors that aided us and are always aiding us in the building up of these missions."[40]

Lest the progress referred to by an industrious but still needy Archbishop be thought to have been reported in an overenthusiastic manner, it is interesting to hear another witness on the same subject. This was none other than the famous Jesuit, Father Peter DeSmet, who, after visiting San Francisco for several days in the fall of 1858, later recorded his impressions as follows:

> ... A dozen years ago, SF was nothing but a very little seaport, with only a handful of inhabitants. Today it is the marvel and the port par excellence of the whole Pacific Ocean. A population of at least 60,000 souls has sprung up, gathered from all the corners of the earth. ...
> But what consoles . . . one . . . is the sweet thought that our holy religion has its share in the astonishing activity of this future great people. Judge of its progress: besides a fair Cathedral, just recently built by its venerable titular, who is an Archbishop, there are five churches, four convents, a college directed by our Fathers and several schools for boys and girls. . . .[41]

One of the primary tasks of a bishop is to teach, and this is ordinarily done by the pastoral letter. It is clear that San Francisco's first Archbishop was far from deficient here also; one of

---

[39] Alemany to Paris Society, etc., May 17, 1858. ASPFP.

[40] Alemany to Paris Society, etc., August 19, 1858. ASPFP.

[41] Hiram M. Chittenden, and Albert T. Richardson, *Life, Letters and Travels of Father Pierre Jean de Smet, S.J., 1801–1873*, New York, 1905, II, pp. 737–738.

his better phrased letters dated from this same year of 1858, and it merited praise from the editor of the New York *Freeman's Journal*. We quote it here as an example of the dignified and paternal tone which marked Alemany's exercise of his pastoral office:

> Our diocese stands in need of spiritual blessings as much as any other. We thank our most merciful God, that through his goodness many churches have been erected within the last few years; many charitable persons have extended their generous hand to the orphan; the holy sacrifice of the Mass is numerously attended, and the number of communions fills with much consolation the hearts of the clergy, who left their distant homes to come and minister to your spiritual wants; yet we cannot but regret that much sin prevails. The sacred name of the Most High is sometimes profaned; the baneful vice of cursing is indulged in by some, perhaps, to the great scandal of the little ones of Christ, and not a few trample upon the holy commandments of God without scruple or remorse, as if they had no soul to save, or Judge to meet, or hell to dread. Finally, indifference is also deluding a considerable number of men, who, forgetting that it was God who made them what they are, gave them what they have, and preserves them by day and by night, and who, to secure their eternal life, endured the most excruciating death, are altogether unmindful of Him—think it too much to say a prayer to Him, and never visit His sacred temple to return Him thanks in an humble and religious spirit. Far be it from our lips to mean an offense to the negligent, or anything but the discharge of our duty. We are clothed with the same sinful mortality as others, yet, by reason of that station, which, though most unworthy, it has pleased Divine Providence that we should hold in your regard, we feel bound to urge all to adore God in spirit and in truth.[42]

Once again, in early 1859 and after serving for six years as archbishop, Alemany could testify to the satisfying and constant increase of Catholicism in his archdiocese. His report to Paris lists the Catholics as numbering about 87,000, Protestants about 82,000, and nonbaptized at 90,000. The number of those making

[42] New York *Freeman's Journal*, December 25, 1858.

their paschal communions had risen to 14,000, and, during 1858, two hundred and fifty adult baptisms had been recorded. There were now fifty-eight priests in the service of the archdiocese, but still none were native-born. The number of churches had risen to fifty-six and there were nine smaller chapels in use. The increase of seven churches and eight priests over the figures of 1857 is pointed out by Alemany as an evidence of slow but steady growth and development. An insistent note is found in the last lines of this report: "Please to assist us both with your constant prayers and with a large appropriation that we may be enabled to pay our debts and better provide for the yet numerous necessities."[43]

By 1859, it was abundantly evident to the Archbishop and to his advisers that steady progress made a division of the over-extended Archdiocese of San Francisco an imperative necessity. That Alemany wished advice on this important matter is shown by a letter which he wrote to Archbishop John B. Purcell, who had ruled the Archdiocese of Cincinnati from its beginning in 1850. Among other points of interest, Alemany's mention of either a division of his territory or the appointment of a coadjutor as his assistant, indicates what is now to become a rather constant refrain—that he would gladly resign and pass on the burden of his rule to another while he returned to his first vocation as a Dominican missionary, which was the role in which, seemingly, he had been the happiest.

For a long time I have considered that it would be of some relief to myself and of very great advantage to religion, to have this diocese of San Francisco divided into two. This has now 57 Churches and 9 Chapels, 60 Priests and several Religious Institutions with a Catholic population of little less than 100,000 or fully that. The Catholics are spread over a very large territory, which renders the episcopal visitation very difficult, and as it necessarily keeps me absent from this city

[43] Alemany to the Paris Society, etc., January 4, 1859. ASPFP.

173

most of the time, business of importance at home remains more or less unattended. Were the diocese divided into two, Religion would doubtless derive an immense benefit from the more particular care and closer attention bestowed on each.

And yet a pious and venerable friend of mine suggests to me to apply for a Coadjutor, that he might divide or share the work with me. I would like this very much, if I could be sure that we both would have the same mind, else I fear that it might occasion disorder and injury. Were I to have a Coadjutor, I would not see the necessity of dividing the diocese so soon.

My object in writing you this, is to ask of you the kindness of your candid advice on the above: that is, whether you would advise me to apply for the division of the diocese only, or for a Coadjutor only, or for both things, or for none.

I would also feel very grateful to you, if you would be so kind as to suggest the names of a few able, prudent and truly pious Priests, who might be recommended for that responsible office. . . .[44]

It would seem that Purcell counseled Alemany to seek rather for the division of his archdiocese rather than to ask the Holy See for the services of a coadjutor bishop. This would give meaning to another letter from Alemany to Purcell, written several months later, in which the former thanks him for having sent him such advice while telling him that he has followed his suggestion that he ask that the northern part of his territory be erected into a diocese or vicariate apostolic. In this same letter, Alemany placed Father Eugene O'Connell as among his choices for the new bishopric; however, in first place he put Father James Croke, his vicar general, while the third name proposed by Alemany was that of Father Thomas Foley, then serving as secretary to the Archbishop of Baltimore. The letter concluded with the request that Purcell join his prayers with those of Alemany that God grant to the Church in California "a holy, prudent and learned Bishop, endowed with apostolic zeal."[45]

While Alemany was discussing this important matter with

[44] Alemany to Purcell, San Francisco, February 8, 1859. MCUND.
[45] Alemany to Purcell, San Francisco, May 25, 1859. MCUND.

Purcell and others, Rome was giving careful, if slow, consideration to the same subject. A letter of Cardinal Barnabò to Alemany, written in August, 1859, discussed the matter and commented on *"de nova erectione in civitate a Sacramento nuncupata"* while expressing the opinion that it seemed feasible to arrange for such a separation.[46] It is proverbial that Rome is seldom, if ever, in a hurry about such things, and therefore it was not until September 27, 1860, that the separation was officially made. On that day, the Vicariate of Marysville in northern California was erected, with its boundaries, all formerly within the Archdiocese of San Francisco, set at that part of northern California from the thirty-ninth and forty-second degree latitude (the latter being the California-Oregon border) and from the Pacific Ocean to the eastern boundary of Nevada. Father Eugene O'Connell was selected as titular Bishop of Flaviopolis and first Vicar Apostolic and on February 3, 1861, he was consecrated in Dublin by Archbishop Paul Cullen. While Alemany had placed him as second on his list of choices, presumably he was pleased, for he had thus written to Purcell concerning Father O'Connell:

> Eugene O'Connell is a man of great prayerfulness, purity of conscience, piety, docility, obedience, humility and apostolic zeal, who moves the hearts of the faithful by his angelic discourses; he has also learning, especially in Theology, speaks the Spanish and perhaps the French languages, possesses sufficient health and has a prudent manner of conducting himself in business negotiations. . . .[47]

Official confirmation came to Alemany of the erection of the Marysville Vicariate and the selection of O'Connell as its head in a letter from Barnabò which was dated October 10, 1860.[48]

[46] Barnabò to Alemany, Rome, August 16, 1859. AASF.

[47] Alemany to Purcell, San Francisco, May 25, 1859. MCUND.

[48] Barnabò to Alemany, Rome, October 10, 1860. AASF. As might be supposed, Marysville was not a universally popular choice for the new Bishopric. "Philos.," writing from Sacramento to the *Freeman's Journal* (issue of May 11, 1861), thus unburdened himself: "We hoped and

One of the first matters which occupied Archbishop Alemany in early 1860 was the further convincing of his financial helpers in Paris that progress in his see was not synonymous with financial affluence: this he did in a letter dated January 4, 1860;

> I had the honor to receive your favor of the 17th of year last, which naturally created much surprise in my mind, as in that our diocese seemed to be thought to suffice for itself, not withstanding the immense necessity under which it labors. Few, very few dioceses in these States, if well examined, will be found to be in greater need.[49]

Evidently, and with good reason, too, Alemany would have considered it a real disaster in the midst of so many real necessities had he not been continued on the list in Paris for continued financial help.

One of the stormier years of the pontificate of Pius IX was 1860, for this year marked a step in the ultimate deprivation by the Italian government of his jurisdiction over the Papal States. What is now regarded as a blessing in disguise was then thought of by most Catholics as a tragedy, and many were the messages which went to Rome expressing sympathy for the Holy Father. San Francisco was not remiss here for, during the months of March and April official sympathy was voiced in a pastoral letter of Alemany to his flock on the papal travails, while the cardinal prefect of Propaganda was informed by Alemany that an address of sympathy was being sent to the Holy Father "accompanied with gifts."[50] After a lengthy dissertation on the papal difficulties

---

expected that Sacramento might also have been selected as the See of a Bishop—as it is the capitol of the state, the second in commerce, population, etc.—the most central and easy of access, and, as its wants and necessities require the constant care of a Bishop."

[49] Alemany to Paris Society, etc., San Francisco, January 4, 1860. ASPEP.

[50] Alemany to Barnabò, San Francisco, notation in Alemany journal for 1860. AASF. An interesting gift sent to Pius IX at this time is mentioned by Alemany in a letter to Barnabò dated April 13, 1860. "Last week, I sent His Holiness testimonials expressing the fealty of the clergy of this diocese; they were placed in a box containing a chalice made of California gold and some other specimens of gold—these were donated by a group of men, all

and their sympathy for the Fisherman by the Tiber (all couched in classical Latin), the signers told His Holiness that they were sending him a "chalice made of the gold of California and wrought here by California craftsmen, together with some other specimens of California gold—to which we add a copy of a volume written by the first Governor of California under the American Flag, the Honorable Peter Burnett. His volume is entitled, *The Path Which Led a Protestant Lawyer to the Catholic Church*, published in 1859."[51]

On June 10, 1861, the beleaguered Pope Pius wrote expressing his gratitude for the warm words of sympathy, as well as for the gifts sent to him from his sons among the Archdiocese of San Francisco; as customary, a paternal blessing was extended to the "Venerable Brother, Joseph Alemany, Archbishop, and to his beloved clergy."[52]

In early June, 1860, Archbishop Alemany probably read with pleasure the following rather grandiloquent lines in a San Francisco daily paper, which quoted them from the *Monitor*:

Only ten years ago, the Catholics of San Francisco possessed but one frame structure in which to worship God with the exception of the old church at Mission Dolores, erected by the missionary Fathers who first planted the cross in California. But how changed! Magnificent Cathedrals resound to the voice of the preacher, the solemn anthems rise Heavenwards from noble edifices built to Almighty God; colleges and other institutions are in operation and the sick and the orphans are cared for by those noble religious Orders which are the boast and the glory of the church.[53]

Although the reference to "Magnificent Cathedrals" was greatly overstated, an event of importance which came to pass in

---

Protestants, who form a corporation called 'Allison's Ranch'—I hope and ask that the Father of all the faithful may accept our gifts and bestow his blessings upon us. . . ." Latin original. APF.

[51] Copy (undated). *AASF.*

[52] "Pius IX, Pope, to our Ven. Brother, Joseph S. Alemany, Archbishop of San Francisco, June 10, 1861." *AASF.*

[53] San Francisco *Herald,* June 2, 1860.

August, 1860, lent partial justification to the reference. This was the dedication by Alemany of the imposing St. Patrick's Church in Grass Valley, an edifice which had been erected through the generosity and faith of the numerous miners of the mountain town. It was second in size only to St. Mary's Cathedral in San Francisco, and, as one paper described it, this "spacious edifice, certainly an ornament to the flourishing town of Grass Valley, was built at a cost of $23,000 of which $10,000 remains unpaid —but it is expected that the debt will be liquidated by January 1."[54] Later on this same year (1860), Archbishop Alemany set off on yet another journey to the more remote areas of his archdiocese, for middle October found him confirming forty persons in Soñora, while other confirmations followed at nearby Jamestown, Chinese Camp, LaGrange, Hornitos, Coulterville, and Big Oak Flat. On this same trip he dedicated three new churches, those of St. Francis Xavier at Chinese Camp, St. Louis at LaGrange, and Our Lady of Mount Carmel at Big Oak Flat.[55] The year came to a close with his celebration of solemn pontifical Christmas Midnight Mass in his yet new St. Mary's Cathedral in San Francisco—an event which a reporter called "in the highest degree edifying, while the demeanor of the large number of our dissenting brethren in attendance was in every way respectful and attentive—the sermon being delivered by Rev. John Prendergast who delivered an admirable discourse, which was listened to with attention and was characterized by great earnestness and feeling."[56]

No doubt, Alemany shared the apprehensions of the rest of the United States of America over the indications, in early 1861, that civil strife was imminent between the North and the South.

[54] New York *Freeman's Journal*, August 11, 1860. This spacious church served the Catholics of Grass Valley for almost a century. Torn down in 1950, it was replaced by a new structure.

[55] This tour, reported by "Philos." from Sacramento, was mentioned in the New York *Freeman's Journal*, December 1, 1860.

[56] *Freeman's Journal*, February 2, 1861.

For a generation and more, there had been only token union between these sections, and the complications of the slavery question, states rights, limited or absolute sovereignty of federal and state governments had all conspired to bring on civil strife. Happily, California was not to become a battlefield, but even so it remained essentially divided in loyalties, there being fierce partisans of both the North and the South in the state. In 1861 it would have been incorrect to call California either a Northern or a Southern state in sympathies. It was rather like a border state, such as Kentucky, than a fully committed state such as New York. While the balance was tipped slightly in favor of the North, it would appear that Northern and Southern sentiments were almost evenly divided. Of the utmost concern for the Archbishop, of course, was the fact that his flock numbered those of two different loyalties. One wonders, from Alemany's knowledge of the problem, whether he agreed entirely with the sanguine opinion of a correspondent that "in political matters, the people are almost unanimously for the Union and opposed to secession."[57] This may well have been true of the writer's own friends, but closer investigation would have made it evident that it was not true throughout the entire state. At any rate, Alemany, like the other religious and civil leaders of disturbed California, would have his work cut out for him in the fratricidal years 1861–1865. In retrospect, Elijah R. Kennedy could remark in a standard account: "The Catholic Archbishop Alemany, owing to the influence of his character and his powerful ecclesiastical position, was equally servicable in the cause."[58] A contemporary writer, in referring to Civil War politics as invading various California pulpits, phrases it as follows: "The Catholic Archbishop Alemany, in anticipation of the oncoming conflict, had issued a pastoral letter . . . of February 25, 1861, in which he spoke out

[57] *Freeman's Journal,* May 11, 1861.
[58] Elijah R. Kennedy, *The Contest for California in 1861,* Boston, 1912, p. 142.

against divorces and duels. He concluded by giving equal con-demnation to the national divorce and duel which seemed to be looming ahead."[59]

Since his pastoral letter is the first official statement of its kind, we may quote it here completely—although, actually, it is a short document. The Washington's Birthday pastoral charge to his flock read as follows:

Dearly Beloved:

It is our painful duty to have to request your prayers for our coun-try. Far be it from us to assume the character of a prophet of evil tidings; equally far be it from our tongue to speak the language of a politician but, in the present crisis, we cannot remain silent. We deplore the calamity and sad consequences of divorce . . . we deprecate still more the unparalleled disaster of the duel . . . but we fear that we are about to witness the most disastrous divorce that can befall the noblest family, and the most calamitous conflict ever witnessed between brothers. Few understand the value of health until they have lost it and few also in our prosperous and dear country will form a proper estimate of the evils of civil war till they see it converted into a large fighting ground—when commerce shall be paralyzed, industry unbe-friended, prosperity checked, the halls of learning mourning in soli-tude, passions unrestrained, hatred enkindled, peace forced to give way to strife, devastation made a virtue, houses and cities wasted and destroyed under the name of triumph, the brave citizens of a mighty nation armed to strike each other, their mother country gaping at the wounds received from the hands of her mad children! Such would Civil War be—an endless duel, on a grand scale—a family of states, destined to be the most prosperous, the most intelligent, the most happy nation of the earth, making themselves so many fighting, suicidal tribes, by struggling to change "E Pluribus Unum" into "Ex Uno Plures." . . . It is not our province to allude to the causes which may have brought our country, perhaps, to the very eve of so many evils: but our only desire is to request you all to raise up your most fervent prayers to the God of All Nations that He may vouchsafe to grant us peace, harmony and brotherly love. God alone can avert the evils that

[59] Ann Casey, "Thomas Starr King and the Secession Movement," in *Southern California Historical Quarterly*, XLIII (September, 1961), p. 267.

our sins may have provoked. . . . "Now the Lord of peace Himself give you everlasting peace in every place." (II Thess, 3:16)[60]

Although the anguished words of the Archbishop were eloquently and sincerely written, like so many others they were of no avail to stay the onrushing conflict. He, too, like others placed in positions of responsibility, was to face many crises in the four years of internecine strife which now confronted a divided house.

One such crisis concerned the issue of what came to be called "flagging the churches." This referred to the demands of Northern sympathizers that the churches of San Francisco display the national colors on July 4, 1861. Agreement as to the propriety of so doing was far from unanimous, and the press of the day was filled with pro and con sentiments. St. Mary's Cathedral, located at California and Dupont Streets, was the principal Catholic Church of the city, and many there were who hoped to see it as the scene of a solid Union demonstration. *The Daily Evening Bulletin,* heavily pro-Union in sentiment, declared:

> We have been told on excellent authority that St. Mary's Cathedral is soon to have a flag reared above it of such dimensions that you could wrap in it all the Secessionists that dare show their heads in San Francisco as in a winding sheet and still have enough left to proclaim with perfect clearness that the Catholic Church is right for the Union.[61]

That this information was incorrect was brought out the following day by the *Alta California,* never loath to prove the *Bulletin* wrong:

> We are informed on good authority that the report to the effect that a flag will soon be raised on St. Mary's Cathedral is without foundation. No intention of the kind is entertained.[62]

[60] San Francisco *Daily Evening Bulletin,* February 25, 1861.
[61] San Francisco *Daily Evening Bulletin,* June 28, 1861.
[62] San Francisco *Daily Alta California,* June 29, 1862. Mention has been made of Alemany's custom of frequent referral to Rome of perplexities regarding his diocese. Another example of this is found in a letter of

It would seem that Archbishop Alemany was convinced that neither his personal patriotism nor that of his flock needed to be proven by exhibiting the American flag on what he considered to be first and foremost the house of God. Credit must be given to him for refusing to panic on the issue, and he remained steadfast in his convictions. St. Mary's Cathedral, as well as the other Catholic churches under his jurisdiction, continued unflagged. Nevertheless, the solid and personal patriotism of Alemany were unchallenged.

Another cause of irritation to San Francisco's first Archbishop was the attitude of the local *Monitor.* It was necessary at times for the Archbishop to emphasize that this Catholic paper was not his official organ, for it so happened that the editor during all the war years, Thomas A. Brady, had been opposed to the Civil War from its beginning. He considered Lincoln responsible for the disasters which marked 1862, and wrote that "for all the blood shed . . . posterity will hold him responsible. And when secession had been made into one vast slaughterhouse, your Christian friend will be ready to mount the butcher's block and preach about crowning mercies and saving grace."[63] With the continuance of his attacks upon Lincoln for alleged dictatorial practices, a sharp division arose among Brady's readers, and one wrote an open letter to the *Daily Evening Bulletin* with the assertion that the *Monitor* was attempting to create conditions that would "imperil the peace of the state . . . and even of the happy city in which we live. It was, therefore, obligatory for loyal men to

---

March 23, 1862, to Barnabò in which Alemany discussed such matters as to what his subjects should be bound in the laws of fasting, the days of obligation for Mass attendance, and other like matters.

Another such proof is found in an exact enumeration of the number of matrimonial dispensations he had granted from 1853–1863 (1366, of which 901 were for mixed marriages and 442 for disparity of cult); he deplored the large number of these latter two classes of dispensations and wrote that he saw no solution in the fluid religious conditions with which he must cope in California (San Francisco, June 9, 1863. APR).

[63] San Francisco *Monitor,* April 2, 1864.

caution against such treasonable publications." The *Monitor* did not speak for the Catholic Church, but, said the correspondent, in order to dispel any false conclusions, Archbishop Alemany should "define the position which . . . this journal . . . bears to the Catholic Church." He should act in such a way that "the foul treason which lurks in their columns may not, in any event, be imputed to those who are innocent of any participation in their guilt." For whatever reason, the very next day, August 28, 1863, the *Bulletin* carried the following card from the Archbishop:

TO THE PUBLIC:

As some journals of this state, alleging in their justification the tone and sentiments of certain so-called periodicals and journals, have assailed and misrepresented the principles of the Catholic Church, I deem it my duty to disavow any responsibility for articles and statements without her sanction and approbation, and to state that the periodicals and journals alluded to not only have not this sanction, but are not always faithful exponents of the doctrines and wishes of the Catholic Church which in this diocese has no official organ.[64]

It would seem that this rather pointed pronouncement did cause Mr. Brady to moderate his attitude somewhat—but not entirely. But even this temporary victory did not save the Archbishop from further concern as weary months of war succeeded each other. On November 2, 1864, with the advent of the presidential election, he found it necessary to issue yet another pastoral letter, written at Sonora, California, and published in a San Francisco paper on November 7 with the following comment:

The following circular by Archbishop Alemany, dated Sonora, California, November 2, 1864, was read yesterday in all of the Catholic churches:

For the past 1800 years Catholics have theoretically and practically maintained that the precept "Honor thy mother and thy father" obliges them to be respectively submissive to authority, both civil and ecclesiastical. This forms part of their religion to such an extent that no Catholic conscience at variant with it can be at rest. . . . So firmly does

---

[64] San Francisco *Daily Evening Bulletin,* August 27, 1863.

the Catholic adhere to authority that the great Doctor of the Church, St. Augustine, would not yield his belief even to the Holy Scriptures unless this were taught him by the authority of the church.

In a similar manner, respectful obedience to their government is enjoined on all Catholics throughout the world . . . and the same will be done to the end of time. This is well known to all Catholics and, with rare exceptions, practiced by them everywhere and at all times. But, as it may occasionally happen that some Catholics as well as others may, in these troubled times, be misguided and made to participate in unwarranted agitations, I have deemed it proper to request of you to warn your flock against such deceits and commotions—and to instruct them to continue to join, with their reverential submission to civil authority, their calm, quiet, peaceful and independent conduct. Princes may sometimes make war but private individuals cannot. The company of seditious men can do no other service than to drag the incautious into excesses, quarrels, enmities, blows—and, not infrequently, into an untimely and unprovided death.[65]

In summary, then, it appears that Archbishop Alemany proved himself completely faithful to that oath of allegiance as an American citizen which he had sworn on October 27, 1845, at Memphis, Tennessee. His fearless actions and attitude must have pleased the majority of his flock who, it would seem, were loyal to the Federal Union—while not always proving so pleasing to certain Southern sympathizers among the Catholics of the Archdiocese of San Francisco.

There were two more notable functions which marked Alemany's episcopal administration in 1861. Despite the intense heat of the day, he laid the cornerstone for a new St. Mary's Church in Stockton on July 21, paying due tribute to the pioneer founder of Stockton, Captain Charles M. Weber, a devout Catholic who had donated substantial sums to aid in erecting the edifice. Finally, on December 7, the day after the eleventh anniversary of his arrival in California in 1850, he dedicated the new St. Joseph's Church in San Francisco, a daily paper there thus reporting the event:

[65] *Alta California,* November 7, 1864.

184

Dedication—The rapid growth of the city toward the Mission Dolores is seen in the erection of a house of public worship away out on 10th St. near Hayes Park. This edifice, built by the Roman Catholics, and which is to be called "St. Joseph's," will be dedicated to the worship of God this morning.[66]

The last two years of the first decade of Archbishop Alemany's rule in the See of San Francisco, 1862–1863, may be quickly summarized. By this time he no doubt had established himself firmly in the minds and hearts of all not only as a zealous bishop, but also as a loyal citizen of his adopted country and state. In some of his less official writings, there was still discernible a quaintness of expression which stemmed from his foreign birth and proficiency in other languages before he had learned English. This was evident in a letter which he wrote in 1862 to the superior of the Jesuit Mission of California, Father Burchard Villiger—unintentionally, but truly, Alemany revealed himself as a devoted shepherd in what he wrote about himself and of his daily routine pursued in the execution of his many duties:

I am sorry that my poor circumstances have forced me, after years' study on the subject, to confine my serving the Faithful personally or verbally to two hours in the morning and two and a half in the evening. Until I can do better, I require the balance for correspondence, saying the office, Mass, taking a little medicine in the shape of exercise, etc. I wish I could be like St. Francis of Sales but *parami desgracia,* I am not like him. Yet any time that any clergyman will have to see me at those hours, I will cheerfully give him the first attention, (unless he comes to kill time): and should anything from them require my immediate attention, a line drawn into my room will soon take me out of it, if I am in. It is to be hoped that I may be enabled with better health and abilities or experience or more aid to do better after *poco tiempo.*[67]

In July, 1862, Archbishop Alemany convened the first synod in the history of the Archdiocese of San Francisco; ten years

[66] *Alta California,* December 7, 1861.
[67] Alemany to Burchard Villiger, S.J., Petaluma, California, June 2, 1862. ASJC.

185

earlier he had presided over the only synod held in the Diocese of Monterey. The decade had marked many notable changes in the California Catholic picture—the young Prelate who then was still feeling his way with the many problems that were his was now archbishop with two suffragan jurisdictions, those of Monterey and Los Angeles and of Marysville. Much of this must have been in Alemany's mind when, on July 17, 1862, he issued a pastoral letter from the Synod at San Francisco in which, among other things, he called attention to this progress:

Assembled in Synod, to deliberate on the best means of advancing the interests of our holy Religion in this Archdiocese, we cannot allow an occasion so auspicious to glide by without addressing you some words of congratulation and warning. Your churches, convents, hospitals, colleges, schools, orphanages and asylums for those who have, by sin, lost their heavenly Father, are proofs of your living faith. Ever ready to help your Pastors, you did not grasp with a miser's hand the gold that allured you from afar, but with wonderful liberality gave the first treasure you drew from the vaults of the mountains to build tabernacles to the God who placed it there—to build homes for his afflicted and houseless children. And whilst grateful to Almighty God, who has imparted to you a spirit of Christian zeal and benevolence, we feel our satisfaction increase to know, that in attending to the exterior wants of Religion, you have not forgotten its life is within; that in building and adorning the material temple, you have not forgotten to build and beautify the temple of the soul. . . .[68]

An outstanding educational event which marked 1863 in San Francisco was the dedication of the new St. Mary's College on Mission Road. Under date of July 9, a simple entry in the Archbishop's diary commemorates the dedication: "I blessed the Chapel of the College of Saint Mary, beyond the Mission Road." A preliminary school called St. Mary's had been meeting for several years, since 1855, in the basement of the cathedral. By 1863, it was possible to dedicate the new establishment located "away out" on Mission Road. In 1857, Alemany had

[68] A printed copy of this pastoral is in AUSF.

endeavored to obtain the services of the Christian Brothers to help him to establish such a college, but he was refused by the superiors of the congregation, beseiged as they were for such aid. Ten years later, in 1867, while in Rome, the ever-determined Alemany appealed personally to the Holy Father for this aid, and a letter written in his behalf to the superior general of the Brothers by Cardinal Barnabò produced the desired results: on August 18, 1868, Brother Justin, as director and visitor, accompanied by a group of seven of his confreres, arrived in San Francisco. On the following Sunday, speaking in St. Francis Church, Archbishop Alemany said: "I made a journey of 20,000 miles to get the Brothers. I have at last succeeded. Let us give thanks to God."

Among the many important items concerning the See of San Francisco which are to be found in the Roman Propaganda Fide archives is a very detailed account of the first decade of Archbishop Alemany's service in the See of San Francisco, 1853–1863. Dated October 29, 1863, and written by Alemany himself exactly ten years and three months since the erection of the archdiocese, this important report began with the statement that, since His Holiness had dispensed him from the obligation of reporting personally in Rome for his *ad liminia* visit, Alemany was forwarding this report to Propaganda through the good offices of the rector of the North American College in Rome. He identified himself as the "unworthy incumbent of the See of San Francisco, fifty years old, a professed friar of the Dominican Order." There followed a description of the large amount of territory confided to his pastoral vigilance in California, together with the observation that he had endeavored to visit each part of his entire archdiocese every two years—and its principal churches at least once a year. His churches numbered fifty, with about eighty mission stations without churches. There were eight churches and seven chapels in his see city of San Francisco. Clerical resources as regards seminarians were placed as ten in his own small seminary at Mission Dolores, while twelve others were studying for the diocese, most of them at All Hallows College, Dublin. An indication that, fifteen years after the discovery of gold in California, Alemany still considered his territory to be missionary in character, is found in the assertion that he regarded his pastors as not being rectors in the full canonical sense, but rather as missionaries with none of the rights of irremovable pastors. Frank admission was made that it was quite difficult to assess the quality of Catholic life in his diocese since all seemed to be constantly in flux. However, a meticulous statement was furnished of the number of Catholics in each of the parishes of the diocese, with the entire city of San Francisco leading with 29,000 Catholics. Alemany's final estimate was that there were, to his knowledge, almost 57,000 Catholics committed to his care. His devotion to the educational work of his diocese was further shown by the figure of twenty-six Catholic schools which in 1863, were educating 4391 pupils—practically all of these had been established while he was archbishop. He was able to report that the sixty-seven priests who shared the work with him were, so far as he knew, good examples of the disciplined clerical life. However, he mentioned by name two former priests who had caused him especial displeasure by opposing his orders. He next referred to the "imprudent zeal" of some of the Jesuit fathers in San Francisco who, unintentionally, he hoped, had effectively helped to set up significant areas of discord between his own priests and themselves by the manner in which they had conducted themselves in St. Ignatius Church. Of the sixty-seven priests previously mentioned, twenty-nine were religious, these being six Dominicans and twenty-three Jesuits. Alemany next expressed his satisfaction with the quality of religious observance being shown by the various communities of religious women on which he depended so heavily for the education of his children. A rather eloquent statement followed concerning the problems priests must face in frontier California, many of which came from the fact that the state had been developed as a melting pot of all the nations with different customs and traditions among the Catholics and none at all among the many outside the Catholic Church. "More than in Italy or in Spain," he added, "fall into such vices as extreme drunkenness and the like." Lest too grim a picture be presented, though, Alemany mentioned that, while there was almost certainly a decrease in the practice of faith in California from 1843–1849—largely because of the effects of the secularization laws passed by Mexico against the mission system as well as, occasionally, by the poor example set by some missionaries—he was happy to report that the situation had, in the main, improved much since 1849. The needs of the diocese included many more priests, especially those who were filled with "a spirit of zeal and a love of poverty," more schools—in fact, more of nearly everything! In the matter of obtaining more recruits to help with the needed work of the diocese, Alemany remarked that, although he was "poor in knowledge, prudence and virtue and wealthy only in his spiritual miseries," he would gladly wish to start a training school for brothers and sisters to help in the works of zeal which must be established here and in other parts of the United States.

It may certainly be doubted whether the average episcopal report reaching the cardinal prefect's desk included two petitions to resign the episcopal office. However, a measure of the humility which Alemany possessed is to be found in the following words in which he sought to resign the See of San Francisco. First, when discussing the fact that, in the eastern part of his diocese, there were some "gentile Indians" for whom it was almost impossible to care, Alemany wrote: "But, if it would please the Holy See to give another shepherd to the diocese, I will freely minister to them with the help of God's grace as Vicar Apostolic or as a simple missionary."

189

Again, at the very end of his report, Alemany again suggests that he be allowed to resign:

Finally, although I have tried to labor diligently for the Spouse entrusted to me by the Holy Father, I feel bound to think of myself as an unprofitable servant—so much so that the greatness of the tasks which are mine in this part of the Church seem to call for a better Pastor. With God's grace, I believe that I could be of more service if, freed from this office, I could devote myself to the giving of missions or of spiritual exercises or if I should be assigned by Christ's Vicar to gratuitously instruct poor children somewhere. I ask pardon from the same Holy Father for my negligences and faults committed in my office, awaiting instructions and corrections from the Holy See and asking a blessing for my Church in California.[69]

Evidently, the first vocation which Joseph Alemany had felt as a Dominican—that to be a missionary of and in his order—was still very much felt by him even though he had advanced, relatively young, to the dignity of metropolitan archbishop.

Previous reference has been made to the simplicity which always marked the manners of the friar-Archbishop of San Francisco. Perhaps as good a manner as any to illustrate this part of his character is to be found in an anecdote related by a pioneer San Franciscan who found himself charmed by seeing the Archbishop at work under rather novel circumstances which he recorded for posterity as follows:

At some of the large fires which devastated the city in the early days, the regular firemen would become wholly exhausted by their prolonged exertions, and some would fall to the ground while working

[69] APF. Entire report is in Alemany's handwriting and signed by him. An interesting reference to Alemany and his attempts to resign the See of San Francisco occurs in Cormier's book, *Vie du Reverendissime Pere A. Vincent Jandel,* Paris, 1896, pp. 494–495. After mentioning that a "special motive which made Père Jandel second the work of the Dominican Order in California was the profound veneration which Archbishop Alemany inspired—truly living in the midst of his flock as the poorest and least of his religious,"—Cormier quoted Jandel as having written to Alemany after one of the latter's earlier attempts to resign: "Don't count on my help— seeing the good that you are doing, my sentiments are in the other direction. . . ."

190

at the brakes. I was always on the spot assisting in my humble way at the engines or in saving property. On one occasion, during a large fire, the firemen of one of the engines were completely worn out, and appealed in vain to the crowd standing around to aid them, until a man came running up, having just rescued two children from a house burning nearby, and called out to the crowd, in English, to go to work, and also spoke in Spanish for others to assist. Immediately they began to work at the engines, relieving the exhausted firemen. When inquiring who this man was, I learned that it was Dr. Allemany [*sic*], the present Bishop of California. Though a small man physically and slightly built, he worked for hours that morning at the engines, and influenced others to do the same. There was not a stronger man for his size in California. There were no important fires in San Francisco where the Bishop and his friend Reverend Mr. O'Connell were absent. The exertions of these clergymen at fires were well known and appreciated by the fireman of San Francisco, by whom, as well as by their own flock, they were beloved and respected, their humble and unassuming manners endearing them to every one. The Reverend Mr. Taylor also, who was one of God's noblest works, was always found in the midst of the greatest danger, whether by fire or accident, helping with his gigantic strength.[70]

It appears evident, then, that the first decade of Archbishop Alemany's rule of the See of San Francisco was a highly successful one. Zeal and hard work and devotion on his part had already justified the wise choice made by Rome for this position.

[70] Francis Cassin. "A Few Facts About California," manuscript (1878), Bancroft Library, Berkeley, pp. 8–9. Cassin, a Catholic layman, was a pioneer who had come to California in 1849.

9

A Dominican Archbishop Jousts with the
Jesuits in San Francisco

THE first decade of Archbishop Alemany's holding of office inevitably brought with it numerous problems and difficulties. Thus a eulogium on Alemany published in 1878 by an enthusiastic admirer, a contemporary of his named Father Hugh Quigley, is so obviously unrealistic as to be almost laughable. After commenting on the Archbishop's prudence and piety, Quigley observes that

his administration of this diocese and province is probably the only one that has never been disturbed by the disobedience of a single subject or even unfavorably commented on or criticized. . . .[1]

In our effort to obtain a clearer perspective of Alemany and his years as Archbishop of San Francisco, perhaps it would be best to begin with this balanced verdict on his personal self:

Though small in stature and plain to a marked degree in appearance and in dress, Bishop Alemany was indefatigable as a worker, though most ascetic in his own life and of a composure of temper that nothing seemed to disturb. In adherence to principle, he was absolutely inflexible, but personal motives seemed to find no place in his springs of action. As Bishop he considered himself the representative of the parochial clergy and guardian of their rights and privileges, although bound by strong affection for the Order (Dominican) which he had

[1] Hugh Quigley, *The Irish Race in California and on the Pacific Coast,* San Francisco, 1878, p. 419.

chosen for himself. The favor he showed to religious orders within the diocese was strictly limited by their utility to the spiritual needs of the diocese. The singular combination of intense enthusiasm for the religious life, with absolute impartiality between its professors and the secular clergy, was a marked feature in Bishop Alemany's striking character. . . .[2]

In this perspective, then, we might now consider the long-standing disagreement which disturbed the relationship of Archbishop Alemany and Jesuit superiors in San Francisco. As in most such matters, neither side could be entirely right—but both could be, and were, it seems, righteous, conscientious, and sincere in their views and contentions. As we shall see, Alemany was not supported in his views by Roman authorities, but neither was he publicly declared wrong, for Rome had great respect for his industry and devotion. Whatever indication he received that he was wrong was done in a somewhat cautious and oblique way by Roman authorities. For our present purposes we shall limit our discussion here to the years 1853–1875; a later phase involving further disagreement will be taken up in a later chapter.

In 1853, when finishing his three years as Bishop of Monterey, Alemany wrote to Father General Peter Beckx of the Jesuit order requesting his support for the educational work at the newly founded Santa Clara College; certainly, his words reveal no animus against the Jesuits—although he was liberally accused of such later on. Mentioning the efforts of Fathers Nobili and Accolti to found a good college for boys at Santa Clara, Alemany asked Beckx to allocate more men to California for this important work. He pointed out the recent growth in San Francisco and vicinity:

The number of residents here in San Francisco grows greater each day and, in this city of San Francisco, in which, five years ago, there was not even a thousand persons, there are now forty or fifty thousand.

[2] Bryan Clinch, "The Jesuits in American California," in *Records of the American Catholic Historical Society*, V, n. 18, pp. 242–243.

The same thing is happening in other parts of this area, and this increase will continue since the "*auri sacri fames,*" the fertility of the land and pleasant climate will attract persons from all other parts of the world; not without reason, therefore, is it to think that our California will develop into a great place. . . . I ask you, therefore, to send me some Jesuit Fathers to help in the conversion of the Indians who again need a shepherd as well as in making of Santa Clara an excellent institution of learning.[3]

A confirmation of this evidence of good will is also found in a letter which Alemany addressed to his Roman superior, Cardinal Franzoni of Propaganda, in which he praised the work of the Jesuits in his diocese and asked approval for various concessions which he had granted them.[4] In 1861, another interchange of letters took place between Alemany and the Jesuit superiors in San Francisco. These superiors, moreover, had been given careful instructions to act so as to give absolutely no offense to the Archbishop. This had been done by Father Felix Sopranis, official Jesuit visitor in San Francisco, sent there in 1861 as part of his visitation of the Jesuit houses in the United States. Emphatic in his written instructions left behind was that the local superiors, in their planning for the future, take care that all such projects receive Alemany's approval, and that any solicitation of funds have his permission and blessing.[5] However, a letter which served to indicate areas of disagreement was written by Alemany from San Francisco on August 7, 1861, and addressed to Burchard Villiger, superior of the Jesuit missions of California:

. . . about ten years ago, because I felt they would do good, I gave to Father Nobili the Congregations of Santa Clara and San Jose. I wished

[3] Alemany to Beckx, San Francisco, August 23, 1853. ASJR. Peter Beckx, S.J. (1795–1887), was Jesuit general from 1853–1883.

[4] Alemany to Franzoni, San Francisco, February 10, 1854. APF.

[5] Felix Sopranis, S.J., "Memorial of the Visitation of St. Ignatius College, San Francisco," May 17, 1861. ASJR. Father Sopranis (1799–1876) was official visitor to the American provinces of his order, 1859–1864. He visited San Francisco twice in connection with the Jesuit difficulties with Archbishop Alemany. Arriving for his first visit on March 25, 1861, he remained about two months. On his second visit he arrived on May 28, 1863, and he remained until November 3, 1863.

to afford the opportunity of some permanent establishment of the good children of St. Ignatius and of St. Dominic, while they would also work for the good of religion, and fight for the holy cause till the day of Judgment. In connexion with this, it would appear that it is not exactly the intention of the Church to place Parishes much under the care of the Religious, nor the object of the Religious to administer them. And it was in order to show my good will to the Jesuit and Dominican Fathers, that I obtained for both some considerable time since what I considered favors. Now I have a kind of presentment, that I may meet with some displeasure from both for not succeeding in obtaining more. And this is the main object of this: namely to see if the *materia prima* of such an unpleasant future different views or disagreeableness might be avoided.

The matter is this: Religious Orders naturally desire to have the Church property, which they administer, vested in themselves. The Decrees of Baltimore governing all the dioceses in the States require the property of parishes and such like to be vested in the bishops. If so, how can Religious have charge of Parishes? This is the grave question. I desired to obviate this difficulty by obtaining from Rome a moderation, or such an entrusting of the Parish as to become impossible for the bishop to change the administration without the previous determination or decision from the Propaganda. But it seems, that the S. Congregation will not likely acceed [*sic*]. It appears to wish, as it is natural, that the emoluments due to the Pastors should be of the Religious serving the Parish; but it contemplates the bishop owner and unrestricted in the government.

I may have presumed too much or undertaken more than I was allowed, when allowing all the offices of a Parish performed in St. Ignatius Church of San Francisco. But now when more explicit instructions are received, and when it is desired to build another Church; what should I do not to displease and yet do my duty?[6]

Evidently, a satisfactory answer was shortly forthcoming from Father Villiger; it has not been preserved, it would seem, but it inspired the following friendly reply from Alemany two weeks later:

San Francisco, Aug. 22, 1861

Very Rev. Dear Father,

I received in Placerville your esteemed favor of the 12th inst. in answer to my proposal of the 7th that seems to ease the main difficul-

[6] ASJC.

ties. . . . this was now my only difficulty in your building a New Church, supposing that you desired that it should be a Parish Church; for then it appeared to me, that I could not allow it, unless you would make me the Deeds of the Church, (which looked at least curious,) or unless I could have obtained permission from Rome that you and the Dominican Fathers might have retained the Deed of the Paroquial or proparoquial [sic] Church, which after the departure of Father Sopranis I learned from Rome the Holy See was not inclined to grant. But as you do not desire to retain the parish, then all the main embarrassment seems to be removed.

Now while I need very badly the prayers of St. Ignatius, and of St. Dominic, and their children almost as bad; yet put in the position in which I am placed, I do not see that I can do differently from what I am doing in these things.[7]

That the matter of the Jesuit position in San Francisco with regard to diocesan authority weighed heavily on Alemany is established by a letter which he addressed in August, 1862 to an old friend, Archbishop Purcell of Cincinnati. In this letter, Alemany mentioned how he had willingly invited some of the Jesuit fathers to work in San Francisco "with a view to have the Catholic boys of this city taught almost gratuitously." The small school which had been opened (St. Ignatius College, founded in 1855) had, he thought, "charged rather too much"; now that other fathers had come, some of whom preached well and to the satisfaction of many, difficulties had arisen which concerned him. Saying that he would like the good will of the Fathers, Alemany added that he could not approve of some of the means which they seemed to have used to attract people to their church on Market Street. He said that he had not yet given any formal document to the Jesuit fathers for their establishment, much less for having a parish church, and he noted that the Jesuits had said that they would prefer not to have parochial responsibilities later on with the further development of their educational work. The perplexed Prelate concluded with

7 ASJC.

196

a request to the more experienced Purcell that he freely give any advice to Alemany which he considered proper and helpful.[8]

It is not known what answer, if any, was returned by Purcell. However, further correspondence on aspects of the matter is not lacking—and a refreshing note is introduced by the fact that tried and true Jesuit friends of the Archbishop did not hesitate to express their views without losing his friendship. Such was Father Michael Accolti, founder, in 1849, of the Jesuit order in California, and who by 1862 was pastor of the parish connected with Santa Clara College. Writing in friendly manner to Alemany, Accolti, after discussing some difficulties which had arisen between them concerning the preparing of parish reports, etc., had the following frank comments to make:

I hope that these dark clouds that are arising from behind St. Mary's Cathedral will soon disappear, and let the sky look clear as before. But should they still persevere in gathering, I will regret with all my heart to have been so foolish as to go purposely to Europe in order to gather Jesuits for California. . . .[9]

Whether Accolti's letter would have caused a delay in an important communication which Alemany addressed the very next day to Father Villiger is only a matter of conjecture. However,

[8] Alemany to Purcell, San Francisco, August 25, 1862. MCUND.

[9] Michael Accolti, S.J., to Alemany. Santa Clara College, Santa Clara, September 9, 1862. ASJC. Accolti's earlier friendship for Alemany is proven by a letter which he wrote to a Missouri Jesuit superior, William S. Murphy, concerning the then Bishop Alemany. He wrote: "And here I must confess for the sake of justice and truth that, if we have laid some solid foundation for our future and permanent existence in California, all this we owe to the disinterested and charitable liberality of the zealous and wise prelate, Bishop Alemany . . ." (Accolti to Murphy, November 8, 1852. ASJM). Again, in addressing the famous Pierre De Smet, S.J., Accolti mentions that the "worthy prelate of the diocese has the best dispositions towards us . . ." (November 20, 1852. ASJM). Similar testimony is given by John Nobili, S.J., who founded Santa Clara College in 1851 at the request of Alemany: ". . . The new Bishop, J. M. Alemany, is one more devoted to our Society in deeds rather than by mere words; recently, in a public address before many people, he praised our Order . . ." (Nobili to Roothaan, November 8, 1852. ASJR).

197

this important decision of the Archbishop, which still has its effects upon the Jesuit order in San Francisco, should be quoted in full:

San Francisco, Sept. 10, 1862

Very Rev. Dear Sir,

I think it is time that I should comply with the wishes of the Church, which directs the Bishops in the United States to have parroquial or proparroquial [sic] churches in their name. This I should doubtlessly have done long before; but desiring always to avoid anything which might have the appearance of unfriendly feeling, I have put that off. Not to fail, however, any longer in this duty, I feel obliged to state to you, that I believe the Deed of your church in this city should be in my name, and that unless it be conveyed to me within twelve months, I will consider you not much interested in keeping the parish in the same church and myself bound to let said parish cease in said church.

Of course, this is not intended to give trouble to anybody: had we marked out more clearly the boundaries of the respective rights of regulars and seculars, perhaps we might have avoided the little trouble which now seems unavoidable. I think, therefore, that the defining now of those boundaries in a way clear to both parties is the only means of dissipating such troubles now and hereafter.[10]

One of the frequently expressed opinions of various Jesuit Fathers in San Francisco at this time, was that the generally mild Alemany was moved to write some rather stern letters to Jesuit superiors at the behest of the members of his diocesan council. For example, Father Nicolas Congiato, who served twice as President of St. Ignatius College (1862–1865; 1866–1869) found occasion to forward to the Jesuit general in Rome a letter of Alemany which had been addressed to him on October 16, 1862, in which a rather uncharacteristically sharp request was made by the writer:

To comply with what I consider my duty, I must inquire of you whether you have permission from the Holy See for the erection of

[10] Alemany to Burchard Villiger, S.J., San Francisco, September 10, 1862. ASJC.

198

your college or institution of St. Ignatius in this city—and, if so, what is the date of this permission? I must also ask of you a list of the Fathers and Brothers attached to St. Ignatius with their respective age, and whether they be professed or simple novices. I fear that there is not prudence enough used by all under your care. The love of God demands that we should be prudent.[11]

In an addition to this letter Congiato added:

Here is another of those sweet and consoling letters which have been emanating from His Grace the Archbishop for the last few months. . . . I am at a loss to understand what the Archbishop means by what he asks and says of us. As far as I know, no imprudence in any way has been committed by any under my care here in San Francisco of late. The poor Archbishop is led by the nose and believes whatever is told about us by those who surround him. God bless him and them. . . .[12]

It may well be imagined that Alemany's letter stirred up much comment when its contents were made known to the Jesuits who staffed St. Ignatius Church and College. Naturally, they would instinctively side with their superior in judging the issues, and this is exactly what they seem to have done. One would imagine that the atmosphere was hardly cleared at all when Father Accolti, good friend that he was, received an almost argumentative letter from Alemany containing the following reflections:

San Francisco, October 23, 1862

. . . I think it would be better for all parties to study as much as possible to have peace with all men. Strong efforts I fear are made to draw parishioners from their parishes in this city. Can the Pastors like that? Could Father Accolti like that Father Vilarrasa would make efforts to draw out postulants and Novices from St. Ignatius to give them to St. Dominic? I do not think that either St. Dominic or St. Ignatius would like it. If I were a Jesuit, I do not think that I could ever see any propriety or utility, or spiritual interests in those efforts, for spiritual or true progess must grow on the ground of "*quod tibi*

[11] Alemany to Nicolas Congiato, S.J., San Francisco, October 16, 1862. ASJC.

[12] ASJC.

non vis fieri, alteri ne feceris." [Do not do to others what you do not wish done to you.][13]

Evidently, Father Accolti was not convinced that the Archbishop was either properly informed or correct in his statements or inferences here. Alemany's letter occasioned a rather eloquent reply to his complaints. After expressing, with considerable literary skill, his distress at the menacing turn things had taken in San Francisco in the Alemany-Jesuit relationship, Accolti wrote:

Now, as to the heavy charges against our Fathers in San Francisco. Indeed I do not understand what Your Lordship means by these great efforts which our Fathers of St. Ignatius are making for drawing people from other Parishes. Does Your Lordship mean that they are soliciting people of other Churches to go to St. Ignatius, or to live within the limits of their own Parish? Indeed I am at a loss to believe it, really I do not believe it, I am astonished that Your Lordship should believe it; and therefore I protest, so far as I can do it as a private individual, against such an acusation. But if the great efforts mentioned by Your Lordship consist of endeavoring to do the best they can to deserve the esteem and confidence of a sensible and not a selfish people, then I think instead of blame they deserve rather commendation.

The clouds of prejudices against us, instead of dissipating, are every day growing thicker and thicker still. But how has it happened? What real cause have we given to disturb that calm harmony which existed among us before, and promised so much good? What great fault have we committed to deserve so many severe and rude dealings. Indeed I cannot answer to such questions which naturally occur to my mind, except by putting the whole concern on the back of the old Nick. Certainly *"inimicus homo hoc fecit,"* the ancient enemy of all good, has stretched his tail and is trying to create disorders in the field of the Lord. What Your Lordship very wisely says in his letter, "it would be better for all parties to study as much as possible to have peace with all men," is very true indeed. But who has disturbed that peace which reigned before? I do not know much about it. Perhaps Your

[13] Alemany to Accolti, San Francisco, October 23, 1862. *ASJC.*

Lordship who is on the top of the mountain may be better acquainted with what passes below. I think that in order to keep peace, a most available means would be not to lend an easy ear to every report; because I know everywhere great is the number of old women of both sexes, who live on scandals as vultures on rotten carcasses, forsooth, all with good intentions. Though not living in San Francisco, yet many things have been related to me by secular persons, as said in different houses and to different persons against us by the Revd. gentlemen of the cathedral and at St. Patrick, which I did not by any means believe, because they betrayed either a great ignorance or a consummate malice; neither of which I can suppose to abide in those Revd. gentlemen, concerning whose delicacy of conscience and ecclesiastical attainments I have never entertained the least doubt.

Let us consider each other not as rival bodies, but as soldiers militating under the same King and under the same Flag of his Cross though organized into different regiments. No matter if our uniforms are of different colors and shape; their stuff is woven with the wool of the same immaculate lamb; let us put aside all petty jealousies and contentions, considering that we have common enemies to fight with: Hell, the world, heresy and infidelity, all arrayed in fierce combat against ourselves and the Church of Christ.

Since by divine dispensation Your Lordship has been appointed as the General in Chief of this apostolical army in California, so everyone has the right to expect from Your Lordship that unbiased spirit of impartiality which is the best cement of union, and constitutes one of the brightest qualities of those who represent upon earth the character of him who in coming into the world announced peace to all men of good will, and in parting from it made to his followers that touching request *"Pacem relinquo vobis, pacem meam do vobis."*

In what I have hereto said I had, Monseigneur, not the least intention to give lessons or suggestions to Your Lordship from whom, a humble disciple, I have only to accept documents of wisdom and perfection. I beg you therefore to take what I have written simply as an effusion of the heart, which without committing sin, may sometimes forget the strict rules of diplomacy. Nevertheless should there have slipped from my pen in the course of this letter any word or phrase capable of giving the least offense, I beg of Your Lordship to give it a charitable construction or consider it as not written at all, because I did not mean to give any "pinch" whatsoever.

201

Let us pray then to the Holy Ghost that he may direct our minds and our hearts to the ways of truth, charity and peace, in which I wish to live and to die.[14]

By this time, it had probably become evident to all concerned that the impasse in San Francisco would eventually find its way to the desks of Roman authorities both of the Jesuit order and of the Congregation de Propaganda Fide. It is not surprising, then, to find in the Roman archives of this latter congregation a four-page statement of the difficulties sent, on December 3, 1862, by Father General Peter Beckx to Barnabò. In effect, it is but a summation of what had transpired up to then with the hope expressed that a happy solution could be arrived at; however, it was not long before a determined Beckx was to write a number of strong letters to Propaganda in defense of the Jesuits in San Francisco.[15] But there were no indications that San Francisco's Archbishop was in a mood to yield his position, for on December 11, 1862, he took the highest possible ground when, in writing to Father Congiato, he remarked: "Rome is my mother and my law, and, no doubt, it is yours. I wrote there long ago . . . begging to be directed. When I am instructed, I will be happy to let you know. May almighty God direct us and assist us to do His Holy Will. Asking your prayers for me."[16] The Archbishop's letters concerning these matters for the year 1862 came to an end with a very frank expression of his views to Father Felix Sopranis, who had returned to Rome after seeing for himself the situation in San Francisco:

Your favor of the 10th of Sept. last reached me safely, and although I wished to reply to it, something or other would make me always

[14] Accolti to Alemany, Santa Clara College, October 29, 1862. Copy in ASJC.
[15] Beckx to Barnabò, Rome, December 3, 1862. APF. Beckx wrote as follows: "Father Villiger writes me concerning the seriousness of matters there. The Archbishop would be pleased, presumably, if we would leave the city. . . ."
[16] ASJC.

postpone it; while, I confess, that I considered I could not persuade you by writing.

I consider it the duty of the Ordinaries in the United States to have in their name the Churches that are parishes or proparishes. You consider the thing differently. But suppose the Holy See directs it as I view it; then there can be no harm either in my requiring it, or in your Fathers complying with it. Should there be any uncheerfulness in children to do their Mother's will? But I have many reasons to believe, that it is our common Mother's will to have such Churches vested in the bishop; therefore, it appears to me, I have no alternative.

Then, having heartily invited your Fathers to Santa Clara, that they might facilitate good solid Christian education, placed almost within the reach of all, and notwithstanding my having made over to them considerable property, yet very very few of my Catholic people can avail themselves of that, owing to the high, too high prices of the College; and I am forced to beg from door to door to make other provisions to have the young educated; and even this, I am told, meets with condemnation.

I invited your Fathers heartily to San Francisco with the express understanding that they should have a kind of free school, or nearly so; now, the way it is, I must have a free school with room for 400 boys (most of other Churches,) at the Cathedral under great expense; and St. Ignatius' issues its tickets of from $4.— to $8.— per month. I think, if St. Ignatius was in California, he would help the little bishop in another way, he might likely take the poor and leave the rich to the bishop. How is this difficulty to be obviated? By creating debts, which may never, or hardly ever, be liquidated?

I thought the Jesuit Fathers would cultivate a due regard for other Priests and other Churches; but I fear they, or some of them, forget that; and the way that they (many secular Priests, and I), were dealt with at last Synod savors too much of it. There are other Churches in this city besides St. Ignatius, and they are much in debt, and are entitled to the support of their respective faithful; if the Jesuit Fathers wish to ignore this, no written agreements can satisfy me.[17]

The stormy year of 1862 came to an end with a final letter from Beckx to Barnabò where, in an Italian four-page *relatio*, a careful statement of the position of the Society against Alemany's claims was made. The Jesuit general expressed sincere regrets

[17] Alemany to Sopranis, San Francisco, December 23, 1862. ASJC.

that a formerly friendly Archbishop seemed now to be arrayed in hostility against the Fathers of the Society in San Francisco. He likewise expressed the hope that peaceful solutions could be worked out successfully, and submitted several documents establishing the legitimacy of what the Society had been doing there.[18]

It will be recalled that in September, 1862, Alemany had served notice that, if the deeds to the St. Ignatius Church property (which he considered to belong to the diocese) were not forthcoming, he would find it necessary to change the parochial status of St. Ignatius. Since both Father Beckx in Rome and local Jesuit superiors had decided that they could not surrender such deeds without compromising a principle of their order which they considered fully protected by ecclesiastical law, it came about that, in the autumn of 1863, Alemany served notice as to his decision to remove this status from the Jesuits in San Francisco. Previously, he had asked the opinion of almost a dozen of his pastors and assistant priests in San Francisco as to what they thought concerning the "harmful" activities of the Jesuits there. First to reply was Father John F. Harrington, assistant pastor at the cathedral, who on June 30, 1863, emphatically stated that he thought that the manner in which the Jesuits on Market Street were diverting other persons from attendance at their parish churches was, indeed, a subject of scandal. This was being done, he said, by encouraging them to join the sodalities of St. Ignatius Church and by a multitude of other methods at all of which, it appeared, the Jesuits were quite adept. After a three-page statement, Father Harrington concluded by stating that he felt that he had spoken freely "what . . . I consider to be the truth before God."[19] Next to reply was Father Peter Grey, pioneer pastor of St. Patrick's Church; since his parish immediately adjoined that of St. Ignatius, his reply was of especial significance. Father Grey opined that "a fourth or more of my

[18] Beckx to Barnabò, Rome, December 24, 1862. APF.
[19] John F. Harrington to Alemany, San Francisco, June 30, 1863. Alemany forwarded the original of the letters here quoted to Barnabò in Rome. APF.

parishioners attend St. Ignatius Church—and these do not contribute to the support of their proper parish." The sodality he considered to be a principal means to draw people to the Jesuit church, and "public blessings and consecrations of old, young and babies . . . contributes much to draw the excitable [sic] of other parishes in that direction."[20]

Father Hugh Gallagher, who certainly was among the most distinguished of the diocesan priests of this era, wrote to Alemany in his capacity as parish priest of St. Joseph's Parish, which was also adjacent to St. Ignatius. A detailed answer based upon a careful investigation made by Father Gallagher had revealed that of 150 unmarried men working at a nearby sugar refinery, two-thirds of those who heard Mass each Sunday did so at St. Ignatius Church, as many were members of the sodality there and had been instructed that they should be in regular attendance at the Market Street church in order to gain indulgences, etc. Father Gallagher had also checked the Hayes Valley part of his parish with about the same result: underlying his report was the obvious perplexity as to how he could run his parish if this condition be allowed to continue.[21]

In an even more dramatic manner, Father Michael King, assistant pastor at St. Patrick's and later on to become famous as a long-term pastor of St. Mary's Church in Oakland, answered Alemany's inquiries. "My observations," he wrote, "justify me in stating that Sodalists, from the moment that they are received into the Sodality, ignore all relations with their own pastors. . . ." He next complains of "constant visits to non-Sodalists—especially to the wealthy families—a certain Rev. Father, well versed in the most approved system of praising the babies and of ingratiating himself in parental favor in a thousand harmless ways, runs through this parish every week asking the ladies where they were at Mass on Sunday, giving them an abstract of his last sermon and expressing the hope that they or their husbands

[20] Peter J. Grey to Alemany, San Francisco, July 14, 1863. APF.
[21] Hugh Gallagher to Alemany. August 24 and 28, 1862. APF.

will be present at his next discourse which is to be on a very important subject seldom treated, etc." Father King also commented on the constant "blessing of babies at St. Ignatius Church and the searching after the unblessed little ones," while reserving his especial scorn for the lavish distribution of the "St. Ignatius Water—this liquid lately become a beverage, in fact superceding [sic] the Napa Soda Water and the various 'nostrums' guaranteed for the infallible cure of all the maladies of human nature." His conclusion is rather firmly stated: "My Lord, I beg leave to state that, it is my firm conviction that the element of meanness predominates in the means used by the Reverend Fathers to 'fill up' their vast hall and alianate [sic] the Catholics of this city from their respective churches and pastors...."[22]

Father Thomas Cian, a Chinese priest brought to California by Alemany to care for his countrymen, was serving as a curate at St. Francis Church when he wrote to Alemany. He was cautious in his comments, noting that "there were many things told concerning the Fathers of St. Ignatius Church but only a few positive facts were taken place [sic] which I am acquainted with as follow"—and he then confirms the general picture regarding the sodality activities conflicting with parish attendance, etc. He ends by asking Alemany's direction as to what he shall tell his penitents when they inquire, as they frequently do, concerning the matter of Mass attendance at their parish church or at St. Ignatius Church.[23] From Stockton, a priest with former experience in San Francisco, Father James Motter, wrote that he was completely convinced that the activities of the Market Street Jesuits had served to demoralize, in part, the ordinary parish workings in San Francisco; he suspects that the unusual religious ceremonies provided there, while good in themselves, have had more of a sentimental effect upon many Catholics who find them only at St. Ignatius Church: "It is known that inuendoes fre-

22 Michael King to Alemany, San Francisco, August 27, 1863. APF.
23 Thomas Cian to Alemany, San Francisco, August 28, 1863. APF.

quently leak out (on such occasions as the frequent visits of the Fathers to the house of the faithful) concerning the jealousy from bishops and priests who are always proclaimed to mean well but to know not what they do."[24] Father Sebastian Wolf, pastor of St. Boniface Church in San Francisco, was less conscious of the difficulties referred to above by his clerical confreres; he simply wrote that, "while able to state that some of my people went to St. Ignatius Church, I am unable to testify whether they did so at the personal invitation of the Fathers."[25]

Father James Cotter, pastor of St. Francis Church, is forthright in asserting that the "policy of the Reverend Fathers of St. Ignatius Church . . . has subverted that order which should exist in the parishes of San Francisco. . . . they . . . should respect the rights of other pastors. Now this, in general, has not been done. . . . the more one considers the matter, the more evident does it appear that the policy of the Jesuits as it now manifests itself is detrimental to the welfare of religion in this city, because it is not in order. . . ."[26] Another priest who is outstandingly worthy in the list of those who served the archdiocese at this time was Father John Prendergast who, later on, several times was to refuse the mitre as coadjutor to Archbishop Alemany; writing from Volcano, Amador County, where he had gone for a few days, he expressed the view that "I have heard much but know nothing from my own experience, as I have not had much time nor many opportunities to observe; however, I am inclined to think that the members of the Sodalities were either lead into error or left in error regarding the conditions necessary on their part to gain certain indulgences."[27]

An important answer was bound to be given by Father James Croke, at that time rector of St. Mary's Cathedral and serving

[24] James Motter to Alemany, Stockton, California, September 1, 1863. APF.

[25] Sebastian Wolf to Alemany, San Francisco, September 2, 1863. APF.

[26] James Cotter to Alemany, San Francisco, September 2, 1863. APF.

[27] John Prendergast to Alemany, Volcano, California, September 7, 1863. APF.

as Alemany's vicar general; it was Father Croke who, in the opinion of certain of the Jesuits, was the spearhead of the "attack" against them as it was he, they said, who was responsible for exercising the most influence on Alemany's views in the whole matter. He answered Alemany at considerable length and, as might be expected, gave what he considered to be his "candid and impartial opinion of the course pursued by the Fathers of the Society of Jesus for the last few years." In a careful and complete review of what Croke considered to be the facts of the case, the Vicar General expressed his conviction that the Jesuits of St. Ignatius Church and College had, for whatever motives, succeeded in effectively disrupting the progress of the parishes in what was still pioneer San Francisco. He was convinced that they had succeeded in persuading many of the faithful that the "Jesuit Fathers alone are the only truly devoted and zealous priests—that the seculars have neither the talents nor opportunities nor education to govern parishes or cure souls, and that many of them are endeavoring to serve two masters, God and Mammon. They openly say that the secular priests have clubbed together to persecute the meek and humble Fathers who have nothing at heart but the glory of God and that the motive of this persecution is a mean jealousy at their superior success in the holy ministry and the general confidence and respect which their zeal and devotedness have inspired amongst the Catholics of San Francisco. . . ." By so doing, added Croke, they had derogated the respect due to the Ordinary of the diocese. "In conclusion, My Lord, allow me to state, as my calm and deliberate opinion—the result of experience and impartial observation—that the course pursued and being pursued by the Jesuit Fathers since the arrival of Fathers Villiger and Bushard, has been anything but conducive to the permanent good of religion, the salvation of souls and what their holy Founder St. Ignatius had so much at heart—the greater glory of God."[28]

[28] James Croke, V.G., to Alemany, San Francisco, September 17, 1863. APF.

No doubt, it was the overwhelming expression of such opinion that caused Archbishop Alemany to write to Father Congiato that while he "desired, with the blessing of our good God, to desire nothing but what be the will of the Holy See for the good order and administration of the diocese," he was far from satisfied with the conduct of the Fathers in connection with the sodalities and other activities of St. Ignatius Church; adding that "notwithstanding . . . I am willing to settle our affairs prudently and quietly, guided of course by any instructions that the Holy See may see fit to give. Let us all join in prayer that all may be well done for the good of religion and the interests of souls."[29] It could hardly have been unexpected then that, two weeks later, a formal letter of importance was dispatched by Alemany to Congiato:

It is now over twelve months since I notified the V. Rev. B. Villiger, Supr. S.J., that to comply with the wishes of the Church, the title of your Church here should be vested in me, and that if this was not done within twelve months from that date—the 10th of Sept./62,—I should declare your Church here to be no longer a Parish Church. Thus, to comply with my duty, I feel very sorry to notify you that within a few days I will make that declaration, as said title has not been conveyed to me.[30]

The next day saw Father Sopranis thus answering the Archbishop:

I acknowledge the receipt of the communication Your Grace was pleased to make yesterday to Fr. Congiato who is prevented by sickness from answering it himself.

As through the kindness of Your Grace, our St. Ignatius had been declared a Parish Church, we cannot have any objection that Your Grace be willing to declare the same church to be no longer a Parish Church.

This, be sure of it Most Rd. Abp., will neither diminish the esteem and the affection which we entertain for Your Grace, nor relax our zeal in cooperating to the spiritual welfare of your flock by the ministrations of our own Institute.[31]

29 Alemany to Congiato, San Francisco, September 9, 1863. ASJC.
30 Alemany to Congiato, San Francisco, September 24, 1863. ASJC.
31 Sopranis to Alemany, San Francisco, September 25, 1863. Copy in ASJC.

A week later Alemany sent a formal notice to Father Maraschi, pastor of St. Ignatius Church:

> As the decrees of Baltimore confirmed by the Holy See require that the Parochial Churches be vested in the Ordinary, and as after my long requesting your Regular Superiors to comply with that regulation of the Church in the case of St. Ignatius, they seem to feel that they should not do so, I believe that duty leaves me no alternative but to discontinue the character of your Church as a Parish, which I do hereby.
>
> To provide for the faithful, I have extended the limits of St. Patrick's from 4th Street to 6th: those of St. Joseph's from 7th to 6th: and those of the Cathedral from O'Farrell to Turk.[32]

Two days later, Sopranis wrote to Alemany to tell him of the submission which had been made very promptly to the latter's will in regard to removing parochial status from St. Ignatius Church. Mentioning that, upon his return to Rome, he would have to report completely concerning the matter both to Cardinal Barnabò and to Father Beckx, Sopranis wrote that he felt bound in duty to explain why the Jesuit order found it impossible to comply with the Archbishop's request that the deeds to their property in San Francisco be sent to him:

> This is therefore my statement: Our Father General not allowing us to invest your Grace with the title of our Church, has made use of the common right which is granted by the Holy See to all religious orders, which can possess property of their own. As our Churches are an essential part of our Colleges which we are authorized by the Holy See to possess as our own, Father General, I believe, wisely, thought that the Holy See would contradict itself if allowing us on the one hand to possess Colleges, she should on the other oblige us to dispossess ourselves of the same by vesting the Bishops with the title of

[32] Alemany to Anthony Maraschi, S.J., October 2, 1863. ASJC. On September 16, 1862, at a meeting of the "Committee on Parochial Boundaries" called by Alemany, the following boundaries had been assigned to St. Ignatius Parish: ". . . Beginning where Fourth St. runs into the Bay, along the Bay to Seventh or Harris [*sic*] St., along Seventh St. to Market St., crossing Market St. to McAlister [*sic*] St., along McAlister to the Ocean, along O'Farrell St. to Stockton St.—crossing Market St. to Fourth, along Fourth to Place of beginning."

our own property. He concluded, therefore, it not to be according to the will of the Holy See that the title which your Grace required from us should be given. And that Rev. Father General has been true in thinking so, it seems evidently proved also by this, that the Holy See allows those religious Orders who, according their institutes, are enable to have Parishes, to possess those Churches as their own; and therefore though the Ordinary has the right to visit them, his visit however is limited by ecclesiastical laws only to what concerns the Sacraments and parochial duties, but he cannot interfere with what concerns the property. And this is the reason, I think, by which the Holy See approving of the Decrees of the Council of Baltimore, with regard to the 5th Decree, made the observation:

In order that it may appear that, by this decree, the Bishops do not wish to injure in any way the Regular Orders, it might be added: "Preserving intact the privileges of the Regular Orders, according to whatsoever has been decreed in Canon Law and the Constitutions of the Roman Pontiffs." And, in accordance with such observation, the words—"The privileges of Regulars," etc. have been added to the 5th Decree. . . .

Our Father General therefore having considered all these things and regarding the 5th Decree of the Council of Baltimore as not affecting us, has deemed not only to be his right, but also to do according to the mind of the Holy See, not allowing us to invest your Grace with the title of our Church. And although on these principles he could perhaps have insisted upon your Grace not to withdraw from us the Parish, in view especially that the Holy See has temporarily enabled us to have Parishes—what we could not, according to our Institute— to supply the want of due foundation for the support of ours, he nevertheless would not. He has preferred that we should submit our-selves to the care of Divine Providence for our support rather than make any opposition to your Grace, to whom our Society is so much indebted for the true liberality with which your Grace has endowed Sta. Clara College.

I beg humbly of your Grace to accept these few words, as I have written them, in a friendly spirit, not to condemn in any way what your Grace has thought in his wisdom to be his duty to do, but only to show the truth of things, as it is in itself on our side.[33]

Joseph Riordan, Jesuit historian of the earlier epoch of his order's history in San Francisco, commenting on this letter of

[33] Sopranis to Alemany, San Francisco, October 2, 1863. Copy in ASJC.

Father Sopranis, expresses the opinion that the latter was firm but polite in presenting his reasons for the Society's course of action. In Riordan's opinion, "His Grace might, if so saw fit, take away the parish; from the reasons adduced for its taking away, the Fathers were at liberty to dissent." A pious note is added with his comment that "years have passed since . . . this question . . . was of any practical interest, and all those who have participated in it are united today in the peace and happiness of eternal bliss. . . . On November 3rd, pained at the failure of his mission, Father Sopranis set sail for New York on his way to Rome."[34]

Before winding up affairs in San Francisco, Sopranis composed a lengthy account of the entire matter which he sent on to Cardinal Barnabò. "The three key points which will have, eventually, to be settled by Rome," wrote Sopranis, "are as follows: 1. Is the Archbishop of San Francisco correct in his demand to have us turn over to him the title and deeds to our church property there? 2. Has a college of the Society been legitimately erected in San Francisco? 3. Are the Marian Sodalities erected in connection with this Church existing legitimately and according to Canon Law?"[35] In checking on the contents of this document, one comes to the conclusion that Sopranis did his work well—there are no impassioned charges of persecution (a note which one comes upon occasionally in Congiato's letters), but rather, a calm statement is given of the Society's case. However, Sopranis does state that, in his opinion, it was not Alemany so much as those who surrounded and advised him who were causing the present furor in San Francisco.

In a previous chapter we recorded a detailed account by Alemany concerning the state of his diocese in 1863. We might here extract from it a sentence relevant to the matter in hand:

[34] Riordan, *The First Half Century of St. Ignatius Church and College,* pp. 130–131.
[35] Sopranis to Barnabò, San Francisco, October 9, 1863. APF.

I have told the Jesuit Fathers here that I think I have jurisdiction over them since they were established here without the permission of the Holy See.[36]

Although, in the strictest sense, it might have been considered true that no explicit document could be produced by Jesuit superiors proving such a permission, it would seem, in retrospect, that this was a petty weapon to be wielded by that Alemany who, on August 23, 1853, had thus addressed himself to the president of the Society for the Propagation of the Faith:

The Fathers of the Society of Jesus have rendered and are rendering considerable service to our holy cause in the diocese, though they have not been many so far. But now it is contemplated to establish a good college to be conducted by said Fathers and others of the same Society that I expect from Europe, for which purpose I give the bearer, Very Rev. Fr. Accolti, Superior of the FF. of the Society here, letters to the General in Rome.

Therefore I cannot but recommend this great affair to the charity of the Society for the Propagation of the Faith, to which the establishing of such institutions is so essential.[37]

When one adds to the above evidence an entry of Alemany written two years later in his "Record of Episcopal Visitations," one is surprised, indeed, at the attitude he assumed when questioning the right of the Jesuits to exist in San Francisco. This important item reads as follows and would seem to indicate, that he had, himself, given permission to the Jesuit Fathers to establish themselves on Market Street in San Francisco:

July 15 (1855)
I bless the Church of St. Ignatius
in the city of San Francisco where the Fathers of
the Society of Jesus are given permission [*auctoritate
donantur*] to have a school and a college.[38]

[36] Alemany to Barnabò, San Francisco, October 29, 1863. APF.
[37] ASPF, Lyons, France. This letter was examined in the chancery office of the Diocese of Fribourg, Switzerland, where, during World War II, the records of the Lyons branch of the Society were brought for safekeeping. They were still there at the time of the author's visit in 1957.
[38] Alemany, "Chronicle of Episcopal Visitations." *AASF*.

Putting together these two statements, one reaches the conclusion that either Alemany had begun to worry too late about the legitimacy of the Jesuit order in San Francisco, or else that he had been made to reconsider the matter at the advice of some of his council who, it was evident, were irritated, not without reason, at the whole local posture of the Society of Jesus.

Father General Beckx was never remiss in his duty to keep Propaganda authorities informed: two letters, of November 25 and 27, 1863, told Barnabò of the latest state of the case.[39] Nor was this all, for under date of January 9, 1863, Beckx sent an extensive account of eleven pages reviewing the entire case from the first arrival of Alemany and the Jesuits in California. He asked that certain principles be clearly established and that they be applied to the case at hand. "Let us have a decision from Your Eminence," asks the General, "as to whether our Order is legitimately established in California; whether, in fact, it has no right to the title to its church in San Francisco because of the decrees of the Second Council of Baltimore and whether it has the right to aggregate its Sodalities with the 'Prima Primaria' Sodality in Rome. In effect," concluded Father Beckx, "we will get no place in this wearying and too long drawn out dispute until a clear answer is afforded to these key questions; failure to settle them will continue to harm the progress of religion in San Francisco."[40] Beckx then carefully proceeded to establish the

---

[39] Beckx to Barnabò. *APF.*

[40] Beckx to Barnabò. APF. Solid evidence that the Jesuit general was determined to allow no cause for further offense to be given to Alemany is furnished by a letter which Beckx wrote to Congiato from Rome, July 16, 1864. He praised the latter for acceding to Alemany's request that he administer confirmation in the nonparochial St. Ignatius Church on June 19, 1863. Beckx wrote: ". . . I think that Your Reverence has done well . . . it is always better, on these occasions, to show ourselves disposed to do all that we can to please. Surely, it would have been a matter of little edification to the faithful to have refused the request under pretext of safeguarding certain rights which do not seem to have been violated. Any such action would be viewed here with disapprobation. Right, strictly enforced in every detail, is always, on the one side and on the other, odious and does not help to conciliate hearts. . . ."

214

legitimacy of his Society's position in California. His main point was that the privileges of regulars were fully protected by the words of the Baltimore decree to the effect that nothing there mentioned should be construed as derogating any of the legitimately approved privileges of religious orders. "If these privileges be honored in other parts of the world, why not in San Francisco?" asked Father Beckx. Here, indeed, would appear to be the principal point, and it was because of this that Alemany eventually lost his case at Rome—although there was only an indirect method used to inform him of his original error.

No one can accuse the Jesuit order of not having represented its case fully, for again, on March 4, 1864, Father Sopranis addressed a fourteen-page statement of the case to Barnabò. That the matter was still prominent with both Archbishop Alemany and the Jesuit superiors in San Francisco is shown by a letter which on September 3, 1864, Alemany wrote to Father Congiato, in which it is evident that he had received no decision from Rome causing him to change his original convictions concernng all the issues at stake. Alemany had been considerably disturbed and irritated by reports that the members of his diocesan council were being blamed for all the opposition between the Archbishop and the Jesuits; then, too, there was Alemany's sensitivity in being represented as the prisoner of his council—that it had forced the issue in such a manner as to leave the Archbishop no alternative. His letter was a vigorous defense of his action in the entire matter:

> While the Son of God promised that the faith of Peter's Chair should never fail, the Prince of the Apostles did not deem it beneath his authority to have himself surrounded by the other Apostles in the Council of Jerusalem, and to determine with them what he might have decided alone. And if Christ's Vicars use a council with advantage, far more will this be useful to other inferior Prelates: at least so it was thought by the Bishops of the United States, when assembled in Council they determined that the Prelates should be exhorted to have Counsellors, where it may be practicable, whose advice they might

request in the administration of the diocese; and this determination was sanctioned by the Sovereign Pontiff. Of such Council the Bishop simply request[s] advice; but he alone is responsible for the final result; so that it is not easily conceived how any reasonable man can protest respect for his Bishop, and censure his advisers.

Regulars may be allowed by the Ordinary in case of necessity, and with permission from the Holy See, to have charge of Parishes: but the law in the United States is that the Parish Church be vested in the Ordinary. When therefore a case presents itself of whether a church building under the Regulars shall be a parochial Church or not; it is optional with them, either to vest the title in the Ordinary or to renounce the proffered parochial charge. But it is not optional with the Ordinary to entrust such a charge and to forego the required condition. And this is what is brought about at St. Ignatius in its actual relations to parochial functions. Twelve months were given to its Superiors to make the choice alluded to at the expiration of which their preferring the retention of the title in their name left no alternative to the Ordinary. And the choice on their part may better suit all parties, for religious persons free from multiplicity of duties consequent on a parochial charge, may devote themselves more easily to the primary and specific object of their religious Institute.

Should there still be any who may deem the above insufficient, I should only recommend him at present a more serious consideration of the divine commandment "Honor thy father and thy mother," and of the injunctions of St. Paul, "Obey your Prelates, and be subject to them" (Hebr. 13.17). Bishops, it is true, are neither impeccable nor infallible. If it should happen at any time, that a Clergyman finds himself aggrieved by them, he may appeal to a higher ecclesiastical tribunal, where his complaints will be weighed in the scales of perfect justice; but it is beneath the dignity of a Bishop to meet them in public discussion before the people.[41]

Troubles extending from San Francisco to Rome would, eventually, come to the attention of many other persons: among these was Bishop Modeste Demers of the Diocese of Vancouver Island, Canada, who, while visiting San Francisco in late 1864, reported to his Archbishop, Francis Norbert Blanchet of Oregon

[41] Alemany to Congiato, San Francisco, September 3, 1864. ASJC.

216

City, that the rift between Alemany and the Jesuits was "scandalous in the extreme." Demers' first opinion, modified a bit in a second letter six weeks later, was that the Jesuits were guilty of an almost complete lack of respect for Alemany's authority, and he was convinced that the "Holy Father will not fail to do justice to the holy archbishop of the diocese." "In all regards, though," concludes Demers, "the dispute is a regrettable one and charity," he suspected, "has been wounded on either side as almost always happens in long drawn out disputes of this sort."[42] These letters of Demers would seem to be the reason why Blanchet wrote to Alemany a few months later to inquire if any decision had in fact been forthcoming from Rome—for, he writes, word had come to him that such a decision, completely in defense of Alemany's position, had come from Rome.[43] Blanchet was mistaken, however.

Actually, not much was changed—if anything—in 1865; this is evident from still another report of Father General Beckx to Cardinal Barnabò which contained the reiterated hope that, soon, a decision would be reached and announced.[44] Another prelate who deplored what was happening in San Francisco was Bishop Thaddeus Amat of the Diocese of Monterey-Los Angeles. In a letter which he wrote to Barnabò from San Francisco on September 11, 1865, Amat told the Cardinal that he thought that the Church and its interests were being seriously hurt by the dispute—"*Religio tota ingemuit*" is the way he phrased it—and he asked the Cardinal to apply due remedies to bring such difficulties to an end.[45] Once again, Bishop Demers entered the picture with a similar letter addressed from Victoria to Barnabò; he stated that he had returned from a seven-month visit to Cali-

---

[42] Modeste Demers to Francis N. Blanchet. Two letters: December 26, 1864, San Francisco, and February 9, 1865, San Rafael, California. AAPO.
[43] Blanchet to Alemany, Portland, Oregon, June 8, 1865. AAPO.
[44] Beckx to Barnabò, Rome, November 15, 1865. APF.
[45] Thaddeus Amat to Barnabò. APF.

fornia where he had found a deplorable "schism" existing between Alemany and the Jesuits in San Francisco. While taking the occasion to launch into a full-scale discussion of his own difficulties with the Oblates in his territory, he took no sides in the San Francisco dispute, but expressed the prayerful hope that all would soon be settled satisfactorily.[46]

By this time, most of those concerned must have wondered when, if ever, Rome would issue a decision on what by now had become almost a *cause célèbre*. On March 3, 1866, the secretary of the Congregation addressed a discreetly worded letter to Alemany, cautioning him that careful examination should be made by him concerning the correct interpretation of the decrees of Baltimore with a "view to the protection of the rights of both sides."[47] One wonders here if this was intended as an oblique way of informing Alemany that such a reexamination of these decrees might convince him that he had been in error in their rigorous and literal application in the case of the Jesuit property in his see city.

Since the impasse was maintained, it is interesting to note that Beckx wrote a friendly letter in 1866 to Alemany. While beginning with the expressed hope that what he wrote would be properly understood, Beckx came to the point quickly by stating that the formerly friendly relationship between the Archbishop and the Jesuits in California seemed to have been seriously weakened amidst the present difficulties. He added that he had no intention of going into details well known to both sides, but that he wrote in sorrow as he reflected that Cardinal Barnabò's hopes for a peaceful solution had not been realized. Rather, recent reports from San Francisco had convinced the General that all was not well there. He felt the greater sorrow about all this

---

[46] Demers to Barnabò, Victoria, Vancouver Island, September 12, 1865. APF.

[47] Annibale Capalti to Alemany, Rome, March 3, 1866. Copy in APF.

when he reflected that Alemany himself was a member of a distinguished religious order and that he, certainly, was aware of what pressures were frequently exerted by various opponents of such orders. Beckx found it all lamentable and perplexing because he had heard and agreed that Alemany's many virtues entitled him to sincere respect. Finally, he implored the Archbishop most humbly to make of himself a cause of strength and comfort to the Jesuits who labored with him for God's glory in California.[48]

It was not until five months later that Alemany replied to this effort on the part of Beckx to reestablish a friendly relationship. Alemany said that the delay in replying was caused by the fact that he had been in Baltimore for some time (at the Second Plenary Council), but he was quick to add that he did not think that the General of the Jesuits understood some of the local happenings in San Franciso which caused him to be rather harsh in his attitude towards several of the Jesuit fathers who, in his opinion, had flaunted diocesan regulations. A frank paragraph followed in which Alemany admitted that he was "but a poor man who frequently falls into error—however, having considered my course of action here, I do not see how I could have acted otherwise." While professing that he wished to do nothing but the will of Christ's Vicar in these matters, he was generous enough to add his conviction that Father Beckx would gladly give his life to obey these same directives of the Holy See. "May Saints Ignatius and Dominic bring about a sweet solution of all," wrote the Dominican Archbishop to the Jesuit General. A pointed remark was phrased as follows: "If you were the Archbishop of San Francisco (an office which I must carry on my unworthy shoulders) you would, beyond doubt, see the necessity that exists of avoiding the occasions whereby religious, perhaps

[48] Beckx to Alemany, Rome, July 24, 1866. Copy in ASJC.

inspired by misplaced zeal, offer occasion of offense and com- plaints to parish priests."[49]

However friendly this interchange was intended to be, it does not seem to have changed the situation substantially. One wonders what portion of blame, if indeed any, should be laid at the doorstep of Roman authorities in their failure to issue some needed and clear-cut directives which presumably would have helped to solve the difficulties. A careful investigation of the documentary evidence in the archives of Propaganda Fide fails to reveal any such directives or decisions. Thus one is forced to wonder whether dilatory tactics (almost certainly deliberate in this case) were, in fact, the best solution here.

Archbishop Alemany went to Rome in the late spring of 1867, and while there he received a communication from Barnabò's secretary which told him that he was being sent "information and letters concerning the present state of affairs between you and the Society of Jesus in San Francisco. Please examine them as the Cardinal Prefect would like you to do."[50] It is practically certain that during this time Alemany had at least one conference with Cardinal Barnabò as well as one with Father Beckx. We can only conjecture, however, whether Alemany was the recipient of some instructions as to what his future course of action in the matters under dispute should be. One thing that is certain, though, is that a year later an interchange of letters between Alemany and Barnabò found the latter acknowledging a previous communication of July 27, 1868:

---

[49] Alemany to Beckx, San Francisco, December 28, 1866. ASJR. That Archbishop Alemany had attained a certain stature by the time of the Second Plenary Council of Baltimore, which he attended in 1866, is shown by a letter of Bernard Chocarne, O.P., to Father Master General Jandel in Rome from Baltimore, on October 19, 1866, Chocarne wrote that "The Order of St. Dominic is represented by Bishop Grace of St. Paul but especially by Monseigneur Alemany who enjoys among his colleagues a very exalted reputation for zeal. He is truly a saint, and I rejoice to have known him. . . ." AOP.

[50] Capalti to Alemany, Rome, July 3, 1867. Copy in APF.

220

I have received Your Reverence's letter, from which I have been enabled to understand thoroughly all the matters which, even now, are obstacles and concerning which I have been given much information from others.

The Sacred Congregation, having considered all these things, has issued an "Instruction" which, I trust, will be communicated to you by the Archbishop of Baltimore when he writes to you on the subject.[51]

Quite naturally, one who investigates these matters is further disappointed when neither the San Francisco Archdiocese archives nor those of Baltimore yield anything here which would enable one to say exactly what transpired in this important matter. However, two revealing letters of Father James Croke, Alemany's vicar general, are extant, and at least in an indirect manner their assertions would seem to justify the conclusion that Alemany had actually lost his case at Rome.

On March 10, 1868, Father Croke left San Francisco on board the *Constitution* en route to Europe via Panama; according to the *Monitor*, he departed "for Europe to recruit his health."[52] Perhaps this was so, but it seems that this was not the only reason: his later letters reveal that he was also sent to Rome by Alemany to discuss the not yet resolved issues between the Archbishop and the Jesuits. Concerning these issues, we are fortunate to have two long and very frank letters from Croke to Alemany which tell us much of what had transpired in Rome on the occasion of his visit there. Unfortunately—although this is not a crippling omission—the first page of the first of these two letters, with the date of its composition, is missing from what is otherwise a most legible and informative letter. In it, Croke tells how he had paid a visit to Cardinal Barnabò and had been closeted with him for some time discussing the conflicts in San Francisco. Barnabò mentioned the continued complaints of Jesuit superiors in Rome and in California, adding that, during Alemany's last visit, the Cardinal thought that all had been arranged amicably,

[51] Barnabò to Alemany, Rome, September 1, 1868. Copy in APF.
[52] San Francisco *Monitor*, March 14, 1868.

whereas the difficulties still continued. Barnabò considered the matters of sufficient importance to schedule another and longer meeting with Croke, during which he exposed at great length the various aspects of the situation as they had reached his desk. The Vicar General wrote:

> . . . The Cardinal dwelt a great deal on the good the Jesuits were doing in the Diocese—the danger of their leaving unless they were treated fairly. He seemed to imply that the parish was taken from them without cause, that some few priests in the neighborhood of the Jesuits were jealous of the great crowds which attended the church— that, although he would ultimately be obliged to settle all these matters, he would not wish to command Your Grace because of the friendship and great respect he bore you.[53]

Croke next commented on the genuine friendliness exhibited by Barnabò who, after hearing his views, remarked that he did not, at the moment, have all the papers at hand which he would need for quotation, and suggested that Croke visit Father Beckx and there enter into an equally frank discussion. Then, Barnabò added, he would expect a return visit from him. Accordingly, the meeting with the Jesuit Father General soon took place, and Croke found Beckx "most amiable and seeming most anxious to settle all things to Your Grace's satisfaction."[54] Croke told Alemany how he had given a long account of the reasons why opposition to Jesuit policies and to several Jesuits personally had marked Alemany's rule in San Francisco in the past few years; as a result of Croke's assertion, Beckx sent for Father Sopranis, the official visitor to San Francisco in 1861. Croke mentioned that he found Sopranis harder to deal with than Beckx, for Sopranis supported "with great warmth" the policies of his Society in San Francisco.

Despite the warmth of Sopranis's rebuttal, Croke was able to assure Alemany that, in the main, their discussions were con-

[53] AASF.
[54] Croke to Alemany, undated. AASF.

ducted on a friendly basis. He was pleased to add that Beckx, while listening intently to the Sopranis statements, did not seem to agree with all of them. This led Croke to say that he thought that Beckx did not know much about all the many circumstances involved, but was dependent entirely upon letters received from San Francisco. The overwhelming wish of the Jesuit General, according to Croke, was to see all the matters brought to a just settlement. After assuring Alemany that he had insisted both with Barnabò and with Beckx that he was not authorized to "interfere" in these delicate matters, Croke mentioned that he was soon to leave Rome for Ireland—but not before having re-visited both Barnabò and Beckx. Implicit is the idea that he would report later on by letter as to these two important visits. He expected to leave Rome by November 6 and to sail for New York about January 1. After then discussing the rumors he had heard in Rome concerning Alemany's possible resignation, Croke brought his letter to an end.

Father Croke's second letter, equally if not more informative than the first, was written in Doneraile, County Cork, Ireland. His purpose was not only to visit relations there, but also to rest after what had turned out to be an exhausting visit to Rome. As he indicated, his letter was written after "many" interviews with Barnabò and Beckx, for the matters had required more than several meetings. Dated December 22, 1868, the letter found Croke telling Alemany that, in fact, he had been detained in Rome much longer than he expected because of these many con-ferences. Since a number of the meetings had been without notable result, Croke had thought it better to wait until the present moment to sum up everything for the Archbishop. A key comment of Barnabò was reported in the first part of this letter:

Having once had pastoral charge, the Jesuits ought not to have been deprived of it in San Francisco—so His Eminence seems to think. If this had been done solely because they refused to vest the church and lot in the Ordinary—he thinks that the decrees of Baltimore do not

223

apply to regulars whose rights are guaranteed by the phrase—*"salvis juribus regularium."* He further said that, as the case was appealed to the Holy See, he would ultimately be obliged to settle it in favor of the Jesuits and that he was on the point of bringing the question to a close—but, in consideration of the respect he bore Your Grace, he would much prefer to have the matter settled by mutual concessions and negotiations, for it would give him great pain to be obliged to interfere as Judge and give a decision which would not be in accordance with Your Grace's wishes.[55]

Croke went on to assure Alemany that he had endeavored to answer all of Barnabò's assertions as they would have been answered by Alemany himself, but he reports that the net result was that Barnabò had ordered him to return to Father Beckx in a continued endeavor to find peaceful solution to the difficulties. Again, and this after several visits to Beckx, he was able to report that he had found the Jesuit General "on all occasions extremely kind and tractable and anxious to have the difficulty settled."[56] Out of these visits came a paper which Croke forwarded to Alemany and which contained some general statements of principles that, it was hoped, would help resolve the problems. "From what I have learned in Rome," warns Croke, "I believe that the two questions [viz., that involving parochial rights, and that concerning the legitimacy of the Jesuit Sodality in San Francisco, which had been questioned by Alemany] will be decided in their favor."[57] Croke was interested to find out from the cardinal that he, together with other diocesan priests, had been reported to Rome because of their unfriendly attitude towards the Jesuits,

[55] Croke to Alemany, Doneraile, County Cork, Ireland, December 22, 1868. AASF. One exception to this lack of correspondence is to be found in a letter of Alemany to Barnabò from San Francisco under date of June 4, 1869. APF. In it he refers to the fact that he had recently received a document from the Jesuit father general entitled "Pro Memoria," in which he was assured that the general "was content to leave all our matters to the prudent decision of Your Eminence. In my reply, I expressed myself as quite content to follow the same course, etc."
[56] *Ibid.*
[57] *Ibid.*

and this caused him to add that, in his opinion, "all that I have heard leads me to believe that the Fathers in San Francisco have not been overscrupulous in the reports which they forwarded to headquarters in which "they have lauded themselves as the chief pillars of the Church in California and the head and center of all piety—in fact, as the sole founder of the Church!"[58]

Although he feared that it would cause anguish to Alemany, Croke wrote that he found it necessary to report that he had learned that the Archbishop had been accused of anti-Jesuit attitudes stemming from his membership in the Dominican order! A candid comment which indicates that Croke had been more than a little uneasy in the interviews and negotiations is found in these lines:

> I fear that I have tired Your Lordship with these long details, but I thought it my duty to give you a sketch of the work in which I have been engaged in Rome. I had no idea of getting into such a mess and feel very happy to have escaped without suspension. Had I any idea of being overhauled I would have kept away from the Cardinal's premises and preserved a strict incognito during my stay in the Eternal City. However, it is probably better that I was dragged into the business as I think I have removed some false impressions and perhaps smoothed the way for a final adjustment of the difficulty.[59]

In a more relaxed vein, Father Croke finished his account by mentioning that a letter furnished him by the always cordial Barnabò had enabled him to have an audience with the Holy Father, Pius IX, who had received him "with his usual kindness" and who, after inquiring particularly for Alemany, had sent him a special blessing. Mentioning several favors granted by the Pope concerning privileged altars, etc., Croke reported finally that Pius had given him leave to "hear Confessions and say Mass at sea and had sent a wig to the pastor of Napa!"[60]

With these candid letters of Alemany's Vicar General, which

[58] *Ibid.*
[59] *Ibid.*
[60] *Ibid.*

must suffice in the lack of more precise documentary evidence, we here bring to conclusion this account of a lengthy and detailed controversy between persons equally convinced of their rights. Viewing the matter from the negative criterion of the almost total absence of letters in the Propaganda files, it would seem that a period of peace set in and presumably was enjoyed by both sides during 1869. It would be pleasant to be able to record that, henceforth, the relations between Archbishop Alemany and the Jesuits of San Francisco were completely friendly, but unfortunately such was not to be the case. Actually, the respite was hardly more than a lull between storms, for, in 1870, other issues split whatever precarious unity and concord had been earlier obtained.

10

Middle Years in San Francisco, 1863–1875

THE San Francisco of the 1860's and 1870's was much different from that seaport where Bishop Alemany had landed on December 7, 1850. The United States Census of 1850 had fixed California's population at 92,597, but, probably because of the continual flux in Gold Rush San Francisco, this figure does not include the actual number of people in the city itself. (While an attempt had been made to take a census there around this time, the results remain a mystery, for the totals were destroyed in one of the many fires which plagued San Francisco at this time.) Another attempt at a census was made in 1852 and San Francisco was credited with 36,751 inhabitants. By 1860, this figure had risen to 56,802 which, while representing a significant increase, could hardly be called spectacular. However, the next decade saw the number of people triple, for in 1870 almost 150,000 were accounted for in San Francisco itself. Obviously, this tripling of population brought the usual problems of growth to Archbishop Alemany.[1]

Pioneer San Francisco had finished the decade of the 1850's with the last duel (officially, at least) to be fought within its limits (or, better, just beyond them in San Mateo County) when, on September 13, 1859, Senator David C. Broderick was mortally wounded by Chief Justice David S. Terry of the State Supreme Court on the "field of honor." Nor did the city sleep

[1] San Francisco in 1964 had a population of 800,000.

quietly all through the sixties, for on Wednesday, October 21, 1868, it was visited by a very severe earthquake which was more intense than an earlier one of 1865. It was the most serious thus far recorded, and the rather light loss of life (five persons) is attributable to the fact that it came just before eight A.M.— when schools and office buildings were not yet in use. Bishop O'Connell's brother, Patrick, a merchant of Oakland, thus reported to the president of All Hallows College, Father William Fortune, concerning the event:

> I presume you know all about our great earthquake of 21st Oct. Your humble servant was in this great city "at the Bay" when it occurred and shall never forget the sensation . . . oh, what a period of time seemed compressed into that moment . . . poor mortal man is never made to feel his own nothingness so thoroughly as during an earthquake—the grasp of the Infinite seems upon him—if anything could make one wish for an earthquake, it were to see our self-sufficient philosophers and intellectual giants of the present day brought under such fire. The noise which preceded and accompanied the shocks was certainly unearthly.[2]

Another important date in the late 1860's is May 10, 1869, which marked the completion of the transcontinental railroad with the meeting of the Union and Central Pacific lines at Promontory, Utah. This significant event brought added importance, of course, to Alemany's see city, and throughout this colorful decade this and other events made of San Francisco a sort of "Silver City," especially when the riches of the Comstock Lode in Nevada were reflected in the plush residences of the wealthiest of the city's people on Nob Hill. (Local historians sometimes refer to these years as San Francisco's "Bonanza Age.") In 1873, the invention of the famed cable car in San Francisco served to open hilly areas of the city to the expanding population, and this caused Archbishop Alemany to think of increasing the number of parishes in the city. Some few final figures will illustrate

[2] San Francisco, December 13, 1868. AAHC.

both the growth and the problems facing Alemany during these years: in 1859, Alemany had estimated the total number of Catholics in his entire archdiocese at 87,000—eight years later, there were 50,000 in his see city alone, while in 1875, at the time of his silver jubilee as a bishop in California, the number of Catholics in the entire archdiocese had reached 200,000.

An interesting matter which will recur in these pages from now on will be the unsuccessful attempts made by Alemany to resign his see. When he finally was allowed to retire (which was not until the end of 1884), he remarked publicly, "I had never thought that I was born to be a Bishop and I had told Pius IX so—but," he added, "nevertheless, they made me a Bishop!" That these were more than mere words is evident by his not infrequent requests to be allowed to deposit the episcopal burden in order to devote himself to the simple work of a missionary in a remote part of California, or, better still, to be allowed to advance a grand design which he cherished for years for the establishment of a missionary college in Spain to train laborers for present or former Spanish-speaking countries, especially to supplement the apostolic workers in California itself.

In September, 1864, Alemany wrote to the newly chosen Archbishop Martin J. Spalding of Baltimore to congratulate him on his appointment. The following lines concerning himself are found in this letter:

> When I am out of place, see that I be succeeded by a man of apostolic zeal, of sound judgment and of ability to manage temporal business. (Entre-nous: Bishop O'Connell is a learned man and a very holy man, but rather limited in temporal administration: Bishop Amat, I fear very much, has not prudence enough.) I have, thank God, a most promising priest, Rev. John Prendergast, but I would feel obliged, at your leisure, if you would suggest me some good names that I might leave behind should death pay me the same sort of visit paid Archbp. Kenrick, as I suffer sometimes from Asthmatic suffocation.[3]

[3] Alemany to Martin J. Spalding, San Francisco, September 4, 1864. AAB.

In late December of the same year, Alemany wrote to Cardinal Barnabò to apologize for his neglect in not submitting a list of priests he judged worthy of the mitre which, according to an instruction of 1861, each American bishop was to send to Rome every three years. He named four priests, three of his own diocese, Fathers Prendergast, Lootens, and Croke, and one of Baltimore, Father Thomas Foley, who was eventually to become the first rector of the Catholic University of America. He carefully analyzed the qualities of each as he knew them; his high praise of Prendergast was notable, while he mentioned, concerning Croke, that there might be cause for concern in the fact that he was inclined to be quite stubborn at times![4] (That this did not automatically disqualify a man from the mitre would seem apparent from Alemany's own career, for he freely owned to the same quality himself.) However, this firmness, the absence of which would have made of him a mere will-of-the-wisp, was occasionally manifested by Alemany in a manner which demands admiration. Thus, for example, when a misunderstanding arose concerning a matter of the supposed refusal of Christian burial to a certain Michael Prefumo, the Archbishop addressed a vigorous letter to the San Francisco *Evening Bulletin* in which he explained the case and related it to the discipline of his Church which, he remarked, is "not a political institution—her Father is God, her birthplace is Heaven, her dwelling place an indestructible rock, her grave shall never be found . . . would to God that her few undutiful children would understand the constitution of her heart!"[5]

In the early months of 1864, Father Herbert Vaughan, future cardinal archbishop of Westminster, was in California on a begging tour for a missionary society which he had founded in England. His penetrating eye took in much, and the literature of this earlier American period of California Catholicism was

---

[4] Alemany to Barnabò, San Francisco, December 26, 1864. APF.
[5] Alemany to editor, San Francisco *Evening Bulletin,* November 18, 1865.

substantially enriched by an article which he published in the *Dublin Review* (January, 1866) and which merited an early reprinting in the *Catholic World*, published in New York. His impressions of Archbishop Alemany should certainly find place here:

We have now to notice the direct action of the archbishop and of the clergy upon the population. The bishop is *"forma gregis facta ex animo,"* "the city on the hill," "the candle placed high upon the candlestick," giving its light around; and on each prelate bestows what gifts he pleases. With these he illumines the world in the person of his minister.

Go, then, up California street, turn round the cathedral of St. Mary's, and you will enter a miserable, dingy little house. This is the residence of the Archbishop of San Francisco and his clergy, who live with him in community. To the left are a number of little yards, and the back windows of the houses in which the Chinamen are swarming. Broken pots and pans, old doors, and a yellow compost, window-frames, fagots, remnants of used fireworks, sides of pig glazed and varnished, long strings of meat—God only knows *what* meat—hanging to dry, dog-kennels, dead cats, dirty linen in heaps, and white linen and blue cottons drying on lines or lying on rubbish—such is the view to the left. The odors which exhale from it who shall describe? A spark would probably set the whole of these premises in a conflagration; and one is tempted to think that even a fire would be a blessing. To the right, adjoining the cathedral, is the yard where the Catholic boys come out to play; and in this yard stands a little iron or zinc cottage, containing two rooms. This is where the archbishop lives; one is his bedroom, the other his office, where his secretaries are at work all day. No man is more poorly lodged in the whole city; and no man preaches the spirit of evangelical poverty, a detachment in the midst of this money-worshipping city, like this Dominican Spanish Archbishop of San Francisco. From ten in the morning to one P.M. every day, and for two or three hours every evening, His Grace, arrayed in his common white habit, and with his green cord and pectoral cross, receives all who come to consult him, to beg of him, to converse with him, be they who they may—emigrants, servants, merchants, the afflicted, the ruined, the unfortunate. The example of such a life of disinterested zeal, holy simplicity, and poverty has told upon the inhabitants of San

231

Francisco with an irresistible power. It has been one of the Catholic influences exercised by the Church on the population.[6]

In early April, 1866, Archbishop Alemany sought permission from Cardinal Barnabò to absent himself from his archdiocese to attend the national council to be held in Baltimore. In the same letter, he requested the services of a priest to work among the German-speaking peoples of San Francisco. He likewise repeated how desirous he was of procuring some Christian Brothers to further the work of education among the children, writing that, so far, he had asked in vain but that he still hoped for success in the matter. Finally, he asked the Cardinal Prefect's counsel as to whether he should go on to Europe from Baltimore, after the national council, to "discuss with you and with the Holy Father the problems which I face here."[7]

It is hardly surprising that a man of such marked devotion to the Holy See as Archbishop Alemany should keep his people informed as to the travails which Pius IX was undergoing at this time. In a pastoral letter addressed to his flock on Ash Wednesday, 1867, Alemany deplored the lack of respect shown Pope Pius IX by those who would deprive him of his temporal power, stating that "it is to be regretted that some of those who constituted themselves as doctors of the Law take pleasure in traducing the Papacy as an obsolete or expiring institution, the funeral of which they have insultingly announced. . . ."[8] Ad-

[6] "California and the Church," in *Catholic World*, II (March, 1866), pp. 808–809. This is a reprint of Vaughan's article from the Dublin *Review*.
[7] Alemany to Barnabò, San Francisco, April 6, 1866. APF. Dublin *Review*, VII, New Series, January 1866, pp. 1–35.
[8] Alemany sent an English copy of this pastoral letter to Barnabò, AAF. In this same spring of 1867, a pastoral visit which Alemany made to administer confirmation in St. Anne's Church, Columbia, caused a correspondent there to send the following bucolic account to the *Monitor*: "Here, in a temple dedicated to the Most High, on the golden soil of Tuolumne where, not thirty years ago, the murderous war whoop of the savage Indian was heard from neighboring ravines, the representatives of most of the civilized races of the earth met in unity and love—united by the bond of the pure faith. Kneeling side by side in fervent prayer, we could distinguish

mittedly, in the light of subsequent history, some of Alemany's arguments for the preservation of the temporal power of the papacy might seem quite vulnerable; however, there can be no doubt as to his sincerity in presenting to his people what amounted to the traditional defense of the Holy See's usurped rights in this regard.

On May 4, 1867, the San Francisco *Monitor* announced that Archbishop Alemany would soon leave for Ireland where he would endeavor to "recruit more priests and brothers to work with him for souls in California"; he would then, it added, go on to Rome to attend some canonizations and for other matters. By the end of June, Alemany was a guest in Rome at the Dominican hospice connected with that convent and Church of the Minerva which he knew so well from his earlier residence there. Uppermost in his mind was to obtain some sort of sanction from the highest authority for his plan to establish a missionary college in Spain to help on the work of the Church in California. Therefore, on June 30, 1867, he sent a letter to Cardinal Barnabò asking him to help him to bring to the personal attention of Pius IX a letter of the same date in which he outlined his project. He envisioned it as a college of Dominicans of regular observance, to be established in Spain under his direction, from which would come forth zealous missionaries to work in the Spanish American colonies—"Cuba, Mexico, Peru and New Granada."[9] There is no explicit mention in this petition of his California needs, and it is possible that, by this time, he had decided to rely upon Ireland for diocesan priests, as well as to build up future priests in the customary ways by providing

the fair-headed German, the swart Mexican, the stately Spaniard and the dark Italian while the generous and ardent Celt mingled his devotion with the native born citizens.

"After the first Gospel, on administering the Sacrament, His Grace delivered an impressive discourse as he addressed himself to the participants in language so touching and eloquently simple, for which His Grace is so eminently distinguished." March 2, 1867.

[9] Alemany to Pius IX. APF.

seminaries for them. Despite repeated attempts, which were to be continued even through his years of retirement in Spain, Alemany was not to see the fruition of his project, however laudable it appears to have been.

Archbishop Alemany finished his visit to Rome by middle August, for on the eighteenth of that month, he wrote as follows to Cardinal Barnabò from Queenstown, Ireland, where he was embarking for home:

> I am leaving here tomorrow for California by way of New York and I am sending you my report i.e. re my diocese as you permitted me to do during my stay in Rome.[10]

Highlights of this interesting report included his mention that he had found it necessary to suspend operation of his diocesan seminary for lack of students, adding that he had twenty in all studying at Santa Clara College as well as at All Hallows' and Carlow in Ireland, Einsiedeln in Switzerland, and the American College in Rome. He had twenty-nine diocesan priests who cared for the twenty-six parishes of his large diocese, and one detects a note of legitimate pride with his mention that the number of Catholic schools had risen to thirty, with about 5600 children enrolled. There were thirty Jesuits and twenty Dominicans at work in his territory; while both groups, as he remarked, *"gaudent bona fama"*—that is, enjoy good reputations—he was convinced that the Jesuits, in their two institutions in San Francisco and at Santa Clara, charged too much tuition. This is why, he added, he wanted to bring the Christian Brothers to his diocese to remedy this situation with the foundation of a school with lower tuition rates. His explicit words with regard to the Jesuits were as follows:

> For the good of souls and increase of religion, the Jesuit Fathers preach, hear confessions and teach the youth who attend their colleges

10 APF.

234

—but I fear that they keep many away from these colleges because they charge too much tuition.[11]

As on the previous Ash Wednesday, Alemany addressed another pastoral to his people on the same day in 1868. Saying that "it is with mingled feelings of pleasure and grief that we have received another encyclical letter from our Sovereign Pontiff," the Archbishop again stated the case for papal claims in the temporal realm, while recalling that, despite their temporary setbacks through the mercy of God, "the enemies of the Church are neither dead nor asleep."[12]

By the middle of 1868, the Catholic bishops of the world had been informed of the forthcoming ecumenical council to be convened in the Vatican in December of 1869. The preparations for it were many, of course, and this will explain a letter of Alemany to Spalding of Baltimore asking him to act for the former in obtaining "an able Divine or canonist for Rome to aid in preparing for the Great Council." A frank note appears in the following lines: "I do not know our clergy in the East and those of our Great West are too young or to be born yet."[13] As events proved, San Francisco's Archbishop was to play an important role in the deliberations which occupied the conciliar fathers at the historic Vatican Council.

Rather frequent correspondence with the authorities of Dublin's All Hallows College during these years reveals that

[11] *Ibid.* It is interesting to note that Alemany makes no reference at all in this report to the current controversy between himself and the Jesuit Order in San Francisco. This is perhaps best understood by the fact that he had just left Rome where he had discussed the matter thoroughly with the authorities.

[12] This pastoral, published in the *Monitor* on March 7, 1868, also appeared in the New York *Freeman's Journal*, April 11, 1868. It caused the following editorial comment in a Presbyterian paper of San Francisco, the *Occident*, March 14, 1868: "Archbishop Alemany has issued his Pastoral Letter, the spirit of which is worthy of commendation. Of course, a Catholic prelate could hardly publish a document of this kind that would be free from sentiments to which Protestants must object, but it is always pleasant to find a spirit manifested that we can honor. . . ."

[13] Alemany to Spalding, San Francisco, July 4, 1868. AAB.

Alemany was always interested in obtaining zealous young priests for the service of the Church in California. Thus, for example, in 1868 he wrote to the president, Father William Fortune, of his happiness at receiving news that seven priests had recently been ordained at All Hallows for such service. "They will be a great help. As our people is [*sic*] always on the increase, particularly in cities and in farming lands, I requested you in my last letter to keep always a good number—say twelve—of good, steady, pious, zealous and talented young students for the diocese."[14] The same letter referred to a significant milestone in Alemany's episcopate when, on Sunday, August 9, 1868, he had elevated Father Lootens to episcopal dignity.

> Last Sunday we had the consolation to have a new Bishop (Rt. Rev. Louis Lootens) consecrated at our Cathedral, Bp. Amat and Bp. O'Connell assisting me in the great ceremony which gave great joy to the immense concourse of people. Yesterday arrived also a nice colony of Christian Brothers to aid us in giving Christian education to our numerous boys.[15]

The always persistent Alemany seemed determined at this time not to let Rome forget his desires in the matter of the missionary college in Spain. Again he dispatched a letter to Cardinal Barnabò explaining the matter and adding:

> Last year, I asked the Holy Father to allow me to resign so that I might devote my time to the founding of several Dominican colleges in Spain of regular observance, common life, etc.—with the intention of preparing missionaries for those parts of America which need them badly. The Holy Father seemed to approve, but indicated that he wished to delay the matter for awhile. You then suggested a Coadjutor rather than my resignation. After prayer, etc., I hereby submit the names of three priests I think worthy of episcopal dignity as my Coadjutor. [He then gave information concerning Father John Prendergast previously mentioned, while adding the names of two Irish priests, Father Bartholomew Woodlock of the Catholic University, Dublin,

14 Alemany to Fortune, San Francisco, August 11, 1868. AAHC.
15 *Ibid.*

236

and Father William Fortune of All Hallows College, Dublin, adding that he had the approval of his suffragans, Bishops Amat and O'Connell, in the matter.] There is no doubt that the church of San Francisco could be well and better ruled by another Bishop. . . . I humbly ask Your Eminence to obtain my resignation from the Holy See, or, at least, to grant me a coadjutor.[16]

Two letters, written on the same day to Archbishops Spalding of Baltimore and Purcell of Cincinnati, asked their influence to further the cause of either his resignation or to aid in the obtaining of a worthy coadjutor.[17] In three weeks he had an answer from Archbishop Purcell to the effect that, since he did not know any of the names proposed, he was unable to help in the matter. However, Purcell added, changed conditions in Spain, which had been undergoing political convolutions at the time, had so altered affairs that he presumed the indefinite postponement of the missionary-college project.[18]

Another event which might have radically changed affairs for Alemany and the Church in northern California happened in early December when, as a letter of Patrick O'Connell informed Father Fortune in Dublin, Archbishop Alemany had experienced a narrow escape from sudden death:

. . . having been thrown from his horse and nearly caught under the vicious brute which, in rearing up after the A.B. [sic] had mounted him, fell back, some of his weight coming on the saintly A.B.'s limbs —his head also received a severe gash. Although rendered unconscious for awhile, he soon rallied and was able to walk up the steps to his door. I believe he was able to appear today in his Cathedral. Oh what a loss this extraordinary man would be to his archdiocese.[19]

[16] Alemany to Barnabò, San Francisco, August 20, 1868. APF. A notation on this letter indicates that an answer was sent to Alemany informing him that the bishops of the United States should be polled concerning their opinions as to the qualifications of the men proposed by Alemany. There is no reference to the matter of his resignation.
[17] Alemany to Spalding and to Purcell, San Francisco, October 15, 1868. AAB:MCUND.
[18] Purcell to Alemany, Cincinnati, Ohio, November 5, 1868. AASF.
[19] O'Connell to Fortune, Oakland, California, December 13, 1868. AAHC.

The next year of Alemany's episcopal reign would be marked notably by his departure for Rome and the Vatican Council. However, before this time came, in thanking the Paris Propagation of the Faith Society for further financial aid (1000 francs, one-fifth of the grant for that year which had been made to him), Alemany reminded the authorities in Paris that "very few, except those placed in my position, could realize my many necessities . . . occasioned by the building of churches, the educating of so many students in a country so young and so rapidly filling up with population."[20] Finally, though, in autumn, the time came for Archbishop Alemany, accompanied by Bishop O'Connell, to leave for Rome; this departure was preceded by another pastoral letter, dated September 15, 1869, which was a scholarly analysis of various situations confronting the Church and which concluded with the hope that "accompanied by your prayers and your gifts [that is, a special collection for the Holy Father], we may safely go and safely return with the priceless blessings of the Vicar of Christ and the heavenly counsels of the Bishops of the world, confirmed by the Chair of St. Peter."[21]

That the two California bishops were journeying to Rome from a colorful and picturesque area was testified to in the fact that Alemany, while stopping en route in Paris at a Dominican convent, there exhibited some gold ingots he was bringing to Rome as a gift for the Pope. Bishop O'Connell brought some ingots of silver for the same purpose.[22]

One of Alemany's early activities after his arrival in Rome was to inform Cardinal Barnabò that a meeting had just been held of all the American archbishops who had arrived in Rome (together with Alemany and his two suffragans) again to dis-

[20] "President of the Paris Society," San Francisco, February 17, 1869. ASPFP.
[21] "To the Clergy and Laity of the Diocese [sic] of San Francisco, September 15, 1869." AUSF.
[22] Reference is made to this interesting detail in a French Dominican periodical, L'Annee Dominicaine, 1869, p. 516. AOPC.

cuss the matter of obtaining a coadjutor for San Francisco. He told Barnabò that five of the prelates had been opposed to the move. In Alemany's opinion, they so judged because they feared that this was but a first step in his relinquishing his office. While thanking them for their desire that he continue as archbishop, he informed them that a coadjutor would enable him to devote time to his favorite project of the missionary college while not necessarily causing him to resign the see—which matter was not to be decided by him but by the Cardinal Prefect of Propaganda himself. And, lest Barnabò had forgotten the state of the question, Alemany next expressed himself in excellent Latin concerning his plans for his desired college.[23]

By the time that Alemany had composed this letter, the Vatican Council had already been in session for about a month. Solemnly opened in December, 1869, it was to continue until circumstances forced its adjournment in late October, 1870. A report of what was keeping San Francisco's Archbishop occupied was sent by him in the following letter to Father Fortune in Dublin on May 9, 1870:

> Since Febr. [sic] we have been exceedingly engaged, at least those Bishops who compose our committee. We had one or two sittings a day, Sundays included, each of 4 or 5 hours, and much study was required to prepare the materials.[24]

As the Council proceeded, it became evident that Archbishop Alemany was to go down in its history as an outspoken advocate of the definition of papal infallibility. He so expressed his views

[23] Rome, January 13, 1870. APF. On March 17, 1870, a St. Patrick's Day oration delivered in the Mechanics' Pavilion, San Francisco, by "the Rev. Fr. Hayes" lauded the absent Alemany. A press report says that Hayes referred in glowing and respectful language to the Archbishop to whose wisdom, piety, and many virtues he paid a high tribute. Pointing to the many churches of his faith, he added that they were "clear and telling evidences of the zealous churchman, the prudent forethought of the faithful, unchanging friend of Ireland and her children, the good and worthy citizen, Joseph Sadoc Alemany, Archbishop of San Francisco." San Francisco *Evening Bulletin*, March 18, 1870.
[24] AAHC.

239

in a speech which he delivered to the Council fathers on May 14; several weeks later, on June 20, he again defended the opportuneness of the definition of this papal prerogative, "but proposed a long insertion in the preliminary part to forestall misconceptions."[25] Alemany introduced a quite practical note in his first address with his remark that, since it was evidently impossible for bishops from distant places such as Australia or America to come frequently to Rome for general councils, "it would seem providential that Christ had bestowed an infallible pope on his church to care for it between such meetings." He added his belief that Christ had so provided, concluding that it was the business of the Council fathers to vote as to their opinions concerning this matter.

In a second address to the Council fathers on June 20, Alemany assured his listeners that the doctrine of papal infallibility was held firmly by Catholics in the United States: a quite lengthy address on this occasion served to establish his command of theology as well as ecclesiastical history, for it abounded in allusions drawn from both of these sources.[26] It was a foregone conclusion, of course, that Alemany's vote would be cast for the definition of papal infallibility on that celebrated July 18, 1870, when, under circumstances of thunder and lightning which accompanied the balloting, 533 bishops shouted their *"placets"* and two voted against the definition. Nor was Alemany slow to inform his flock as to the events which he had just witnessed: a pastoral letter "Given at Rome, out of the Flaminian Gate,

[25] See Cuthbert Butler's, *The Vatican Council: The Story Told from the Inside in Bishop Ullathorne's Letters*, 2 vols., New York, 1930. Alemany is mentioned five times in connection with his attendance at and participation in this Council. The quotation is from Butler, II, p. 100. See also James Hennesey, S.J., *The First Council of the Vatican: The American Experience*, New York, 1963, where the author records Alemany's participation in this Council.

[26] Alemany's two speeches are included in Mansi, *Collectio Conciliorum*, etc., *Passim.*

240

Feast of St. Symmachus (July 19) A.D. 1870"[27] gave the news of the definition which had been voted on the previous day. That its author was not without a sense of the dramatic is evident from first to last:

> Yesterday, for the first time in our life, we witnessed the clapping of hands and waving of handkerchiefs in a sacred Basilica—yesterday was repeated in St. Peter's what over fourteen hundred years since took place in the Third General Council at Ephesus, where, as soon as the Fathers announced the decree proclaiming the Blessed Virgin to be the Mother of God, and to be entitled to be honored as such, the faithful multitudes became seized with holy enthusiasm, and, unable to restrain their joy, rent the air with loud applause. At the appointed hour commenced the holy sacrifice of the Mass, followed by the Litanies of the Saints and the solemn invocation of the Holy Ghost by the Sovereign Pontiff, echoed by the assembled Bishops, all on their knees; and, after many prayers offered to the Almighty for his divine light and heavenly assistance, one of the Fathers read aloud the Constitution on which the votes were about to be taken, and which had been the subject of discussion for a few months; after which the vote of each was distinctly asked and registered. This being ended, the Holy Father was formally informed, that, out of the 535 prelates, 533 voted in favor of its decrees, and 2 against them; and then the Sovereign Pontiff, with a clear and majestic voice, approved and confirmed the Constitution. No sooner was the word *Confirmandum* uttered, than the assembled multitude and Fathers, as if moved by one electric sentiment, gave vent to the feelings of joy which filled their hearts in repeated rounds of applause, filling the immense Basilica with their evivas and clapping of hands, which the Masters of Ceremonies had no small difficulty to subdue. Absent, therefore, from you in body, but present in spirit, we beg of you to render thanks to God for having made us children of the Catholic Church and to pray sincerely that, in His infinite mercy, He may vouchsafe to bring the erring into the one fold. Let us also continue to implore your supplications to God, not only for the General Council, but also for the peace of the world,

---

[27] "Pastoral Letter on the Definition of the Infallibility of the Pope Addressed from Rome by Joseph S. Alemany, O.P., Archbishop of San Francisco, to the Faithful of His Diocese," San Francisco, 1870. AUSF.

that through the most powerful intercession of the immaculate Mother of God, and through the infinite merits of Christ, we all may live and die in His holy peace and divine love.[28]

Whether the editor of the *Monitor* in San Francisco knew of this pastoral letter so soon is not evident; however, the issue of July 23, 1870, published less than a week after the definition of papal infallibility, mentioned that "Archbishop Alemany is in good health and his people will be delighted to see him back among them in sound health, pursuing his pious labors for the advancement of God's Church." With the proroguing of the Vatican Council in October, 1870, it was not long before Alemany returned to his pastoral duties in San Francisco. Arriving home on November 15, two evenings later he addressed an overflow congregation in his cathedral on the work of the Council. In a long address the Archbishop expressed his gratitude to God for "guiding me safely across land and ocean to the Eternal City and back to my home." The service was concluded with a solemn *Te Deum* intoned by Archbishop Alemany himself in gratitude for the successful completion of his journey.[29] Only a few days later, Alemany wrote to Cardinal Barnabò to tell him of his safe arrival:

With God's blessing, I arrived home in good health and have felt the sympathy of the faithful here for the oppression dealt out to the Papal States for the liberty of which we all hope. I take the liberty to include a copy of my pastoral letter concerning the Council.[30]

The active sympathy which Alemany showed so publicly for Pio Nono in his many travails took another and very explicit form again in the summer after his return from the Vatican Council. In honor of Pius' twenty-fifth anniversary as pope, a public procession was planned through the downtown streets of

[28] *Ibid.*
[29] San Francisco *Bulletin,* November 18, 1870, which reported the event as happening on the previous evening.
[30] Alemany to Barnabò, November 24, 1870, APF.

242

San Francisco. This event was announced by Alemany to Monsignor Simeoni, Secretary of Propaganda:

> We are getting ready to have a grand procession *"per tutta la città"* to celebrate with thanks to God the 25th anniversary of the Holy Father—*"quem Deus diu nobis incolumen servet. . . ."*[31]

It was, indeed, to be a grand procession and demonstration of loyalty to the Holy See, as well as one of affection to the person of Pio Nono. It was estimated that on July 2, more than 20,000 persons participated in the march up Market Street—although the *"tutta la città"* was clearly an exaggeration, the ceremonies of the day undoubtedly attracted much attention.

In keeping with his yearly custom, Alemany issued a pastoral letter at the beginning of the Lenten season, 1872. He informed his flock that, since his return from the Vatican Council, he had visited nearly all the parishes of the archdiocese, and that these visits had occasioned his giving thanks to Almighty God for what he called "the many evidences of Christian piety experienced in most of them." True to his concept of his pastoral office, though, the Archbishop, after praising those who were ever faithful to their religious duties, gently reproved those who were remiss in their fulfillment. An exhortation to Christian education was followed with pleas for cooperation "when we are about to establish in this city a large school under the Christian Brothers." Finally, in an explicit use of his episcopal authority, Alemany announced that he was revoking any special privilege of the Spanish-speaking people of his archdiocese in the matter of the use of meat on days of abstinence, admonishing them that they must conform to general usage in this regard.[32]

On August 17, 1872, Alemany wrote again to the president of the Paris Society for the Propagation of the Faith. He thanked him for a long series of benefactions to his diocese (the last had enabled him to retire the debt from the French national

[31] APF.
[32] AOPC.

243

parish in San Francisco—an item which must have especially pleased his French correspondents), but this was quickly followed by a reminder to them that the needs of the ever-growing Church in California and adjacent territories were still tremendous. All, or nearly all, of his churches and convents were still heavily in debt, he added, for they were built in many cases when Catholics were neither numerous nor wealthy, and when a great deal had to be done in a short time. Two local convents of the Presentation Sisters, educating some 1,600 girls between them, were heavily in debt, and Alemany's desires to extend his parochial school system to what he called the larger towns of his diocese had not yet come to fruition. An additional burden sprang from the state of the Church in Utah which was under his jurisdiction at this time—for there were problems of a unique character there involving Mormonism which called for special handling and which would be solved, if ever, only by financial help from outside, since the handful of Catholics in that territory could hardly be expected to contribute very much in this regard.[33]

A unique phase of the history of the Catholic Church in San Francisco is to be found in that Sisterhood of the Holy Family which, in 1872, was founded, with Archbishop Alemany's sanction, by his devoted vicar general, Father John Prendergast. Miss Elizabeth Armer was the foundress of the group; and to her, when she was conversing with Alemany concerning her desire to enter one of the already existing religious communities, the Archbishop said:

Father Prendergast and I have another work for you to do. There are the little ones to be cared for while their mothers are off to work. And who is to instruct the children of a big city in the ways of faith, hope and love? . . . There are the poor to be visited in their homes. There are hearts to heal and souls to save in our busy city streets. This is the work God wants you to do, Elizabeth.[34]

[33] ASPFP.
[34] Quoted in *Monitor*, April 20, 1962.

The work envisioned by Archbishop Alemany and Father Prendergast has through the years brought about a sizable increase in the numbers of those who have entered this Sisterhood. The multitude of tasks successfully performed by these sisters reflects glory upon their founder and the one who authorized their coming into being as "San Francisco's Own"—an unofficial title which is proudly held by these sisters.

By the spring of 1873, the time had come for Alemany to renew some Roman faculties customarily granted to bishops for a period of ten years. To do so, he had to itemize the number of times he had made use of certain dispensations concerning marriages, and this he did, with customary meticulousness, in a letter to Cardinal Barnabò on April 27. From 1863–1873, there had been 2,659 such dispensations granted, the larger number of these concerning dispensations for the marriage of a Catholic with a non-Catholic—there being 1,835 of these. In addition, 622 cases were listed of marriage of Catholics with those not of the Christian faith; a positive note was added by Alemany when he informed the Roman Cardinal that, "as a result of these many dispensations, much good results, i.e., children are brought up in the Catholic faith, conversion of non-Catholic spouses sometimes results, etc."[35]

Evidence of the solid work now being done "for Romanism" by Archbishop Alemany and his loyal cohorts among clergy, sisters, and laity is to be found in the following account from a local newspaper of the time:

. . . The San Francisco diocese has 104 churches and chapels and 92 priests. Among the convents are "Presentation Convent" and Dominican monastery, on Bush St. the Convent of the S. Heart and several others. The majority of these establishments have schools attached, and it is noticeable in these as in all other institutions of this church that women are employed most unhesitatingly in the most responsible positions. One cause of the success of Romanism is found in the fact

[35] APF.

that it opens so many avenues for women, cultivated and otherwise, to engage in legitimate work.

. . . Here, then, is a simple presentation of the status and power of Romanism in the U.S. If the network of this organization which covers the land could be someday suddenly presented before the public gaze in its entirety, like the instantaneously illuminated powder traceries of a fourth of July fireworks exhibition, people outside of the Roman communion would be greatly startled. . . .[36]

Signs of mature growth were far from lacking, then, as Archbishop Alemany, in 1874, entered into his third decade as archbishop of San Francisco. Indeed, quite a new note was sounded by him on February 5 in a letter which he wrote to Father Fortune at All Hallows concerning prospective subjects for his diocese; informing the All Hallows' president that he would not have to recruit subjects for San Francisco, Alemany wrote:

I fear I will have to request from now that, next Sept., no new ones be added to my subjects, as our population, how well supplied with priests, is not increasing but very little [sic].[37]

Another significant sign of solid growth under Alemany's administration was made evident with his calling of the First Provincial Council to be held by the Catholic Church in California. It met in San Francisco in St. Mary's Cathedral from April 26 to May 2, 1874, with some private sessions in the Archbishop's residence; and while delayed some years because of the fewness of the number of bishops in California, it now witnessed an Archbishop gathered with three others of episcopal rank: Thaddeus Amat of Monterey and Los Angeles, Eugene O'Connell of Grass Valley and Francis Mora, Coadjutor Bishop of Monterey and Los Angeles. On May 3, 1874, a joint pastoral letter was issued over all of their signatures in which the purpose of the Council ("the regulation of morals, the correction of abuses, allaying of controversies and the accomplishment of such things

[36] Clipping dated September 21, 1873, is from an unidentified San Francisco newspaper.
[37] AAHC.

246

as are enjoined by the Sacred Canons") was fully explained, while an exhortation to greater fidelity in the faith comprised most of the remaining part of the letter. The minutes of the Council were kept faithfully by Bishop O'Connell as secretary, and they were sent by him, as required, to Propaganda Fide in Rome. From them we learn that, in the first private meeting of the Council, primary attention as given to approving Alemany's reiterated desire to have a coadjutor archbishop appointed by Rome as soon as possible. At another private meeting held on May 2, Bishop O'Connell's proposal to have a coadjutor bishop appointed to assist him also won approval.[38] Another document in the Propaganda Fide archives amply demonstrates that the cardinals of the Congregation performed their usual careful scrutiny of the acts and decrees of the San Francisco Synod, and that, while they approved in the main of what had been done, they had some small points to call to Alemany's attention. For example, he was reminded to furnish an adequate index to his *Acta* when and if another such council was held under him, while other minor corrections were indicated to make the San Francisco decrees conform more perfectly with Roman usage. Finally, indication was made that the Sacred Congregation was

[38] APF. A pithy reference to this Council appeared in a hostile San Francisco publication, Thistleton's *Jolly Giant*: the *Critic*, May 2, 1874: "The Roman Catholic Bishops and priests of this coast are now in session in this city. What they are doing is a mystery to all save themselves. This is Catholicism all over . . . However, it matters but very little, the present council will not affect the enlightened people of this city very much. . . ." Partial file, Gleeson Library, University of San Francisco. In an earlier issue of the same *Jolly Giant*, February 21, 1874, Alemany had been made the recipient of some sarcastic abuse because he had, in the judgment of the *Giant's* editor, deprived the San Francisco German Catholics of their rights and thus, in effect, favored the Chinese. ". . . we would not be at all surprised to see the Chinese worshipping Josh in St. Mary's Cathedral . . . as it is, they have Alemany pretty well surrounded and a stranger who might visit Chinatown now, would be very likely to take St. Mary's for a China Josh house. . . . There are burning tapers and statues in both, and the worshippers or visitors resemble each other in so much as they both go through much the same forms of bowing before images . . . the Catholic form of worship is taken from Paganism. . . ."

willing to approve the decrees of this first Provincial Council although the approval was, in fact, a very cautious one: in answer to the proposal that it go on record as saying that the Council in San Francisco "merited the simple recognition and approval of the Sacred Congregations," the answer was given that it "is sufficient that the Decrees of this Council be hereby recognized."[39]

Another of what now must be judged to have been valiant attempts to obtain a coadjutor for his see was made by Alemany in a letter to Cardinal Alessandro Franchi who, in 1874, had succeeded Barnabò as prefect of the Congregation de Propaganda Fide. He reminded the Cardinal that, some years ago, he had made a similar request which was not then approved by the American archbishops. Adding that they had again been canvassed and now approved, Alemany noted that after "twenty-four years of useless labors on my part, my body is growing weary, while my resources both of mind and of heart are not sufficient to let me continue to rule my continually growing diocese as I should—wherefore I humbly ask you to request the Holy Father to grant me, together with such a coadjutor and successor, His apostolic blessing."[40] Franchi was rather prompt in his reply for, less than a month later, he answered Alemany:

I proposed your request concerning a Coadjutor to the Holy Father [Pius IX] and he grants you permission to institute the customary proceedings in the matter—i.e. submitting a list of candidates, asking advice concerning them of your brother American Bishops, etc.[41]

San Francisco's "little bishop" (as he frequently called himself) had discovered that the mitre which he had accepted out of obedience to the same Pius IX in 1850 was not to be easily laid aside. When Archbishop Alemany mentioned that he was growing old in the episcopal office he was but stating the facts, for, on July 29, 1875, he solemnly celebrated the silver jubilee of

[39] APF.
[40] Alemany to Franchi, San Francisco, October 6, 1874.
[41] Franchi to Alemany, Rome, November 11, 1874. APF.

his consecration as a bishop. As might be expected, the San Francisco *Monitor* devoted much space to the joyful events which marked the occasion, and both the editorials and news articles in its various issues at this time indicate a sincere affection for the prelate who had administered the San Francisco see for so many fruitful years. The *Monitor* thus commemorated the event:

> Today, the twenty-fifth anniversary of the consecration of Archbishop Alemany and his transfer from Monterey to this diocese, is recorded the grandest celebration ever conducted on the Pacific coast under the auspices of the Catholic Church, excepting only the demonstration in honor of Pio Nono. Special masses were in all the churches of the diocese, with a general communion. At nine o'clock this morning the principal services were held in the Cathedral which had been specially decorated with flowers and evergreens. The solemn Pontifical Mass was celebrated by His Grace the Archbishop and one hundred priests were in attendance, including Bishops Amat and Mora of Los Angeles, and O'Connell of Marysville. Long before the opening hour the church was densely packed and many were turned away unable to gain admittance. The exercises were more than usually impressive and lasted an hour and a half.
>
> At 1 o'clock the clergy took dinner in the basement of the Cathedral, on which occasion Very Reverend Father Prendergast delivered an address on behalf of the clergy of the Archdiocese. After the address a magnificent set of pontifical robes were presented by the clergy to the Archbishop. The robes are of exquisite workmanship and are valued at $1,500.
>
> At 3 o'clock this afternoon the Archbishop was serenaded by a brass band, after which he received a large delegation of ladies and gentlemen. Among the many presents he received was a purse of $6,000, and a handsome carriage and pair of horses presented by Peter Donahue.[42]

Nor did the jubilee go unnoticed in other parts of the country, for as the Philadelphia *Catholic Record* reported shortly afterwards:

> On the occasion of this Jubilee . . . His Grace received a purse of $5000 in gold from his people who celebrated the day with much

[42] *Monitor*, July 29, 1875.

249

pomp. From half a dozen priests, a few old ruined Spanish churches and a concourse of rough and uncultured people, mad to accumulate wealth by any means, has been developed, in the course of a quarter century, an orderly and settled population of 200,000 governed by an Archbishop, 3 Bishops, 193 priests and worshipping in 187 churches.[43]

Archbishop Alemany was determined to sing his *"nunc dimittis"* as soon as possible after this significant milestone in his episcopal career had been reached. Accordingly, he went ahead busily in the summer of 1875 with plans to get Rome to give him the desired coadjutor. His efforts were reported to Propaganda by Bishop O'Connell of Grass Valley, acting as secretary in a meeting of the California bishops which had included a discussion of the appointment of a coadjutor for Alemany. O'Connell reported that the Archbishop "who has served for twenty-five years and is now advanced in age and filled with the labors of the years" had met with Bishops O'Connell, Amat, and Mora in San Francisco on July 28, 1875, and had received their approval to ask for a coadjutor bishop. The report went on to say that they had all agreed on the following three names as suitable candidates for the position: 1. the Reverend William Fortune, president of All Hallows College, Dublin; 2. the Right Reverend Thomas Foley, bishop-administrator of the diocese of Chicago; 3. the Reverend John Prendergast, vicar general of San Francisco. O'Connell added that it was the opinion of Alemany himself and Mora that, if Prendergast be chosen, he should not be given the right of succession to the see of San Francisco; he added, though, that Amat (always an independent spirit, it would seem) had disagreed and proposed that Prendergast's name be sent to Rome with the recommendation that, if selected as coadjutor to Alemany, he be given the right of succession to the see.[44] Much of what O'Connell reported was confirmed in a covering letter written by Alemany several days later in which he also included

[43] Philadelphia *Monthly Catholic Record*, September, 1875, p. 318.
[44] O'Connell to Franchi, San Francisco, July 28, 1875. APF.

the O'Connell report.[45] Additional evidence of the determination of Alemany to get action from Rome at this time is made evident in a very frank letter which he sent, only two weeks later, to the unofficial primate of the American Church, Archbishop Bayley of Baltimore:

> The Holy Father having kindly allowed me to petition for a coadjutor, on the return of Bishop Amat from Europe all the Prelates of this little province met and commended for that office to the Holy See the following subjects.
> 1. Very Rev. William Fortune, of Dublin:
> 2. Right Rev. Thomas Foley, D.D. of Chicago;
> 3. Very Rev. John Prendergast, my Vicar General.
> The first is no doubt a Priest of very great ability, learning, prudence, activity and amiable disposition; he has discharged with much credit for many years the duties of President of the College of All Hallows': and as most of our Priests were educated in that college and the majority of our Catholics are Irish or descendants of Irish, it is, hoped that he would administer this diocese would [sic] care and success. I consulted Cardinal Cullen on his fitness in Rome in 1870, and again more recently by letter, and he considers him worthy to be promoted to that dignity. He was already appointed by the Holy Father to some See in Australia; but he succeeded in having his resignation accepted on the ground of bad health. Yet he has been able to continue to attend to the onerous duties of that large college; and as our climate is doubtlessly one of the most salubrious in the world, I should think his excuse would not hold good in our case.
> The second I suppose is well known to Your Grace, it appears that he is administering well the diocese of Chicago, which makes me believe that he would make a good Archbishop.
> The third is a talented, well informed, eloquent and good Priest (fellow student of the first, both equally admired in college for their superior talent and now both 40 years old). But Father Prendergast is naturally inclined to be serious, not open, or too reserved, and for this reason some in our meeting thought that he should not be commended as if wanting that good spirit of charity which a Bishop should have; and I must confess that though he could give me much assistance in my very many labours, he scarcely ever gives me any aid

[45] Alemany to Franchi, San Francisco, July 31, 1875. APF.

unless when I be absent. And yet he has always quietly attended well to the duties assigned him these fifteen years. He also seems to have some dislike for temporal administration (most important here), but he is able to do justice to it, and when charged with it, I think he would find a way to have it attended to. However, we sent his name, and in doing so we thought it necessary to petition the Holy See, that if he be appointed, it be *sine jure successionis*.

I must now request Your Grace to have the kindness to communicate your views on the above to his Eminence Cardinal Franchi, and to pray Almighty God to give us a good, holy, wise, prudent, zealous and apostolic successor.[46]

However, Archbishop Alemany was yet to serve his archdiocese for another decade that is, until December 28, 1884, when his resignation was accepted by the Holy See. Evidently, Rome thought with good reason that the "little bishop" of San Francisco was doing very well in that frontier of the faith called California.

[46] Alemany to James R. Bayley, San Francisco, August 11, 1875. AAB.

11

Further Disputes with the Jesuits— and Dominicans as Well

AMONG the more distinguished ecclesiastical gatherings on the Pacific Coast in the late nineteenth century was that of Sunday, February 1, 1880, when the Jesuit fathers solemnly dedicated their third St. Ignatius Church in San Francisco. The ceremonies of blessing and dedication were performed by Archbishop Alemany, who also pontificated at the Mass which followed. The occasion was so impressive as to cause the official chronicler of a later date to become well nigh rhapsodic in his words:

> The altar in its magnificence, bright with myriads of lights and costly flowers . . . the beautiful vestments of the participating clergy, the mitre and crosier and the modest pious man that bore them, he as much an honor to them as they to him—all tended to elevate minds above the sordidness of earth and fix them on realms above the skies. . . .[1]

Magnificent it may all have been, but the solemn blessing by Archbishop Alemany of this impressive structure erected on what was officially known as "Block 74 of the Western Addition" had been preceded, literally, by years of disagreement between the Archbishop of San Francisco and the Fathers of the Society of Jesus. To the details which marked these years and this story we shall now give our attention.

In the beginning of December, 1870, Father Joseph Bayma,

[1] Riordan, *First Half Century*, etc., p. 235.

253

then rector of St. Ignatius College on Market Street, had written to Archbishop Alemany concerning the desire of the Jesuit Fathers to remove their church and college to another part of the city, stating that the location on Market Street between Fourth and Fifth streets was growing more unsuitable for their purposes with the passage of the years. The central artery of San Francisco presented quite a different aspect in 1870 from what it had appeared in 1855, when Alemany had commissioned Father Anthony Maraschi to "build anywhere out there!" Now the Jesuits were located and, in a sense, caught, by their location in a too central part of San Francisco; the tax rate was rising, there was no room for expansion, and little quiet was afforded for the succesful pursuit of the educational processes which the Jesuits considered their chief work in the city. To Father Bayma's information that the Society was considering removal to a part of the Western Addition in the general area of Hayes Street and Van Ness Avenue (though no property had as yet been acquired there), Alemany thus replied:

The places you suggest for the future St. Ignatius College are too near Parishes already established, which naturally would be subject to the old troubles. This is what I should state after serious reflexion and sound counsel. After the same I would propose that your new place follow the Rule found necessary to avoid trouble between Churches, namely to have them thirteen or fourteen blocks from each other. Should this rule be unacceptable, I believe that I might offer the Church of St. Francis, or that of St. Bridget's, or that of St. Peter's, or any place east of Third and Harrison Sts. Of course whatever I would propose should finally meet with the approval of the Holy See. I beg that you charitably join me in offering the Holy Sacrifice and many Rosaries that through the powerful intercession of the holy Patriarchs St. Ignatius and St. Dominic, all may be well settled and turn to God's honor and glory.[2]

Since the views of the Archbishop had been expressed so definitely, the whole matter was dropped until some years later

[2] Alemany to Bayma, San Francisco, December 5, 1870. ASJC.

when, as Father Riordan remarked, "circumstances over which the Fathers had no control, necessitated action and established church and college where they now are."[3] However, although the more active phases of this newest disagreement did not come to pass until 1877 (and resulted, ultimately, in the events of February 1, 1880, referred to above), the years in between were to be marked by signs of less than perfect agreement between Alemany and his Jesuit co-laborers in San Francisco.

Perhaps the best documentary evidence as to these continuing difficulties is to be found in a long report which Alemany sent to Cardinal Franchi of Propaganda under date of February 8, 1875. In it he again went into the details of the disputes already reported in an earlier chapter, while again indicating his fears that any removal of St. Ignatius Church and College in San Francisco would be attendant with even more difficulties, which he professed himself as wishing to avoid. In a rare witticism, Alemany reminded Franchi that "since the Vatican Council has not declared the infallibility of the little Archbishop of San Francisco,"[4] he could only hope to present his side of the matters under dispute and await the decision of Rome.

In May, 1875, a much more significant document was received by the Cardinal Prefect: indeed, even now, the more one peruses it, the more one is impressed with the document when one takes note of the impressive positions occupied by its fifteen signers. Ten were the fathers general of the most important religious orders and congregations of the Catholic Church; six of the signers acted in their capacity as vicars general of their respective orders and congregations, while the one remaining signature was that of the secretary of the Society of Jesus in Rome who represented his father general. There appears to be no way of learning whether this extraordinary and explicit criticism of Alemany's policies regarding the Jesuits of San Francisco was

[3] Riordan, *First Half Century,* etc., p. 164.
[4] APF.

255

ever called to his attention. However, whether it was or not, it is certainly a revealing statement of what these important Roman religious superiors thought of the activities of an archbishop in far off California. Indeed, it would appear from a careful reading of the nineteen printed pages of the document that they considered his views on the rights or non-rights of religious as constituting a *cause célèbre* which should not go unnoticed by them in their several capacities as defenders of these rights. It would appear that their indignation was spurred by their reading of that decree of San Francisco Provincial Synod of April, 1874, which stated that "Parish Churches which have been committed to the care of Regulars, belong to the Ordinary just as do other ecclesiastical properties." The signers evidently had enlisted the professional skill of their own canonists as they proceeded to demolish the synodal assertion with methodical precision. (In the light of the decision taken by Rome and previously reported in these pages, it would appear that the Roman superiors general were correct in their careful analysis of the errors inherent in the Synod's position, as well as in their recognition of the perilous consequences which would result if these views were allowed to stand.)

An interesting point is that these responsible men with worldwide concerns saw fit to seize upon the stubbornly maintained views of a Dominican Archbishop in far-off California as an opportunity to reaffirm the rights of religious orders throughout the world. Among the fathers general who signed what amounted to a severe critique of the Alemany policies with regard to the Jesuits in San Francisco were those of the Silvestrian Fathers, the Cistercians, the Friars Minor, the Augustinians, the Servites, the Capuchins, the Calced Carmelites, and the Passionists. The vicars general and procurators included those of the Benedictines, Dominicans (!), Mercedarians, Friars Minor Conventual, Congregation of English Benedictines, and the Carmelites of the Ancient Observance. As previously mentioned, the

256

Jesuit general, Father Peter Beckx, had his secretary general (Father Torquatus Armellini) sign in his stead. It can hardly be doubted that this formidable array of signatures must have caused Cardinal Franchi to peruse the views expressed in this document. Indeed, this report may well carefully have been one of the controlling reasons why, ultimately, Alemany was to lose in his desire to keep the Jesuits from their Hayes Street-Van Ness Avenue location in San Francisco—for the document had analyzed so closely the rights of religious orders in such matters as, perhaps, to make his intransigence unacceptable to authorities in Rome. However, the years between this report and the dedication of the Hayes Street-Van Ness Avenue Church, 1875–1880, were to see the usual (by now) interchange of letters, with, presumably, either side convinced that it was right—in this sense, the whole matter may be considered as a continuation of the disputes earlier recorded.[5]

By 1877 it was evident to Jesuit superiors that they would have to face the continuous opposition of Archbishop Alemany in their desire to remove to the Western Addition in San Francisco. On June 10, Father Aloysius Varsi, then president of St. Ignatius College, departed for Italy to discuss the entire matter with Jesuit and ecclesiastical authorities in Rome. The motives for removal of church and college from Market Street had become so pressing that delay meant serious if not irreparable loss. In the rapidly developing city, it was imperative that opportunities offered to acquire desirable property not be neglected, while the annual tax burden of $12,000 was beyond the immediate resources of the Fathers. In addition, they knew that this rate would increase as their property on Market Street grew in commercial value. Father Riordan thus reports the sequence of events:

The Fathers had no choice; they must leave the property on Market St. The matter was thoroughly discussed with the Very Reverend

[5] APF.

257

Peter Beckx, General of the Society of Jesus, and, having received his approval, was submitted to the Propaganda for decision. Father Varsi had an interview with His Eminence, Cardinal Franchi, Prefect of Propaganda and submitted maps of San Francisco and indicated two lots somewhat nearer Market St. than at present occupied as possible locations for the new buildings. On being asked whether the Fathers might go on with the project: "Facciano Pure," answered the Cardinal; "Let them by all means." The matter therefore was definitely settled. A site a little more removed from Market St. than those first thought of was ultimately chosen, but of this a little later.[6]

Actually, the year 1878 was to be the year of extended disagreement between Alemany and the local Jesuits concerning the removal. This year had hardly gotten under way before the epistolary war was resumed. On January 15, 1878, Alemany wrote Varsi that he could not in good conscience approve of the latter's desire to remove St. Ignatius College to "Block 74" of the Western Addition, alleging that it was too close to St. Joseph Church, at 10th and Howard streets, where he wished to erect a new cathedral. The proposed Jesuit church would be only a few blocks away, and, in Alemany's opinion unpleasant complications were bound to result. He continued:

. . . In a country like this, where we have to depend exclusively on the offerings of the people attending church, the Cathedral could have no support, if you locate near it, or the lot where it has to be. Some time ago I expressed my views on such matters to some of your Superiors, (Father Masnata or Father Ponte, I think); and independently of that I think that afterwards I invited you to San Jose, Santa Clara and San Francisco to aid me, —out of good will because troubled by bad people elsewhere. I think you might consider a little before establishing yourselves where your Church will unintentionally but surely swallow up the congregation and offerings of the Cathedral. Were it not for that, I would not object to your choosing the most desirable and central place in this city.[7]

[6] Riordan, *First Half Century*, p. 205.
[7] Alemany to Aloysius Varsi, S.J., San Francisco, January 15, 1878. ASJC.

258

As an evidence of his good will, Alemany suggested an alternate site a few blocks west of the proposed one and ended his letter with the words: "Believing that if you were the Bishop, you could not act differently, I remain, etc."[8] However, Father Varsi made it very evident in a prompt and lengthy answer dated January 20, 1878, that he considered it necessary that they proceed with their plans to obtain Block 74 for the new church and college. He reminded Alemany that the news concerning the proposed cathedral was a complete surprise to him, and that he had proceeded in good faith to negotiate for the Hayes-Van Ness site without the slightest knowledge of the Archbishop's now revealed plans to transfer his cathedral to a location a few blocks away. Alemany was informed that, in October, 1877, the Jesuits had bought Block 74 for the sum of $200,000. Varsi wrote:

During my last visit to Rome, acting under instructions of my Superiors, this whole question was fairly and honestly submitted to the Cardinal Prefect by the Rev. Fr. Weld, Assistant of V. Rev. Fr. General, and myself. Your views, as expressed in the letter to Fr. Bayma of 1870, which are not materially different from those of January 15th 1878, as well as our views were stated. The map of San Francisco with the division of Parishes, etc. was exhibited; two different lots, both nearer to St. Joseph's than our block 74, were pointed out to His Eminence as being adapted to our purposes of College and Church; and finally, when I asked His Eminence, whether under the existing circumstances it would be right and safe for us to proceed at once to the contemplated removal of St. Ignatius, we received from Him this answer "*faciano pure.*"

Having now, by the force of circumstances, purchased a lot less objectionable than either of the two shown to His Eminence, as being further yet from St. Joseph's, I believe that we are still more deserving of his approval.

And now I do hope and pray that Your Grace will not refuse the favor which again I most humbly ask of you, namely, of giving your

[8] *Ibid.*

259

CALIFORNIA'S FIRST ARCHBISHOP

blessing upon this important undertaking. By so doing, Your Grace will acquire a new claim to the gratitude and prayers of the Society, and of the many souls under your charge who may be brought into the fold of Jesus Christ by our humble ministrations.[9]

Despite the conciliatory tone adopted by Father Varsi, Alemany answered that, with the advice of his council, he still found it necessary to refuse approval of the Hayes Street-Van Ness Avenue site, although, as he added, "the city is very large, and, if you propose some other place, I will do what I can without injury to other churches."[10] Varsi's answer was quick in coming:

We have seriously considered Your Grace's suggestion about proposing some other place; but I must confess that we are at a loss to find any that would meet with Your Grace's requirements unless we go to the outskirts of the City, which I am not authorized to do.

I conclude by expressing my deep regret that Your Grace thought it necessary to protest against our removal to Block 74 in the Western Addition However, I have performed my painful duty of transmitting it to the proper authority. And I pray to God that differences of opinion will not sever the union of hearts.[11]

By this time, both parties were following earlier patterns in appealing their respective cases to Roman authorities. Thus, Alemany, under date of January 24, 1878, presented his arguments in a four-page letter to Franchi,[12] while Varsi, writing to the Cardinal on April 4, 1878, far exceeded the length of Alemany's letter when he sent a detailed thirty-one page resume of the whole matter. Nor was Father General Beckx any more remiss in his defense of Varsi's case than he had been, years before, in defending the same or related rights with Franchi's predecessor, Cardinal Barnabò. Two letters went in quick succession, one to Franchi, recently made papal secretary of state,

9 Varsi to Alemany, San Francisco, January 20, 1878. ASJC.
10 Alemany to Varsi, San Francisco, February 10, 1878. ASJC.
11 Varsi to Alemany, San Francisco, February 20, 1878. Copy in ASJC.
12 Alemany to Franchi, San Francisco, January 24, 1878. APF.

and the other to his successor as prefect of Propaganda, Giovanni Simeoni; in both letters Beckx, while supporting Varsi's views, asked for a favorable decision so that an end could be put to the delay in San Francisco which was causing superiors there much worry and financial concern.[13]

It was not long before a decision was reached by the new Prefect of Propaganda. On May 24, 1878, he sent a letter to Alemany in which, quite diplomatically but also quite firmly, he told him that he was to yield in his opposition to the removal of St. Ignatius Church and College from Market Street to the new site at Hayes Street and Van Ness Avenue in the Western Addition. Simeoni said that he had investigated the whole matter quite thoroughly and that he was convinced that, among other reasons, the financial loss which would be entailed if the Jesuits were forced to relinquish their new property would be sufficient to justify their removal to this new site. He added that he was not overly impressed with Alemany's arguments that such a relocation would cause damage to the prospects for a proposed new cathedral—the Jesuits were to build a new college and they had a right guaranteed to them to have a church for public worship in connection with this new college: cathedral or no cathedral, this right was theirs and they were not to be deprived of it by Alemany. However, perhaps to mollify the feelings of the Archbishop, Simeoni went on to add diplomatically that, if it indeed could be shown that such financial harm had, in fact, resulted, he presumed that Jesuit superiors could be counted on to indemnify the archdiocese in due time.[14] While this firm statement must have disappointed Alemany, he was docile in his

---

[13] Beckx to Cardinal Secretary of State Franchi, May 9, 1878; Beckx to the newly appointed Cardinal Prefect of Propaganda, Giovanni Simeoni, May 10, 1878. APF. After serving as prefect of Propaganda from March 10, 1874, to March 13, 1878, Franchi had been appointed papal secretary of state. His successor, Cardinal Simeoni, served as prefect from March 15, 1878, to January 14, 1892.

[14] Simeoni to Alemany, Rome, May 24, 1878. Copy in APF.

reply, writing on July 22, that he was willing to yield to the Society of Jesus concerning the new location in San Francisco—but that he was not pleased at the direction things had taken seems evident from the following words: "I bow my head and accept your decision with holy resignation."[15] This submission, however painful, caused Simeoni to answer Alemany on August 26 in words of praise for his acceptance of the decision, while he added that the apostolic benediction asked by Father Varsi of Pope Leo XIII for the new St. Ignatius Church and College would be forthcoming shortly. Evidently, Simeoni wanted to make it clear that the whole matter was over and finished and that this blessing of the Holy Father would seem to be the best way to convince Alemany of this fact.[16]

Now that Rome had spoken, there remained only an exchange of letters on the local scene to confirm details. It is not surprising, then, as the letters here quoted will reveal, that the final exchange was to be more official than personal—at least on Alemany's part. Magnanimity is always easier on the part of a victor—and thus, perhaps, it was not difficult for Varsi to express his sentiments as follows:

I have received information from V. Rev. Fr. General Beckx that it has been decided in Rome by the proper authority that we are at liberty to remove St. Ignatius Church and College to lot 74 of the Western Addition; and Fr. General says that we should commence at once the new buildings.

This decision relieves me of very great anxiety; but yet I should feel very grieved if I were to proceed in this important affair without first obtaining Your Grace's blessing on it. I therefore most humbly beg Your Grace, for the love of Jesus' Sacred Heart and of St. Aloysius whose feast we celebrate today, to grant us this favor; for which we shall ever feel most grateful.[17]

15 Alemany to Simeoni, San Francisco, July 22, 1878. APF.
16 Simeoni to Alemany, Rome, August 26, 1878. APF.
17 Varsi to Alemany, San Francisco, June 21, 1878. Copy in ASJC.

It was some weeks before Alemany answered this letter. Finally, on August 5, he replied to Varsi:

> The Cardinal Prefect informed me, that considering what had been done—the immense injury which would accrue to you if your new building was not built in your new lot purchased with a most heavy sum etc. you may be allowed to proceed; consequently I can have no objection. The Cardinal, however, intimates that should any injury result to the Cathedral (and I will request the same in regard to St. Joseph's) from your proximity, it would become necessary to have such compensated. When answering His Eminence, I stated that in case, to avoid trouble, it was deemed prudent to build a new Cathedral elsewhere, and the heirs of N. Hawse would sue and recover the lot donated for a Cathedral at cor. of 10th and Howard Sts., I should expect to be indemnified.[18]

On August 20, 1878, a gracious cablegram addressed to Father Varsi from Cardinal Nina, papal secretary of state, brought the promised blessing of Pope Leo XIII:

> The Holy Father with all his heart blesses the new building containing church and college.[19]

In mid-September, Archbishop Alemany was asked to give the address on the occasion of the laying of the cornerstone for the new St. Ignatius Church and College. He replied by saying that, while he intended to perform the ceremony itself on Sunday, October 20, 1878, he would not be able to "make an address on the occasion."[20] Actually, when the time arrived for the ceremony, Archbishop Alemany was not present, since he had delegated Bishop O'Connell of Grass Valley to represent him and to perform the ceremony. It is not evident whether this was a deliberate abstention on Alemany's part; however, it would not seem to be exceeding the facts to conjecture that he would not have been exactly at ease had he been present for the laying of

18 Alemany to Varsi, San Francisco, August 5, 1878. ASJC.
19 Riordan, *First Half Century,* etc., p. 223.
20 Alemany to Varsi, San Francisco, September 26, 1878. ASJC.

the cornerstone at a site concerning which he had considerable misgivings. A contemporary account mentions only that "His Grace, the Most Reverend Archbishop being prevented by previous engagements from officiating, his place was supplied . . . by Bishop O'Connell."[21]

As already indicated, on the day of the blessing and dedication itself, Sunday, February 1, 1880, the pontifical celebrant was Archbishop Alemany. A masterful sermon was preached by Bishop James A. Healy of the Diocese of Portland, Maine. During the Mass, there were between three and four thousand persons crowded within the new and quite magnificent St. Ignatius Church, while it was estimated that, in the course of the day, more than fifteen thousand persons entered the portals of this third and newest of the St. Ignatius churches in San Francisco.[22] Eventually, as matters turned out, no new cathedral was erected in the area of St. Joseph's Church, just a few blocks away. Instead, property was bought for the new St. Mary's Cathedral at Van Ness Avenue and O'Farrell Street; dedicated in 1891 (three years after Archbishop Alemany's death in Spain), it served until its destruction by fire on September 7, 1962. Alemany had planned it and bought the property for it, but it was to be his successor, Archbishop Patrick Riordan, who would bring it to completion. Before turning our attention to another set of disagreements between Alemany and, in this case, the friars of his

[21] This detail is found in a manuscript in ASJC. Written on the day of the cornerstone laying itself, October 20, 1878, it was cast in the form of a letter addressed to the editor of the New York *Freeman's Journal*. It was signed simply "Pacific Coast" with no further indication as to authorship.

[22] This, the third St. Ignatius Church in San Francisco, was destroyed by fire following the earthquake of April 18, 1906. The present St. Ignatius Church at Fulton Street and Parker Avenue, dedicated on February 2, 1914, is the fifth in the series—a temporary church at Hayes and Shrader streets served from 1906–1914. It is interesting to note that Bishop James Augustine Healy (1830–1900), who preached on this occasion, was the only Negro to hold an American see. He served as second Bishop of Portland, Maine, 1875–1900. His Jesuit brother served as president of Georgetown University. See Albert S. Foley, S.J., *Bishop Healy: Beloved Outcast*, New York, 1954.

Dominican Order, it might be well to repeat the graceful words used by Father Riordan on the occasion of Alemany's retirement:

> On the 19th of May, 1885, Father Sasia, in company with Fathers Kenna and Congiato, waited on the Archbishop to wish him Godspeed and, five days later, he departed. Whatever differences had existed between him and the Fathers had long since been healed—differences, in fact, which were rather due to external influences which had been brought to bear upon the pious prelate than to anything spontaneous on his own part. An ornament to his noble Order and to the Archdiocese, he left behind him no sincerer admirers of his many virtues than the Fathers of St. Ignatius. . . .[23]

Whatever is to be thought of this magnanimous attitude which the San Francisco Jesuits are said to have had concerning Archbishop Alemany, the record would seem to be clear that there were some of his brethren in the Dominican Order who did not share this opinion. For one of the interesting anomalies which one encounters in the story of the Archbishop is that he was involved in some serious and long-standing disputes with the members of his own religious order who worked with him in northern California. A previous chapter has detailed some such disagreements which happened while he was the young provincial of the American Dominicans in the late 1840's in Kentucky and Ohio. However, the opposition manifested by Alemany to the Dominicans in California (an opposition which they seem to have returned quite liberally) is quite another sort of thing. It finally reached dramatic proportions when the five friars who composed the council of St. Dominic's Priory in San Francisco wrote to their master general in Rome in 1880 that they "dared to say that no other Bishop in any part of the world is acting so irrationally with regard to Dominican rights and privileges as is this Dominican Archbishop here."[24]

[23] Riordan, *First Half Century,* etc., p. 267.
[24] Benedict McGovern, O.P., Bernard Doogan, O.P., Anthony Rooney, O.P., Thomas O'Neill, O.P., and John Murphy, O.P., to Father Master General Joseph Larroca, O.P., San Francisco, April 12, 1880. AOPR.

As a necessary prelude to the understanding of a delicate situation, mention should be made that the sturdy and stubborn Dominican Prelate who came from "that part of Spain where people have strong heads" was matched all during his many years in California by Francis Sadoc Vilarrasa, O.P., who was, like Alemany, a Catalan, and whose life-span practically parallels that of the Archbishop. As we noted earlier, Vilarrasa had not been at all pleased with the rule of Alemany as his provincial, as documents preserved in the master general's archives make clear. However, even though it is evident that Alemany knew of this opposition, the newly consecrated Bishop of Monterey asked Vilarrasa to accompany him to California both to help him and to offer aid in the project of founding the Dominicans there. One who studies Vilarrasa during the years in which he served his order with genuine distinction and devotion must become convinced of his worth. Father Vilarrasa continued to rule his order in California as commissary general until his death in Benicia on March 17, 1888—just a month previous to that of Alemany in Spain on April 14.[25]

Even though Father Vilarrasa was to accuse Alemany, and this many times in official correspondence to Rome, of being hostile to religious orders in his diocese, there is no indication that he was ever constrained to think of him as anything but a loyal Dominican in his ideas and, as far as possible, in his personal way of life. For example, when in 1874 Vilarrasa wrote an interesting account of his years in California, he was careful to mention that, in the earlier years during which Alemany served as bishop of Monterey, 1850–1853, Alemany "made it a point to be present at all of the [Dominican] community exercises when he was at home and able to do so."[26] However, near the

[25] O'Daniel, *The Dominican Province of St. Joseph,* New York, 1942, p. 173.

[26] Vilarrasa, "Chronica Pro Historia FF. Ordinum Praedictorum in California, 1850–1874." AOPR.

end of this same informative chronicle, the frank Vilarrasa thus declared himself on the progress—or lack of it, as he saw it—of the Dominicans in California:

> The Order has progressed slowly up to now [1874] but if it be recalled . . . that the order received little or rather no incentive from the Archdiocese—indeed, that grave impediments were placed in its way from time to time, then it will seem wonderful that there are now found in California two houses of the brethren with seventeen priests, six students . . . and six lay brothers. . . .[27]

An explanation of the attitude of Alemany towards both the Jesuit and the Dominican orders in his diocese should be sought in the fact that, being a religious himself, he was apparently determined to be scrupulously objective in administering his diocese when there was question of anything involving the respective rights of his diocesan clergy as contrasted with those of the members of these two Orders. That this attitude took unfortunate and even exaggerated forms at times is a matter of record; perhaps, though, given the circumstances and the character of the man himself, most of what is here recorded seems to have been somewhat inevitable.[28]

On January 3, 1861, while engaged in earlier difficulties with the Jesuits, Alemany wrote Barnabò to report that the same, or nearly the same, situation existed with regard to the Dominicans; they felt that they should retain ownership of the parishes committed to their care. As in the case with the Jesuits, Alemany added that he would leave the entire matter to the Cardinal for his consideration and decision.[29] Seemingly, though, he inter-

[27] Vilarrasa, "Chronica," entry for 1874.

[28] Correspondence between the author and the Reverend Reginald M. Coffey, O.P., previously mentioned as archivist of the Dominican Province of St. Joseph, Washington, D.C., was supplemented by use of the archives there and several conversations on the matters relating to Alemany—especially the relationship between his membership in the Dominican Order and his episcopal capacity.

[29] Alemany to Barnabò, San Francisco, January 3, 1861. APF.

preted Barnabò's answer as a justification for the following lines which he sent to Vilarrasa several months later. He indicated that a letter from Barnabò had convinced him that

... the Sacred Congregation does not seem to approve the permitting of churches as parishes to belong to Regulars. He rather intimates that I should not deprive myself and successors of the right to the goods and property properly belonging to the parishes themselves.[30]

The next significant indication that not all was well between Alemany and the friars of his order is contained in a letter written by Vilarrasa to Father Jandel, Dominican master general, from Benicia on February 8, 1867. In this letter, Vilarrasa bluntly states that "the Archbishop is not favorable to religious Orders—indeed, he does what is possible to impede their endeavors. . . . I write you these things as I feel that you should be informed concerning them."[31] Almost ten years later, Vilarrasa found himself forced to send another like lengthy statement; according to the Dominican Commissary General, Alemany had been making impossible demands on the friars considering their quite limited manpower—as well as trying more than once to exercise a dominative power in their councils in which, as a Dominican himself, "he should know that no Bishop should intrude."[32]

Further details were furnished at considerable length in another letter of Vilarrasa which he wrote to Jandel on August 18 of the same year.[33] Apparently, the awkward situation had not

[30] Alemany to Vilarrasa, San Francisco, June 4, 1861. AOPC.

[31] Vilarrasa to Jandel, Benicia, California, February 8, 1867. AOPR. Vilarrasa adds many details here concerning the points in which he considers Alemany to be trespassing on Dominican rights and privileges in his episcopal rule and contacts with the Dominican friars in his diocese.

[32] Vilarrasa to Giuseppe M. Sanvitò, O.P., vicar general of Dominican Order. Benicia, California, June 15, 1876. AOPR.

[33] Vilarrasa to Sanvitò, August 18, 1876. AOPR. Vilarrasa here adds some details concerning points still at issue between Alemany and himself—notably that the former is demanding that the few friars at St. Dominic's, San Francisco (because of their proximity to Calvary Cemetery) accept the burden of officiating at practically all the funerals there without compensa-

much improved two years later, for Vilarrasa then wrote to the procurator general of his order to report more infractions by Alemany on what he considered to be inalienable Dominican rights.[34] The same tone is found in yet another letter two months later in which Vilarrasa reports that Alemany had managed to "find still other ways to harass the friars in the proper exercise of their priestly ministry in San Francisco."[35] In this letter it is evident that Vilarrasa's patience was running out at the seeming and long-standing usurpation of Dominican rights by an archbishop of their Order. And so things went until, on April 12, 1880, the five friars previously referred to sent to Rome from St. Dominic's Monastery, San Francisco, a formidable and eloquent Latin statement of all that Vilarrasa had been writing for years—plus some interesting additions of their own. They wished, they wrote, to protest as vigorously as possible concerning the arbitrary actions of Archbishop Alemany, and proceeded to spell out very eloquently what they considered these actions to have been. "Tyrannical have been these actions in the extreme," they reported, adding that it has been "frequently an occasion of wonder to us how an Archbishop who is regarded as so pious by all would dare to spurn, rather to crush under his feet, rights and privileges guaranteed to our Order by the Holy See itself!

---

tion and at considerable inconvenience to themselves as well as disastrous results to their Dominican observances. "How can the Friars observe their rule of choir, etc.," asked Vilarrasa, "with these obligations thrust upon them by one who, above all, should know how serious these same obligations are?"

[34] Vilarrasa to Raymond Bianchi, O.P., procurator general of the Dominican Order, Rome. Benicia, October (exact date not given), 1878. AOPR.

[35] Vilarrasa to Sanvitò, Rome; Benicia, December 10, 1878. AOPR. An indication of Vilarrasa's feelings at this time is found in a blunt letter which he wrote to Alemany on October 7, 1878. Vilarrasa told Alemany that the friars could not undertake the permanent care of some Indian missions around Mariposa and in Mono County, although "Fr. William Dempflin, O.P. can make occasional visits as he does." He then states: "Had I been a prophet, I would never have consented to come to California—and I can assure that many times have repented [sic] of having done so. . . ." Copy in AOPC.

Either ignorance or pride moves him; indeed, it is possible that he has a false conscience on the matter!"[36] There followed a detailed and indignant enumeration of the "long sufferings" which the friars had been made to undergo by their Dominican "brother"—added justification for their present communication was found, they added, in the fact that "our most excellent Father Vilarrasa has requested us to write this letter and thus to enter our protest against what has been happening here with us these many years." The impassioned letter finishes with the hope and prayer that remedies may be applied immediately by Roman authorities to correct a situation which had resulted in so much harm to religion and to the Dominican Order.

As it became evident in the Jesuit-Alemany disputes, the latter was never one to confine himself to Roman correspondence alone—he was always ready to write to people on the local scene when occasion demanded. Middle August, 1880, therefore, saw Archbishop Alemany complaining rather bitterly in a long letter which he wrote to Vilarrasa concerning the tone of a communication which he had received from Father Benedict McGovern, the prior of St. Dominic's Monastery. Alemany protested that some of McGovern's language was insulting in the extreme, especially when he found himself accused of most flagrant and extravagant injustices and of inflicting treatment on the Dominican fathers which was usually reserved to slaves! The irate Alemany thus wrote to Vilarrasa:

> I was thinking that I had done pretty well, considering my ability and the circumstances, for the existence, permanency and advancement of the Order in this diocese; but the Prior takes me to task, as if having inflicted the greatest injury to the Order and being the main cause of its not prospering. In its boldest and most disrespectful manner the letter calls me to an account for all my sins committed and omitted which I will not now enumerate.
>
> My object at present is to state: 1. that I protest against my ever

having had any other intention than that of promoting the good and prosperity of the Order, as far as means and providence could allow: 2. that whatever I wished the Dominicans to do, was, as I thought, and as I have reason to think yet, within my authority. I may have been mistaken, and I may not. This shall be examined, and accordingly remedied or confirmed, or prudently modified if I have the right. But what is altogether very wrong, under the color of right, is the insulting manner in which a bishop is addressed. Suppose I was wrong in my construction of the Papal Constitution and acted accordingly; could he not write a respectful letter? And if not satisfied, could he not refer the case to you? And if he found no remedy could he not appeal to the General, who could have settled all in a most easy way? . . . Decisions of the Holy See seem to me to justify my acts, which he calls, by turns, unjust, invalid and most tyrannical—most flagrant and extravagant injustice—the treatment inflicted on slaves and even worse than such!

If I have erred in the interpretation given to the Papal Constitutions, it was an error of the head, not of the heart I hope. Such error he might and could have had easily corrected by the ordinary process or means pointed out by the discipline of the Church; but the means adopted by him in his style are not the best to favor the progress which I have at heart as much as he. Personally I can let him call me all the hard names he pleases, but as a bishop I believe I must not let this pass unnoticed.

As such letter dwells on many real or imaginary grievances, I shall have to refer to it on some other occasion. I repeat, that nothing shall be required by me, but what after due examination shall be found to be demanded of me by the will of the Church and the interests of the Order.[37]

A week later, Vilarrasa expressed his regret to Alemany that McGovern should have phrased his complaints in such language as reported by the offended Prelate. However, he added that "while I disapprove of the language, Father McGovern is a good priest and a pious religious and he has great respect for authority: I believe it was a want of reflection rather than malice that caused him to use that stile [*sic*]. I believe you when you

[37] Alemany to Vilarrasa, San Francisco, August 17, 1880. AOPC.

say that you have always desired the good of our Order and done what you thought prudent for its welfare. In order to avoid any future misunderstandings, if you have no objections, I will collect the principal points that give dissatisfaction and we will endeavor to settle them in a most convenient manner and if you prefer it (which I believe would be more secure) the General may be consulted. But I will not do it unless you say so. . . ."[38]

This interchange of letters between Alemany and Vilarrasa was finished, it would seem, with another letter from the former, dated September 5, 1880, in which the Archbishop, while thanking Vilarrasa for his "kind letter with regard to Father McGovern," added that he had received a note from the Prior of St. Dominic's "which he intends as an apology, but which is rather a confirmation or justification of his previous one."[39] Evidently, the embattled superior of the Dominicans in San Francisco was not of a mind to retract the essential accusations which he had expressed, perhaps too enthusiastically, in his former letter to Alemany. Presumably, too, the latter's peace of soul would not have been increased had he ever had occasion to come by a letter which Father Antoninus Rooney, one of the five signers of the letter of protest to the master general, sent to Father Vilarrasa several months later. In this letter, Rooney told Vilarrasa that he had visited Father Varsi the day before at the Jesuit residence, and the two had agreed that it might be well to join forces and send to Rome conjointly one memorial containing all of the charges against the Archbishop!

He was much pleased at this view of the case, regards it as just to ourselves and as calculated to give us strength in Rome. . . . He says that he has already directly sent nearly all his complaints to the Holy Father and he assured me that he is quite certain that the Ordinary has received a letter from the Pope commanding him not to molest

[38] Vilarrasa to Alemany, Benicia, California, August 24, 1880. Copy in AOPC.

[39] Alemany to Vilarrasa, San Francisco, California. AOPC.

the Jesuits. . . . Fr. Varsi is very communicative, knows his rights and fears nothing.[40]

While it might appear that the time had been reached when more letters were unnecessary between Alemany and Vilarrasa, such was not to be the case, for on February 6, 1881, the latter returned to the fray with another frank letter in which he continued to take issue with the Archbishop on several matters. He informed Alemany that it was simply impossible for the Dominicans to furnish further help in various parishes in San Francisco and vicinity, and that he could not commit his priests to give one quarter of the retreats and missions in the diocese as requested by Alemany—"such a promise would indicate that we have been previously unwilling. Not so. Actually, we probably have given as many as one quarter already. We'll continue to do the best we can. We are not only willing, but anxious. Same thing about confessors of nuns—we shall do the best we can."[41]

When, in 1881, the Dominican master general, Father Joseph Larroca, made a journey to New York from Rome to make an official visitation of St. Joseph's Province, Vilarrasa made an unsuccessful effort to get him to continue on to California as support to his endeavors to defend Dominican rights and privileges. He thus wrote to Larroca's companion to ask his help in getting the Master General to come to California:

Though the Father General will not find here things entirely as he would wish, yet I am confident that, as a general rule, he will find the Fathers well disposed. This visit would give great encouragement and it would enable him to be acquinted [sic] with the circumstances of this country.

Your second letter was received whilst we were assembled in Benicia for our Biennial Chapter. I communicated to the Fathers the

[40] Anthony Rooney, O.P., to Vilarrasa, San Francisco, November 29, 1880. AOPC.
[41] Vilarrasa to Alemany, Benicia, California, February 6, 1881. Copy in AOPC.

approaching visit of Father General in St. Joseph's Province. It was unanimously resolved to send a petition (which I enclose here) begging Father General to come to California. Moreover, it was also unanimously resolved that California, *must* supply all the expenses for the voyage.[42]

It would appear, though, that Larroca did not intend to go to California, for, in a letter which he sent to Rome, after mentioning his arrival in America, he adds that, while he would like to go to California to make a visitation of the Dominican brethren there, he wonders if he can spare the time. "And then there is that blessed Archbishop, *mi e poco simpatico!*"[43] Evidently, Larroca thought that little or nothing constructive would be accomplished by any visit to California at this time. (However, as will be indicated later, it is quite possible that Alemany's long-standing stubbornness might finally have counted against him in the fulfillment of the project so dear to his heart—the founding of an apostolic college in Spain to train Dominicans for the Spanish-speaking areas of America with the retired Archbishop Alemany as superior and director of the enterprise.)

Holy Week of 1882 witnessed a new area of conflict arising between Alemany and the friars of St. Dominic's Monastery. Since pontifical requirements at the principal Mass on Holy Thursday—that of the blessing of the holy oils—required the presence of many assistant priests, Alemany reiterated an order, which he had issued two years previously, that five of the six priests assigned to St. Dominic's Church be with him to assist him with these ceremonies. This put a grievous burden on the understaffed friars who had reported to Rome in 1880 that only three of their number were actually able to be present; they had been interested to note that only six of the eighteen Jesuits of

[42] Vilarrasa to Joseph Carberry, O.P., Benicia, California, June 3, 1881. AOPC. Carberry was an Irish Dominican who served as secretary to Father Larroca on this visit to the United States.

[43] Larroca to Bianchi, New York, June 10, 1881. AOPR.

St. Ignatius College were present, while the pastors of the city were represented by only two of their number. Perhaps correctly, they felt that an injustice was being worked upon them—and that this was but another attempt on the part of Alemany to exert undue pressure upon them. Indeed, he had remarked in an earlier letter on the subject that, while considering himself completely within his rights in ordering the friars to be present at this Mass, "if we wished a fight, he was quite prepared to have one." On July 11, 1882, Alemany wrote to Larroca enclosing a letter for him to read concerning the matter and asking the Master General to send it on for him to Cardinal Simeoni, prefect of Propaganda.[44] Another letter of a few months later reiterated Alemany's firm stand on this matter—although there is no indication that any final decision was issued by Roman authorities.

In any event, it would seem that Alemany was too busy in 1883 and the final year of his reign, 1884, in the matter of obtaining his coadjutor and successor to have any more encounters with Vilarrasa or his Dominican brethren. If he did, available documentary sources are silent on the matter. One wonders how much of all that has here been told had been forgotten—when, on Tuesday, May 19, 1885, among those present at an official farewell for Alemany before his departure for his native Spain were four of his Dominican Order. One of these was Father Bernard Doogan who, as sub-prior of the St. Dominic's community in San Francisco, had four years previously been among the signers of the solemn protest against Alemany. One thing remains certain—that Joseph Sadoc Alemany ever regarded himself as a Dominican unto the end, and he testified to the fact when, on July 24, 1886, in a letter of congratulation written from his place of retirement in Valencia, Spain, to the newly created James Cardinal Gibbons of Baltimore, he began with

[44] AOPR.

the words: "Permit this old Dominican in the old world to congratulate you," and signed it in the customary Dominican manner, despite his episcopal rank: "Br. Joseph S. Alemany, O.P., Abp. of Pelusium."[45]

[45] AAB. "Pelusium" refers to the titular see assigned to Alemany upon his retirement from the See of San Francisco. It is an ancient see in Asia Minor.

12

Final Years in San Francisco

THE San Francisco of the 1870's and 1880's is frequently referred to as the Silver City because of the influences which the riches of the Comstock Lode in Nevada had upon its economic development. San Francisco had reached its centennial year in 1876 and Alemany was a prominent participant in the attendant commemorations. During the last full decade of his administration, it was more than evident that the infant pueblo of pre-Gold Rush days, which had been hurried into manhood by the discovery of gold in California in 1848, had arrived securely at a place in the sun of civilization. San Francisco had just about everything that a colorful metropolis should have during these years. Emperor Norton and Denis Kearney, as well as a multitude of lesser lights, must be counted among the leading celebrities—and the steady growth of the city was evident, among others, to its Archbishop who always had to consider the problems which came with just such growth. Almost 150,000 persons lived in San Francisco in 1870, and this number included an impressive aristocracy of wealth, although relatively few of the "nabobs" who dwelt on Nob Hill were subject to Alemany's spiritual jurisdiction. It may be doubted that the simple tastes which had marked Alemany from the beginning needed to be satisfied by any invitations to the tables of Leland Stanford, Mark Hopkins, Collis Huntington, and Charles Crocker or their associates; Alemany, while conscious of the importance of these

277

builders of the transcontinental railroad and of the other enterprises which marked their lives, counted little upon their support in his work.

As Alemany entered his final decade as archbishop, official census figures revealed that San Francisco had risen in population to almost 234,000—quite an advance since the last decennial census. This impressive figure represented about one-fourth of all the population of California. Men outnumbered women by two to one, and this continuing disproportion brought its own pastoral problems. Since older men dream dreams, it would not seem completely chimerical to think that Archbishop Alemany must have reflected many times concerning the changing scene since his arrival, three decades before, in Gold Rush San Francisco as the newly consecrated bishop of the Diocese of Monterey. Some of his present problems would be left to his successor to solve; others represented a later and more developed phase of some of the earlier perplexities which had been his since the beginning. One which was constantly on his mind concerned the founding and successful manning of the seminaries which would have to provide priests to carry on the work of a former generation. Judging from the amount of documentary support one finds here in the form of letters, petitions, and the like, this was one of Alemany's main objects for many years— during which time he suffered some severe disappointments, though his efforts laid the groundwork which was used by his successor. But though Alemany retired from his see in 1884, the problem of getting priests to man his seminary was not yet solved.

In 1840, California's first bishop, the Franciscan Garcia Diego, opened a small seminary at Mission Santa Barbara; in the short six years of his administration, 1840–1846, he ordained six secular priests for his vast diocese of Upper and Lower California. However, for only two of these years did the seminary remain at Santa Barbara, for, after an interval, it was transferred to Mission Santa Iñes. Opening there in 1844, it operated for about ten years, with its history marked by many difficulties and dark moments. In 1853, Bishop Alemany opened a new seminary at Mission Dolores in San Francisco, but again the time proved to be inopportune, and later, in 1866, much to Alemany's distress, this seminary was forced to close its doors. The three students were transferred to other seminaries outside of California to continue their studies. For almost two decades he was to be dependent upon such outside sources as the Irish and other European seminaries for most of his priests—and, as indicated, this was a matter of deep concern to him. This is made evident by a notation in the minutes of a meeting of the California bishops which was held in San Francisco in 1876 and which was reported by Bishop O'Connell, acting as secretary for the meeting. He mentioned that "the Archbishop proposed to prepare the way to open a Provincial Seminary (which idea pleased all of us) as did, also, his proposal that we all endeavor to seek out a religious Order or Congregation which would be willing to staff such a seminary."[1]

In November, 1876, Alemany was able to inform Cardinal Franchi that he had entered into correspondence with the superior general of the Sulpicians in Paris and hoped to persuade him to send some of his subjects to inaugurate the work in California; in this hope he was to be disappointed, for it was not until the time of his successor, Archbishop Patrick W. Riordan, that the Sulpicians arrived in California.[2] Two years later, since the matter had not been brought to any conclusion, Cardinal Franchi himself wrote to the Sulpician superior enlisting his aid in behalf of Alemany.[3] On November 14, 1878, Franchi wrote encour-

[1] O'Connell to Franchi, San Francisco, February 12, 1876. APF.
[2] Alemany to Franchi, San Francisco, November 5, 1876. APF.
[3] Franchi to Père Icard, Superior General of the Society of St. Sulpice, August 27, 1878. Copy in APF.

279

agingly to Alemany to say that he had received a favorable answer from Paris; the Sulpician general had replied that he would do all in his power to assist the Archbishop in his needs with regard to the staffing of a seminary in his archdiocese where, after arrival, they would hope "to train his men with the same solicitude with which we train our own subjects."[4] By the next year, however, it was evident that the Sulpicians could not fulfill their intentions, and Alemany began to correspond with the Marist fathers in Lyons in the hope that they would come to his aid. In early 1879, a delighted Alemany reported to Rome that he had high hopes of getting the services of several such Fathers, and asked help from Franchi to have the matter arranged "before the arrival of my coadjutor."[5] (Actually, Alemany was yet four years away from the appointment of his coadjutor and he was to wait three more years before the Marists finally arrived to staff the seminary.) On July 7, 1882, Alemany wrote Franchi's successor, Cardinal Simeoni, that he had virtually completed arrangements with these Fathers, and it was a happy day when, in 1882, four Marists arrived from France to open a diocesan seminary at Mission San Jose.[6] This they staffed for only two years, however, and no doubt their departure was an added affliction for Alemany. On July 25, 1884, he thus wrote to Bishop Patrick Manogue of the Diocese of Grass Valley:

I tried my very best to avoid the sad event of the Marist Fathers abandoning the post they accepted without giving me time to look elsewhere. God's Will be done. They are now all gone. We must not close up the seminary which would be a lasting damper and discouragement. Besides the 5 seminarians, we have from 4 to 8 on the way; so we must strain every nerve to bridge over the time till God grants us some good Sulpitians [sic] or others. I wrote to P. Icard. Perhaps you might repeat your earnest prayers to him. . . . They say the

[4] Franchi to Alemany, Rome, November 14, 1878. Copy in APF.
[5] Alemany to Simeoni, San Francisco, March 2, 1879. APF.
[6] APF.

Basilian Fathers of Canada are very good for this object. But I would rather wait if we could receive any kind of encouragement from the Sulpitians. Now I would ask: have you any suitable priest to spare to conduct the Seminary pro tem. If not, I will try to get two or three myself, although a little cramped.[7]

In a somewhat limping fashion, several priests of the archdiocese carried on at Mission San Jose until June, 1885, when, with the continued non-appearance of the Sulpicians, the seminary was closed and the few students sent to Baltimore to complete their studies.

Alemany's earlier request in 1868 for a coadjutor had been blocked by the expressed opinion of some of the American bishops that he should remain at the helm for some time more. When in 1875 the *terna* or list proposed by Alemany and the several other bishops of California faced the complication that Father Prendergast, Alemany's vicar general and the one most favored to be his coadjutor, absolutely refused to be considered for such an office, it behooved the bishops to rearrange this list. Thus it was that, gathered in episcopal conference in San Francisco in February, 1876, Alemany, joined with the other California prelates, received their approbation to substitute the name of Bishop William Henry Elder of Natchez, Mississippi, for that of the reluctant Prendergast. "All," reported Bishop O'Connell, "agreed unanimously with the Archbishop in the substitution of Elder's name."[8]

Several days later, Alemany wrote to the Cardinal Prefect to tell him of what he had learned concerning the estimable qualities of Bishop Elder and why he thought that his appointment to San Francisco with the right of succession would be a good and acceptable move. Presumably, though, he was not yet con-

---

[7] Alemany to Manogue, San Francisco, July 25, 1884. It would appear that Manogue had forwarded Alemany's letter to the Cardinal Prefect in Rome. APF.

[8] Minutes of Meeting by Bishop O'Connell. February 12, 1876. APF.

versant with Elder's own views; these became apparent in due time in a letter which the latter sent to Cardinal Franchi wherein he gave detailed reasons why he should not be translated from Mississippi to California—or to any place else. Elder wrote that he thought that such a change as was contemplated could not be affected without grave detriment to both Natchez and to San Francisco. Moreover, his diocese had many unique problems resulting from the ravages of the Civil War and was encumbered with a substantial debt. Therefore, it was Elder's conviction that he should be allowed to remain at his post and to finish his work there. In addition, Elder was convinced that he was not endowed with the considerable talents which he considered indispensable for one who would assist and then succeed Alemany in a growing jurisdiction such as that in California. "I have a disposition along lines of an active missionary life and am ill suited to be the sort of administrator and corrector of the clergy that would be required of me . . . in California . . . actually, I would freely lay down the episcopal burden entirely lest my responsibilities continue to grow—for all of which I know I must account to the Supreme Pastor of souls."[9] Elder ended by indicating what he considered to be his other shortcomings, and earnestly implored the Cardinal to entreat the Holy Father not to order the change.

Elder, of course, did not much want to go to California—which was very much of a "far country" in the 1870's. However, he was not to escape so easily as by writing a letter. Since no coadjutor for San Francisco was forthcoming, two years later Alemany renewed his request that something be done. At length, on May 6, 1878, Propaganda authorities decided that Elder should go to San Francisco as they had previously desired; in this decision they were supported by Leo XIII, who, in an audience granted to the Cardinal Prefect on May 12, confirmed the

[9] William Henry Elder to Franchi, Natchez, Mississippi, April 21, 1876. APF. Elder served as third bishop of Natchez, 1857–1880.

appointment.[10] Several months later, a curious comment appeared in the columns of the Portland, Oregon, *Catholic Sentinel*:

> The daily press of San Francisco have this week been discussing the pros and cons on the question of an appointment of a Coadjutor for this Archdiocese. Some of the journalists have attributed the change to motives far at variance with the truth, one journal alleging that the Jesuits were at the bottom of the movements, whilst every Catholic knows that the Most Reverend Archbishop has been for many years seeking to retire from the active management of this vast and rapidly growing field of missionary enterprise.[11]

Roman authorities lost no time in sending on the bulls of Elder's appointment to San Francisco. Under date of May 16, 1878, Alemany was informed that his coadjutor had been appointed and that the necessary documents had been forwarded to him.[12] However, as he may well have suspected by this time, it was one thing to have a coadjutor appointed and quite another thing to have him delivered safely to San Francisco! This is precisely what he was to find out in the present circumstances. Elder again represented his position to Propaganda, this time adding that his diocese was in distress and disorganized because of cholera attacks which had resulted in a considerable number of deaths among both clergy and laity. In his opinion, this was even a worse time to contemplate his translation to San Francisco than had been the previous attempt two years before. Evidently, Rome was impressed with the reasons of the still reluctant Elder, for Alemany was informed, at the close of 1878, that at least for the time being Elder would remain in Natchez "because of conditions prevailing there."[13]

That Alemany himself had not been unacquainted with the

[10] Minutes, meeting of plenary session of cardinals of Congregation de Propaganda Fide, May 6, 1878. APF.

[11] Portland *Catholic Sentinel*, August 29, 1878. "Letter of An Oregonian Abroad."

[12] The decree of Propaganda which gave Alemany the good—if premature—news of his reception of a coadjutor is dated May 16, 1878. APF.

[13] Simeoni to Alemany. Rome, December 31, 1878. Copy in APF.

283

reluctance of Elder to come to California as his coadjutor is shown by a letter which he had written earlier to Simeoni in which he had proved himself quite conversant with the whole matter, while leaving the final decision to Roman authorities.[14] In 1880, Bishop Elder was selected as coadjutor to the aging Archbishop Purcell of Cincinnati. The news that he had, in effect, lost his coadjutor to Cincinnati was known to Alemany by February, 1880. It caused him to write to Simeoni from San Francisco on February 16, 1880: "By the direction of Divine Providence, I see that my coadjutor, Bishop Elder, has been granted to the Archbishop of Cincinnati as his coadjutor. I therefore ask Your Eminence whether I should now submit another name for this position here (after I have consulted my brother Bishops) since I so much need such a helper. . . ."[15] Simeoni replied on March 21, 1880, that Alemany should indeed start the selection of such another list.[16] Finally, to make certain that there be no confusion in the matter, Simeoni wrote Alemany that he hoped that the latter had received his telegram "informing you that, under date of February 4, I sent Bishop Elder his Briefs as Coadjutor of Cincinnati and a copy to you. I hope that you received them safely."[17] So, by 1880 and after much tribulation, Archbishop Alemany and the See of San Francisco were still without benefit of a coadjutor Archbishop. It was to take three more years before the matter was to be finally settled with the appointment of Father Patrick Riordan of Chicago.

Perhaps another reason why Alemany's petitions to resign his see were received unfavorably in Rome was his success in managing the finances of his growing archdiocese. It may be also that one of the main reasons why the Roman authorities deferred action for so very long in the matters of his resignation and the appointment of a coadjutor was simply because they were convinced

14 Alemany to Simeoni, San Francisco, November 25, 1878. APF.
15 Alemany to Simeoni, San Francisco, February 16, 1880. APF.
16 Simeoni to Alemany, Rome, March 21, 1880. APF.
17 Simeoni to Alemany, Rome, April 29, 1880. Copy in APF.

that a very competent administrator was at work in far-off California. Spain and an apostolic college headed by Alemany could wait; meanwhile, the Spanish Dominican friar was to continue serving his Church in the western United States. An instance of Alemany's business acumen is to be found in a letter which Alemany wrote to Archbishop Bayley of Baltimore in 1876 about the best financial arrangements to be made concerning the North American College in Rome:

. . . I am still of opinion that the best friends of the American College should and could find some Priest in Mass. or Kentucky, who could be constituted Procurator of the College and who could keep the Students sufficiently well clothed with $50.— a year (the Holy Father don't [sic] spend more) and sufficiently well boarded with $150.— (I doubt whether the Holy Father eats more). From the price of provisions in Rome in 1870, I am inclined to think that a really good economist could run the College at $200 a piece, no matter how few the students might be. Dr. Chatard is an admirable man and is well in his post; but he may not be an economist, and likely would be glad to have one near him charged with that department. I think the College should be kept all the time, for our greatly growing Church in the States will always demand ecclesiastics well educated, but it seems to me clear that in order to have a sufficient number of Prelates interested in this, the expenses should be brought low or within the moderate bounds of other colleges.[18]

Further evidence of a sustained interest in the North American College was given by Alemany at the end of the following year when, after writing some characteristically frank and blunt advice to Father Chatard, its rector, Alemany thus expressed his opinion of the prospects for the College:

The Church in our country, with God's blessing, is obviously destined to be prominent in talent, erudition, efficiency and numbers. The astonishing increase within a few dozen of years in its dioceses, colleges, convents, Priests and Catholics promises a most properous condition in the near future.

To guide that prosperity it will be necessary to have men possessed

[18] Alemany to Bayley, San Francisco, February 19, 1876. AAB.

285

of solid ecclesiastical learning and a sound spirit of devotion to Rome and Roman sentiments. The College in Rome would be one of the principal means to secure those attainments, hence all efforts should be used to secure the permanence, enlargement and prosperity of that College.[19]

No doubt, Archbishop Alemany had always been quite proud of his American citizenship, which in 1845 he had received while serving in Memphis, Tennessee. Now, in 1876, with the centennial year of national independence at hand, Alemany rejoiced in the opportunities which it would afford him and his flock to thank Almighty God publicly for the blessings of the century. To prepare the Catholics under his care for the advent of July 4, particularly significant in the centennial year, the Archbishop issued a pastoral letter calling special attention to "Our Nation's Feast and to its due celebration."

This is the Centennial year of our proud independence as a nation. A hundred years since, our country was a wilderness, her lands untilled, her resources undeveloped, her population sparse, and war being waged against the thirteen poor colonies by one of the most powerful Governments of modern times. But thanks to the noble patriots of the Revolution, who, yielding to none—not even to the historic Spartans—in their devotion to liberty, honor and chivalric aims, we came through the ordeal a glorious and free people. They left us their Declaration of Independence as a model of sublimity for the admiration of mankind. They framed for us a Constitution whose provisions secure for every soul that dwells beneath it—together with ample protection for "life, liberty and the pursuit of happiness"—as much genuine freedom as is the happiness of man to enjoy, if not the fullest enjoyed in any portion of the civilized world. Under the benign influence of the Republic our disenthralled country has experienced a hundred years of wonderful success, and has made gigantic strides towards prosperity and refinement. . . . We ought, therefore, to thank God from our hearts for mercifully bestowing upon us such choice favors and with such a lavish hand.[20]

[19] Alemany to Very Reverend Francis S. Chatard, San Francisco, December 31, 1877. Copy in AAB. Chatard served as rector of the North American College in Rome, 1868–1878.
[20] Pastoral letter. San Francisco, June 26, 1876. Copy in AUSF.

286

Civic and church authorities had agreed that one of the outstanding events of the centennial commemoration would take place at Mission Dolores on the anniversary of its foundation on October 8, 1776. As was to be expected, Archbishop Alemany was to play a principal part in this celebration. (Several months before he had dedicated the new St. Vibiana's Cathedral in Los Angeles. At the dinner which followed, he had delivered an address on the foundation of the earlier California missions. With obvious emotion, he saluted the "early trials of our Christian Fathers in redeeming from savagery our fair and prosperous state."[21])

The centennial celebration took place on Sunday, October 8, 1876. The compiler of a very complete account called *Our Centennial Memoir*[22] waxes rhapsodic as he records the principal events of the day:

> Although the dawn was overcast and broke over the green hills somewhat inauspiciously—spiritualizing, mayhap, the ordinarily bright skies of our favored clime—the genius loci seemed, as it were, to shine through the gloom and to invest the festal occasion with a halo.[23]

The pontifical Mass which marked the occasion was offered in the Mission grounds by Bishop O'Connell of Grass Valley.[24] A generous outpouring of clergy and laity were present. Archbishop Alemany had arranged to have another Dominican bishop, Thomas Grace of St. Paul, deliver the sermon. However, the latter's sudden and unexpected illness made it necessary for the Archbishop himself to do the honors. Calling the day one "of

[21] San Francisco *Monitor,* May 13, 1876.
[22] The full title of this valuable book is *Our Centennial Memoir. Founding of Missions. San Francisco de Assisi in Its Hundredth Year. The Celebration of Its Foundation. Historical Reminiscences of the Missions of California* (San Francisco, 1877).
[23] *Ibid.,* p. 57.
[24] *Ibid.,* where O'Connell is called, incorrectly, the "Bishop of Marysville." At the time of this Mass, his service as vicar apostolic had been terminated and he had been translated to the newly created diocese of Grass Valley, which had been formed out of the old vicariate of Marysville.

joy and exultation," Alemany, who could certainly consider himself a part of what he spoke because of his more than quarter century of service as a bishop in California, outlined the history of his adopted state and said that he rejoiced in commemorating the "hundredth anniversary of the existence of San Francisco as a civil and religious community, because we are especially interested in the establishment and prosperous duration of its double edifice [mission and presidio] which were laid in this place by our forefathers a hundred years ago."[25] Alemany's sermon, which he gave first in English and then in Spanish, was a lengthy one and concluded with some well-chosen words:

> Well may California be proud of her heroic, disinterested Christian pioneers who, in a short time, transformed numberless barbarous tribes into comparatively well-civilized Christian communities; and well may we echo today with sweet strains of joyous melody the solemn *Te Deum* intoned here for the first time one hundred years ago.
>
> In conclusion, let me pray that the Mission of the Franciscans—the establishment of Christianity in this country—may ever prove successful, and that our prosperous city may ever be favored with God's choicest benedictions, which will be the case if its citizens will be guided by the Christian counsels inaugurated here a century ago. . . . It is obvious that we shall not witness the next Centennial here; but I hope and pray that we may all see it from on high, celebrated here again with Christian spirit and becoming solemnity.[26]

The centennial Mass was followed by an elaborate parade made up of fifteen divisions which marched all the way to Portsmouth Plaza and then back to the Mechanics' Pavilion on Mission and Eighth streets. In the afternoon, 11,000 persons crowded into the spacious Pavilion and listened to addresses by many dignitaries including the remarks of Governor William Irwin.

[25] *Ibid.*, p. 60. Some students of local history, including the present writer, would not agree with Alemany's date as to the founding of San Francisco. However, a digression on this rather complicated point would take us too far afield.

[26] *Ibid.*, p. 68.

Although the main addresses were delivered by General Mariano Guadalupe Vallejo and the Honorable John D. Dwinelle, Archbishop Alemany and Bishop O'Connell occupied prominent places in the orchestra section of the Pavilion. Both prelates must surely have been pleased with the ringing words with which Dwinelle brought his oration to an end:

> Behold the contrast. A hundred years ago today not fifty people were present when the foundation of the city of San Francisco was laid. Today, thousands assist at this celebration. . . . Then, there was absolutely no population. Now, there are upwards of 300,000. In another hundred years . . . I cannot doubt that San Francisco will be the largest city on the Pacific Ocean and that at least twenty millions will occupy territory ceded by Mexico to the American Union; nor can I doubt that in that territory, the Catholic Church will maintain her comparative strength. I have not, on this occasion, uttered a word in praise of the Holy Apostolic Roman Catholic Church. If I had been one of her sons, I should have given her such a tribute as full of gratitude as of truth. . . . But, Protestant as I am, I am not afraid to say that I rejoice in the strength and prosperity of the Holy Apostolic Roman Catholic Church; and that, when I predict that a hundred years from now, she will be stronger than ever, and that her greatest strength will be in the United States, it is because my heart goes with the prediction.[27]

In the afternoon, both Archbishop Alemany and Bishop O'Connell returned by carriage to Mission Dolores, where the Archbishop laid the cornerstone for a new church alongside the old Mission Dolores.[28] A large assemblage of the faithful was

[27] *Ibid.,* p. 96. Dwinelle's predictions and projections were not too wide of the mark. As these lines are written in 1965, California, with a population of more than 18,000,000—ranks as number one in this regard in the American Union.

[28] The "new" Mission Dolores Church, whose cornerstone was laid on this occasion, was built of brick and was so badly damaged by the San Francisco earthquake and fire of April 18, 1906, that it was torn down. Meanwhile, the old adobe mission next door suffered only relatively minor damage. Evidently, the Franciscan padres built their thick, well-buttressed adobe walls with care and after earlier experiences with earthquakes.

on hand to witness the simple ceremony which was performed by Alemany without benefit of any more speeches; presumably, enough had been already said on that Sunday to satisfy all!

It was perhaps too much to expect that Protestant extremists would take too kindly to what some called the "Romish celebrations" of that Sunday. We may first quote a comparatively dispassionate mention of the general Catholic picture in 1876 in San Francisco as it appeared to B. E. Lloyd, author of a popular history of the city which appeared a month before the centennial celebrations:

> The Roman Catholic influence is very great in San Francisco, though not so preponderating as might be thought, when we recall the fact that California was at one time controlled by the Jesuit priesthood [!]. This, however, furnishes no criterion by which to judge of the religious status of California today. Perhaps none of the native Californians accept any other religious belief than that taught by the Catholic clergy, but the native Californians are fast disappearing from the stage . . . but many of those who have sided in wresting from the well-disposed natives their title to their mother territory, are strong adherents to the Catholic faith. Particularly is this true of the foreign population. It constitutes the principal strength of Romanism in San Francisco.[29]

Not nearly so objective was the obvious disgust registered in the columns of the Methodist paper, the *California Christian Advocate*, only a few days after the events of October 8:

> Disgraceful! We are humiliated that Governor Irwin, Mayor Bryant, a number of Judges, City Supervisors and other officials gave their sanction, by their presence, to the Romish pageant last Sunday. When the public sentiment of evangelical Christendom is trampled underfoot by such desecration of the Lord's Day by the rulers of the people—it indicates a state of morals deplorably low. . . . The usual High Mass and the parade . . . filled the streets for several hours—greatly to the annoyance and disturbance of worshipping congregations whose rights on such occasions are utterly ignored. It seems that the Sabbath in this

[29] B. E. Lloyd. *Lights and Shades in San Francisco* (San Francisco, 1876), pp. 496–497.

city—as in other places where the papal church is numerically strong —is utterly abolished.

Judge Dwinelle, who claims to be a Protestant, was the orator. He is reported to have conceded to the Romish Church the parentage of "modern civilization"—of a certain species, it is, unquestionably, the mother: such civilizations as flourishes in Spain, in central America, in portions of Mexico and in all other countries where Protestant influences do not exert an appreciable influence. The civilization of medieval times is a fair specimen of what the church produces. Whoever gives that effete ecclesiasticism credit for any modern progress in the arts of civilized life simply stultifies himself.[30]

Perhaps, after all, there was some ground for alarm and for concern on the part of those, who like the *Advocate* editor, feared Roman Catholicism, for there was abundant evidence of the solid growth of Catholicism in northern California. As of the centennial year, the Catholic population of the entire archdiocese was estimated at about 120,000, served by 93 churches, 16 chapels, 121 priests, 51 regulars and 70 secular priests. When it is reflected that, in 1849,

a small wooden shanty erected upon the site of the present tasteful church of St. Francis, Vallejo St., was, with the exception of Mission Dolores, the only house of prayer in the commercial metropolis of the Pacific Coast, the march of Catholic progress is evident. . . . The numerous religious edifices throughout the city are monuments of the piety and munificence of the Catholic community.[31]

Although Archbishop Alemany was much too realistic and appreciative of others' efforts to relate all of this progress to himself, it is obviously true, of course, that he must receive due credit for much of this progress of which he was the architect and the builder.

Frequently, one arrives more quickly at historical truth when one comes upon a private expression of opinion not written with thought of publication. Of this type of evidence concerning the

[30] California *Christian Advocate* (San Francisco), October 12, 1876.
[31] *Our Centennial Memoir,* p. 156.

contemporary esteem felt for Archbishop Alemany by at least one of his priests (and, presumably, by many more, too) is the testimony written by Father Hugh Lagan, a young Irish priest who was a curate at St. Mary's Church in Oakland when, on October 24, 1876, he wrote to Father Fortune, then serving as president of Lagan's alma mater, All Hallows College in Dublin:

> Bright days are in store for the Church on this Coast. 25 years ago the tiny mustard seed—today, a truly gigantic growth. . . . What a future 25 years from now! It is watched over by a saintly Archbishop, a man for prudence, learning and piety not equalled in the American Episcopate; a man whose like we shall not see again. He is cruel with himself, indulgent and kind to others, ready to obey, reluctant to command. He is deeply loved and respected by all his priests.[32]

Brighter days were indeed in store for the Catholic Church in northern California—and not all of them were to wait a quarter century for their dawning. One, certainly, dawned on November 11, 1876, when Archbishop Alemany welcomed to San Francisco three members of a Dominican sisterhood which would figure largely and successfully in the future work of the archdiocese. Originally a German congregation from Ratisbon, Bavaria, these sisters had come to the United States to teach the children of German immigrants. In 1853, they had founded the Convent of the Holy Cross in Brooklyn, and, in time, this convent was responsible for ten other distinct offshoots of the Dominican family in the United States. Among these must be counted the Congregation of the Queen of the Holy Rosary with present-day headquarters at Mission San Jose.[33]

Not all the events of the 1870's in Alemany's episcopate were as peaceful as the successful introduction of another sisterhood

[32] AAHC.

[33] *Historical Sketch of the Dominican Congregation of the Queen of the Holy Rosary, Mission San Jose, California*, by a "Member of the Order." 1926. The story of the foundress is best told in *Her Days Unfolded—Reverend Mother Pia Backes, O.P.* (St. Benedict, Oregon, 1953).

to his diocese. The latter years of this decade were marked by the agitation of a labor leader, Denis Kearney of "The Chinese Must Go" fame. Since this Irishman, who had deserted his faith, recruited his supporters in large part from the native Irish Catholic laborers of San Francisco—or from those who were first-generation Irish—it was only to be expected that his rabble-rousing tactics and incendiary commands would become an object of grave concern to Alemany. Kearney, born in Ireland in 1847, had arrived in San Francisco in 1868 as the first mate of an appropriately named vessel, the *Shooting Star*—for such he was destined to be in the history of the city.

The middle and late years of the 1870's were, in part, years of financial distress and failures in northern California—largely because of economic difficulties on the Comstock Lode in Nevada, which was joined quite closely to the financial sinews of San Francisco. Many deserving breadwinners were unemployed, and Kearney let it be known that much of the trouble could be blamed upon the flood of cheap Chinese labor which had appeared throughout northern California when the completion of the transcontinental railroad in 1869 had rendered unemployed these same Chinese track-layers and unskilled laborers.

To the agitator Kearney, the solution was simple—he would form a political group and then make it into a party, the Workingmen's Party, and this he succeeded in doing in the late 1870's in San Francisco. Inflammatory speeches marked the sandlot meetings which he addressed as frequently as he could when, shaking a fist in the direction of Nob Hill—where the wealthy had their mansions—Kearney would threaten vengeance, suggest hanging parties, and shout defiance with such slogans as "Judge Lynch is the only Judge we want" and "Bullets will replace ballots—Hemp! Hemp! is the cry of freedom!" Most of his speeches ended with the refrain already quoted: "The Chinese Must Go—Denis Kearney Says So!" Since many of Kearney's fervent and frenzied followers were Catholics, Alemany felt it his duty to issue several pastoral charges denouncing the excesses of the entire movement. At the height of the agitation, and under date of July 25, 1877, the courageous Prelate issued a pastoral letter which was read in the pulpits of all of his churches. In it he remarked that he deemed it not out of place to call upon all good citizens, the Catholics in particular, to stand by authority. While freely admitting that the flood of Asiatic immigrants let loose upon California had grievously afflicted the workingmen of his flock, Alemany insisted that lawful redress must come from the government and that anarchy was not the answer. In a pointed conclusion to his short but incisive letter, Alemany wrote:

> Our people of California are, as a rule, strictly subordinate to authority, although a few may be misguided occasionally by unprincipled leaders. Hence I feel it my duty in these dangerous times to counsel all to shun suspicious company, to listen to no declaimer conniving at the subversion of quiet and order, to participate in no unauthorized move and to sustain to their utmost the legally constituted authorities.[34]

The *California Christian Advocate*, always quite eager and willing to criticize the Catholic body, had its own opinion of the Alemany letter. The editor expressed his thoughts thus:

> Do you wish proof that Romanism has trained a most violent and dangerous group in our population? It is at hand in a convincing though unexpected form. . . . I refer you to Archbishop Alemany's recent letter of admonition and entreaty to his people. The venerable prelate is doubtless a sincere and singularly simple-minded man. He must be so—to placard before the people such a damaging document. There are many poor people in the branches of the Protestant churches. Suppose a Methodist or Protestant Episcopal Bishop . . . were to issue an exhortation to their members to abstain from violence, incendiarism and murder; not to join the hoodlum mob, nor promote rioting in the streets. The whole nation would laugh out loud. . . . But, did

[34] Alemany's pastoral letter was printed in the San Francisco *Alta California*, July 26, 1877.

anybody think it unfit or untimely for the Archbishop publicly to advise his people in that way? No, for the reason that every man knows that the Papists of our cities are the fiercest, least self-governed, most unreasoning and furious mob element. The Proclamation was fit enough in point of time, import and authorship—but what of the system which prepared a people to need it? . . .[35]

As the crisis continued to mount, it became evident that Alemany would have to issue an even more direct prohibition to his flock in the matter of attending the Kearney meetings. Such a move could backfire, and, perhaps, cause more harm than good—and the record makes it clear that Alemany, firm but never rash in action, thought much before finally issuing such a prohibition. In middle November, 1877, the *Monitor* urged all Catholic workers to avoid the Kearney meetings. The July pastoral of the preceding year had been occasioned in part by some riots which had disturbed San Francisco, and, with their outbreak again in the spring of 1878, Alemany thought it his duty to be even more explicit in his pastoral advice. On Sunday, April 7, 1878, every churchgoer in the archdiocese heard Alemany's second letter, dated two days previously, in which he again denounced the excesses of the Workingmen's Party. After a brief but well-phrased resume of the situation, the Archbishop invoked his legitimate authority in the concluding words: "We, therefore, admonish and even require, everyone to stay away from such seditious, anti-social and anti-Christian meetings."[36] Several days later, the *California Christian Advocate* was prompt to add its helpful comment: "If the good Bishop's advice is heeded and the Romanists abandon such meetings, there will be but a thin attendance!"[37]

On May 9, the *Monitor* stressed the courage which animated the Archbishop in issuing this pastoral, while praising Alemany

[35] *California Christian Advocate*, August 23, 1877.

[36] Alemany's second pastoral appeared in the *Alta California*, April 9, 1878.

[37] *California Christian Advocate*, April 11, 1878.

for "forbidding his faithful children from associating themselves with any secret organization and also from attending any meetings at which sedition was spoken or threats of violence indulged in." In the editor's opinion, "this was the first serious check put to the mad course of the disturbers. Many of the workingmen of the city, probably a majority, are Catholics and, of course, they listened respectfully to the voice of their beloved prelate. In consequence, the attendance at the sandlots began to diminish."[38] It was proably because of such a diminishing attendance that, in the middle of 1878, Kearney went to the east coast to extend there the blessings of his movement. Returning to San Francisco several years later, he was to find himself pretty much without a following. It may well be imagined that he had no specially fond memories of Alemany who had, by courageous action, done much to destroy the base of his influence.[39]

It has been indicated that Alemany came in for his share of notice in the vigorous papers which comprised the Protestant press in the San Francisco of his day. But it is to be noted that, with the exception of the scurrilities which marred the columns of a bigoted paper such as the *Jolly Giant*—and which, obviously, Alemany would never stoop to notice—the occasional journalistic attacks were directed rather against institutionalized Catholicism as the Protestant editors understood it rather than the respected person of the archbishop himself. However, when in 1877 a pastoral letter was issued treating of mixed marriages, signed jointly by the three Catholic prelates of California, Arch-

[38] San Francisco *Monitor*, May 9, 1878. Editorial: "The Workingmen's Party—Past and Present."

[39] An interesting sequel to the Kearney story was that, by the middle 1880's, he was out of politics and into real estate with consequent solid pecuniary gains. With the inheritance of a fortune in Imperial Valley holdings in southern California, Kearney became quite indifferent to the plight of the workingmen—opining, on one occasion, that "watching the wheat game is harder business than excluding the Chinese." Losing his comfortable home in San Francisco in the fire and earthquake of 1906, Kearney went to live in Oakland where he died, almost forgotten, on April 24, 1907.

bishop Alemany, Bishop O'Connell, and Bishop Amat of Monterey and Los Angeles, a Presbyterian paper, the *Occident*, became indignant at the very idea "that a trio of old bachelors should thus dictate to the young men and women of this free land in regard to 'mutual affection,' 'matrimonial engagements,' and the 'education of children.' . . . What can they know about such matters? Rome says her pastors must not marry—and yet they claim the right to tell others who and how to marry! . . . give these Bishops the power and they would re-enact all the tyranny and cruelty of the past. Thank God, they can only fulminate pastoral letters now! They have no Inquisition to carry out their fulminations!"[40]

When, on February 7, 1878, the death of Pius IX ended his long reign of thirty-two years (1846–1878), Archbishop Alemany was surely among those with most personal memories of this Pontiff. It was Pio Nono who had summoned the 36-year-old Father Alemany in Rome in 1850 and ordered him to accept episcopal consecration. He it was who had sent him with the words ringing in his ears: "Others go to California to seek for gold—you are to go to seek the gold of souls." Alemany could take legitimate pride, too, in the fact that, after naming him to the comparatively brief stewardship of three years as bishop of Monterey, the same Pope had demonstrated his confidence in him by appointing him as first archbishop of San Francisco. So it was with a full heart that Alemany offered a pontifical Mass of requiem for the beloved Pio Nono in St. Mary's Cathedral on February 12, 1878. Heartfelt, too, must have been the words of the affectionate eulogy which Alemany pronounced at the end of the Mass. And on the very next day, he wrote to inform Cardinal Franchi of his sorrow in the death of Pius. "With the most profound sorrow, I have received the sad news of the death of the Holy Father, our most loved and venerated Pius IX. The populace here in general, including Protestants and the public

[40] *Occident* (San Francisco), December 19, 1877.

297

press, have had nothing but praise for such a good Pope. Let us hope that God, out of His goodness and love for his Holy Church, will grant us a new Pope according to the heart of Pius IX."[41]

At the end of 1879, Archbishop Alemany wrote to Cardinal Simeoni asking to be dispensed from the obligation of holding a provincial council. In this regard he was but repeating a similar request made by him in 1876 and then granted. His reason then had been the poor health of Bishop Amat and the fact that there would be only himself meeting with his other suffragan, Bishop O'Connell of Grass Valley.[42] Evidently, Alemany thought himself justified in making a similar plea three years later. He informed Simeoni that "we three Bishops do not think it expedient to summon a second Provincial Council; since we are only three, there would be little solemnity attached; besides, many of our parishes have only one priest, who could ill be spared for any such Synod; finally, the decrees of the Councils of Baltimore, which have force here, seem to cover the main points which would have to be discussed."[43] Roman authorities acquiesced in his request concerning the postponement of the otherwise required provincial council.

By the late 1870's, James Gibbons, then Archbishop of Baltimore and later Cardinal, had emerged as one of the most influential men in the American hierarchy. So it was that Alemany, who outranked him in seniority, wrote to him concerning a matter of vital importance—the obtaining of some more teaching brothers for the educational needs of his diocese. His letter, familiar in tone, read as follows:

Most Rev. Dear Sir,

Although we have suffered much difficulty in procuring lots, building Churches and managing debts created on that account, we feel that we must redouble our energies to procure the Christian education

[41] Alemany to Franchi, San Francisco, February 13, 1878.
[42] Alemany to Simeoni, November 30, 1876. APF.
[43] Alemany to Simeoni, December 19, 1879. APF.

of our boys. The good Christian Brothers have done far more than could be expected in that line; but they cannot expect additional numbers from the east or from Europe, and these formed here are not sufficient to attend to the various places requiring some such Brothers.

My object then is to ask you to aid an old friend both with your advice and in any other possible way. We live here at the end of the world, and I have not a fair chance to know where to apply to, and who are the best. I have Sisters of the Holy Cross from Indiana, and they do well, although (*entre nous*) they have shown a little small bit of want of holy and perfect docility. I have a confused idea that the Brothers of the Holy Cross did not always give full satisfaction. Good Archbp. Spalding commended to me once the Xaverian Brothers and promised me (in his name and that of his successor I should think) to aid me in procuring them. But at that time I had already had some understanding with the Christian Brothers, with whom I am very much pleased. Besides the above, I think that the Marist Brothers carry on schools successfully in England and Ireland. I would now request you to aid me with your views and directions on the above all important affair, and I will be very grateful.

How is your health? . . . When will you pay a visit to this beautiful Pacific?[44]

It was not long before Alemany again wrote to Gibbons—this time about an even more vital need, that of obtaining a co-adjutor now that Cincinnati had claimed Bishop Elder:

From a recent letter of the Cardinal Prefect I infer that my coadjutor will have to go to Cincinnati immediately; and thus I will have to continue to carry along the heavy load of this peculiar Diocese, which demands much care, especially in the temporal Administration.

Ergo, please help the old man by giving me a short list of young energetic and zealous Bishops, who besides prudence and some ability for preaching may be known as capable of attending to the temporal affairs. I have lived so long in this remote west, that I do not know much those in the east. I voted against my Coadjutor going to Cincinnati, because I think more of San Francisco than of Cincinnati; but as I fear I can no longer count on him, I would wish to be ready to present the name to the Holy See of some one else, well known for prudence, zeal and ability especially in temporal matters.[45]

[44] San Francisco, December 10, 1879. AAB.
[45] Alemany to Gibbons, San Francisco, February 24, 1880. AAB.

That Alemany was indeed feeling the need of some one to assist him seems evident from yet another dispensation which he felt obliged to ask in the middle of 1880. This time it was to be excused from journeying to Rome for his *ad limina* visit. This he requested of Simeoni in a letter of August 28, 1880, in which he mentioned the fact that he had forwarded an account of the state of his diocese—"it is late, but there is so much to be done here by me. Since it seems impossible for me to leave my diocese now, I ask to be excused from the 'ad limina.' However, I shall willingly present myself, if you should wish this of me."[46]

One wonders if the long-suffering Alemany was not more than a little piqued at Rome's failure to send him the much desired assistance. Surely, no one had more right to plead excessive obligations at home than this same Alemany who, by now, presumably had come to realize that more than one can make use of delaying tactics! At any rate, he was pleased to hear from the Prefect that he was, in fact, to be dispensed from the *ad limina* visit to Rome. "The report of your diocese for 1880, I have given to my consultors for their scrutiny. His Holiness dispenses you from the obligation of the "ad limina" which you should make at this time—however, when the impediments to such a visit disappear, you should make it."[47] In the event, some criticisms were made of Alemany's rule by an archbishop of the Propaganda staff who was deputed by Simeoni to scrutinize carefully the 1880 report forwarded to Rome by Alemany. The Roman prelate, whose name is partially illegible on his signed report, found Alemany's reasons for postponing his provincial synod rather unconvincing. In addition, quoting the Tridentine decrees, he insisted that Alemany be informed that he must open a seminary very quickly, and that here, too, his reasons for keeping the former seminary closed were not entirely convincing. The

[46] Alemany to Simeoni, San Francisco, August 28, 1880. APF. This important report, mentioned by Alemany and which was forwarded to Rome by him, could not be found by the author in APF.

[47] Simeoni to Alemany, Rome, October 12, 1880. Copy in APF.

rather hard-hitting assessment contained no praise of Alemany's stewardship (perhaps such would have been out of place in a factual summation), but presumably, after long years in the "ruling of the portion of the church of God committed to his care," Alemany had learned that Rome was spare in its praise—if, indeed, it accorded any at all to hard working prelates!

Following the rule of trying again when not successful, Archbishop Alemany spent quite a bit of time in 1881 memorializing Rome in the matter of the nonappearing coadjutor. As should be abundantly clear by this time, his patience had been severely tried by the delay of years—after all, his first request was dated 1868 and now, thirteen years later, he was still at it. He continued to write to various American prelates asking for their suggestions and in certain cases for their aid. When he had obtained the opinions and advice of some of the leaders in the American hierarchy, Alemany methodically summed up all their opinions in a letter to Simeoni dated January 18, 1881.[48] His principal points had already been expressed by Bishop O'Connell, acting again as secretary of the meeting of the California hierarchy which had convened in Alemany's residence on January 17, 1881. O'Connell's minutes related that the three bishops (Alemany, himself, and Mora) had been joined in consultation by the recently consecrated Patrick Manogue, Coadjutor Bishop of Grass Valley. The important resolution approved by the California bishops finds this expression in Bishop O'Connell's minutes:

After the Archbishop had reported on all that he had been able to find out concerning the qualities to be sought for in his coadjutor, and after we had read the letters which he had received from many Bishops and from Cardinal McCloskey, we all agree unanimously that the Holy See should be humbly asked to appoint a Coadjutor Archbishop with right of succession from the three following Bishops—namely,

Right Reverend John J. Keane, Bishop of Richmond
Right Reverend John L. Spalding, Bishop of Peoria,
Right Reverend William H. Gross, Bishop of Savannah.[49]

[48] APF.
[49] O'Connell's report is dated January 17, 1881. APF.

Yet another disappointment came Alemany's way when he learned that the first choice of this list, Bishop Keane of Richmond, was in such poor health as to be threatened with blindness. Hence, in telling Simeoni what he had learned, he added that he felt an obligation to acquaint the Cardinal with this important bit of information.[50]

Once again, a perplexed Alemany wrote to Gibbons in Baltimore to ask advice and continued aid, informing him of his regrets that he was not worthy to have "good Bishop Keane" as a coadjutor, Alemany added that he must again select three names and asked that Gibbons give some thought to the matter. With Keane out of the picture, Alemany remarked that he thought that Bishop Gross would suit remarkably well, and mentioned several other prelates, including bishops Kain and O'Farrell.[51]

On August 22, 1881, a very remarkable document concerning the selection of a coadjutor for Alemany was signed by many priests, two of the Jesuit Order and the rest of the diocesan clergy of San Francisco. Their unanimous choice of the post was, again, the beloved vicar general of the archdiocese, Very Reverend John J. Prendergast (1834–1914). In words indicative of the most sincere esteem for a splendid priest, the petition read:

We the undersigned secular and regular Clergy of the Archdiocese of San Francisco, California having learned that a Coadjutor is to be appointed to our Venerable Archbishop most respectfully submit to Your Eminence for the consideration of the Sovereign Pontiff the following statement:

That among the names forwarded to His Holiness occurs, as we understand, that of the Very Rev. John Prendergast, Vicar General of this Diocese. That his name should have been so submitted has caused us much gratification, but no surprise, for mentally, morally and phisically [sic] we regard him as possessing the qualifications requisite for so important a position, and that in so eminent a degree that we

50 Alemany to Simeoni, San Francisco, June 17, 1881. APF.
51 Alemany to Gibbons, San Francisco, August 21, 1881. AAB.

have felt impelled to manifest in this rather unusual manner the unanimity of the Clergy in favor of Father Prendergast, as may be seen from the signatures hereunto appended. His faithful services during the past twenty years, his intimate knowledge of the wants of the Diocese and the experience received from his position of Vicar General seem to us to render his appointment particularly appropriate. Therefore, in as much as we believe Father Prendergast possesses every requisite, learning, piety, zeal, prudence, we sincerely trust that the Sovereign Pontiff will be graciously pleased to listen to our petition for which act of Sovereign Clemency we shall be profoundly grateful.[52]

It would appear that Archbishop Alemany was pleased with the confidence which his priests had expressed in his Vicar General. However, he was quick to inform Cardinal Simeoni that he did not think it possible, barring an explicit order of His Holiness himself, that Prendergast would accept if chosen. He added that, when the petition had come to the Vicar General's attention, he had promptly stated that he would not willingly accept the appointment to be Alemany's coadjutor or to any other see—he simply did not wish to be a bishop and insisted that he had good reasons, including those of conscience, which demanded that he refuse any such burden. Alemany recalled, too, how Father Prendergast had been proposed earlier as co-adjutor to Bishop O'Connell in Grass Valley before Bishop Manogue's final selection there—and how promptly the Vicar General had made known his displeasure at having his name proposed for this other dignity. So it would appear that, while Alemany was far from opposed to Father Prendergast, he did not consider him seriously in the running because of his complete opposition to the assuming of the mitre.[53]

A month later, Alemany had an answer from Simeoni in

---

[52] Among the signers of this unique petition were such earlier co-laborers with Alemany as James Croke (formerly his vicar general) William Gleeson, Michael King, Sebastian Wolf, Joseph Gallagher, and John McNally. The two Jesuits who signed were Nicolas Congiato of San Jose and John Pinasco of Santa Clara. In all, there were forty seven signers. APF.

[53] Alemany to Simeoni, San Francisco, August 22, 1881. APF.

which the Cardinal said that he had received the petition of the priests and would follow the usual protocol of including Prendergast's name in the list of those proposed. He added, however, that the bishops of the province remained free to propose other names for the Cardinal's guidance.[54] One can but imagine Prendergast's perturbation when, under date of December 9, 1881, he received a lengthy letter from Simeoni. In it he was told that nothing was more pleasing to Roman authorities than to hear a priest praised as he had been by bishops, priests, and laymen alike. The shrewd observation follows that "although not always true, this is generally a sign of a man's true worth." Simeoni then continued:

> So I congratulate you, indeed, on having the confidence of your Archbishop and of the Bishops of the Province who wish you as Coadjutor Archbishop, and whose desire is shared by the clergy and laity alike. Since you have been placed on the terna, I exhort you to do nothing to frustrate the proposal of your name to the Holy Father. It belongs to His Holiness alone to make the choice—do not oppose the will of Christ's Vicar on earth—whatever the decision may be. I have decided to let you know how the matter stands before I present the list of names to His Holiness on behalf of this Sacred Congregation.[55]

No decision was forthcoming during the remainder of 1881, so we may remit further details concerning this matter to a later page.

As far as significant events of the remainder of the year are concerned, the most important would appear to be a short pastoral letter, dated September 28, 1881, which concerned the building of a new cathedral because of what Alemany called the "evident necessity of removing our Cathedral from its present objectionable location to some more respectable and more suitable part of the city."[56] In the following spring, beginning on April 30, 1882, Alemany presided at the convoking of the

[54] Simeoni to Alemany, Rome, September 30, 1881. Copy in APF.
[55] *Ibid.*
[56] This pastoral was printed in the *Monitor,* September 30, 1881.

Second Provincial Council which had been summoned by him and by the other two ordinaries of California, Bishops O'Connell and Mora. They were joined in their deliberations by Coadjutor Bishop Manogue and the large number of priests who had been assigned to attend the Council. St. Mary's Cathedral was the scene of this meeting, which lasted until May 4 when the decrees were promulgated, duly notarized by Father Prendergast who acted as secretary, and finally signed by the four California prelates in attendance.[57] These decrees generally concerned themselves with such pastoral considerations as usually mark such meetings. Evidently, Roman authorities found little to change, since, after due inspection, only a few minor changes were proposed, and the decrees were solemnly approved a year later by Pope Leo XIII.[58]

A month before convening the above mentioned council, the California prelates had again tried their hand in the matter of a coadjutor bishop for San Francisco. This time the four bishops proposed a different list:

1. Right Reverend John Joseph Kain, Bishop of Wheeling.
2. Right Reverend William Gross, C.SS.R., Bishop of Savannah.
3. Right Reverend Stephen W. Ryan, C.M., Bishop of Buffalo.

Also, they again added the name of Father Prendergast with the note that, if Rome so wished, his name could be placed third on the list in place of Bishop Ryan. At least they were on record again in the matter of a needed coadjutor.[59] As usual, Alemany forwarded the list with a letter of his own in which he listed the qualities of the ones there named as he had been informed of them by various bishops of the United States.[60] After the usual

[57] APF.

[58] The Jesuit Cardinal Franzelin headed the commission which examined these decrees of the Second Provincial Council of San Francisco. Copy in APF.

[59] This *terna*—or selection—was signed by the four bishops of California on March 7, 1882. APF.

[60] Alemany to Simeoni, San Francisco, March 8, 1882. APF.

discussion of a committee of cardinals associated with Propaganda, it was finally decided to return to the name of Bishop Spalding of Peoria, Illinois, who, in 1881, after he had been approached as to his willingness to accept the position of coadjutor to Alemany, had been successful in his refusal, alleging among other reasons that the climate of San Francisco would not be good for his health! In Spalding's letter of refusal, he proposed the name of the one who would, eventually, become Alemany's coadjutor and successor. This was Father Patrick W. Riordan, then pastor of St. James's Church in Chicago. Now it was decided that Cardinal Simeoni again write to Spalding in an endeavor to obtain his consent. If Spalding still remained unwilling, Bishop Kain of Wheeling should then receive a similar letter. Under date of July 21, 1882, John Lancaster Spalding, distinguished orator, scholar, and Bishop of Peoria, received the prescribed letter in which Simeoni said that the Propaganda cardinals wished him to withdraw his opposition to his appointment to San Francisco. Simeoni continued in rather a pointed fashion:

> I hope you will do what the Cardinals want for, if the reasons advanced by you do not satisfy them, neither should they satisfy you! Your reasons are praiseworthy, but more praiseworthy would be the yielding of your will to the good of the church by following the will of these Eminent Fathers. I do not doubt that you will soon let me know of your change of mind and of your acceptance of this appointment. I earnestly urge you to do so.[61]

[61] Simeoni to Spalding, July 21, 1882. Copy in APF. Bishop Spalding's refusal to go to San Francisco revealed a conviction which may be traced to an earlier expression of his concerning California. While in Louisville, he gave a public lecture, January 21, 1872, entitled: "Views and Persons and Things in California" in which he remarked: "San Francisco is not likely ever to be of much greater importance than it is at present. . . . The Queen of the Golden Gate is not destined to fulfill the promise of her earlier days. . . ." David F. Sweeney, O.F.M., *The Life of John Lancaster Spalding, First Bishop of Peoria, 1840–1916* (New York, 1965), p. 94.

On August 30, 1882, Spalding wrote to Archbishop Gibbons of Baltimore: "There is an impression in Rome that I may be induced to accept the coadjutorship of San Francisco. This is a mistake. . . . My conscience will not permit me to go to San Francisco. . . ." *Ibid.*, p. 135.

Despite the urgent tone of Simeoni's letter, Bishop Spalding remained adamant in his refusal of his proposed appointment to San Francisco. By this time, Simeoni had written to Bishop McQuaid of Rochester, already a very outspoken and influential American prelate, to ask his opinion about the whole matter. McQuaid answered as follows:

> Without any doubt, San Francisco is an episcopal See of the highest importance and of great influence. It must receive a prelate with virtue and zeal, one who possesses a certain independence in his character and who will know how to temper his judgment in many things. In San Francisco is to be found a mixed population composed of many nationalities—to harmonize all these, no one would be more acceptable than a native American. . . . The West Coast comprises a veritable Empire in itself and, in the circumstances which will occur, it will be necessary for the Bishops there to turn to San Francisco for their leadership. If the Archbishop there be a man who successfully combines prudence with courage, an immense amount of good will result for religion.[62]

Bishop McQuaid continued by asking where such a man could be found—he added that he did not know those proposed sufficiently well to comment upon them, but urged the Cardinal to take into consideration the name of Bishop Chatard of Vincennes who, in McQuaid's judgment, possessed all of the necessary qualities. Bishop McQuaid's opinion caused Bishop Chatard to be placed on the ever-changing list for San Francisco. The solution was further complicated for Simeoni, perhaps, by a blunt answer sent him by one who had also joined the list of those who had refused the appointment. This was Bishop John J. Keane of Richmond, who wrote to the Roman Cardinal on August 18, 1882, that he had "but an imperfect knowledge of the peculiar difficulties which, serious and many as they are, I have heard to exist in this Archdiocese—i.e., of San Francisco."[63]

[62] Bernard J. McQuaid to Simeoni, Rochester, New York, August 5, 1882. McQuaid served as first bishop of Rochester, New York, 1868–1909.
[63] John J. Keane to Simeoni, Richmond, Virginia, August 18, 1882. APF. Keane served as fifth bishop of Richmond, 1878–1888.

Quite probably, Keane's reluctance and that of some of the other American bishops requested for San Francisco was in part due to what they had heard about the difficulties which Alemany had been facing, and perhaps in part causing, in his see.

Before proceeding to the events which resulted in the promotion of a Chicago pastor, Father Patrick William Riordan, to the post of coadjutor archbishop of San Francisco with right of succession to Alemany, we might pause briefly to cite yet another example of the pastoral solicitude and exactness with which Alemany fulfilled his episcopal responsibilities to the end of his reign. On February 13, 1883, the year during which, finally, he was to receive his coadjutor, he dispatched a letter to Simeoni requesting the necessary renewal of the requisite faculties or permissions which he had to ask for every ten years. From 1873 to 1883, he told the Cardinal, he had either personally or by delegation granted a total of 2,450 matrimonial dispensations. More than 600 of these involved disparity of cult while the large number of 1,846 involved mixed religion. Alemany's comment on these dispensations was enlightening and one which certainly came from the wealth of years of experience in the matter:

> It is a matter of sorrow, indeed, that so many dispensations would have to be granted. But, lacking them, almost all these marriages would take place before Protestant ministers or civil judges with people lost to the Church—and their children, too.[64]

In early 1883, Alemany was asked to let Rome know his reactions to the possible appointment of either Bishop Chatard of Vincennes (McQuaid's candidate) or Father Patrick Riordan of Chicago (Spalding's proposal) as his coadjutor with right of succession. Simeoni told Alemany that, on January 15, 1883, the Sacred Congregation of Propaganda had discussed anew the question and had decided that, while Bishop Kain of Wheeling,

[64] Alemany to Simeoni, San Francisco, February 13, 1883. APF.

West Virginia, possessed excellent qualities, he might not be sufficiently equipped with the necessary talent for the temporal administration of the Archdiocese of San Francisco. Hence, Alemany was to be asked concerning Chatard and Riordan, with Simeoni concluding that "we are hoping to settle this question with the appointment of one of these two men—please give us your views so that we may proceed to the appointment."[65] As a result, Alemany wrote to various American bishops, as he had done so frequently before, and was able to reply in mid-March that, conscious of Spalding's glowing recommendation ("I think that there is none more worthy of the See of San Francisco than Father Riordan"), and conscious, too, that this high opinion of Father Riordan was shared by his ecclesiastical superior, Archbishop Feehan of Chicago, as well as by Archbishop Ryan of St. Louis, he was quite willing to receive Riordan as his coadjutor and as, eventually, his successor. Bishop McMullen of Davenport, Iowa, happened to have visited San Francisco about this time, and since, earlier, he had been vicar general of the Chicago archdiocese, he was able to assure Alemany of Father Riordan's fine qualities.[66] At long last, the impasse concerning this appointment was to be solved—much to the delight of Alemany and much to the benefit of the Catholic Church in northern California.

On June 18, 1883, the cardinals of Propaganda proposed and approved the name of Patrick William Riordan as Alemany's coadjutor, with definite approval—and actual appointment—being made by Pope Leo XIII in an audience granted to Archbishop Persico, the secretary of Propaganda, on June 29. On the next day, Cardinal Simeoni was quick to inform Alemany of the welcome appointment, "which has been approved by the Holy Father. I will send you as soon as possible the Brief appointing Father Riordan your Coadjutor with right of succession

[65] Simeoni to Alemany, Rome, January 24, 1883. Copy in APF.
[66] Alemany to Simeoni, San Francisco, March 15, 1883. APF.

309

to your See."[67] Whether Riordan had heard of his elevation to the episcopacy prior to his official notice from Rome is not known, but if the enjoined and customary secrecy was observed (and very likely it was), it was not until his reception of a letter included in one for Archbishop Feehan from Simeoni, dated July 13, 1883, that the news reached him. In this letter, after informing the Chicago pastor of his promotion and congratulating him, Simeoni wrote: "I know that you will do well there for the good of the souls committed to your care."[68] On the same day, Simeoni wrote also to Archbishop Feehan of Chicago (the Riordan letter, as we noted above, was included in the one to Feehan). This, then, was the first official notification of both Riordan and Feehan:

> I include here a letter for Father Riordan. Please give it to him. At the same time, I congratulate you for having a parish priest so adorned with the qualities that he has been found worthy of such high office.[69]

[67] Simeoni to Alemany, Rome, June 30, 1883. APF. As expected, San Francisco's local press engaged in speculation concerning the prospective appointment. In a Chicago dispatch, the *Examiner* reported, on July 3, 1883, that "although official notification has not reached Chicago or San Francisco, there is no doubt that P. W. Riordan, pastor of St. James Church of this city, has been selected by papal authorities for Coadjutor to the Archbishop of San Francisco with right of succession. The news reached this city through Coadjutor-Archbishop Elder of Cincinnati who has peculiar facilities for knowing all about the matter. . . . Father Riordan is greatly loved—perhaps admired would be the better word. . . . The Irish Catholics here predict for him a brilliant and useful career in one of the most important dioceses in America. . . ." The next day, the *Monitor* assessed other such reports which had been appearing in San Francisco's newspapers. Commenting on their general inaccuracy, the editor remarked that Riordan was reported as being 67 years old—whereas he was but 43: "He will have to live until 1903 until he reaches the patriarchal age [!] given him!" The editor was obviously annoyed at the Chicagoans who created "unsubstantiated" rumors concerning the San Francisco appointment.
[68] Simeoni to Patrick W. Riordan, Rome, July 13, 1883. Copy in APF.
[69] Simeoni to Patrick Feehan, July 13, 1883. Copy in APF. Feehan served as first archbishop of Chicago, 1880–1902. On July 25, the *Monitor* mentioned that it had just received word from Alemany of the Riordan appointment. Its August 1 issue included a sketch of the new coadjutor.

Two weeks later, Archbishop-Elect Riordan received another letter from his new ecclesiastical superior, Cardinal Simeoni: "I send you two documents—one appointing you Titular Archbishop of Cabasa, another officially appointing you Coadjutor Archbishop of San Francisco with right of succession to that See. Although I shall inform Archbishop Alemany concerning these documents, be sure to let me know yourself about your receiving them, that all may be done properly. Again, I congratulate you."[70] When Riordan read the brief of his appointment, he was informed therein that he had been appointed since Archbishop Alemany, "both because of advanced age and poor health," had requested just such assistance as was now being extended to him.

Father Riordan's acceptance of the episcopal office was expressed in two letters to Cardinal Simeoni which were spaced ten days apart. In this first, dated August 8, 1883, he thanked His Eminence for his letter of July 13 notifying him that he had been chosen "as auxiliary [sic] Bishop to the Archbishop of San Francisco with the right of future succession." Adding that although he felt entirely unequal for such a task, he hoped, with divine help, to prove worthy of the task. He also affirmed that he would leave nothing undone so that "in the extensive regions within the San Francisco Archdiocese, our divine religion may always increase and spread."[71] Whatever Riordan may have

[70] Simeoni to Riordan, Rome, July 30, 1883. Copy, APF. Patrick William Riordan (1841–1914) was born in Chatham, New Brunswick, on August 27, 1841. When 7 years old, his parents moved to Chicago; after pursuing priestly studies in Rome and Louvain, he was ordained on June 10, 1865, in Louvain. For several years after his return to Chicago, Father Riordan taught at St. Mary of the Lake Seminary there. After preliminary parochial assignments, in 1871 he was made pastor of the large parish of St. James in Chicago. His twelve years there found him quite successful, and, undoubtedly, it was this work plus his liberal endowment of intellectual and other qualities that caused him to be considered for elevation to the episcopacy.

[71] Riordan to Simeoni, Chicago, Illinois, August 3, 1883. APF.

understood by the words that he had been chosen "auxiliary Bishop" to Alemany was clarified in his second letter, written on August 18, wherein he thanks Simeoni for a letter received only four days previously which had contained two apostolic briefs. By one, he noted, he had been appointed titular Archbishop of Cabasa in Egypt, while the other had confirmed his appointment as "Coadjutor Archbishop of San Francisco in California. Again I thank Your Eminence for the confidence reposed in me that, despite my complete unworthiness, I have been selected for the office of bishop. The Archbishop of Chicago has designated September 16th for my consecration. May God grant that He dower me with the heavenly gifts which I will need to fulfill the episcopal office."[72] While it would appear almost certain that an immediate interchange of letters occurred between Archbishop Alemany and his newly appointed Coadjutor, these are not on record; —it is known that Archbishop Riordan disposed of a portion of his personal papers later on during his long reign of thirty years in San Francisco.

Soon the *Monitor* found it necessary to refute a rumor that Alemany was to leave for New York en route to Rome and that he planned to stop in Chicago to attend the consecration of his Coadjutor. "It is well known here that His Grace does not design subjecting himself to the fatigues of such a journey." While not attending the ceremony personally, Alemany sent his secretary, Father George Montgomery, as his representative. (Montgomery, the nephew of the Dominican of the same name whose refusal of the See of Monterey in 1850 had caused Alemany's appointment, later served as coadjutor to Archbishop Riordan.)

---

[72] Riordan to Simeoni, Chicago, Illinois, August 18, 1883. APF. Seemingly, Riordan was touched at Alemany's courtesy in going to Ogden to meet him when he was en route to San Francisco. Alemany is said to have thus answered Riordan's remonstrance: "I am only following a tradition of the Spanish people that when a prince visits a province, he is always met at the frontier."

It was in his own parish church that the pastor of St. James Church was raised to the episcopal office by Archbishop Patrick Feehan, who was assisted, as co-consecrators, by Coadjutor Bishop John Ireland of St. Paul and Bishop Francis Chatard of Vincennes, Indiana, who, it will be recalled, had been proposed for San Francisco by Bishop McQuaid of Rochester. It was appropriate that the sermon was preached by Bishop John Lancaster Spalding of Peoria, who was largely responsible for Riordan's choice after he had himself renounced the appointment to the Far West. Riordan's consecration furnished an apt occasion for a pastoral letter written by Alemany concerning the implications of the event. Dated San Francisco, September 14, 1883, it recalled that the day of Riordan's elevation "was a day for many years expected and desired by us." Noting the growth of Catholicism which demanded such an appointment, Alemany remarked, too, on "the increasing number of our grey hairs," while rejoicing that "in the decline of our life, we are provided with a young pontiff with the right of succession." He extolled Riordan's qualifications, saying that his protracted residence abroad would especially equip him for his new task amidst many nationalities in the see of San Francisco. But the pastoral had another dimension in addition to that of an affectionate welcome. Many quotations from the Fathers of the Church concerning the episcopal office revealed that Alemany was, indeed, well read in patristic literature. It was a learned letter, rightly called "beautiful and instructive" by the editor of the *Monitor* in the issue of September 19, 1883, in which the pastoral appeared. Meanwhile, on September 26, the *Monitor* published a complete account of Archbishop Riordan's consecration and added an appreciation of the pioneer work of Alemany, who had proved himself "eminently entitled to be enrolled among the good and faithful shepherds." Commenting on the fact that people still lived in San Francisco who could remember the one wooden church which served the city proper on Alemany's arrival in

313

1850, the article went on to assert that Alemany's name "was inscribed in every grateful Catholic heart and his memory will be enshrined in the history of this diocese as the pioneer prelate."

On October 21, the *Monitor* reported that Alemany had left for Utah where he would await the coming of Archbishop Riordan. This meeting took place at the railroad station at Ogden on Saturday morning, November 3. The next morning, in the only Catholic church in Salt Lake City, Riordan offered a pontifical Mass and Alemany preached the sermon. Early on the evening of Tuesday, November 6, 1883, the two prelates, whose joint years of service in the see of San Francisco were to number over sixty, arrived at their destination. A delegation of clergy and laity met them and they were escorted to the episcopal residence on California Street for a gala reception which included the presentation of an ornate mitre given by Mrs. James G. Fair.

Alemany had preceded his journey to Utah to greet Riordan with two letters to Simeoni. On October 17, he had asked that the customary faculties be forwarded for his coadjutor,[73] while the earnestness with which he desired his own retirement was voiced in a letter of the next day which included these lines: "Now that my fine Coadjutor has been consecrated and is on his way here shortly, let me resign and retire to some convent of my Order."[74]

A Congregational paper of San Francisco, the *Pacific*, had this rather sardonic welcome for Archbishop Riordan:

From the papers we learn that an assistant to the Roman Catholic Archbishop of this diocese arrived last week and received a cordial welcome. So far as we have any right to do so, we give him welcome. If he prove to be the sort of man and ecclesiastic called for by the situation, we shall be thrice glad for his coming. Romanism on this coast needs attention, especially in its moralities. When such an enormous proportion of all crime is committed by Romanists and so many

[73] Alemany to Simeoni, San Francisco, October 17, 1883. APF.
[74] Alemany to Simeoni, San Francisco, October 18, 1883.

314

of the vilest places are in their hands—something is the matter, and we respectfully commend an investigation to the coadjutor to the Archbishop.[75]

As expected, the next few weeks witnessed a series of receptions for the newly arrived Coadjutor Archbishop. In reading the *Monitor* and other press reports, one is impressed by the manner in which Alemany remained in the background on such occasions. Indeed, he did not attend many of them with Riordan since he evidently felt that it was enough to have one guest of honor on such occasions.

Although Alemany now had his coadjutor, he was still the ordinary, and, in this capacity, he wrote a very interesting statement to Simeoni concerning things which he thought should be brought to the attention of Rome in matters involving episcopal rule in the United States. The report was impressive for two reasons. First, it was based upon his more than thirty years of experience as a bishop in California, and also it revealed that his views on some topics which had involved him in earlier controversies had changed but little—if at all. Reminding Simeoni that the reason for his report was that Roman authorities were shortly to meet with some American bishops in Rome to discuss such things as Alemany wishes to mention, the veteran Archbishop, by this time one of the senior members of the American hierarchy, first went on record as approving the idea of having lay consultors to assist bishops with details of temporal administration. The lay consultors should have a consultative vote only, he wrote, but their advice should be welcomed and sought by busy bishops so burdened with many details that they could not cope well with all their problems without such help. Alemany next reiterated his earlier stand that the "title or 'dominium' of churches should be in the hands of the Ordinary of a diocese— lest his spiritual jurisdiction suffer harm." He went on to insist

[75] Editorial in *The Pacific* (San Francisco), November 14, 1883.

that legislation should be passed in Rome providing that the pastors of churches be not deprived of revenues needed by them to build schools by priests of religious orders who, by their preaching of novenas and missions, attracted large crowds and took away much needed revenue from a parish by their collections. An adjustment here, Alemany felt, would result in considerably more peaceful relations between diocesan and regular clergy.[76]

It would appear that, barring any complications resulting from ill health or the like, Rome ordinarily wishes bishops contemplating retirement to remain on sufficiently long enough to acquaint their successors with the problems facing them. Perhaps this is why Alemany's prompt haste in almost immediately offering his resignation with the coming of his coadjutor did not meet with Propaganda's favor. At all events, it brought the following reply from Cardinal Simeoni:

> Your proposal to resign in favor of your Coadjutor and that you should retire to a House of your Order does not seem opportune at this time, when your Coadjutor is so new to his office. It seems much better that you should continue there for awhile with the aid of your Coadjutor. For this purpose, you now have permission to delegate or subdelegate any faculties you may have to him for the administration of the diocese. Thus, you will be able to enjoy some respite while continuing to serve the church in San Francisco. With the thought in mind, though, that the time is not far off when you will be able to lay down the burden of the rule of your diocese, please let me know what sum of money you think you will need for your sustenance.[77]

Since Alemany had assumed the episcopal dignity only out of obedience, it was characteristic of him that, with Rome's word thus given, he should continue the administration of his diocese. Early 1884 found him performing the usual round of episcopal duties—with the help, in some cases, of Archbishop Riordan.

[76] Alemany to Simeoni, San Francisco, October 3, 1883.
[77] Simeoni to Alemany, Rome, December 13, 1883. Copy in APF.

On February 24, he pontificated at the opening of the new church at Mission Dolores which was dedicated to St. Francis. Archbishop Riordan, whose oratorical talents were considerable, preached on the occasion. Several short pastoral letters of these months likewise testify to Alemany's continuing rule. It was in the fall of 1884, though, that Alemany wrote his last lengthy pastoral letter which concerned the Third Plenary Council of Baltimore scheduled to meet in early November. Dated October 13, 1884, this pastoral letter may be considered a model of a learned treatise on the meaning of such meetings.

Previously, it had been a matter of some consolation to Alemany to be invited to take an especially active part in the deliberations of this Council. Writing to Archbishop Gibbons on several conciliar matters, Alemany said:

I duly received your two esteemed favors—on the Schema "De Curis Episcoporum" and the sermon, "De Sacerdotio," for which I am obliged. I will try to attend to both cases in the manner you propose, provided you do not monopolize all Red Hats in the East. I take it for granted that, as my dear Archbishop Spalding said to me at the last Plenary Council, such orations are delivered by reading them; otherwise, please correct me.

I conveyed to my dear Coadjutor that you expected him to preach some day during the Council, which I have no doubt he will do and do it well, for he is very gifted.[78]

At the end of October, Alemany left San Francisco en route to the Council at Baltimore. His companion was Bishop Eugene O'Connell, now retired as Bishop of Grass Valley. Because of their joint years of service by this time, the two California bishops were among the seniors in the American episcopate, although the Nestor of the Council was Archbishop Peter Richard Kenrick of St. Louis, who, consecrated nine years before

[78] Alemany to Gibbons, San Francisco, April 14, 1884. AAB. Alemany was also appointed chairman of the committee for the revision of the *Baltimore Catechism.*

317

Alemany, had served the See of St. Louis since 1841. That Alemany's seniority was respected was evidenced by his selection, in late November, as celebrant of the pontifical requiem for all the prelates who had died since the convening of the Second Plenary Council in 1866. By the middle of December, as the *Monitor* noted, Archbishop Alemany had returned to San Francisco from this Council "feeling in first rate health."

Three days after returning home, Alemany wrote a letter to Simeoni which would appear to be the last of a long series of such letters which he had written for so many years. He told the Cardinal Prefect of his recent return from the Council, and said that he was sending to him the collection made in his diocese for the Holy Father, adding that "with it, I offer to His Holiness the profound respect of all my diocese, ask for him length of days and implore the apostolic benediction." It seems quite appropriate that one whose long service in the episcopate had been marked with such loyalty to the Holy See should thus bring to an end his official correspondence as Archbishop of San Francisco.

Earlier, on July 3, 1884, Simeoni had written to Archbishop Riordan. In this letter the Coadjutor of San Francisco was told that, in the light of Alemany's decision to relinquish the see, it would be well for him to know that "we have told him that he is to keep command until you are ready to take over. Do you think that this moment has already arrived? Please let us know about this matter."[79] On July 10, Alemany wrote to Pope Leo XIII requesting that at long last he be allowed to put down the episcopal burden. This important letter may be quoted in full:

For many years I have greatly desired to devote my strength to the work of that Dominican Order which I joined many years ago—my especial wish being to help in the increase of my Order in Spain.

Among other reasons, I had this one very much in mind when, for such a long time, I sought a Coadjutor. Now that Your Holiness has

[79] Simeoni to Riordan, Rome, July 3, 1884. Copy in APF.

granted me such a fine one with right of succession, one who is endowed with great learning, eloquence of speech and experience as well
as prudence in his manner of acting, I ask you in all reverence to free
me from the episcopal office which I have tried to fulfill for thirty-four
years—however uselessly—so that my Coadjutor may succeed me as
soon as I finish some necessary work upon which I am engaged concerning the Ordinary Process for the beatification of the servant of
God, Magin Catala, once a missionary in this territory. I hope, then, to
be able to place myself under the complete direction and obedience of
the Father General of the Order of Preachers.[80]

On the same day, Alemany wrote to Simeoni to remind him
that he thought there could be no difficulty arising concerning
the amount of pension which he would need for his support, for
he believed that this matter might best be left to the Dominican
master general, who, he was confident, would attend to it.[81]

It was not long before the energetic and competent Riordan
sent an answer to Simeoni as to whether he was ready and
thought it opportune to accede to the See of San Francisco. He
reminded the Cardinal that this was a rather hard question to
answer—to write about himself and what he thought of such
an immediate occupancy of Alemany's see. He then divided his
answer into a consideration of the spiritual and temporal state
of the archdiocese. With regard to the first, Riordan thus expressed himself:

I see no pressing difficulties, those excepted which are simply part
of the administration of a diocese where there are too few priests.
In this city, there are 150,000 Catholics who are served by 32
priests. Some serve small parishes while others have such very large
flocks committed to their care that some people do not receive proper
attention, and, therefore, they gradually lapse into indifference. To perform properly the apostolic task in this city, first and foremost we
need more priests.

[80] Alemany to Leo XIII, San Francisco, July 10, 1884. Since Alemany's
letter to the Holy Father concerned Propaganda, it was forwarded there.
APF.
[81] Alemany to Simeoni, San Francisco, July 10, 1884. APF.

The German people in this city are especially in need of pastoral care. I have been told on good authority that, of the 10,000 German Catholics within this city, only about 500 attend Mass on Sundays and days of obligation. It would be most useful, indeed, if some priests of the religious Order, especially those of the Redemptorist Congregation —who work well among these people in other cities—would be assigned to this work here.

The Jesuit and Dominican Fathers who have two churches in San Francisco would be of great help to us if their churches would be made into parishes, with their limits precisely indicated. All of our churches, with three exceptions, are small and built of wood and are old. It will be necessary soon to rebuild in more solid materials.

The same must be said about our parochial schools, which are few in number and sparsely attended. San Francisco has, at the minimum, 20,000 children born of Catholic parents, and 16,000 of these go to the public schools. Since this is so, it is hardly possible to avoid the situation of these children being raised to the detriment of the practice of their faith. These are the principal problems of a spiritual nature facing this diocese—they are neither light nor may they be neglected.[82]

Turning his attention to the temporal side, Archbishop Riordan noted:

There are also some problems of a temporal nature which, however, I do not doubt can be conquered with patience and diligence. The diocese is encumbered by a debt which rises daily. According to figures recently compiled at my request, the amount of money owed by the Archbishop (not counting parochial and parochial school debts) comes to $600,000. On the other hand, the diocese possesses certain properties which can be sold. I don't know but that buyers for some of these could be found right now. But the revenue from our cemetery as well as those monies from the Mexican government which can be used for other purposes hardly suffice to pay the interest on this debt. Such is the state of affairs regarding money in this diocese: unless great prudence is exercised, there will be danger of a failure to honor the obligations of our creditors. . . .

There remains only for me to add that I am prepared to assume the burden of rule, even though, for many reasons, I am unworthy of the charge. However, I am ready not only to devote myself to the solicitous

[82] Riordan to Simeoni, San Francisco, July 24, 1884. APF.

320

administration of this diocese but also to obey the will of Your Eminence regarding it. Whatever is to be done, it remains evident that much will have to be changed both in spiritual as well as in temporal matters that religion here may flourish. If it seems good to the Apostolic See that the Archbishop's renunciation be accepted, I earnestly ask that he not leave here before these temporal matters be cleared up and all placed in order. For the state of affairs in many things is preserved in his memory rather than in the books.[83]

There is a directness and an honesty in this first report of Riordan on the diocese which would shortly be his responsibility. Riordan had been asked for an honest statement of affairs as he saw them—and he had given it. In other statements, he was at pains to express his sincere admiration for Alemany's labors. An example of the solicitude with which he regarded his predecessor was shown in a letter of Riordan's in late October when he wrote to Simeoni that, in his opinion, the pension proposed for the retiring Archbishop was not sufficient: "While ... Diocesan funds could easily supply the '500 scudi' you mention, I don't think that the Archbishop's annual pension should be kept as low as this."[84]

That Archbishop Alemany was quite determined to finish his days as a member of the Dominican Order is evident from a letter written by him on January 7, 1884, to Father Larroca, still master general of the Order of Preachers. In it he mentioned that, now that his coadjutor had been appointed, he hoped that the day of his resignation would not be long delayed and that he wished to retire to a convent of the Dominican Order for two reasons—first, because he was a member of the Order and wished to live as such; secondly, because he hoped, in any such convent to which he might be assigned (evidently, he had Spain in mind), to lay the foundations for that missionary col-

[83] Ibid.
[84] Riordan to Simeoni, Chicago, Illinois, October 29, 1884. APF. Riordan wrote from Chicago whither he had gone after making a pastoral visitation in Utah.

321

lege of friars which had been his desire for so long. "The doctors tell me that I am good for twenty more years," Alemany wrote, "and therefore I can start this college under the obedience of our Order."[85] Presumably, Larroca took the matter under consideration, and it appears quite probable that the failure of the highest authorities in the order to implement Alemany's plan (for it never was fulfilled) was, at least in part, caused by their fear that, judging from his rather tempestuous record in San Francisco regarding the Dominicans there, he and his project might cause more headaches than it was worth.

Although the precise event was unknown to Alemany on the day on which it happened, the important matter of the acceptance of the resignation of the See of San Francisco had been formally brought to the attention of Leo XIII on December 21, 1884. This was attended to by Cardinal Simeoni himself who, ten days later, wrote to Alemany:

On December 21, I asked His Holiness what his will was with regard to accepting your resignation. His Holiness, having heard and pondered your serious reasons for this act, has deigned graciously to approve.

Certainly, you have labored long in your episcopal care and you have cultivated the vineyard of the Lord with untiring labor. Therefore, I do not take readily to the idea that your archdiocese should be deprived of its pastor; on the other hand, it is but right that you should be given the opportunity to rest from your strenuous labors and live the rest of your life in peace and tranquility, freed from all the solicitudes of rule. I trust that your Coadjutor is ready to take over this rule. I will obtain a titular See for you and, since it is but right that you should be supported by the diocese where you have labored, you should receive due support from it; please settle this detail with Archbishop Riordan. Likewise, you will kindly inform your Coadjutor of your resignation and of his accession to the See of San Francisco. Please delegate to him all necessary faculties, etc.[86]

[85] Alemany to Larroca, San Francisco, January 7, 1884. AOPR.
[86] Simeoni to Alemany, Rome, December 31, 1884. Copy, APF.

322

From Alemany's answer it is evident that he did not learn what was for him the truly happy news that he could now sing his *nunc dimittis* from the burdens of episcopal rule until late January, 1885. On February 10, 1885, he thus answered Simeoni:

With a thankful spirit, on January 25, I received the letter from Your Eminence informing me that the Holy Father has accepted my resignation and containing also your kind words written with excessive love about my former labors here. I thank you for these kind words also while hoping that the merciful God will deal mercifully with me concerning both what I have neglected to do and what I have done so badly. I hope that the new Archbishop Riordan will rule this diocese very well. I trust that Your Eminence will obtain for him the necessary faculties to confer Orders and perform other functions even before the reception of the Sacred Pallium.

Your Reverence's humble and devoted servant,

Joseph Sadoc, O.P., Archbishop (Resignatus) of San Francisco[87]

Official sources have consistently listed the date of Riordan's succession as second Archbishop of San Francisco as December 28, 1884—although, as we have just seen, Alemany and Riordan were not acquainted with the papal acceptance of Alemany's resignation until January 25, 1885. However, careful reading of the letter by both men concerned made it apparent that Leo XIII had, in fact, accepted Alemany's resignation on December 21, 1884, and that the cardinal had given him permission to implement and effect it at his will. Apparently, therefore, it was

[87] Alemany to Simeoni, San Francisco, February 10, 1884. APF. It would appear that Archbishop Riordan's statement in the article on his predecessor which he wrote for the Catholic Encyclopedia (I, pp. 282–283) that Alemany had "resigned in November, 1884" is incorrect. The *Catholic Directory* of the Archdiocese of San Francisco annually prints the correct date—e.g., Alemany is noted as having "Resigned and appointed Titular Archbishop of Pelusio, December 28, 1884" (1963 edition, p. 261). The first official mention in the *Monitor* of Alemany's resignation was not made until its issue of February 4, 1885. The editor wrote: "It has long been an open secret that Archbishop Alemany has wished to resign his charge. A letter received last week from the Pope acceded to his request."

323

decided that it was better to have his succession date from the latter part of 1884, with December 28 being chosen as the official date of the resignation of Joseph Sadoc Alemany as first Archbishop of the see which he had administered for thirty-one years. A coadjutor with right of succession is automatically elevated to a see with such a resignation—so that Patrick William Riordan may be said to have begun his thirty years as archbishop of San Francisco on the same day, December 28, 1884.

13

Retirement and Death

THE early months of 1885 proved to be very busy for the retired Archbishop as well as for his successor. Two letters which he wrote during this period to brother Dominicans serve to illustrate that, despite long years of episcopal rule, and despite, too, serious areas of disagreement between himself and the Dominican friars in his archdiocese, Alemany still considered himself a child of that Order. On January 25, 1885, he wrote once more to Father Larroca in Rome concerning the steps he should take to retire to a Dominican convent in Spain. While informing the Master General of his satisfaction at having had his resignation accepted by the Holy See, Alemany also remarked with how much joy he was looking forward to spending the rest of his days as a simple Dominican friar. On the next day, January 26, Alemany addressed the following letter to Father Vilarrasa, with whom he had been locked in active conflict on more than one occasion:

Yesterday I received the happy news that the Holy Father has finally accepted my resignation, for which I had been working these last seventeen years. The Cardinal Prefect in sending me that communication seems to intimate that I remain under a sort of annual pension. But I will at once write to the General to dispose of me any where he may see fit. But until I hear from him I must ask you several questions and permissions.

I will naturally have to remain here settling affairs, conveying church properties to Archbishop Riordan etc., etc. Hence, until, under the direction of the General, I go to some convent, may I not continue as heretofore chiefly about the office and Mass?

I may receive some little presents, besides some little pension; therefore, may I continue to give some little alms to the poor, and provide myself with moderation and prudently give and take? Moreover, my work for the next month or two will have to continue pretty heavy, while my stomach has become semiprotestant, and several Doctors say I should not eat fish; ergo, may I use some power to dispense myself, under a prudent confessor, in matters of fasts and abstinence of the Order?[1]

At this time, too, the press of San Francisco published the news of Alemany's resignation, and the comment of the *Morning Call* was typical of several graceful tributes paid to him:

The news of the near separation of Archbishop Alemany from his charge will be received by the large Catholic community of San Francisco with the deepest regret. He has grown up with his people. In joy and disaster, in times of trial and jubilation, at the great sacrifice of the church, at the baptismal font, the marriage feast, and in the supreme moments of final dissolution, he has been at their side. Of a nature that has endeared him to all, with a far-reaching sagacity that could appreciate the future development of a great city from a few scattered hills and sand dunes, with a kindly heart, and an open hand, few men on the Pacific Coast have created so strong and lasting an impression on his contemporaries as Joseph Sadoc Alemany. Not only the Catholics of San Francisco will miss him, but also every good citizen of our city. With those of his own faith the loss will be felt to be almost irreparable, and especially by those of more mature years. It is seldom that in any community can a man be found whose absence from it will be felt so deeply as will be that of Archbishop Alemany when he leaves San Francisco for his old home in Spain. He will carry with him the deepest gratitude of the host of those whose spiritual welfare he has been instrumental in securing.[2]

It was natural that the *Monitor* would have some comment to make also. In an editorial published on February 4, 1885, while mentioning that the news was far from unexpected, the editor

[1] Alemany to Larroca, San Francisco, January 25, 1885. AOPR. Alemany to Vilarrasa, San Francisco, January 26, 1885. AOPC.
[2] San Francisco *Morning Call*, January 28, 1885.

paid deserved tribute to the Dominican friar who had so successfully headed the See of San Francisco for more than thirty years:

> For more than a third of a century (1850–1885) Archbishop Alemany has been the spiritual father, the friend and God-given guide of the Catholics of California. . . .
>
> It is only 36 years since a small wooden shanty on Vallejo Street sufficed to hold the Catholics of San Francisco whenever they desired to worship Almighty God. The churches in the other portions of the vast diocese were merely the ruined adobe buildings left by the missionary Fathers. The native congregations were scattered and rapidly disappearing, but our venerable Metropolitan has lived to see this spiritual wilderness blossom as a rose, and has been the husband-man of Heaven who has labored to bring about this state of Christian cultivation in the Lord's vineyard.
>
> More than 150 churches and chapels erected to the glory of God attest to the zeal of the pastor and the generosity of the flock. Nearly 200 priests, the majority of whom were educated and ordained for this diocese, lift up their voices to the throne of God and ask Him Who sent them such a beloved bishop to bless his last days even as his whole life has been blessed. A theological seminary, 6 colleges, 18 academies, 5 asylums, and 4 hospitals are all living monuments of the watchful care of the prudent pastor for his people. . . . The flock which has grown up from a few hundred to 200,000, finds itself surrounded by churches, schools and institutions wherein they can find salvation for their souls, solace for their afflictions, mental strength to serve God in their religion, or to preserve their faith while fighting the battle of life.
>
> We would not dare to offend the well-known humility of our holy Archbishop by any reference to his corporal works of mercy. The recording angel will reveal them on the last day. . . .[3]

By this time, Alemany was on the friendliest terms with the future cardinal of Baltimore, whose elevation to the sacred college would come after Alemany's retirement to Spain. Accordingly, he wrote about his resignation to Archbishop Gibbons in the following lines:

[3] *Monitor,* February 4, 1885.

I suppose that by this time Your Grace knows the great secret of my renuntiation [*sic*] having been accepted by the Holy Father the 21st of last Dec. I am happy to be relieved from my great responsibilities. I do not know yet where Divine Providence will send me; but wherever I may be, I will always remember your sweet kindness and prudent charity. May God reward the Church of Baltimore and its worthy Pastor with the foreshadowed honors.[4]

While Alemany was busy informing others of his resignation, Archbishop Riordan was establishing his hold upon the government of the archdiocese. In middle February, 1885, he wrote to Simeoni to reply to an official communication which had informed him of his succession to the see. While stating his realization that the burden had been placed upon his "unworthy shoulders" and thanking the Cardinal for reposing such confidence in him, Riordan expressed the hope that God would grant him the grace to be a good shepherd, "utterly devoted to his sublime task of saving the souls committed to his care." He respectfully requested that the sacred pallium be forwarded to him at the hands of some cleric who might be journeying from Rome to San Francisco in the near future, and ended with a formal request that the faculties to act as a metropolitan archbishop before its reception be granted to him.[5] It would seem that this letter was the occasion of a reply from Simeoni several weeks later in which the Cardinal Prefect expressed himself with regard to the situation in the Archdiocese of San Francisco:

Certainly, the resigning Archbishop, now so advanced in years, has labored long and with diligence in bearing the burdens of episcopal rule in his far flung Archdiocese. It now belongs to you to cultivate this vineyard and to free it from cockle, and thus continue to bring forth abundant fruit.

I know, indeed, that the Archdiocese is burdened with difficulties of no light character; however, I count upon your knowledge, prudence

[4] Alemany to Gibbons, San Francisco, February 12, 1885. AAB.
[5] Riordan to Simeoni, San Francisco, February 16, 1885. APF.

and administrative ability to overcome all those things which are opposed to the religious progress we all want—so that all may be well done for the good of your Archdiocese.[6]

Even though officially retired, Archbishop Alemany continued in the exercise of some episcopal functions. On Holy Thursday, 1885, as he had done for many years, he blessed the holy oils in St. Mary's Cathedral (one senses a nice delicacy in Riordan in thus allowing the retired Archbishop to perform a function generally performed by the Ordinary himself). On April 19, he confirmed a large class of 250 children at St. Francis Church, and, on the following Sunday, he again administered confirmation—this time at the French Church of Notre Dame des Victoires. This occasion was marked, according to a press report, by an "extended discourse in French in which he explained the Sacrament of Confirmation, etc."

In May, 1885, Alemany received word from Rome that a titular see had been assigned to him and that he was now the head of the ancient (and suppressed) See of Pelusium in Egypt. Simeoni was gracious in communicating this news: "I congratulate you on this act of His Holiness, who has not wanted you to be deprived of a See now that you have resigned your position in San Francisco."[7] Only a few days previous to this appointment, Alemany had written to him concerning some financial matters affecting his former archdiocese. After stating the financial picture in broad terms, he added that if Simeoni wanted any further details, it would be well if he wrote Father Peter J. Grey, long time rector of St. Patrick's Church in San Francisco and now chancellor of the archdiocese. Evidently, the time was approaching when Alemany would be making his final farewells in preparation for his return to Spain.[8] This was further confirmed

[6] Simeoni to Riordan, Rome, March 9, 1885. APF.
[7] Simeoni to Alemany, Rome, April 17, 1885. Copy in APF.
[8] Alemany to Simeoni, San Francisco, April 6, 1885. APF.

by him in another letter sent in early May to Father Larroca in which he made mention that he was about ready to send on to the proper authorities in Rome the canonical process with which he had been occupied in the matter of the possible beatification of Father Magin Catala, O.F.M., pioneer missionary at Mission Santa Clara.[9]

It was quite appropriate that the grateful beneficiaries of Alemany's long years of service should see to it that his departure be not uncommemorated. Accordingly, in late April, 1885, a committee of prominent Catholics of San Francisco was formed to consider what form this commemoration might take. Headed by Joseph A. Donohoe and Dennis J. Oliver, the committee announced that "after his distinguished services, rendered to two generations, we cannot afford to allow that, in his modesty and humility . . . Archbishop Alemany . . . should depart from among us forever without some tribute on our part to the unselfish effort, the devoted zeal and the large public spirit he has displayed during so many years." Out of a series of such conferences came plans for the various events which were to mark Alemany's departure for his native Spain.

When the news was made public that the time for the Archbishop's departure was not far off, the *Monitor* in an editorial published in early May again eulogized Alemany for his long service:

[9] Alemany to Larroca, San Francisco, May 2, 1885. AOPR. Magin Catala, called the "holy man of Santa Clara," was born in Montblanch in the province of Catalonia, Spain. Receiving the Franciscan habit in Barcelona in 1777, he was ordained in 1785 and sailed to America in 1786 for work in the foreign missions of his order. He labored at Santa Clara Mission for thirty-six uninterrupted years, 1794–1830. His reputation for sanctity was widespread during his lifetime, and this provided the reason for Alemany's canonical investigations with a view to submitting his cause to Rome for official consideration. It was the final preparation for this cause which was among the reasons for Alemany's delaying his departure from California in 1885. However, it would appear that the cause was found defective in its preparation—allegedly, this is the reason why progress was not made in it and why it is still not progressing at the present time.

In a few days now the connection which has subsisted for the life time of a generation between California and its first Archbishop will close forever. Archbishop Alemany will take his departure for Rome in obedience to the call of his superiors, and the revered figure which we have grown to regard as almost an essential part of the Church itself will be seen no more among us.

For thirty years he has been coming and going among us, ruling the Church in California as its head, and yet as humble as its youngest child. Indefatigable in work, yet never allowing his anxieties and toils to ruffle his uniform serenity, and as sparing of others as he was severe to himself. That a man should devote his life freely to the benefit of his personal friends and family or native land for no earthly reward, would be in itself a rare heroism, but it was not to his own people Archbishop Alemany's life had been devoted. In the discharge of his high office, he had to deal with men of every race, of every profession, clergy, laity, and religious, and among them all he held the strictest justice, unswayed as far as the human eye can judge by any partiality whatever.

Choosing deliberately a life of poverty and obedience at his entrance into the Order of St. Dominic, he was removed from that obedience and poverty by the express command of the Sovereign Pontiff, and ordered to live as a ruler of the Church in a distant land. How earnestly he threw himself into his appointed task, how he travelled and discharged the duties of a priest as well as those of a ruler of a diocese, we well know. Beyond what was needed for the simple necessaries of life, he has not drawn a single dollar from the revenues of the Archdiocese in exchange for his long labor, and now that he returns to seek an asylum of his chosen Order in his old age, he does so in poverty as perfect as when he first took its Habit as a religious. . . .[10]

[10] *Monitor,* May 6, 1885. On June 3, 1885, the *Monitor* carried an interesting reprint of an appreciation of Alemany's years of service to California which had appeared in the New York *Freeman's Journal.* Praising Alemany, the *Journal* said of him that

He ascended the steps of his episcopal throne with all the dignity that became a prelate—but the poor knew his humility and those nearest to him knew also that, out of all the revenues of his rich diocese, he took nothing for himself but the barest necessities. He was the almoner of God.

His Order, which he loved so well, now opens its arms for the son weary with the cares of the Shepherd and the weight of a mitre. . . .

331

When it was announced that the Archbishop had decided to make his departure from San Francisco on the afternoon of Sunday, May 24, 1885, after due religious ceremonies in the morning at St. Mary's Cathedral, it developed that the preceding week would be marked by more than one farewell ceremony. The first was held on Tuesday afternoon, May 19, when the clergy gathered in the parlors of the cathedral rectory to express their sentiments and to present Alemany with a purse of almost $10,000. Over fifty priests waited upon the Archbishop on this occasion. Father Croke, pioneer vicar general in the 1850's, was there, as was the present vicar, Father Prendergast, who made the presentation. First listed among the three Jesuit fathers present (evidently, the invitation list was restricted because of the limitations of space in the rectory) was Father Nicolas Congiato. It was he who, as president of St. Ignatius College from 1862–1865 and again fom 1866–1869, had been quite adamant in opposing Alemany's views in the issues which were aired during those earlier years. Four Dominican friars were also present, among whom was Father Bernard Doogan who, four years previously, had been among the signers of the solemn protest against Alemany which had been sent to Rome. Father Prendergast gave an eloquent summation of Alemany's distinguished services for the Church in California, as well as a sincere tribute to the esteem in which the clergy of the archdiocese held him:

> . . . For you have been a father to us and have ruled with a father's hand. Just, yet never severe, patient but not weak, charitable more than human tongue can tell, apparently preoccuppied in active duties yet finding time for meditation and prayer, high in office yet

---

He came to San Francisco a poor Dominican friar and he left the episcopacy as he entered it. . . . He turns himself towards Rome penniless, to seek for admission to a convent of his Order. It was a moving and pathetic spectacle, strange and unusual in an age of materialism.

lowly in personal bearing and life, you were truly the pattern of your flock and could justly say with the Apostle, "*Estote imitatores mei....*"[11]

It was apparent that Archbishop Alemany was deeply moved by the tribute which had been so eloquently voiced by his Vicar General. In a trembling voice, the Archbishop replied in a graceful manner to what had been said about him. After giving abundant credit to his co-laborers among the clergy for what had been accomplished during the almost three and a half decades of his episcopal rule in California, Alemany concluded with these words:

I do not think I was born to be a Bishop and I told Pope Pius IX so, but nevertheless they made me a Bishop. Now in my old age it has seemed best to resign the arduous task into younger hands. . . . I thank you most sincerely for your kind words and for your handsome gift. I hope you will pray for me that God may preserve me through life, and particularly at the hour of my death.[12]

The next afternoon, Wednesday, May 20, it was the turn of the laity to express their affection for their departing shepherd. A prominent Catholic layman, John T. Doyle, was their representative in a scene somewhat like that of the previous day. Echoing Father Prendergast's sentiments, Doyle remarked that "we would be unjust to ourselves if we fail to add that during the thirty-five years you have passed among us, two generations of Californians have learned not only to respect you as a minister of God but to love you with the affection of children to a devoted father and loving friend."[13] A purse of $8,000 was presented to Archbishop Alemany on this occasion.

Once again, the affectionate words uttered by Doyle brought forth an equally affectionate reply from Archbishop Alemany:

[11] San Francisco *Call*, May 20, 1885. Cf. Appendix II of this volume for the complete text of Father Prendergast's address and Archbishop Alemany's reply.

[12] *Ibid.*

[13] San Francisco *Call*, May 21, 1885.

Let me say now at my old age I want to enjoy a little rest, and yet when I say this, when I say that I want to go away, my heart is again pained for I know that with departure I sever the bonds of a great love, the love I have for you my children. . . . I seek your prayers for my welfare wherever I go, that I may be kept safe from all harm. My children, my body goes, my heart is with you and will remain with you.[14]

On Thursday and Friday, Alemany met with various Catholic societies for the last time. He found especially moving a last farewell with a delegation of Chinese people, many of them converts, who assembled with their pastor, Father Gregory Antonucci, whom Alemany had brought to the diocese in 1881 for pastoral work among them.

Quite naturally, all of the above mentioned farewells were intended only as preludes to that scheduled for the following Sunday in St. Mary's Cathedral. On Saturday evening, Archbishop Alemany sat for the last time in his confessional there and absolved many of his penitents whom he had nurtured spiritually for many years. His last day in California, Sunday, May 24, 1885, was marked, first, by his celebration of Mass at 7:30 A.M. Although the cathedral was thronged and most approached the altar rail for holy communion, the Archbishop insisted that he be given no help, since he preferred to give the holy Eucharist himself to each of the communicants to whom he also imparted his individual blessing. (Later on, he was to refer to this crowded day as the most eventful in his life.) After a short respite, Alemany returned to preside at a pontifical Mass offered by Archbishop Riordan, at the conclusion of which he walked to the center of the sanctuary and there combined a farewell sermon with an address to several hundred children who were to receive the sacrament of confirmation from his hands. He was deeply moved and his voice quivered as he spoke with affection to all those present. It was perhaps characteristic

[14] *Ibid.*

334

that he should turn, after a few moments, to some final thoughts on the immortality of the soul; a reporter thus recorded the scene:

> As the Archbishop concluded his eloquent address, he was over-come with emotion. Tears were in the eyes of those with him on the altar, and the audience was moved deeply by the words which seemed to them as authoritative as though they had fallen from the lips of a prophet of old. The congregation left the church sadly, and the Archbishop repaired to his rooms for a slight rest before undertaking the final ordeal of parting finally from his friends.[15]

After a quiet dinner with Archbishop Riordan and the priests of the Cathedral, the hour came for Alemany to leave the scene of his long years of service. At two o'clock, Dennis J. Oliver, who had come on the *S.S. Columbus* to California with Bishop Alemany in 1850 and who, in the ensuing years, had become a wealthy and prominent figure in San Francisco, called with his carriage to take the two archbishops and Father Prendergast to the Oakland ferry. Almost a hundred persons crossed the bay with the party and assembled at the Oakland Station for the departure of the train which was to remove a beloved shepherd from their midst. A special car had been provided to take some of the clergy and laity as far as Port Costa where the final fare-wells had been agreed upon. When still another ferry had brought additional persons who wished to witness the departure, it was found that, with characteristic modesty, Archbishop Ale-many had taken his place very quietly in the last seat of the special car while awaiting the moment of his departure. He was persuaded to impart a final blessing from the rear of the car to those who knelt outside to receive it, and, later, final benediction was repeated in a brief stop at the station in Oakland. A reporter thus described the scene:

> The train drew away from the kneeling people and, as the Arch-bishop stood in reverent attitude, the wind blew his gray locks and a tear came to his eye. The train gathered speed and soon was whirling

[15] San Francisco *Call*, May 25, 1885.

along the shore and out of sight of the heavy-hearted people, who were rising with the sunlight and the archbishop's blessing on their heads.[16]

As the train approached Port Costa, the Archbishop rose to take final leave of the men who had been laboring with him for so long. With one accord, clergy and laity alike knelt in the aisle and received a final blessing, which the departing Archbishop imparted with great affection. As he passed through the cars to a Pullman car at the head of the train, Alemany was greeted with evident respect by all. As the train ran on the ferryboat which then served between Port Costa and Martinez, Joseph Sadoc Alemany, San Francisco's "Little Bishop," stood on the platform and waved a final farewell to his friends.

The Archbishop was accompanied on his final transcontinental tour to New York by two close personal friends, Daniel T. Murphy and James A. Donohoe. A stop was made in the nation's capitol where the Catholic General William Rosecrans had Alemany presented to President Grover Cleveland, who received him with marked respect. An unexpected event marked Archbishop Alemany's stay in New York, for while there it was his sad duty to preside at the funeral of his travelling companion, Daniel T. Murphy, who had died suddenly in New York. On June 5, 1885, Alemany thus wrote from New York to his former secretary, Father George Montgomery:

After attending the funeral of dear Marquis Murphy [Murphy had been made a Papal Marquis at Alemany's request because of extensive

[16] *Ibid.* On May 28, 1885, a San Francisco denominational paper, *The Pacific* (Congregational), paid graceful tribute to Alemany in these words:
   Archbishop Alemany of the Roman Catholic diocese of San Francisco, on account of growing infirmities of age, has resigned and retired and will return to Spain, the land of his birth, to spend the evening of his days. . . . The Archbishop has well earned all the rewards he has received. He has been efficient and laborious. In particular he had [*sic*] administered the finances of his charge, as well as his own, with diligence, economy and safety. Modest in deportment and small in person, he has been always at his post and done the work of a giant. We hope he may live long and enjoy a green old age, amid the scenes of his earliest memories. . . .

benefactions to the Church in San Francisco] I have been getting ready to sail tomorrow in the *Etruria.*

I brought over with me from Philadelphia dear Bp. O'Connell who may probably go back to St. Thomas Seminary. But he is anxious to be cured from his ailments before hand. . . . When I can rest a little, I will set aside some old papers and send them to you.

Any letters for me sent to the care of Very Rev. Dr. Schulte— American College, Rome, will reach me if God grants me to arrive there safely.[17]

It would seem that Archbishop Alemany's voyage to Europe was not marked by any startling events. By the last week of July, 1885, he had arrived in Rome (possibly, he had made a slow journey there, stopping en route to visit both Ireland and France). He performed a charitable favor for his friend, Bishop O'Connell, now like himself retired from his diocese in California, when he wrote in Rome to Cardinal Simeoni to tell him that he did not think that Bishop Manogue, who had succeeded O'Connell in the See of Grass Valley, was doing all that he should do for the retired prelate in the matter of paying him a sufficient pension. Adding that, in his opinion, O'Connell had not received sufficient respect and deference from his successor, he called Simeoni's attention to the fact that, because of insufficient income for his support, Bishop O'Connell had to worry much about the matter, while, because of his modesty, he was not one to enforce his rights. On July 24, while still in Rome, Alemany wrote to Simeoni from "Via San Sebastiano, n. 10," to thank the Cardinal for assigning him the titular See of Pelusium. "I would have thanked you and His Holiness earlier," wrote Alemany, "but preparations for my long voyage have occasioned this delay."[18]

[17] Alemany to the Reverend George Montgomery, New York, June 5, 1885.

[18] Alemany to Simeoni, Rome, July 24, 1885. APF. It would appear that Bishop O'Connell was quite restless in the first stages of his retirement in 1884 (he had resigned some months before Alemany). On August 8, 1885, Archbishop Ryan of Philadelphia, where O'Connell had been staying for a short time, wrote to Simeoni: "He is a pious man but, perhaps, inclined to scrupulosity." APF.

Ten days later, Archbishop Alemany wrote a more significant letter to Simeoni, giving the Cardinal his views concerning the territory which should belong to the newly established diocese of Sacramento, which had been created to supplant the earlier jurisdiction of Grass Valley in northern California. "My dear successor, Monsignor Riordan," wrote Alemany, had informed him that he should add his views on the subject to those of Riordan himself, for, as frequently happens in such matters, there were areas of disagreement between the newly appointed Archbishop and Bishop Manogue concerning the territory which was to be included in the new diocese. Riordan's referring the matter to his predecessor for an expression of his views would appear to be but another instance of the courteous deference which he always showed to Alemany.[19]

That Alemany had been, in fact, deeply moved at the warm sentiments expressed concerning him when he left California was shown by a long and affectionate letter which he addressed to the editor of the *Monitor* from Rome on August 22, 1885, and which appeared in full in the issue of September 23. After expressing his gratitude to all whom he considered joined to himself by a lasting spiritual relationship, Alemany asserted that it was precisely because of this sentiment that he had said that, even with his going, he would leave his heart in California. This was, he added, not a passing emotion, but the spontaneous manifestation of a deep-rooted sentiment. Although he thought of his leaving California as the fulfillment of the will of God, he mentioned how, in his daily Mass and prayers, he would see to it that the close bond be maintained.

After a stay of some weeks in Rome, Alemany went north to

[19] Alemany to Simeoni, Rome, August 3, 1885. APF. It was such examples of the cordial relationship between Riordan and Alemany that could cause the former to include these words in the sketch of Alemany which he wrote for the Catholic Encyclopedia: ". . . from his first meeting and until his death, the closest and tenderest friendship existed between them. . . ."

Viterbo, a city of memories for him, since he had been raised to the priesthood in its cathedral some forty-eight years previously. What occasioned him to make a will there, dated September 5, 1885, is not known, nor why, a month later, on October 9 in Rome, he made yet another will. In the first, after commending his soul to God and his body to the earth, Alemany left all his personal possessions to the Dominican master general, naming both Larroca and Archbishop Riordan as joint executors of the will. The second will was couched in more literary terms and made explicit mention that it was the testator's desire that he be buried with simple rites and with little or no external pomp which might accrue to him in virtue of his episcopal consecration. He made more explicit provision for the transfer of any financial assets which he might have for his projected missionary college by appointing several Spanish Dominican priests as his executors in this regard. (This was possibly the chief reason for the second will—to preclude any future difficulties in the matter of the missionary college.) His Roman sojourn had included an affectionate visit with Pope Leo XIII, who received him with the sentiments one would expect owing to a bishop who had served so long in the episcopal office. By the end of October, 1885, Alemany was back in Spain in his native Vich, where he took part in the celebration in honor of the Holy Rosary and assisted in the dedication of a new Dominican convent. Now that he was back in Spain, the time had come for him to make more plans for his projected missionary college.

With regard to this prospective foundation, Alemany must have been heartened by the fact that the situation had changed appreciably for the better since he had left Spain as an exile in 1835. In 1851, the Church had relinguished any further claims to the formerly expropriated properties of the secular and religious clergy, while in compensation the government promised support to the clergy to some limited extent. The concordat carried the provision that "the government proposes to improve the colleges for overseas missionaries and will, therefore, make the necessary arrangements for the establishment . . . of religious congregations and houses of St. Vincent de Paul, St. Philip Neri and another Order from those approved by the Holy See."[20] But in the ensuing ebb and flow of Spanish politics, the Church's position had not been honored, and it was only as late as 1875, with the accession of Alfonso XII as king, who promised justice in these matters, that things began to improve for the embattled Church in Spain. The King kept his word during the decade in which he ruled Spain, 1875–1885, but with his death it remained to be seen what the regent, Queen Christina, would do in regard to the religious situation. While considerable governmental interference was experienced, it would appear that, in the main, she wished to continue Alfonso's favorable attitude. This, then, was the general situation as Alemany returned to Spain in the fall of 1885. His thought in establishing a Dominican missionary college in Spain was twofold: not only would it develop vocations for the American missions, but he hoped that it would serve to restore the earlier suppressed Aragon Province of his Order. Both prospects were most pleasing to Alemany. That he would seem destined to success was made more evident by the fact that he had arranged to use for this purpose the substantial sums which had been given to him by clergy and laity on his departure from San Francisco: these funds he had left in San Francisco with Archbishop Riordan with the explicit provision that they would be forwarded to Alemany when he needed them for his college. If (as actually happened) he was unable to start such a college, the money was to go to Archbishop Riordan for the work of the archdiocese.

After visiting various localities in Spain, Alemany took up temporary residence with the Jesuits in their college in Valencia

[20] cf. E. Allison Peers, *Spain, the Church and the Orders*, (London, 1939) p. 83.

while reaching a decision as to whether he should remain in Valencia itself and there initiate his long anticipated college. Finally, he chose this city because it was large and prosperous and noted for its solid devotion to such Dominican saints as Vincent Ferrer and Louis Bertrand. Alemany found that the large church of Nuestra Senora Del Pilar was located next to a former Dominican convent which was then occupied by soldiers as a barracks, and he was hopeful that the government could be persuaded to remove the soldiers and allow the building to be brought back to its former religious use. With this in mind, Archbishop Alemany secured a residence at 46 Maldonado Street,[21] almost diagonally across from the church, with a Dominican confrere, the French Father Albert Gebhart, first sharing the apartment with him as companion and secretary. The Archbishop's quickly established routine included the daily celebration of Mass at the Blessed Virgin's altar in the adjacent church of Del Pilar, while his long manifested zeal for the confessional found him quickly in demand in this regard. In the next several years, he wrote many letters to Father Larroca in Rome concerning important details as he valiantly endeavored to get Dominican support for his missionary college in Valencia. Thus, for example, in February, 1886, he assured the Master General that Cardinal Monacillo of Valencia had indicated gracious support of the venture and had blessed it. A few days later, he wrote that the same Cardinal would welcome the assigning of several Dominican friars to the work. Soon he reported that,

[21] In June, 1963, the author visited the house on Maldonado Street, Valencia, where Alemany had lived in retirement and where he died. He was told that the façade had been altered since Alemany's time and, upon visiting the rooms on the upper story, now occupied by a commercial enterprise, it was apparent that it was impossible to identify exactly the room in which Alemany had died. The same situation was found true in the nearby church of Del Pilar; it was almost entirely gutted and destroyed by the Reds in the Spanish Civil War and although restored, the original altar at which Alemany offered Mass almost daily is gone.

despite Father Gebhart's discouraged feelings arising from the fact that he could not preach or hear confessions in the adjacent church because of language difficulties, he was, in Alemany's judgment, a child of obedience and would serve well as novice master in the training of the young Dominicans who, it was hoped, would be the first enrolled in the contemplated college. Several other such letters written during 1886 indicate the zeal with which the retired Archbishop was endeavoring to establish his college.[22]

A letter of sincere congratulations went from Valencia to Baltimore in mid-summer, 1886, when Alemany heard the expected news that Archbishop Gibbons had been elevated to the college of cardinals:

> Valencia, Spain, Maldonado St. 46
> Jul. 24/86

Your Eminence,

Permit this old Dominican in the old world to congratulate you on your high promotion, the highest in the Church under that of the Sovereign Pontiff, so richly deserved by your able and unceasing labors in defending the cause of the Pope—the cause of Christ's Kingdom. The same is doing [sic] our distinguished Cardinal Monicillo, who recently has published a lengthy, eloquent and profound Pastoral in defence of the interests of the Church. May God grant you, Most Eminent Sir, to continue your eminent work Ad Multos Annos.

I am here trying to lay the foundation of the dear project of my heart, that of reestablishing the Dominicans in this part of Spain. I have some hope of succeeding, if God spares my life, and blesses me with his temporal and spiritual aid.[23]

The failure of Father Larroca to support Alemany's plans with the sending of several friars to help him did not seem to affect

[22] These letters of Alemany to Larroca bear the following dates: (all were written in Valencia) February 1 and 13, 1886; March 3 and 23, 1887. All are signed "Fr.—i.e., Frater (Brother) Alemany, O.P."—an indication that Alemany quickly returned to former Dominican usages after retirement from active episcopal duties. AOPR.

[23] Alemany to Gibbons, Valencia, July 24, 1886. Archives, AAB.

their personal relationship. Thus, before Christmas, 1886, Alemany wrote to congratulate Larroca as the latter observed his golden jubilee in the priesthood.[24] However, by this time the not unastute Alemany must have realized that his plans were not winning any substantial backing at Dominican headquarters in Rome. Larroca was a native of Spain and knew the needs of his country quite well, but the reasons for his lack of support are not completely evident.[25] However, as previously indicated, it is quite possible that the intransigent attitude shown by Alemany with regard to his Dominican brethren in San Francisco might have militated against providing him with full cooperation—though this is merely conjecture and not supported by any known documentary evidence. The letters to Larroca continued throughout 1887 (no one ever accused Alemany of giving in easily!), but, as in the preceding year, the attitude of noncooperation of the Master General seems to have been maintained without change.

A human touch concerning this period of Alemany's life is afforded by the letter which he wrote, on Good Friday, 1887, to an old friend in San Francisco:

Valencia, Espana, Maldonado 46
April 8, 1887

Dear in Christ Miss Jones:

As I cannot pay your father and mother and their dear children an occasional visit, I will send you this note to let you know that I am yet in the land of the living in this city, the native place of St. Vincent Ferrer, of St. Louis Bertrand and of many more. I like this place very much for its climate, large beautiful churches, many religious feasts, good music and the piety of the people. We have, of

24 Alemany to Larroca, December 20, 1886. AOPR.
25 Considerable searching in the Dominican Master General's Archives, Santa Sabina, Rome by the author has convinced him that, for reasons not immediately evident, Larroca did not enter into much correspondence with Alemany concerning the Valencia venture—or, if he did, that copies of this correspondence were not kept. However, there seems to be no doubt concerning Larroca's continued coldness to Alemany's proposals for his missionary college.

course, a few bad persons, but the vast majority are very religious. To give you an idea, we have just had today three hours devotions in our church of Pilar, commencing at noon and ending at 3 o'cl. with rich music and seven sermons, one on each of the last seven words of Our Saviour. The vast edifice commenced filling two hours before the beginning of the function and many ladies had to occupy the sanctuary and very many could not get in. The two orators were truly eloquent, though plain in style. Many a tear were [sic] dropped on the Passion of the Saviour. The same ceremony was performed in several other churches with, no doubt, a great concourse of people.

With the exception of a few days, we have had a very mild winter with plenty flowers [sic] all along. The summers however are rather warm. We have everything desirable except good government.

How are your parents, your brothers and sisters? Kind regards to them, and to the good sisters of Notre Dame.[26]

It would appear that the "many years" promised Alemany by his doctor in San Francisco when he retired as archbishop there would not mean perfect health for him, for by July, 1887, he was forced to ask a special permission from Cardinal Simeoni:

I must tell Your Eminence that my sight is weakening so much that I cannot read much now for any length of time.

Taking advantage of the kindness which you have ever shown to me, I ask Your Eminence to obtain permission for me to offer the Votive Mass of the Blessed Virgin Mary.[27]

An interesting account of a visit paid to the retired Archbishop by a priest who had known him well in California appeared in the San Francisco *Monitor* in July, 1887. This was Father Michael Wallrath of Colusa, who reported his visit with Alemany as follows:

As the innumerable friends of the venerable Archbishop Alemany will hear with pleasure the report of a visit to him, I send you these few lines. Yesterday morning I arrived here early by a circuitous route from Rome, chosen by me for the purpose of seeing once more our

[26] Alemany to Miss Maria Jones, Valencia, April 8, 1887. Original in possession of Dr. Susan Carroll Jones, M.D., San Francisco.

[27] Alemany to Simeoni, Valencia, July 8, 1887. APF.

dearly beloved former prelate, the greatest benefactor of California Catholics.

It was my good fortune to meet His Grace at home last Monday morning in his quarters at Valencia. You may imagine my feelings of joy on beholding in that far-off land the well-known features of the aged pioneer of Catholics in California, and I dare say it appeared to me that the good Archbishop felt equally glad on seeing a visitor from the land that will remain most cherished in his heart to the end of his life. I found the venerable prelate in good health, with the same smiling countenance and winning tone of voice.

He is dwelling in the second story of an humble house on Maldonado Street, No. 46, Valencia, with only a servant boy and lady housekeeper as his attendants, and is living in a most simple, unpretentious manner. His house is quite near to the old Dominican church of Our Lady of the Pillar [*sic*]. This church, where the Archbishop celebrates mass, is fairly large, has many side chapels, a magnificent gilt altar of rich and antique ornamentations, though on the whole it needs much repairing. The convent adjacent to the building, which was in former times the Dominican novitiate, is now a barrack of soldiers.

The Dominicans, of whose order the prelate is a member, possessed still another church and convent in Valencia, which last is in the same condition. When expelled from all Spain by the Government, they had to abandon also their sanctuaries in Valencia. They have at present re-established some nine new convents over the kingdom, but none as yet in Catalonia; hence the Archbishop is laboring to gradually re-establish a house of his order also in Valencia, and he has good hopes of success.

On my leaving, the Archbishop graciously loaded me with hearty greetings to all in California.[28]

The anticipated success regarding Alemany's desired Dominican foundation in Spain was still not within sight in early 1888 —when he had been at work on the project for over two full years. On the feast of the Epiphany, January 6, 1888, he suffered a cerebral hemorrhage while hearing confessions before Mass in the Church of the Pilar. Additional evidence of his already demonstrated physical stamina manifested itself when,

28 *Monitor,* July 13, 1887.

345

after a week in bed, he was judged sufficiently recovered to offer Mass several times. This he did for the last time about a month after his stroke when, finding his memory failing and discovering that his formerly excellent knowledge of the rubrics had deserted him, he decided not to try to offer Mass again unless he underwent a notable improvement. However, he showed his customary devotion to the confessional. On his patronal feast day, that of St. Joseph, March 19, 1888, he again became quite ill, but was not considered to be in danger until several more days had passed. On March 28, he received viaticum with evident piety and a slight recovery ensued. Two weeks later, however, Alemany suffered a second stroke, and, since he was judged close to death, the last rites were administered to him. He remained in a somewhat comatose condition until Saturday, April 14, when, just at the hour of the evening Angelus, he died. Since a law prevailed in Valencia that prevented his body being brought to the church, the remains of California's pioneer prelate were embalmed and he lay in simple state in the house where he had died. On Tuesday, April 17, a solemn requiem Mass was offered for the repose of his soul in the parish church of the district of Valencia where he had lived. (Del Pilar was not a parish church, and, consequently, the obsequies took place in the church of Santos Juanes.) The aged Cardinal Monacillo of Valencia was unable to be present, but both Church and state were officially represented at the large funeral which witnessed more than one hundred priests in attendance, as well as a capacity number of the faithful. The dean of the basilica, Dr. Jose Cirujeda, presided at the office for the dead and offered the solemn Mass which followed.

Archbishop Alemany had wished to be buried in his native Vich, and this wish was honored when his two priest brothers, Father Ignacio and Father Miguel, accompanied his remains by train from Valencia to Vich after the morning services. That evening, upon arrival in Vich, a procession of priests and people met the train and, while the bells of all the churches tolled, the cortege moved through the crowded streets to the Dominican Convent of the Annunciation where the body lay in state throughout the night. The next morning, at ten o'clock, a second solemn requiem Mass was offered for the repose of one who had so honored the name of Vich in far-distant California. The Bishop of Vich, Dr. Jose Morgades y Gili, presided, and the funeral oration was delivered by Canon Narvisso Vilarrasa, nephew of Father Sadoc Vilarrasa, Alemany's brother Dominican. The rites were brought to a close when the Archbishop's remains were interred in the Chapel of the Blessed Sacrament to the right of the central nave of the venerable church of Santo Domingo where, many years before, Joseph Sadoc Alemany had vowed his life to the service of God in the Order of Friars Preacher.

More than two weeks after Alemany's death, the *Monitor,* not yet knowing of the event, mentioned his recent illness as "reported by Very Rev. Joachim Adam, V.G., who informs us that he recently visited Archbishop Alemany to find that, the victim of brain fever, he had been prepared for death." The editor expressed the hope that Alemany would recover. It was not until the following Saturday, May 5, that the same editor received word, in another letter from Father Adam, of Alemany's demise several weeks before. Adam had written from Valencia on the day of Alemany's funeral, April 17, 1888, to report fully the details of the passing of the prelate whose "pure and holy soul," he wrote, "returned to God last Saturday, April 14, at about six p.m." Adding that Alemany's two-year stay in Valencia had endeared him to many, Adam described the simplicity of the wake which was held in the house where the Archbishop had died.[29]

Sincere tribute was paid to Archbishop Alemany in the same

[29] *Monitor,* May 2; May 9, 1888.

issue of the *Monitor*. Commenting on his passing, the editor referred to him as "perhaps the best known man in California," adding that

. . . his small, slight figure and his ascetic countenance were familiar to all classes and creeds in this city, from the millionaire to the newsboy, and down to the inmates of the prison which he frequently visited in discharge of his pastoral duties in common with the humblest priest under him. While not an eminent preacher, he was an excellent administrator, and under his direction the archdiocese kept full pace with the wonderful growth of the state at large.[30]

It so happened that Archbishop Riordan was absent from San Francisco en route to Europe when the news arrived of the death of his predecessor. This will explain why the month's mind Mass which was offered in the cathedral which had been built by Alemany was not offered by his successor. As expected, St. Mary's Cathedral was crowded beyond capacity on Monday, May 14, when Father John Cottle celebrated the solemn requiem as a month's mind Mass for the lamented shepherd. At its end, the eulogy was delivered by the vicar general who had known Alemany so well and who, as we have seen, could have succeeded him were it not for his steady refusal of the honor—Father John Prendergast. The sermon was reported as having been marked with affection as he described the long years which Alemany had devoted to the upbuilding of the Church in California. Included in it were "many anecdotes illustrative of his purity of character, benevolence and simplicity." Prendergast also took the occasion to deny the rumour that had been circulated to the effect that Alemany had taken one million dollars with him to Spain. Father Prendergast remarked that, while the clergy had freely subscribed $10,000 as a gift out of love for Alemany, he had declined to take it with him but had decided to leave it with Archbishop Riordan with the stipulation that, if he could establish his missionary college in Spain, the money would be de-

[30] *Monitor,* May 9, 1888.

voted to this end—if, however, this proved to be impossible, then Archbishop Riordan was to devote it to charitable purposes. The *Monitor* account concluded by stating that "the oration was an eloquent eulogy of a noble man."[31] Thus did a grieving flock in San Francisco sincerely honor the memory of the one who had been for so long their devoted father in God.

[31] *Monitor,* May 15, 1888.

14

Alemany's Character and Influence on Catholicism in California

WHILE it would seem obvious that much of the character of California's pioneer archbishop has been revealed in the preceding chapters, it would appear that this present study would be incomplete were not some attempt made at its end to assess the man and to weigh the extent of his lasting influence upon the history of the Catholic Church in the area which he served. This, then, is the purpose of this present chapter.

We shall divide this assessment into three parts: first, we shall attempt to sum up Alemany's personal characteristics as revealed in his background, ante-episcopal and episcopal career as well as by various authenticated sources. Since his chief importance lies in the fact of his long service in California as Archbishop, we shall next examine critically his stewardship in this responsible position; although his reluctance to be a bishop as well as his numerous attempts to resign the burden of this office are well known by now, Alemany was a prelate with an extraordinarily long episcopal rule; hence, it will be necessary to pass judgment upon him and upon this rule on the basis of all available evidence. Finally, by a sampling of various contemporary and later opinions of the man and his work, it is hoped that his central position in the earliest American Period of the Catholic Church in California will be made evident.

In the first chapter of this study, evidence was cited to establish the substantial character of the ancestral background of the future pioneer Archbishop of California. From the time when the Alemany family first entered the history of Vich (about 1610) and continuing, indeed, to the present day, the name has been one held in respect among the inhabitants of Vich and of the surrounding area. It is not at all difficult to note a certain sturdiness in Alemany all through his life and it is hardly exceeding the known facts to attribute this, in good measure, to his solid and substantial ancestry. As has been seen, both good and less good qualities, perhaps, can be attributed to this same font of origin and ancestry.

A quality which had the deepest roots in Joseph Alemany was the constant and unobtrusive piety which marked his life. The recollection of the proper Christian example given him by devoted parents seems always to have been with him, and when it is recalled that, of his eleven brothers and sisters, four sons became priests while two daughters entered the cloister as nuns, it would seem that ample testimony is afforded as to the religious environment which marked his family. So perhaps it is not really surprising that Alemany should have demonstrated a piety of life that was the object of admiration of those who watched him and his work. In building his first Cathedral in San Francisco, for example, he found that a room next to his bedroom could be made into a sort of private oratory with a small window overlooking the sanctuary; here, it was reliably reported, San Francisco's first Archbishop spent, unobserved, many a nocturnal hour in quiet prayer. Since such prayer would almost certainly have served to preserve the apostolic spirit which he had manifested earlier as a Dominican missionary on the Kentucky and Tennessee frontier, it is not surprising to learn that Alemany maintained a confessional in his Cathedral for many years; when at home, too, it was noted that he insisted on taking his regular share of parochial duties as much as time would allow. This consideration of his zeal leads us into a con-

351

sideration of the poverty and simplicity which ever marked his life.[1] We are fortunate in having examples of each left for our consideration.

It was known that Archbishop Alemany insisted on living according to the prescriptions of his Dominican rule rather than in the customary style of prelates. He cared for his own room, made his own bed, and dressed habitually in his home and adjacent office in the Dominican habit rather than in the customary episcopal purple—which he donned, rather reluctantly it would seem, only when necessity demanded it. A simple pectoral cross supported by a green cord, plus the episcopal ring which went with his office, were the sole signs that the white clad Dominican friar was, indeed, a consecrated successor of the apostles. When, in 1875, on the occasion of the silver jubilee of his episcopal consecration, he was presented with a fine carriage and team of horses, he was courteous in his grateful acceptance—but it was not long before he sold both carriage and team because he needed some money to devote to his orphans. His comment on the occasion was an interesting one as he remarked that "The Archbishop's carriage are the horse cars of this city!"

Additional evidence of Alemany's lack of ostentation was had in the fact that, at first, he would allow no throne in his Cathedral, contenting himself with a simple chair for use when he either presided or officiated there. Later on, he was persuaded that more was required and expected of him as Archbishop and, with some reluctance, he allowed a modest and still quite simple

[1] Much of what follows is based upon an unpublished manuscript written by the Right Reverend Antonio Santendreau (1853–1944), who was a native of Catalonia like Alemany and who, after ordination to the priesthood in 1876, began a period of service in the Archdiocese of San Francisco which lasted for sixty-eight years. He first served as a curate in the Spanish National Church of Nuestra Señora de la Guadalupe in San Francisco and later, in 1889, became pastor there, a post which he filled until his death in 1944. For eight years he served under Alemany and this fact makes his memories of the Archbishop both contemporary and valuable. Written about 1906, they were later incorporated into the unpublished manuscript of the Reverend Alberto Collell, O.P., which has been previously mentioned.

throne to be placed in the sanctuary. It was once remarked that if Archbishop Alemany ever, indeed, possessed the *cappa magna* used by bishops on ceremonial occasions, his possession of such a garment was a carefully guarded secret, for no one ever saw him wear it! It is a matter of history that he shunned portraiture of any kind and it was only by strategy that Ernest Narjot was enabled to capture his figure, the absence of which would have represented quite a loss to future generations.[2]

Pastoral visitations of the vast area of his archdiocese, done regularly and with commendable fidelity, always found Alemany willing to aid his priests in their ministry as occasion offered. In 1871, after a visit of this sort to Placerville, a correspondent sent a letter to the *Monitor* remarking that "he left the impression that he is even too unassuming to be a prince of the church!"[3] (Alemany must have been amused at the reference to his being a "prince of the Church"—obviously, he did not regard himself as such.) A characteristic note occurs in an Alemany letterbook where, addressing the Jesuit, Father Benedict Piccardo, who attended the New Almaden mines from Santa Clara College, concerning a prospective visit there, he records that he wrote Piccardo somewhat cryptically: "Will go to Almaden on Saturday, November 17. Will hear confessions. Any bed will do,

[2] Ernest E. Narjot was born in France in 1826 and died in San Francisco in 1898 after a distinguished career in the field of art and portraiture. (Cf. Albert Dressler—*California's Pioneer Artist. Ernest Narjot, A Brief Resume of the Career of a Versatile Genius.* San Francisco, 1936.) After Archbishop Alemany refused to sit for a portrait, Narjot resorted to the strategy of sketching him on several occasions when the Archbishop was preaching in St. Mary's Cathedral. From these informal (and surreptitious) sketches came a splendid painting which, in fact, furnishes the basis for practically every representation which is seen of Alemany. Painted in 1878 and signed by Narjot, the painting has long been in the possession of Miss Frances Molera, hanging in her home on Sacramento Street in San Francisco. Miss Molera kindly consented to have her cherished painting of Alemany photographed for reproduction in this work. In 1965, Miss Molera gave the portrait to the Holy Family Sisters—a group founded by Alemany. It now has a place of honor in the novitiate house of these Sisters in Mission San Jose, California.

[3] *Monitor,* May 27, 1871.

please—no ceremonies about it, anything will suit me."[4] Other examples of the sort could be multiplied, but it is believed that they would be unnecessary: almost certainly, the simple pattern of Alemany has already been made evident.

A spirit of charity and kindness was joined with the above-mentioned simplicity of the Archbishop: thus, on one occasion, when two seminarians arrived unexpectedly and much too late for supper at the cathedral rectory, their scrambled eggs were prepared for them by the Archbishop who then escorted them to some friends to get lodging for them since all of the rooms of the rectory were occupied. Again, that he was not without a certain wry sense of humor was shown one Sunday morning when, having agreed to preside in his Cathedral at the first solemn Mass of a newly ordained priest, he found, after quietly slipping into his place in the sanctuary, that the celebrant had not yet appeared in the sacristy. Inquiry brought the information that the delay was caused by the failure of a servant to shine the shoes of the young priest—whereupon Alemany remarked that, if the young priest did not appear promptly, his Archbishop would go to him and shine his shoes for him. Presumably, it was not long before the tardy celebrant was at the altar!

Anyone in Alemany's position would have to face numerous occasions when the use of authority would be necessary. Several examples are on record that show that he never lacked the firmness necessary in such cases. Thus, as we have seen, when pressure was brought on him to allow the American flag to fly from his Cathedral during Civil War days as an evidence of patriotism, he was firm in his refusal, telling, on one occasion, a somewhat aroused group outside who were demanding the "flagging," as it was called: "There will only be a cross on my Church; there will be the American flag flying from my home."

[4] Alemany to Benedict Piccardo, S.J., San Francisco, November 17, 1867. Copy in Alemany Letterbook, *AASF*.

354

Evidently, Alemany was not one to panic under pressures of this sort.

Since a study of the Narjot portrait of Alemany reveals the Archbishop as being of a definitely ascetical and serious mien, it is necessary to record that his rigorous sense of justice was ever tempered by the quality of mercy. Those who, upon occasion, felt the full weight of a decision involving themselves were frequently made conscious that the decision had been reached only after reflection and prayer—and then, only with reluctance. Thus, for example, on one occasion he carried around in his satchel for several days a copy of a reprimand which he felt he had to impose upon a recalcitrant priest. When it was finally delivered, the accompanying letter read as follows:

Reverend Father:
You know that I have loved and do love you as a dear son. I have admonished you and advised you as a Father—and you have turned a deaf ear. This I feel very deeply in my soul, but, as a Bishop, I feel myself obliged to take away your faculties. But remember that, when you repent and behave yourself and do as you are told, I am ready to lift the suspension.[5]

When it is recalled that Alemany had done a distinguished course of studies in the Dominican Order, it comes as no surprise to find that he was always held in high regard as a scholar. Alemany had that versatility in languages common to educated Europeans, although his correspondence and sermons reveal a certain quaintness of expression which always remained with him in his use of the English language. Thus, for example, he thanked a benefactor for "your beautiful check" of $100 for the orphans of San Rafael, and he also expressed his gratitude to the Dominican Sister Superior for a letter concerning some business—with the additional lines, "The six thousand dollars are all right and safe. Please live long to keep the poor

[5] Santendreau, "Notes Concerning Archbishop Alemany," p. 11. Cf. above, Note 1.

Bishop in socks!" Another letter to the same Mother Mary Joseph, Dominican Superior at San Rafael, asked her to tell "Sister Mary Joseph that the Bishop is not mad; that, when he does not write, it is a sign that he is not mad but that he has the hands full of business."[6] It would appear that his mastery of English was quite sufficient for his needs, but he never pretended to have the fluency that marks the orator—actually, his sermons were like the man, simple and sincere with a minimum of flowery expression.

A bishop plays more than one role in the administration of his diocese; obviously, one of the things which must be considered in forming opinions or judgments about him will concern his business acumen or, more generally, his administrative ability. While there is no evidence that Alemany was so outstanding as to be considered unusually gifted here, there is certainly no evidence that he was not quite competent in these same areas. His earnest efforts, for example, with regard to the Pious Fund indicate that he was not afraid to come to grips with a difficult and touchy question, and there is not lacking solid evidence that Alemany was a man of vision who saw the future of San Francisco in such a manner as to provide well for the needs of his flock inasmuch as his limited resources would permit. Archbishop Riordan's comments, quoted in an earlier chapter, as to the work which remained to be done should not be interpreted as a stricture on the lack of business sense of his predecessor: he simply remarked that Alemany had formed the habit of keeping too much in his head.

Thus far, we have endeavored to point out those qualities of Alemany's character and personality which were commendable and which seem to have been verified in his life; when one

[6] The two letters were written to Mother Mary Joseph Dillon, O.P., Superior at Dominican College, San Rafael, and are dated, respectively, April 12, 1871 and January 3, 1873. Originals in Dominican Archives, San Rafael.

comes now to view the opposite side of the coin, it would appear that the chief criticism which might be directed against him is one which, presumably, he would have been quite willing to admit. The reference is to his stubbornness which showed itself in his firm persistence in his own opinions and convictions even when, upon occasion, matters had been decided against him. He was not wrong when he wrote that he came from "a part of Spain where people are stubborn": he did and was! A partial key here may be provided in a letter which Alemany wrote to Cardinal Barnabò in 1872 in which he apologized for "being such a disturbing person to bother you constantly about matrimonial dispensations—if I appear to be strict in such matters, it is because I conceive it to be the only way open to me in my work with the souls committed to my care."[7] Earlier, indeed, Alemany had disparaged his own abilities when, in writing to Archbishop Spalding of Baltimore, he had commented that he was happy to see the intelligent preparations being made for the forthcoming Council in Baltimore, adding, "You must not mind me, whose head is entirely too small to attend to any serious matter, but I will say 'amen' to any good proposed."[8] Physically, his head may have been small, indeed, but it was, undeniably, a stubborn one!

A question about which there may always be room for legitimate disagreement would be as to whether this intransigence was so marked at times as to constitute what could properly be called a major flaw in the Archbishop's character. The present writer is inclined to favor the opinion that Alemany did, in fact, exceed in occasional demonstrations of such stubbornness; indeed, a careful reading of the Alemany correspondence has convinced him that rarely, if ever, did Alemany *really* change his views about any of the questions under dispute. While "kiss-

[7] Alemany to Barnabò, San Francisco, December 5, 1872.
[8] Alemany to Martin J. Spalding, San Francisco, May 15, 1866.

357

ing the sacred purple with great respect," as he wrote upon several occasions—i.e., showing respect to the Cardinal Prefect who had informed him of an adverse decision—there is no real evidence that Alemany did more than merely follow, in obedience, the letter of the decision. As we have written earlier, he was certainly not always right, but he was too, and this almost certainly, always righteous. Beyond this point in the analysis of his conduct in the situations referred to, it seems impossible to go.

Stubborn as Archbishop Alemany may have been, he was always and ever, it seems, also the solicitous shepherd. An example of this quality was found in a letter which he wrote, towards the end of his episcopal rule, to a certain woman in his Archdiocese.

> Although not good, yet I should be a good Bishop and, as such I should make the episcopal visitation and take an interest in the spiritual welfare of all the spiritual sheep and know them and use my little spiritual means to direct them right.[9]

Any attempt to analyze Alemany as a bishop must necessarily include his position as a member of the Dominican Order before consecration as well as the fact that, while necessarily dispensed from certain obligations in the exercise of episcopal jurisdiction, he always kept a filial feeling towards the Order. As we have seen in considerable detail, he did make foes among some of his brethren in California but that did not alienate him from the Dominican spirit which had been his earliest love. It would seem that, in his case as in the case of many others who have been called to the episcopate from the ranks of religious Orders, a certain tension was set up which, perhaps, was almost impossible to avoid entirely. With episcopal consecration accepted, as in Alemany's case, under explicit orders from the Vicar of Christ came assignment to service in a given portion of the

9 Alemany to Louisa Lynch, San Francisco, July 31, 1882. Copy in *APF*.

Church. Without extinguishing previous loyalties, Bishop Alemany, who still considered himself as a religious, had to pursue a wary path so as not to be unjust to the rights of either his diocese or of his Order. When, as in the present case, that same Order formed part of the clerical personnel of the diocese with the same Father Vilarrasa as Superior who had disagreed with Alemany earlier in the missionary years in Kentucky and Ohio, it was but natural, perhaps, that areas of conflict would present themselves. Some of Alemany's challenging language which was used in various letters to his Dominican brethren in San Francisco reads like the language of controversy ordinarily used quite familiarly between persons who know each other very well! However all this may have been, it would appear that, with the passage of time, a kindly verdict was passed on San Francisco's first Archbishop by members of both the Jesuit and Dominican Orders who looked back upon the earlier years of dispute.

It is interesting to read the description of Alemany's physical appearance joined with a character analysis which was written in 1905 (a full quarter century after the earlier disputes between the friars and the Archbishop) by the same Father James Benedict McGovern, who, in 1880 as Prior of St. Dominic's Church in San Francisco, had been deeply involved in the controversy. It will be recalled that, in a letter previously quoted, Alemany had written to Vilarrasa to express indignation at some of the language used concerning him by McGovern; it may be recalled, too, that Alemany was not at all satisfied with the sort of "retraction" made by the Father Prior at Vilarrasa's insistence. (McGovern's later reflections concerning his former adversary are contained in an unpublished description which is in the Dominican Archives in Washington, D.C. As indicated, the passage of time seems to have mollified the sentiments of the once pugnacious Prior.) First, with regard to Alemany's physical appearance, McGovern notes that the prelate was small, built slenderly with a broad and towering forehead indicating, the author asserts, "a man of great intellect—and such he was." He adds immediately that Alemany was "one of the brainiest and most cultured of the prelates that have adorned the American hierarchy." His lips, thin and closely set, "pointed out a strong and firm character. This, too, he was in a marked degree." His attractions, as McGovern recalled them from earlier days, were of the "spiritual rather than of the physical . . . he was . . . meek, humble, kind, generous, friendly, condescending, forgiving—and all almost to a fault—he won the hearts of all of those with whom he came in contact." Continuing in the same mellow tone, McGovern adds:

> Though twenty-one years have come and gone since his retirement, he still lives in the memories and affections of the Catholics of San Francisco. His name is a synonym for all that is good, holy and true.[10]

In this case, time seems to have wrought a mighty change in Father McGovern's sentiments. Perhaps, indeed, it will not do to take all of the above tribute to Alemany in a completely literal sense; here the language of eulogy is, as always, suspect. At any rate, some had not agreed with the euphoric lines later penned by McGovern. Of this class are the lines which were written in rather a venomous manner by the editor of a Masonic magazine of San Francisco: they were published in 1893, when Alemany had already been dead for five years but, seemingly, this key fact was yet unknown to his hostile critic! He wrote:

> Archbishop Alemany, a few years since, after having secured all of the finest pieces of real estate he could for the papal power in this state, returned to his native country of Spain, entered a Dominican Convent of which he was a monk of that order [sic] and, about two years ago, like all old spiders of the tarantula order, who have spread

[10] James Benedict McGovern, O.P. (1836–1918) was ordained in 1863 and, as we have seen, was Prior of St. Dominic's, San Francisco in the early 1880's when the Dominicans were frequently at odds with Alemany. His interesting memoir of Alemany is in the AOPW.

360

their webs and consumed all the flies they are able to catch and consume, crawled into his hole, pulled down the lid and, in his own self-made sarcophagus, awaits the fiat of the Almighty.[11]

It is evident, of course, that such virulent stuff should hardly be taken into account in a serious endeavor to assess the position and lasting worth of Archbishop Alemany. However, as indicated above, neither should the uncritical pean of praise of a McGovern be accorded complete credence. In this latter class, too, must be placed the opinion of Father Hugh Quigley who, writing in 1878 while Alemany was still active in the See of San Francisco, praised him with obvious exaggerations. According to Quigley, as we have seen, Alemany's reign was one of complete harmony which "is probably the only one that has never been disturbed by the disobedience of a single subject or even unfavorably commented on or criticized" [!].[12] Of much more worth is the solid portrait, also previously mentioned, given by a prominent architect of San Francisco, Mr. Bryan Clinch, who knew Alemany well. In Clinch's judgment, "the singular combination of intense enthusiasm for the religious life, with absolute impartiality between its professors and the secular clergy, was a marked feature in Bishop Alemany's striking character."[13]

There is a short but incisive portrait of Archbishop Alemany as he appeared to an Irish Jesuit who was laboring in San Francisco in 1872, which is included in a longer account on the Catholic Church in San Francisco. His brief summation of Alemany notes that "the Archbishop, learned, pious, humble and a strict observer of ecclesiastical discipline, does honor to his high

[11] Edwin A. Sherman, "Romanism in San Francisco," in *The Trestleboard*, a Monthly Masonic and Family Magazine, San Francisco, VII, n. 12 (December, 1893), p. 547.

[12] Hugh Quigley, *The Irish Race in California and on the Pacific Coast* (San Francisco, 1878), p. 419.

[13] Bryan J. Clinch, "The Jesuits in American California" in *Records of the American Catholic Historical Society* (Philadelphia) XVII (1906), p. 131.

office and commands the respect of the professors of every religion, while he is revered by those of his own."[14]

Another substantial tribute to the general esteem in which Archbishop Alemany was held is found in an extensive memoir which was written in 1875 by Mariano Guadalupe Vallejo, the "Lord of the North," so well known in the California story. For reasons of his own, Vallejo had not been impressed with the first Bishop of the Californias, the Franciscan Garcia Diego, and he used the dislike he had for him to contrast his completely affable relations with Alemany; Vallejo's words are as follows:

Some years ago, I met Messrs. David Spence and Jose Abrego at Monterey, and we were comparing present times with those past. The conversation turned to Bishop Garcia Diego and his arrogance. David Spence said at that time that we ought to pardon Bishop Garcia Diego his shortcomings, in view of the virtues which characterized Archbishop Alemany. He said that the latter's affability was proverbial and in more than one instance it served to put back upon the path of cordial relations prelates who suffered from an excess of silly pride and to back up his assertion he told the anecdote which I shall now relate.

Said Mr. David Spence, "It was in 1863, when I was on a visit to San Francisco and met the Reverend Lossa [sic], present bishop of Guadalajara, who had been banished from Sinaloa by General Placido Vega, governor of that State. He told me that to a certain extent he was grateful to General Vega for exiling him, because in San Francisco he had learned lessons in affability, kindness and liberality from Archbishop Alemany which in no way detracted from the high position he occupied as prince of the Catholic Church, but which, rather, helped to win him the good will of the faithful who, attracted by his practical wisdom and excellent treatment, flocked to him spontaneously to offer themselves for the service of the church, whether with their personal services or with their worldly goods and that should Divine Providence permit him to return to his own diocesis [sic], he would not fail to profit by the lessons which Archbishop Alemany had unwittingly given

[14] Michael O'Ferrall, S.J., "Five Years at the Golden Gate" in *Monitor*, March 2, 1872. Father O'Ferrall, an Irish Jesuit, was loaned to the staff of St. Ignatius College, San Francisco for several years and his interesting reminiscences are an observant commentary on Catholic life in San Francisco in the 1860's.

him. He thought the archbishop should be taken as a model by the worthy clergy of Mexico and Spain who perhaps, as in his own case, carried away by mistaken ideas, had been assuming an attitude which repelled, rather than attracted penitent Christians."

To what Bishop Lossa [*sic*] said I will add that in the course of my life I have had repeated opportunity for contacting Archbishop Alemany, who has sometimes deigned to honor my home with his presence and I, as well as the other members of my family, could not help but admire his humility, affable manner and the unquestioned liberality which he showed to the poor who appealed to him. Would to God there were many Catholic prelates who, rising to the heights of his noble mission, would take as their model the worthy archbishop who has so striven to bring luster to the Catholic Church in the Californias.[15]

Certainly, one of the worthiest priests who worked with Archbishop Alemany was that Father John Prendergast who, as we have seen, had refused promotion as Alemany's Coadjutor Archbishop. Ordained in 1859, he knew Alemany for the almost quarter century which found them closely associated and it was a graceful tribute to the latter that Prendergast published in 1911, three years before his own death at the age of eighty:

Archbishop Alemany was the first Bishop of the new era that dawned so suddenly on California. He was a happy choice. No man was better qualified than he to be the connecting link between the old and the new. A Spaniard by birth and a fine type of his noble race, he was held in veneration by the Mexican people alike for his office and his personal virtues; an American by adoption and by years of missionary work in Ohio and Tennessee before he became Bishop, he was in full sympathy with American ideas and principles and enjoyed the unqualified respect of the American people. He spoke four or five languages fluently and idiomatically, which enabled him to enter into pleasant communication with the many-tongued people who sought these shores. Moreover, with a constitution which no labor could tire and an Apos-

15 "Historical and Personal Memoirs Relating to Alta California Written by Mariano G. Vallejo, Military Commandant of Alta California from the year 1836 to the year 1842." Translated from the Spanish by Earl R. Hewitt. A gift of the author to Hubert H. Bancroft, San Francisco, April 10, 1875. Original manuscript in Bancroft Library, Berkeley.

tolic spirit that shrank from no sacrifice, Archbishop Alemany was able to visit periodically the most remote parts of his diocese in days when there were no railroads and when long distances were covered by the crowded and uncomfortable stage. It was nothing extraordinary to see the Archbishop of San Francisco on the top of the stage with a Chinaman seated by his side. Under Archbishop Alemany's administration the old gradually passed with honor; the new began on strong and deep foundations.[16]

Several years earlier, the *Overland Monthly*, which had been founded in San Francisco in 1868 by Bret Harte, had published an interesting article entitled: "What the Catholic Church Has Done for San Francisco" which included the following graceful tribute to the city's first Archbishop:

In many respects, the period during which he served was the most critical and vital in the history of San Francisco. Just as the name of Junipero Serra brings to our minds the California mission regime, and that of Archbishop Riordan the era of modern San Francisco . . . so that of Archbishop Alemany stands out as the apostle of the strenuous days of gold.[17]

A sufficient sampling has now been made to testify to the solid esteem in which Joseph Sadoc Alemany was held by practically all who came under his influence during his long years as the first Archbishop of San Francisco. However, it is thought that such testimonies may well be concluded with some mention of that sincere tribute to his successor which was paid by Archbishop Riordan in a warm and informative sketch which, in 1907, he contributed to the *Catholic Encyclopedia*. Students of Riordan's own distinguished years in the See of San Francisco quickly become convinced of the excellent qualities of this second Archbishop—and chief among them was a certain bluntness and sincerity which make one feel that he was recording

[16] Right Reverend John J. Prendergast, V.G.; "Laying the Foundation— A Glance Backward" in the *Monitor*, September 23, 1911.

[17] Hamilton Wright and F. Marion Gallagher, "What the Catholic Church Has Done for San Francisco" in *Overland Monthly*, vol. L, no. 5 (November, 1907), p. 407.

what he felt to be the absolute truth concerning his predecessor. Commenting on the appropriateness of the choice of Alemany for the episcopal office in California in 1850, Riordan points out that he was almost ideally prepared for it: a cosmopolitan viewpoint, a decade of service in the United States before coming to California and the firmest of loyalty to the United States of America as a naturalized citizen. "Born in Spain," says Riordan, "educated in Rome and long resident in America, his experience and command of several languages put him in touch and in sympathy with all the elements of his diocese . . . while . . . his humility and simplicity of manner, though by nature retiring, drew to him the hearts of all classes . . . The episcopal office which he had accepted only under obedience was, in a human sense, never congenial to Archbishop Alemany—his whole temperament inclined him to be simply a missionary priest; in a large sense, he continued to be such up to the day of his resignation. . . ."

As to the genuine and lasting accomplishments of Alemany, Riordan is quite explicit:

. . . When he began his work, there were but twenty-one adobe mission churches scattered up and down the state and not more than a dozen priests in all California. He lived to see the state divided into three dioceses, with about three hundred thousand population, many churches of modern architecture and some of respectable dimensions, a body of devoted clergy, secular and regular, charitable and educational institutions conducted by the teaching orders of both men and women, such as to meet, as far as possible under the circumstances, the wants of a constantly growing population. . . .[18]

This biography has endeavored to avoid glossing over what may be considered to have been Alemany's mistakes in judgment, for the desire in these pages has been not to write eulogy but to present as complete a portrait of the man as is possible

[18] Alemany, Joseph S.: Sketch by P. W. Riordan, Catholic Encyclopedia I (New York, 1907), pp. 282–283.

from the available sources. Although evidence is not entirely lacking that the precise and rather strict nature of the Archbishop made him appear rather at times small-minded, this observation is easily counter-balanced by the magnanimous spirit which he customarily showed in the industrious and long years during which, with admirable selflessness, he devoted himself to his pastoral tasks in administering the Archdiocese of San Francisco. In an earlier sketch of Alemany written by the present author, the reflection was made that

> . . . the deeds and the daring of the one who habitually called himself the "little Bishop" . . . will . . . always remain among the more precious pages in the book of California Catholicism. At the end of his long years of service . . . . Alemany remarked: "I do not think that I was born to be a Bishop and I told Pius IX so; nevertheless, they made me a Bishop." Shall we not agree that Pius IX has never had any reason to regret, either in time or in eternity, having called Joseph Sadoc Alemany to the plenitude of priesthood?[19]

Nothing that the present writer has learned in the long period of research which necessarily has preceded the writing of this book has caused him substantially to change these views. The Catholic Church in California and San Francisco were, in the light of precise historical truth, richly dowered with the presence of Joseph Sadoc Alemany, O.P. as the first Archbishop of San Francisco. He was, indeed, a "great priest who in his days pleased God."

[19] John B. McGloin, S.J., "The Coming of Joseph Sadoc Alemany, O.P., Pioneer Prelate of El Dorado" in *Records of the American Catholic Historical Society of Philadelphia,* LXII, n. 4 (December, 1951), p. 212.

An Essay on Sources

IT is here proposed to group and discuss the main source and other materials which have been consulted in the making of this book. We shall first indicate the principal archival collections in Europe and the United States which were used; next, some items which concern Alemany directly will be listed; finally, a selected and varied list of subsidiary materials will be named. It is felt that this listing, joined with the many books and other sources quoted in the text, will provide a sufficient overview of the sources of the present study.

1. DOCUMENTARY COLLECTIONS

It might be expected that the prime source for this study would be the Archives of the Archdiocese of San Francisco which had Alemany as its first Archbishop, 1853–1884. As will be seen, materials are there in sufficient number as to be of prime help. However, the Roman Archives of Propaganda Fide provide other and extensive coverage also. We shall here list the main informative fonts in the Archdiocesan Archives as preserved in the Chancery Office, San Francisco. As a partial background for the state of California Catholicism in the decade preceding Alemany's arrival as Bishop of Monterey in 1850, the *Libro Borrador* kept by his predecessor, the Franciscan Bishop Garcia Diego y Moreno, is of substantial value—especially since Alemany added some items of his own after his coming to California. Under date of December 30, 1850, three weeks after this arrival, Alemany wrote thus in the *Borrador*: "This book will now be officially devoted to the records of my official diocesan business as Bishop of Monterey." The fourteen pages which follow in Alemany's handwriting, 1850–1882, furnish incomplete but occasionally important details concerning such matters as the 1850 arrival, the question of title to mission lands and buildings, the Pious Fund, and the separation of Baja California from his diocese. Another valuable record book is that which, called *Liber Visitationis Episcopalis, 1850–1853,* has some satisfying details concerning Alemany's first activities in California. A continuing chronicle brings the story of such activities through 1875 and quickly reveals that, although Alemany's handwriting at times leaves much to be desired, he was, indeed, a methodical keeper of records. Still another, *Liber Gubernii Sedis S. Francisci,* is invaluable for its detailed accounts of ordinations, appointments, details of the erection of the archdiocese in 1853, etc. A very large journal of Alemany's correspondence (408 pages) gives a detailed account of this facet of his life, 1862–1868. Much diocesan history is inescapably brought to light here. Several other books of varying size continue the same story through 1881. A volume called *Liber "E" Dioceseos S. Francisci* contains copies of many important Roman documents, 1851–1861—there are about one hundred documents in all. But it is in another such volume that we come on the richest treasure, for this contains the originals of such Roman documents to 1861. Here we have the official notification to Alemany of his forthcoming consecration in Rome with a reminder by the master of ceremonies to be in the sacristy by "8¼" A.M., etc.! Several other volumes also contain originals of other such key documents. The two final volumes of use here were found to be a journal which Alemany kept of correspondence and episcopal activities (actually a sort

368

of diary, etc.) 1855–1863, and an important minutes book of the meetings of the Archdiocesan council, 1862–1879: here one reads the "inside" details which accompanied the extended controversies between Alemany and Jesuit superiors in San Francisco.

Both complementary and supplementary to the materials mentioned above are those which were consulted, in two extended searchings, in the Roman Archives of the Sacred Congregation de Propaganda Fide. These consultations in the fall of 1957 and the spring of 1963 amounted to almost six months in the aggregate: the first visit found the author studying much more than the Alemany story in an endeavor to put it in eventual perspective and focus. On this occasion he was limited by the customary hundred years' rule to materials up to 1857. The second visit found an appreciated relaxation of this same rule and extensive records were consulted up to and including 1888, the year of Alemany's death. It was a satisfying—if expected—thing to note how conscientiously Alemany fulfilled his obligations concerning various reports to the cardinal prefects of Propaganda who were his immediate superiors because his territory, missionary as it was considered all during his years of rule, was directly under them. It is no exaggeration to say that thousands of pages were turned to document the Alemany years in California: some letters were quite routine (that is, matrimonial dispensations and the like), but the occasionally wearisome search had its rewarding moments as when, for example, one came on detailed and satisfyingly complete accounts in Alemany's own handwriting of the state of his diocese at given times. These have never before been used. (A general account of the contents of these Archives is provided in the author's "The Roman Propaganda Fide Archives: An Overview and an Assessment," in *Church History*, XXXIII, no. 1, March, 1964, pp. 84–91.) The Vatican Archives, although duly checked, contained only background materials antedating Alemany's rule: as indicated, American prelates, including San

Francisco's first archbishop, reported to Propaganda rather than to other Roman congregations.

The pages of this book abound in references to the important materials consulted in the Paris and Fribourg, Switzerland, Archives of the missionary aid organization still known as the Société pour la Propagation de la Foi. There were two branches, one in Paris and one in Lyons. For safety, the Lyons records were removed in World War II to Fribourg where they were consulted by the author. The Society quite naturally wanted precise statements of needs, etc., before dispensing funds to Alemany and other American pioneer prelates: this necessitated a careful filling out of forms and answering of many questions, which reporting was almost always accompanied by additional details in letter form. It may be well imagined how rewarding such reports were in endeavoring to reconstruct the story of California's pioneer archbishop. Like the Propaganda sources mentioned above, these letters to Paris and Fribourg as written by Alemany are used for the first time.

The well-preserved Archives of All Hallows College in Dublin also furnished considerable additions to the Alemany story. He had much correspondence with authorities there concerning the sending of Irish priests "over to Macedonia" to help him. In the 1957 visit to Ireland, incidental materials were found in the Archives of several other missionary colleges there.

Certainly most worthy of special mention and expression of gratitude is the complete cooperation afforded the author by the highest authorities of the Dominican Order. Very Reverend John Driscoll, O.P., American Assistant in Rome to the Most Reverend Master General of the Order, obtained complete access for the author to important records preserved in the Master General's Archives; the same sort of cooperation, and this over an extended period of time and accompanied by courtesies and helps too numerous to be mentioned, was extended by the Reverend Reginald Coffey, O.P., archivist of the Province of St. Joseph, Washington, D.C. Similar courtesies came from the Reverend Charles Hess, O.P., archivist of the Province of the Holy Name, San Francisco. The archives of the author's own Jesuit Order in Rome and in San Francisco yielded many letters and other accounts of the Alemany-Jesuit differences. As indicated by their use in the book, the Archives of the Congregation of the Oratory, Birmingham, England, provided an account for some interesting epistolary interchanges between the then Father John Henry Newman and Alemany. In the United States, successful recourse was had, among other archival holdings, to those of the Archdiocese of Baltimore which yielded some vital reports on the state of California Catholicism at the time of Alemany's appointment there. These would appear to be the principal archives worthy of mention here—although others were consulted with only partial success or, in some cases, with a negative yield.

2. Printed Materials Concerning Alemany

Even though there is a part Spanish, part Catalan biography of Alemany by his grandnephew, it would seem that first mention of printed materials concerning the man and his place in California Catholic history should go to the extremely well done unpublished master's thesis called "A Preliminary Survey of the Life of the Most Reverend Joseph Sadoc Alemany, First Archbishop of San Francisco." Its author is Sister Gertrude Mary Gray, S.H.N., who presented this study at the Summer Branch of the Catholic University of America in 1942. Indeed, this was among the present author's first contacts in the field of Alemany, and his admiration for the detailed and high quality of work put into this study has increased with the years. This is why he places mention of it ahead of the biography mentioned above. The title of this biography, by Antonio Alemany Comella, already identi-

371

fied as the Archbishop's grandnephew, is *Ilustrisimo y Reverendisimo Fray Joseph Sadoch Alamany Conill, O.P., Obispo de Monterey y Primer Arzobispo de San Francisco de California* (Vich, Spain, 1925). This affectionate account, compiled mostly from family letters and the like, numbers 151 pages of scattered but invaluable memorabilia: the chief value lies in the fact that much of these materials were later destroyed by the Communists in Spain's Civil War when they occupied Vich and burned the diocesan archives there. In 1925, when Alemany was joined to the immortals in the Gallery of the Illustrious Citizens of Vich, a panegyric was preached by a brother Dominican, Manuel Montoto, O.P., whose discourse was printed with the title, "El Excmo. y Rvmo. Sr. D. Fr. Jose Sadoc Alamany y Conill de la Orden de Predicadores, Primer Arzobispo de San Francisco de California." This account provides valuable details concerning Alemany's later life as a retired archbishop in Valencia. This was added to, twenty years later in 1945, when on the occasion of the rededication of the gallery of Vich's illustrious citizens (destroyed during the Civil War), another Dominican, Jose de Garganta, O.P., delivered a similar discourse with approximately the same title and content (Vich, 1945). Two other sketches which should be mentioned here are that by Francis J. Weber entitled *A Biographical Sketch of Right Reverend Joseph Sadoc Alemany, Bishop of Monterey, 1850–1853* (Los Angeles, 1961), and that by Peter T. Conmy dated 1943, and circulated privately, which is entitled "The Friar Joseph Sadoc Alemany, Bishop of Monterey, Alta California, 1850–1853, Archbishop of San Francisco, 1853–1885."

A generation and more ago, Canon Raymond Casadevall of the Vich Cathedral Chapter determined to devote himself to the production of a complete and scholarly account of Archbishop Alemany's distinguished career. All of the family papers were put at his disposal and all went well until the Spanish Civil War ravaged the country and Vich was occupied by the Communists when all such papers were burned. Subsequently, with Canon Casadevall's death and the return of peace, Father Alberto Collell, O.P., a Dominican friar stationed in Barcelona and on excellent terms with the Alemany family, endeavored to continue the work despite the obvious handicaps resulting from such loss. His work remains unpublished and was put at the disposal of the present author by Father Collell himself. Entitled "Biografia del Exco. y Rdmo. Fray Jose Sadoc Alemany, O.P., Primer Arzobispo de San Francisco de California," the six chapters, which Father Collell put together so painstakingly, end with Alemany's going to California as Bishop of Monterey in 1850. As is evident, this material has been heavily relied upon in the earlier chapters of this study. Another somewhat similar source is the unpublished manuscript of the Right Reverend Antonio Santendreau (1853–1944), a Catalan like Alemany who came to San Francisco in 1876 and who served under Alemany for eight years. His "Notes Concerning Archbishop Alemany" contain some valuable information and some shrewd observations concerning his countryman.

Some standard sketches of Alemany appear in various encyclopedias—the best of them is that written for the *Catholic Encyclopedia* (vol. 1, pp. 282–283) by his successor, Archbishop Riordan. This is an accurate account by one who lived with Alemany for a year as his coadjutor. Others are those in the *Dictionary of American Biography, Dictionary of Catholic Biography*, Reuss' *Biographical Encyclopedia of the Hierarchy of the United States*; in addition to the Riordan sketch, Thomas Meehan added another accurate account of Alemany in his article in the *Catholic Encyclopedia* on San Francisco (vol. XIII, pp. 439–443). Such standard sources as the *Records* of the American Catholic Historical Society of Philadelphia as well as the American Catholic Historical *Researches* and the *Catholic Historical Review* contain occasional references to Alemany. Among such accounts are Gaynor Maddox's "Joseph Sadoc Ale-

373

many, O.P., Archbishop of San Francisco," in *Historical Records and Studies*, VIII (June, 1915) pp. 223–228; and Bryan J. Clinch's excellent sketch entitled "The Jesuits in American California," in the *Records of the American Catholic Historical Society of Philadelphia*, XVII (1906) pp. 48–66, 125–143. The latter contains a penetrating analysis of Alemany's character and influence. Although the present study may lay claim to be the first full-length biographical study of the man, it is evident that Alemany's name must necessarily appear in numerous accounts in the field of American Church history. Several such mentions of special interest will be listed shortly.

3. Some Subsidiary Materials

The name of Victor F. O'Daniel, O.P. (1868–1960), will always loom large in the field of American Dominican historical studies. While quite opinionated and even dogmatic in his assertions and while betraying a too obvious bias in places, O'Daniel's works cannot be entirely neglected. It is not surprising that Alemany should figure rather prominently and favorably in several of O'Daniel's volumes. Notable in this connection are his *The Dominican Province of St. Joseph: Historico-Biographical Studies* (New York, 1942), where (pp. 172–173) O'Daniel is almost certainly excessive in his praise of Alemany. See also (in collaboration with Reginald Coffey, O.P.) his *The First Two Dominican Priories in the United States: Saint Rose's Priory, near Springfield, Kentucky: Saint Joseph's Priory, near Somerset, Ohio* (New York, 1947), where an interesting background is provided for Alemany's missionary years in those states and his brief rule as prior provincial there. His work in Tennessee is satisfactorily described in O'Daniel's *The Father of the Church in Tennessee—or the Life, Times and Character of the Right Reverend Richard Pius Miles, O.P., The First Bishop of Nashville* (Washington, D.C., 1926).

374

Since all of Alemany's active years in the episcopate were passed in California, it will help to provide the briefest survey of the literature concerning the Church there. Alemany finds considerable and substantially accurate treatment in volume IV of the standard work of Zephryin Engelhardt, O.F.M., *Missions and Missionaries of California.* Several of the same author's individual accounts of various missions contain incidental accounts of Alemany also. Gerald Geary's *Secularization of the California Missions, 1810–1846* (Washington, D.C., 1934), and his *Transfer of Ecclesiastical Jurisdiction in California, 1840–1853* (Washington, D.C., 1932), are valuable for apposite subject matter involving Alemany. William Gleeson's *History of the Catholic Church in California* (2 vols., 1872), while pretty much a museum piece now and not without inaccuracies concerning Archbishop Alemany, manages to afford a contemporary portrait. In addition to Francis Weber's already mentioned sketch of Alemany as Bishop of Monterey, the same author has published *California's Reluctant Prelate: The Life and Times of Right Reverend Thaddeus Amat, C.M. (1811–1878)* (Los Angeles, 1964), which, while concerning Alemany only secondarily, has some interesting details concerning the controversies which the two California prelates engaged in over a period of years. Joseph Riordan, S.J., in his *The First Half Century of St. Ignatius Church and College* (San Francisco, 1905), must needs give much space to the Archbishop who figured so largely in Jesuit history in San Francisco. While largely benevolent in tone, the Riordan synthesis is quite helpful in assessing various parts of the Alemany story. The present author's *Eloquent Indian: the Life of James Bouchard, California Jesuit* (Stanford, 1949), contains a bibliography of the Catholic Church in California as well as an extensive treatment of Alemany in its pages. The second chapter is entitled "They Made Me a Bishop: A Pioneer Prelate Arrives in El Dorado," which, obviously, is concerned entirely with Alemany.

Contemporary Catholic newspapers formed a considerable part of the author's research in this book. Notable was the representative file of such papers long of use to students which are housed in the Library of the American Catholic Historical Society of Philadelphia. Of especial use because of the Gregory Phelan reports which have found occasional quotation in these pages were the files of the New York *Freeman's Journal and Catholic Register*. As expected, though, the chief newspaper source was the San Francisco *Monitor* which was founded in 1858 and became Alemany's official organ in 1877, although it contained much about him in its earlier or unofficial years. While there is no complete file of the *Monitor* in existence because of destruction by fire, etc., a sufficient run exists to make this a primary font of information. Notable, for example, is the accurate account by Joseph Gleason called simply the "History of the Archdiocese" which appeared in the *Monitor's* Golden Jubilee Edition of January 23, 1904. Monsignor Gleason's acquaintance with people and places looming large in the Alemany story makes his comments concerning the Archbishop of special value. Then, too, the files of local newspapers such as the San Francisco *Alta California* and others served to flesh out the story in places.

Mention should be made of some of the periodical articles on Alemany. Sebastian Bohan, O.P., is the author of an article on Alemany in *Dominicana* (Washington, D.C.), June and September, 1916, which is of real merit because based on original sources. However, Alemany's years as archbishop receive only general treatment with the main strength of the article concerned with the years up to 1853. In earlier years when *Dominicana* was published in California (1900–1906) its pages contained several good articles on the Dominican story in California by Sister Mary Aloysius, O.P. Obviously, Alemany figures largely in these accounts which are to be found in the January, February, April, May, and June issues of 1901. The present author contributed three earlier articles to as many publications

376

concerning the subject of this now completed biography: cf. "The Coming of Archbishop Alemany to California," in *The Historical Bulletin* (St. Louis University), November, 1949, pp. 5–7; "The Coming of Joseph Sadoc Alemany, O.P., Pioneer Prelate of El Dorado," a paper originally read at the thirty-first annual meeting of the American Catholic Historical Association, Chicago, December 29, 1950, and printed in the *Records* of the American Catholic Historical Society of Philadelphia, LXII (December, 1951), 203–212; "California's First Archbishop: a Visit to Vich," in the *American Ecclesiastical Review,* CXLIII (August, 1960), 112–116.

Here, then, is an overview of the location and value of the chief source materials which were used in the writing of this present volume.

APPENDIXES

Appendix One

WE here reproduce the printed form of the address to the newly arrived Bishop Alemany which formed part of the official welcome extended to him by the Catholics of San Francisco.

ADDRESS TO THE BISHOP OF CALIFORNIA

The following Address to the Rt. Rev. Dr. Alemany, Catholic Bishop of San Francisco, adopted by a General Meeting of the Catholics of the city, John A. McGlynn Esq., Chairman, and Geo. O'Doherty, Esq., Secretary, was presented to him on Tuesday evening, Dec. 10, 1850. The Committee chosen on behalf of the meeting was Messrs. John A. McGlynn, Hugh O'Donnell, P. Moffat O'Brian, M.D., Charles D. Carter, Geo. O'Doherty, Thos. Jefferson Smith, Dennis McCarthy, and R. F. Ryan.

To the Right Reverend,
    Joseph Alemany, Bishop of California [sic]:
Right Reverend Sir: —The Catholics of San Francisco, in public meeting assembled, feel bound to express our gratitude to Almighty God for the signal favor He has conferred upon us, in sending "an exalted teacher to govern and instruct his Church" in this part of the world. As your spiritual children in Christ, we rejoice to meet you as our Father and Prelate, and we bid you a hearty welcome to this land.

The distinguished position to which you had been already raised in the Church, the estimation in which you were held by the Hierarchy of the United States who nominated you to the Holy See for our Bishop, and the reputation you have long enjoyed for those virtues and qualifications befitting an ecclesiastical dignitary, give us the most

381

assured confidence that you are worthy of the Episcopacy, and that your career among us will furnish an exemplification of the character described by the inspired writer: "Behold a great priest who in his time pleased God and was found just, and in the time of wrath was made a reconciliation."

We feel deeply sensible of the exertions you have made to secure for us the services of a zealous and devoted Priesthood from Spain, France, Ireland and the United States; and we are sure the whole community will participate in the pleasure it has afforded us to learn that you have also taken measures to enlist in the cause of religion here, the Sisters of Charity—those self-sacrificing handmaids of Christ, who are everywhere found ministering angels to suffering humanity.

Upwards of two centuries have passed away since the standard of the cross was first planted on this soil, since the sons of St. Ignatius, St. Francis and St. Dominick [sic] first impressed the heart of the Californian savage with the benign influences of the gospel: and we dwell with pleasure on the contemplation, that for you and your fellow laborers, it may, in the providence of God, be reserved, to complete the good work then so zealously commenced, by diffusing, not only among the aboriginal inhabitants, but the unconverted also, who have come hither of late years from the various nations of the world, a knowledge of that faith by which alone their temporal and eternal happiness can be truly secured. No portion of this great Continent presents a more inviting or more interesting field for the Missionary of the Gospel than California. Every bay and river, every mountain and valley, throughout the length and breadth of this beautiful land is, in the name it bears, a silent but unimpeachable witness of the efforts of your predecessors in extending the Kingdom of Christ. And although the civil government which formerly ruled here, has of late years been supplanted by another, the spiritual government of our Holy Mother the Church, the spouse of Christ, continues unchanged and unchangeable; and your presence here this day is a proof, that she is still as solicitous to secure the eternal welfare of her children as she had been centuries ago, when she sent her missionaries to preach the same glad tidings of redemption on the shores of the Pacific.

On the part of our separated brethren in this city who are American citizens, we also venture, Right Reverend Sir, to welcome you. Your lengthened residence in the United States, your attachment and reverence for our Constitution and laws, and your having long adopted our country as your home, will give you, we feel assured, a pre-eminent claim on their confidence and esteem.

382

As to our fellow citizens who are natives of the soil, and who are your kindred in language, religion and blood, we are confident we but faintly express the rapture with which they hail your arrival, when on their part also, we bid you a cordial welcome.

In conclusion, Right Reverend Sir, we all unite in tendering to you our warmest congratulations, on this auspicious and eventful occasion; and we earnestly pray Almighty God to bestow upon you his choicest blessings; "to fill you with the spirit of wisdom and understanding," and long to preserve you among us to carry on the work of the ministry, for His glory and the salvation of souls.

San Francisco, Dec. 10, 1850

To which the Rt. Rev. Bishop replied in substance as follows:

My dearly Beloved Brethren in Christ—I should offer violence to the feelings of my heart, were I to remain silent after the manifestation of your sentiments by the happily chosen organ that has just expressed them. I can read in your countenances that they are a sincere welcome of a religious flock to their pastor. Such a warm manifestation being directed to the high office lately vested in the unworthy person who addresses you, excites in me the liveliest feelings of gratitude. I thank you from my heart. I feel sincerely grateful for your kind welcome, and rejoice at your religious joy.

A long journey through rough, inhospitable countries, a sea-voyage through unfriendly, boisterous and incessantly threatening waves, naturally covers with gloom the heart of the traveller; but on the other hand if befriended by nature, he finds some relief from the unavoidable tediousness and fatigue of the way. Such is the feeling experienced by a pastor, whose lot is cast in a good flock, with this difference, that while the frowning elements may finally overwhelm the vessel, the ship that is piloted by Him who commands the winds and the sea cannot be wrecked. Human nature may be depressed by fear, imagining Providence to look on unconcerned; but it will be emboldened by the inspirations of faith to dispel all gloomy apprehensions. Impious and designing men may threaten, imprison, or exile a pastor; but they cannot subvert the authority of His church, which is the work of the hands of the Almighty, immortal like its author. I would, on this occasion, direct my thoughts to the brother of the pious prelate who consecrated me, the gloriously suffering Archbishop of Turin, but the joy of this happy meeting forbids me.

Your religious feelings, on this occasion, permit nothing but happy

383

prospects to the clergy of California. As long as the faithful will appreciate the worth of religion, and will receive its divine influences, so long can their spiritual prosperity be guaranteed. This is one of the principal reasons why our church in the United States has attained in a few years a growth, like that which San Francisco has made in a few months. Two or three years ago, the insignificant town of San Francisco could scarcely meet the eye of the student of geography; to-day the name of this large and important city resounds throughout the world. About a half a century ago, one bishop, a few priests and some thousand Catholics formed our Church in the United States: it now probably numbers over two millions of Catholics, more than a thousand clergymen, an equal number of churches, and a hierarchy of twenty-five Bishops and six Archbishops. The faithful were always ready to gladden the heart of the wandering missionary priest; they were his aid, received the instructions of his ministry, and God blessed them.

With equal devotion from the faithful in California to their clergy, equal prosperity may be prophesied. That God may prosper and bless his people, and that you may always invoke His blessing upon me, is the prayer of my heart.

Appendix Two

THIRTY-FIVE years after the address of welcome to Bishop Alemany (cf. Appendix One), the Catholics of San Francisco bade
him farewell as he prepared to go to Spain in retirement. The
following address of Father Prendergast, given in the name of
the clergy on May 19, 1885, as well as Archbishop Alemany's
reply, are reproduced here:

Most Rev. Archbishop:
   After repeated efforts and supplications, you can at length give effect
to your long-cherished desire. You have transferred the episcopal
sceptre to the hands of a worthy successor and you are now free to
withdraw, not to a life of ease, but to a sphere of less responsibility.
While we accept, we hope, with unfeigned though painful submission,
the decree which separates us, it is our sad privilege to gather round
you once more before you leave us in order to give expression to our
gratitude, to assure you of our unchangeable affection and veneration,
and to receive your parting blessing. We know, indeed, that you
shrink from praise and complimentary demonstrations; but this consideration, far from releasing us from the duty we owe you, only
renders our obligation the more sacred and imperative.
   Citizens by birth or by adoption of California, we lament, Most
Rev. Archbishop, with all our fellow-citizens, irrespective of religious
faith and political affiliation, your departure from our shores. More
than most other men, you were identified with this State. You have
seen it at its birth and in its glory; you have loved it as if your father-
land, and devoted to it your life; and, surviving most of the energetic
men who founded and formed it, you seem like the last of a vanished
generation.

But you were more than a prominent and honored citizen. You were another Serra for California when California was re-born and became the splendid inheritance of a new race. It is now more than thirty years since you were called by Pius IX of blessed memory from your humble labors in a western State, from your peaceful cloisters and from your brethren to become a bishop in this distant land. California was already an integral portion of the American Union and the Stars and Stripes waved upon its shores; yet it was virtually a foreign country if not a wild one. Here you found yourself amid social conditions absolutely unknown before; among a population drawn from all parts of the world and comprising all classes; sent to build on lines as yet untraced and for a future which only a prophet could forecast; compelled to create all the manifold agencies your sacred mission required—schools, hospitals, asylums, churches, clergy; deprived by two oceans and impassable mountains of the wisdom and treasured experience of your episcopal brethren. No imagination can conceive the countless difficulties that confronted you, or the rare combination of mental and moral qualities your work demanded, and only those who have been with you from the beginning know how truly you were of the number of those apostolic men of whom it is written that they went along the highways of the nations weeping—"*Euntes, ibant et flebant, mittentes semina sua.*" But you were happily chosen for the work you had to do. Your hopeful temperament, your patience and forebearance, your activity and your perseverance, your inflexibility of will joined to gentleness of manner, above all, your spirit of prayer and your unfaltering trust in God, have enabled you not only to surmount all obstacles, but also to accomplish more than the first bishop of any other American See and to return in advanced age amid the lamentations of your people.

Born in historic Spain and possessing many of the best characteristics of your race, you forgot, like Abraham of old, your country and your kindred and your father's house, and, emulating the example of St. Paul, became all things to all men to gain all to Christ. Your very first care as bishop was to draw around you priests of their own blood for those who constituted the dominant element in the Catholic population. At the same time your pastoral solicitude embraced all nationalities. Even the pagan children of China were the objects of your concern and zeal, for, in the hope of converting them, you brought to San Francisco a highly-educated priest of their own race, and afterward other experienced missionaries and native catechists to take his place. Your unceasing interest in this people was the more praiseworthy inasmuch as the experience had amply demonstrated that the most generous efforts on their behalf were not likely to produce large results. We claim no superiority in intelligence and zeal as we acknowledge none; but we possess the important advantage of long and close observation, and we know how inaccessible are the Chinese in our midst to the Catholic faith, partly because of their peculiar social organization, and partly because of the inherent difficulty of detaching this ancient people from their ancestral ways, unless by luring them with the hope of immediate or prospective temporal gain, and thus compromising religion in its first principles and very essence.

And, like a general in the army's van, you were always prepared for every good work. Burthened with the care of a diocese always large in territory and once imperial in its dimensions, travelling over dangerous trails in crowded conveyances, happy if you found at night a rude cabin wherein to rest, administering confirmation, hearing confessions in many languages and preaching in many tongues, you bore the two-fold character of bishop and missionary; and when you returned from your visitation it was not to seek much-needed repose but to resume at once the weighty work of your double administration. And what was the reason and the aim of this tireless activity? It was nothing personal. You expended nothing on yourself; you did not divert one fraction of the revenues of the Church to private use; neither did you lay up anything for sickness or old age; but, trusting in the providence of God and true to the principles of your Order, "having food and wherewith you were clothed—with these you were content." And you close your long episcopal administration and arduous labors as poor as you began. No; it was not the material benefit of any individual that inspired and sustained you. Your sole object was to enlarge the kingdom of Christ and give eternal life to men. This was your high aim, this your sacred ambition; to this you consecrated your whole being, untroubled if here or there some ignorant or worldly-minded man misjudged your character or your motives.

But, Most Reverend Archbishop, to your clergy in particular, this hour which severs our official relations with you and which recalls so many memories, is one of deep and universal sorrow, for you have been a father to us and have ruled us with a father's hand. Just yet never severe, patient but not weak, charitable more than human tongue can tell, apparently preoccupied in active duties yet finding time for meditation and prayer, high in office and authority yet lowly in personal bearing and life, you were truly the pattern of your flock and

387

could justly say to us with the Apostle: "Be you imitators of me." It is our fault if we have not profited by so excellent an example; but it is sure to affect us more powerfully the farther it recedes from our view.

But we must turn away for a moment from the irrevocable past to the future, for we hope and pray that you may yet see many days of peaceful and fruitful labors. You have been blessed with venerable age but you are likely to live yet for a long time and not die until you reach the patriarchal years of your fathers. Thanks to an originally vigorous constitution, to abstemious and regular habits, to active occupation, your mental faculties are unimpaired and your bodily strength gives no warning of exhaustion and decay. And we take it that you feel in yourself the promise of many years, for we understand that, instead of closing your life in honored repose, you purpose devoting what remains of it to the realization of a new project for the propagation of the Faith. Therefore we beg you to take from us the gift we offer you to be used as you choose. We regret that it is not worthier of your acceptance; but such as it is we present it, in the hope that as you have been ours through long years we may claim you still and may have some small share in your labors and sacrifices to the end.

And now, Most Rev. Archbishop, as you will always retain a large place in the hearts of your priests, we hope you will never forget us. The separation is inevitable but not everlasting. Through your prayers and the inspiring memories of your life and example we hope to be found worthy to meet you again, and to be numbered with you in the fold of the Eternal Shepherd.

At the close of Father Prendergast's address, Archbishop Alemany replied as follows:

I am thankful and grateful, reverend gentlemen, for your presence and for the kind words you have been pleased to address me. I hope you will make up with your prayers whatever may be wanting in my speech. As to the success achieved for the Church of God, whatever it may be, it is not my work exclusively; but to you, to your co-operation, I owe it. It is true that as the Bishop is at the head of the Diocese, the success and the mistakes are attributed to him, but in fact they belong to both Bishop and Priests.

There was, indeed, in those days, great want of clergy. These came along in time, and increased as the wants of the Diocese increased until they have become numerous, both secular and regular. To their co-

388

operation with me whatever has been done is due. I hope you will continue that generous co-operation with my worthy and devoted successor. It is a happiness for me to think that I have such a successor— able, zealous, earnest, with great powers of administration, both for the temporal and for the spiritual concerns of the Diocese. The work of the priesthood is the grandest upon earth; when compared with other vocations or avocations of life, they sink into insignificance. Their work at best is perishable; ours is lasting, is eternal. The physician can do no more than ease a little the pains of life. He cannot keep up man's vitality. The lawyer, if he gains his suit, can preserve to his client a little bit of land, perhaps; but even this must soon be left behind.

But ours, the priest's mission, might be envied by the angels. We instruct the minds of men unto salvation. We train up the hearts of the dear young children to know God and serve him. We teach them truths that are to endure for all time to come, and to make their souls, if faithful to that teaching, shine as the stars of heaven. Our mission is, besides, by gentleness and kindness and holiness of life, not only to keep up to that faith the children of the Church, but to edify and to attract those outside of it.

If needs be, I pray God that you may in all this emulate one another in co-operating with the new Archbishop for all things connected with this mission, but, above all, in the building of churches and schools.

The education of the young, of the dear, innocent, beautiful little children, so numerous in our city, is one of the great cares of the bishop and the priest. I pray you to sustain his efforts on all this. Little by little education is becoming infidel. This we must counteract by making sacrifice in behalf of Christian education. Help him, too, in the support of the seminary. The expense is great, but thanks be to God, the number of students is increasing all the time. This, too, must be sustained by your zealous assistance.

As to my future, it might be better for me to retire completely from active work, but I have been so long in the harness that I feel I would hardly feel easy. Besides I am tempted for other reasons to embark upon a missionary work on a small scale. I, together with many of my brethren of the Dominican Order, was driven from my native land; with a stroke of the pen we were banished. Though Spain has still her troubles, times have changed and there are some there who are in a better frame of mind. I would like very much to establish there some kind of house for the training of young missionaries to teach the people those great truths of our holy faith, to make the people see the great crime of persecuting the servants of God, the Jesuits, and others devoting their lives to the good of their neighbor. But this we shall have to recommend to God.

I do not think I was born to be a Bishop, and I told Pius IX so, but nevertheless they made me a Bishop. Now, in my old age it has seemed best to resign the arduous work into younger hands.

I thank you most sincerely for your kind words and for your handsome gift. I hope you will pray for me, that God may preserve me through life and particularly at the hour of death.

Appendix Three

THE following letter was written by Archbishop Alemany to Mother Camillus, superior of the Sisters of Mercy at Rio Vista, California, on November 26, 1883. It is here reproduced because it gives an indication of the spiritual reflections of Alemany as addressed to some of the co-workers whose labors he appreciated so much.

ST. MARY'S CATHEDRAL
628 California St., San Francisco

Dear in Christ Sister,

I am glad, and grateful to Almighty God, that, after much expecting, a nice learned, able, prudent and good-hearted Coadjutor has been sent to aid me in the administration of the diocese. This having been always on the increase required an increase of aid which having come, I hope that we will be able to aid others a little better. And from the start I must promise myself a visit to you, and to the whole Community and to the holy hopes—the young ladies confided to your care by Almighty God to have them well adorned in their minds for good society here, and especially for the grand, brilliant Society of the countless angelic intelligences in heaven.

But as it may yet take me some time, before I can visit St. Gertrude's, I will now write a few lines, exhorting you all to hold fast to the crown, that Christ has prepared for the good Sisters. He did not promise the Apostles rich dresses, splendid eating, honors or good cheer in this world; on the contrary he foretold them, that they would not be treated differently from the way they treated him, that the world would rejoice and be merry, but they would have occasion to weep; but that in the end in a short while, all would be changed and that their joy would be great in heaven. Consequently, since the Mission of the Sisters of Mercy is a sort of Apostolic Mission, somewhat similar to that of the Apostles, it necessarily follows that now they must labor in an Apostolic manner, and expect no pay until they wake up in heaven. And in order to succeed, they must practice what the Apostles practiced, and what the Lord of heaven taught them to practice, namely to renounce all our possessions, i.e. father, mother, brothers, sisters, even *our own selves.* This last is likely the hardest; and yet, unless we do that, we cannot be his disciples. We must deny our own selves, that is our own will. At our profession we take in our own hands our own will, and put it on the Altar of God, and offer it to him. So if we go back to the Altar and take it away from Almighty God, we make a sort of breaking the seventh commandment, with a kind of profanation worse than that of the material temple. And displeasing and offending the good God thereby we lost the privilege of being his disciples, and the crown of unending glory.

I should therefore beg, then, all the Sisters of St. Gertrude's to hold fast to the crown and sail to the haven of heaven in the ship of holy Rule—holy obedience to Rule and unreserved obedience to God who says to the Superiors, "he that heareth you heareth me." So that to obtain heaven the Sisters must be like the wheels in a good watch. . . . If a wheel does not like to be where a watchmaker placed it, the watch is all wrong, but when each wheel is entirely at the disposal of the watchmaker, the nice little watch is an admirable piece of workmanship, and very useful. And as a bad watch is laid aside in disgust by the owner, so the unwilling Sister would be put away by our Lord and Master.

This heaven is worth working for; the Apostles are there for eighteen hundred years and over, and thousands and thousands of holy religious are there too, but none through any other road but that of Christ, who came not to do his will, but that of his heavenly Father.

With best regards to all the Sisters, and commending myself to their prayers and yours in particular, I remain

Yours truly in Christ
J. S. Alemany, A.S.F.

(Original in Archives of Sisters of Mercy, Burlingame, California.)

Appendix Four

A UNIQUE event in the annals of California Catholicism took place in San Francisco on Saturday, February 6, 1965. On that day, before five of his suffragan bishops, the fifth Archbishop of San Francisco, Joseph T. McGucken, pontificated in a requiem Mass in the presence of the returned remains of the first pioneer prelate of the See of San Francisco, Joseph Sadoc Alemany, O.P. The site itself was historically significant, for Old St. Mary's Church, situated on the fringe of Chinatown of today, was formerly Alemany's cathedral, dedicated by him on Christmas night, 1854.

It had been Alemany's request that he be buried in the Church of Santo Domingo, Vich. This request was duly honored, and from April 19, 1888, his remains lay buried in this church where he had been received into the Order of Preachers in 1830. However, in 1921, Edward J. Hanna, third Archbishop of San Francisco from 1915 to 1935, formally petitioned the Cathedral Chapter of Vich to permit the translation of Alemany's remains to San Francisco so that the church there might properly honor in death the Catalan prelate who had given it such laborious years of service. The petition was refused, and Hanna was told that "Vich truly loves this great man and wishes to have his memory kept green with the continued possession of his venerated remains."

In 1934, with the planning of a Dominican house of studies

in Oakland, the Dominican prior provincial, desiring to give these remains honored sepulture under the altar of this College of St. Albert the Great, renewed the earlier petition and was encouraged by the tentative reply which he received. However, the Spanish Civil War broke out, and nothing resulted. Finally, the renewed petition of San Francisco's fourth Archbishop, John J. Mitty, who ruled the see from 1935 to 1961, seemed to have initiated a more favorable attitude both on the part of ecclesiastical authorities and members of the Alemany family in Vich and Barcelona. However, the latter made the provision that preliminary steps looking to the possible beatification of Archbishop Alemany be instituted in return for the release of the remains to the Archdiocese of San Francisco. Archbishop Mitty found these conditions impossible to accept, saying that he could not bind either himself or his successors to such things; and again, the matter came to a rest. There, seemingly, it would have remained but for the persistent efforts of the Reverend Francis J. Weber, archivist of the Archdiocese of Los Angeles. Father Weber, after prolonged negotiations with the Spanish government, the Alemany family, and authorities in Vich, finally succeeded in having permission granted to disinter the remains of Archbishop Alemany. This was done on January 20, 1965, and, after requiem services the next day, the remains were flown to California. On February 5 they were solemnly received by Archbishop McGucken at Old St. Mary's Church, and on the next day, before a congregation which included the Spanish ambassador to the United States, pontifical Mass was offered. Interment followed in the crypt of the bishops in Holy Cross Cemetery.

Index

Adam, Joachim, Vicar General of Monterey-Los Angeles: visits retired Alemany in Spain, 347.

Ajello, O.P., Vincent, Master General of Dominicans: appoints Alemany Prior Provincial of American Dominicans, 56; writes to Bishop Alemany re certain permissions requested by him, 110.

Alemany, O.P., Joseph Sadoc (1814–1888): San Francisco boulevard bears his name, 26, n.1; ancestry, 27; parentage, 28; birth in Vich, 28; his esteem for parents, 29; education in primary schools of Vich, 30; enrolled in diocesan seminary there, 30; attends classes in nearby Moya, 30; enters Dominicans in Vich, 32; pronounces solemn vows, 33; receives religious name of "Sadoc" after early Dominican martyr of Poland, 33; sent to Tremp for philosophical studies, 33; assigned to Gerona for studies in theology, 34; expelled, with other friars, from convent there as result of Secularization Law and forced to return to Vich, 34, 35; continues studies privately while living with relatives at Gurb, 35; leaves Spain for Italy to continue studies, 35; arrival in Rome and audience with Gregory XVI, 35, 36; sent to Viterbo and there assigned to convent of S. Maria dei Gradi, 36, 37; ordained to priesthood in Viterbo, 37; first Mass there, 38; made assistant master of novices in convent of La Quercia, Viterbo, 39; first sermon, 39; public defense in theology, 39; assigned to Dominican Church of S. Maria sopra Minerva, Rome, 40; volunteers for foreign missions, 41; assigned to American missions of his Order, 41; studies English at Urban College of Propaganda, Rome, 42; made lector of sacred theology, 42; leaves for America from Leghorn, 43; arrival in New York, 44; in Pittsburgh, 45; reaches Cincin-

Alemany—*cont.*

North American College, Rome, 285; preaches at Centennial Commemoration at Mission Dolores, 288; present at civic celebration of same event, 289; tribute of one of his priests, 292; troubles re anti-Chinese activities of Denis Kearney, 293–294; pastoral letter forbidding Catholic participation, 295; offers Requiem for Pius IX, 297; again attempts to obtain coadjutor, 299; approves petition of his priests that Father John Prendergast be appointed, 303; calls Second Provincial Council, 305; background for eventual appointment of Patrick Riordan as his Coadjutor with right of succession, 306–309; Riordan appointed and accepts, 309–311; Alemany's pleasure at this appointment, 311; sends Fr. Montgomery, his secretary, to represent him at consecration of Riordan in Chicago, 312; goes to Ogden to meet Riordan and accompanies him to Salt Lake City for Pontifical Mass there, 314; expresses views to Rome re episcopal rule in U.S.A., 315; favors appointment of lay consultors, 315; proposes his resignation to Rome but is told to wait until Riordan is further established in San Francisco, 316; attends Third Plenary Council of Baltimore

where, as one of senior prelates, he offers memorial Mass for deceased American prelates, 317–318; Riordan writes requested reports to Rome on his succession to See when Alemany's resignation is accepted, 318–320; Alemany writes to Dominican Master General on his desire to return to Order after his resignation, 321–322; outlines his plan for a missionary college in Spain, 322–323; resignation accepted, 322–323; letter to Vilarrasa asking various permissions as Dominican, 325; comments of local press on his resignation, 326; final functions as retired Archbishop, 329; appointed to Titular See of Pelusium in Egypt, 329; various farewell commemorations, 332–334; final Mass in St. Mary's Cathedral and departure from San Francisco, 334; goes to New York and to Washington where he is presented to President Cleveland, 336; arrives in Rome and goes from there to Spain, 337; visits his native Vich, 339; further plans for his missionary college, 340; decides to live in Valencia with Dominican priest companion, 341; various letters from there, 342–343; visited by Father Wallrath from California who reports about Alemany in San Francisco *Monitor*, 344–345; ministry as confessor

St. Joseph's, first Dominican Province in U.S.A.: Alemany as Prior Provincial, 56ff.

St. Joseph's Church, San Francisco: dedicated by Alemany, 1861, 184.

St. Mary's Cathedral, San Francisco: cornerstone laid by Alemany, 142; dedication, 161; described by Alemany in letter to his mother, 161–162.

St. Mary's College, San Francisco: dedicated by Alemany, 1863, 186; describes his earlier efforts to obtain Christian Brothers, 186–187.

St. Patrick's Church, Grass Valley: dedicated by Alemany, 1860, 178.

St. Rose's: pioneer Dominican convent near Springfield, Kentucky, 46.

St. Vibiana's Cathedral, Los Angeles: dedicated by Alemany, 287.

Salvatierra, S.J., Juan Maria: founder of first permanent mission in Baja California, 1697, 66; called "Father of Catholicism in California," 66, n.1.

San Carlo al Corso, Rome: Church of Alemany's consecration as Bishop of Monterey, 26, n.1. (Also Church of future consecration of Angelo Roncalli, Pope John XXIII, 94.)

San Jaime de Pallars: Dominican Priory in Catalonia where Alemany studied philosophy, 33.

Santa Barbara, California: Bishop Alemany arrives there in 1850 to present credentials to Franciscan administrator, 112; pontificates on New Year's Day, 1851, 113.

San Francisco, *Daily Alta California*: inaccurately reports Alemany's arrival, 1850, 111, n.25.

Santa Clara College: mentioned by Alemany in Paris report, 125.

Santa Maria sopra Minerva, Rome: Dominican Church served by Alemany as young priest, 25.

Santendreau, Rev. Antonio: valuable recollections of Alemany years in San Francisco, 352, n.1.

Santo Domingo Church, Vich: Alemany buried there, 26.

Santos Juanes, parish church, Valencia, Spain: scene of Alemany obsequies, 346.

St. Louis *Shepherd of the Valley*: records Alemany's arrival in England en route to Monterey, 104.

Sieneguita, near Santa Barbara: Alemany blesses Indian chapel, 1851, 114.

Simeoni, Cardinal Giovanni, successor to Fransoni as Prefect of Propaganda Fide: receives firm letter from Beckx (q.v.) re Jesuit-Alemany troubles in San Francisco, 261.

Society for the Propagation of the Faith, Paris: Alemany asks for financial aid for his return journey to America, 1850, 64. (For various reports and informative letters, cf. chapters 7, 8, and 10, *passim*.)

Somerset, Ohio: site of St. Joseph's Convent, pioneer Dominican foundation, 46.

Sopranis, S.J., Felix, official Roman Jesuit Visitor in California, 1862: Alemany writes him a frank letter, 202–203; (cf. *passim*, chapter 9 re Sopranis' key part in Alemany-Jesuit troubles in San Francisco).

Spalding, John L., Bishop of Peoria: proposes Father Riordan of Chicago as successor to Alemany, 306; preaches at Riordan's consecration, 313.

Spalding, Martin, Bishop of Louisville: informed by Eccleston that Alemany is being proposed for See of Monterey, 89; Alemany's later letter when Spalding is Archbishop of Baltimore re his successor in San Francisco, 229.

Stefanelli, O.P., Giovanni, Dominican Archbishop: co-consecrator of Alemany, 95.

Stevenson, Colonel Jonathan, U.S. military commander in California: writes to Eccleston as non-Catholic observer of sad state of California Catholicism, 1848, 72; letter forwarded to Rome, 72, n.9.

Taney, Chief Justice Roger B.: consulted by Alemany regarding Church lands in California, 134.

Timon, John, Bishop of Buffalo: proposed for See of Monterey, 79.

Valerga, Joseph, Patriarch of Jerusalem: co-consecrator of Alemany, 95.

Vallejo, Mariano Guadalupe: delivers address at Centennial commemoration in San Francisco, 289; impressive testimony re Alemany's character and influence, 362.

Van de Velde, S.J., James, Bishop of Chicago: approves of Alemany for See of Monterey, 90.

Varsi, S.J., Aloysius, President of St. Ignatius College, San Francisco: goes to Rome to discuss change of location of St. Ignatius College with Jesuit General, 257; (cf. chapter 11, *passim*, for Alemany-Varsi letters on this matter).

Vaughan, Rev. Herbert: visits California from England in 1864 and publishes glowing tribute to Alemany in his report on Catholicism in California, 230–232.

Vilarrasa, O.P., Francis Sadoc (1814–1888): sketch, 48–49, n.10; describes missionary life in Ohio, 48; opposes Alemany's selection as Prior Pro-

411